Step Language for Everyday Life
Forward

Step-By-Step Lesson Plans

SERIES DIRECTOR
Jayme Adelson-Goldstein

1

Jenni Currie Santamaria
Christy M. Newman

OXFORD
UNIVERSITY PRESS

OXFORD
UNIVERSITY PRESS

198 Madison Avenue
New York, NY 10016 USA

Great Clarendon Street, Oxford OX2 6DP UK

Oxford University Press is a department of the University of Oxford.
It furthers the University's objective of excellence in research, scholarship, and
education by publishing worldwide in

Oxford New York

Auckland Cape Town Dar es Salaam Hong Kong Karachi
Kuala Lumpur Madrid Melbourne Mexico City Nairobi
New Delhi Shanghai Taipei Toronto

With offices in

Argentina Austria Brazil Chile Czech Republic France Greece
Guatemala Hungary Italy Japan Poland Portugal Singapore
South Korea Switzerland Thailand Turkey Ukraine Vietnam

OXFORD and OXFORD ENGLISH are registered trademarks of
Oxford University Press

© Oxford University Press 2007

Database right Oxford University Press (maker)

Executive Publisher: Janet Aitchison
Editorial Manager: Stephanie Karras
Editors: Sharon Sargent, Glenn Mathes II
Art Director: Maj-Britt Hagsted
Senior Designer: Claudia Carlson
Layout Artist: Colleen Ho
Production Manager: Shanta Persaud
Production Controller: Eve Wong

Printed in China

10 9 8 7 6

ISBN-13: 978 0 19 4392280 STEP-BY-STEP LESSON PLANS
ISBN-13: 978 0 19 4398350 STEP-BY-STEP LESSON PLANS WITH CD-ROM (PACK)
ISBN-13: 978 0 19 4398367 CD-ROM

This book is printed on paper from certified and well-managed sources.

Many thanks to Sharon Sargent for her guidance
and encouragement; Jayme Adelson-Goldstein
for her insight and leadership; and Meg Araneo,
whose copyediting makes my writing look good.
I am also grateful to Jean Rose and my colleagues
and students at ABC Adult School for their
constant inspiration.

Special thanks to Tony and Amaya, whose love
and laughter keep me going.

Jenni Currie Santamaria

I gratefully acknowledge the dedication and
expertise of Jenni Santamaria, Jane Spigarelli,
Stephanie Karras, Sharon Sargent, Glenn Mathes,
Kathryn O'Dell, Meg Araneo, Niki Barolini,
Colleen Ho, Maj-Britt Hagsted, Shanta Persaud,
and Eve Wong. Special thanks to Jenni for
bringing her exceptional "multilevel" talents to
all four books.

For Norma, who always taught that the best
lessons come from the learner.

Jayme Adelson-Goldstein

Acknowledgments

The publishers would like to thank the following for their permission to adapt copyright material:

p. 72 "Americans Spending More Time on Themselves, Says NPD Study" used with permission of The NPD Group
p. 144 "General Facts" used with permission of www.greetingcard.org

Illustrations by: Silke Bachmann, p.6 (man and woman), p.43 (kitchen), p.47, p.71 (supermarket), p.114, 118; Barb Bastian, p.17, p.52; Ken Batelman, p.53, p.56, p.97, p.109, p.128; John Batten, p.43 (two women), p.48 (top illus.), p.68, p.83 (clothes), p.104, p.130 (split screen); Annie Bissett, p.24, p.58 (map bottom), p.73, p.145; Dan Brown, p.5, p.101; Claudia Carlson, p.173 (map); Gary Ciccarelli, p.2 (top and bottom illus.), p.112; Sam and Amy Collins, p.100; Laurie Conley, p.113; Lyndall Culbertson, p.61, p.148, p.152, p.155, p.158, p.159; Jeff Fillbach, p.12, p.31, p.34 (phone conversation), p.70 (cartoon); Debby Fisher, p.4, p.16, p.64 (activities); Martha Gavin, p.30, p.54, p.66, p.78, p.90; Paul Hampson, p.32, p.80, p.106, p.127, p.139 (cartoon); Mark Hannon, p.9, p.18, p.79, p.102, p.116, p.126, p.130 (911 emergencies), p.138; Michael Hortens, p.19, p.48 (article), p.49; Rod Hunt, p.40, p.41; Jon Keegan, p.46 (note), p.77, p.108 (OTC medicine); Uldis Klavins, p.124, p.125; Shelton Leong, p.10 (conversation), p.22 (realia), p.35, p.42, p.58, p.60 (home emergencies), p.72, p.82 (two women), p.94 (cartoon), p.103, p.140; Scott MacNeill, p.8, p.38, p.54 (locations), p.60 (poster), p.82 (realia), p.91, p.132 (car), p.144; Kevin McCain, p.137; Karen Minot, p.28 (family album), p.34 (calendar), p.46 (utility bills), p.59, p.83 (receipt), p.94 (menu), p.95, p.121, p.139, p.142; Derek Mueller, p.89; Tom Newsom, p.65, p.88; Terry Paczko, p.3 (numbers and addresses), p.70 (office actions), p.71 (office actions), p.76, p.84; Geo Parkin, p.136; Roger Penwill, p.10 (cartoon), p.15, p.27, p.44, p.51, p.63, p.75, p.87, p.99, p.111, p.123, p.135, p.147; Karen Prichett, p.28 (people), p.29.

We would like to thank the following for their permission to reproduce photographs:

Alamy: oote boe, p.13 (money exchange); Banana Stock, p.19 (Asian female), p.22 (Indian female); Bluestone Prod., p.67 (grocery clerk); Rolf Bruderer, p.20 (laughing man); Comstock, p.108 (doctor and patient); Dennis Kitchen Studios, p.15 (students); Design Pics, Inc., p.13 (flag); Dynamic Graphics, p.13 (doctor); Justine Eun for OUP, p.44 (women eating lunch); Fogstock, LLC, p.13 (construction worker); Getty Images: Photodisc, p.134 (road work sign); Michael Goldman, p.39 (Hispanic male); Henry Westhein Photography, p.22 (Chinese wedding couple); IndexOpen: Ablestock, p.12 (adult students); Inmagine: Creatas, p.12 (woman reading), p.13 (teacher and student), p.36 (large family), p.134 (children crossing sign); Jupiter Images: Comstock, p.12 (two women talking); Kim Karapeles, p.134 (no parking sign); Masterfile: Dana Hursey, p.13 (men talking); Ryoko Mathes, p.20 (angry man); Medio Images, p.108 (man running); MIXA Co., Ltd., p.36 (mother and adult children); Omni Photo, p.20 (hungry dog); Photodisc, p.19 (Asian senior); Photo Edit Inc.: Michelle D. Bridwell, p.127 (anchorwoman); Punchstock: Corbis, p.20 (tired man), 44 (window washing); Purestock, p.108 (woman eating apple); Anthony Redpath, p.19 (Hispanic female); Bryan Reinhart, p.20 (graduate and parents); Shelley Rotner, p.130 (ambulance); Royalty Free Division, p.115 (reading newspaper); Rubberball Productions, p.22 (African male); David Schmidt, p.19 (Asian male); Stockbyte, p.12 (student on campus), p.120 (time clock); SuperStock: Powerstock, p.20 (worried mother); Thinkstock, p.36 (small family); Transparencies, Inc., p.134 (speed limit sign); Scott Tysick, p.44 (woman cleaning); Jim Whitmers, p.7 (Hispanic male).

Contents

Introduction to *Step Forward Step-By-Step Lesson Plans*

Welcome to *Step Forward Step-by-Step Lesson Plans*. These lesson plans are your guide to *Step Forward*, the adult English language course designed to work in single-level and multilevel classes. In addition to being a step-by-step lesson-planning tool, this book is also a rich collection of tips, strategies, and activities that complement the lessons in the *Step Forward Student Book*. In keeping with current, scientifically based research on language acquisition and instruction, these lesson plans provide a variety of instructional strategies and techniques that work across methodologies and learner populations.

What is *Step Forward*?

The *Step Forward* series is

- the instructional backbone for any standards-based, integrated skills, English language course;
- a program that teaches the skills needed for everyday life, the workplace, the community, and academic pursuits;
- a ready-made framework for learner-centered instruction within a single-level or multilevel environment; and
- a four-skills program that develops students' listening, speaking, reading, and writing skills, as well as their grammar, pronunciation, math, cooperative, and critical-thinking skills.

Step Forward's communication objectives are authentic and taught in conjunction with contextualized language forms. Research shows that when lessons are based on authentic communication and there is a focus on form within that context, learners incorporate new and correct structures into their language use.[1]

What's in this book?

The *Step Forward Step-By-Step Lesson Plans*, a comprehensive instructional planning resource, contains detailed lesson plans interleaved with *Step Forward Student Book* pages.

Each unit in the *Step-By-Step Lesson Plans* follows this format.

Student Book pages are next to lesson plan pages for easy reference.

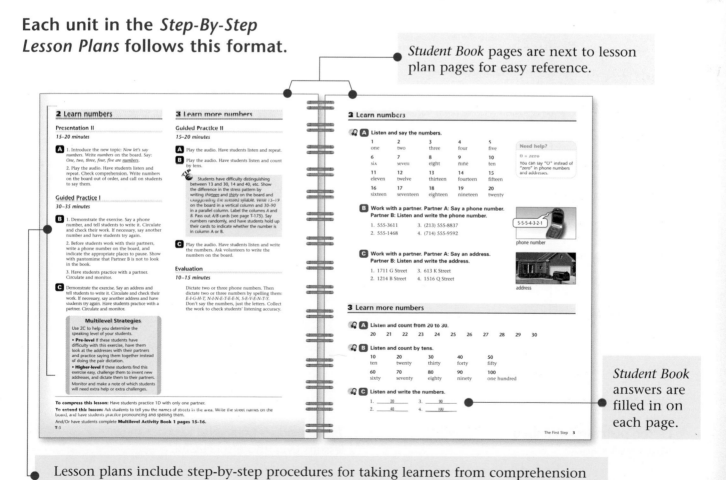

Student Book answers are filled in on each page.

Lesson plans include step-by-step procedures for taking learners from comprehension to accurate production to meaningful and fluent interaction.

---

[1] Rod Ellis, et al., "Doing focus on form," *Systems*, 30 (2002): 419-432.

Each lesson references related *Oxford Picture Dictionary* topics for further vocabulary development.

Every lesson in *Step Forward* is correlated to CASAS competencies, Florida's Standardized Student Syllabi (LCPs), Equipped for the Future (EFF) standards, and the Secretary's Commission on Achieving Necessary Skills (SCANS).

A general lesson information chart provides multilevel objectives, support-skill focus, and correlations.

Unit 1 Lesson 1

Objectives	Grammar	Vocabulary	Correlations
On-level: Identify classroom directions and classroom objects **Pre-level:** Recognize classroom directions and classroom objects **Higher-level:** Talk and write about classroom directions and classroom objects	Regular singular and plural nouns (*a pen, pens*)	Classroom directions, classroom words For additional vocabulary practice, see this **Oxford Picture Dictionary** topic: A Classroom	**CASAS:** 0.1.2, 0.1.5, 7.4.5, 7.4.7 **LCPs:** 32.01, 33.06 **SCANS:** Listening, Seeing things in the mind's eye, Self-management, Participates as member of a team **EFF:** Cooperate with others, Listen actively, Observe critically, Reflect and evaluate, Speak so others can understand

Warm-up and Review

10 minutes (books closed)

Ask *What's this?* as you point to a table, a desk, a chair, and a clock and as you hold up a book, a pen, and a pencil. If a student calls out the answer, write it on the board. Spell the words aloud, pointing to each letter as you say it, and have students repeat chorally. Repeat problem letters. Call on volunteers to spell each word aloud. Say: *Can you spell book, please?*

Introduction

5 minutes

1. Above the words on the board, write *classroom*. Ask: *Can you name other things in a classroom?* Point to additional items students might be able to name.

2. State the objective: *Today we're going to talk about a classroom.*

1 Learn classroom directions

Presentation

20–25 minutes

A Direct students to look at the pictures. Ask: *Is she a teacher or a student?* [a student]

B 1. Have students listen to the audio. Ask them to point to the correct picture as they listen. Circulate and monitor.

2. Check comprehension. Pass out *yes/no* cards (see page T-175), or have students hold up one finger for *yes* and two for *no* in order to get a nonverbal response. Play the audio and mime

each action. Tell students to hold up the *yes* card if your action matches the audio and the *no* card if it doesn't.

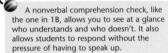
TIP A nonverbal comprehension check, like the one in 1B, allows you to see at a glance who understands and who doesn't. It also allows students to respond without the pressure of having to speak up.

C Ask students to listen and repeat the words.

Guided Practice I

15–20 minutes

D 1. Have students complete the sentences using the new vocabulary.

2. Encourage students to take turns reading the completed sentences in pairs.

Multilevel Strategies

For 1D, pair same-level students together. After they complete the exercise, provide more vocabulary practice targeted to the level of your students.

• **Pre-level** Ask these students to practice together by pointing to the pictures in 1B and saying the correct words.

• **On-level** Ask these students to work in pairs, covering the words and testing each other on the vocabulary. Have one student point to the pictures while the other student says the correct word.

• **Higher-level** Ask these students to dictate the words to each other.

T-4

Lesson plans are organized into seven stages.

Tips provide insights and ideas to make lessons even more successful.

Time guidelines help you pace the class.

2 Talk about a classroom

Guided Practice II
35–40 minutes

A 1. Ask students to repeat the words from the warm-up. Introduce the new topic: *Now let's talk about a classroom.*

2. Group students and assign roles: leader, fact checker, recorder, and reporter. Write the roles on the board. As you explain each role, pantomime the duties you expect that person taking the role to perform. Explain that students work with their groups to match the words and pictures in 2A.

3. Check comprehension of the exercise. Pantomime the duties of each role again as you ask about it. Ask students to raise their hands when you say their roles. *Who looks up the words in the picture dictionary?* [fact checker] *Who writes the numbers in the book?* [recorder] *Who tells the class your answers?* [reporter] *Who helps everyone?* [leader]

4. Set a time limit (three minutes). Ask the groups to work together to complete the task. While students are working, copy the wordlist on the board.

5. Call "time" and have the reporters from each group take turns calling out the numbers for the wordlist. Record students' answers on the board. If groups disagree, write each group's choice next to the word.

B 1. Ask students to listen and check their answers.

2. Have students correct the wordlist on the board and then write the correct numbers in their books.

3. Tell the groups from 2A to break into pairs to practice the words. Set a time limit (two minutes).

C 1. Point out the *Grammar note.* Have students repeat the singular and plural forms.

2. Have students complete their charts. As they work, copy the chart on the board.

3. Ask volunteers to complete the chart on the board as their classmates dictate the answers.

Communicative Practice and Application
10–15 minutes

D 1. Model the example with a volunteer. Then model it again with new directions. Say: *Point to the clock. Open the notebook.*

2. Set a time limit (five minutes). Ask students to practice the classroom directions with several partners.

> **Multilevel Strategies**
>
> For 2D, use mixed-level pairs.
> • **Pre-level** Pair these students with on- or higher-level students. Direct them to listen to their partners and follow their commands.

Evaluation
10–15 minutes (books closed)

TEST YOURSELF

1. Make a two-column chart on the board with the headings *Directions* and *Classroom Words.* Have students close their books and give you an example for each column.

2. Have students copy the chart into their notebooks.

3. Give students five to ten minutes to test themselves by writing the words they recall from the lesson.

4. Call "time" and have students check their spelling in *The Oxford Picture Dictionary* or another dictionary. Circulate and monitor students' progress.

> **Multilevel Strategies**
>
> Target the *Test Yourself* to the level of your students.
> • **Pre-level** Have these students work with their books open.
> • **Higher-level** Have these students complete the chart and then write three directions by combining words from both columns. *Point to the pens*

Multilevel Strategies help meet the varying needs of all learners in the classroom.

To compress this lesson: Conduct 2A as a whole-class activity. Have students practice 2D with only one partner.

To extend this lesson: Dictate short sentences using the lesson vocabulary. For example, *Point to the chair.* Allow students to look in the book for spelling help.

And/Or have students complete **Workbook 1 page 2** and **Multilevel Activity Book 1 page 18.**

Tips on how to compress or extend a lesson aid time and classroom management.

Unit 1 Learning Log for _____ Date: _____
(name)

I can
- ❑ use classroom directions and name things in the classroom
- ❑ write my name, telephone number and signature
- ❑ use the verb be (*I am a student. She is a teacher.*)
- ❑ introduce myself to people.
- ❑ understand ways to learn English.
- ❑ say my goals.

My favorite exercise was _____

I need to practice _____

I want to learn more about _____

Unit 2 Learning Log for _____ Date: _____
(name)

I can
- ❑ use words for time and the calendar.
- ❑ write about myself.
- ❑ use yes/no questions and answers (*Is Trang happy? Yes, she is.*)
- ❑ talk about marital status.
- ❑ understand a population map.
- ❑ understand a graph about population.

My favorite exercise was _____

I need to practice _____

I want to learn more about _____

Unit 3 Learning Log for _____ Date: _____
(name)

I can
- ❑ name family members.
- ❑ write about my eye and hair color.
- ❑ use possessives (*Her eyes are brown.*)
- ❑ say dates.
- ❑ understand information about American families.
- ❑ understand a pie chart about American families.

My favorite exercise was _____

I need to practice _____

I want to learn more about _____

T-176   © 2007 Oxford University Press • Permission granted to reproduce for classroom use.

O

Unit 8
Exercise 47   Name: _____
             Date: _____

A. Complete the sentences. Use the words in the box.

every day	once a week	twice a week
three times a week	four times a month	

1. Maria eats breakfast at home ____once a week____. (on Monday)
2. Miguel shops for food _____. (seven days a week)
3. Jim and Trang play soccer _____. (on Tuesday and Thursday)
4. I eat dinner with my mother _____. (every Sunday)
5. Mr. Smith teaches English _____. (Monday, Wednesday, Friday)

B. Look at Ann's schedule. Circle the correct answer.

1. How often does Ann have lunch at home?
   She (always /never) has lunch at home.
2. How often does she have breakfast in a restaurant?
   She (usually / never) has breakfast in a restaurant.
3. How often does she have breakfast at home?
   She (always / never) has breakfast at home.
4. How often does she have lunch at school?
   She (usually / sometimes) has lunch at school.
5. How often does she have lunch at Tim's?
   She (always / sometimes) has lunch at Tim's.
6. How often does she have dinner with her mother?
   She (sometimes / never) has dinner with her mother.

Monday
• Breakfast at home
• lunch at school
Tuesday
• Breakfast at home
• Lunch at school
Wednesday
• Breakfast at home
• Lunch at school
Thursday
• Breakfast at home
• Lunch at school
Friday
• Breakfast at home
• Lunch at school
• Dinner at Mom's
Saturday
• Breakfast at home
• lunch at Tim's
Sunday
• Breakfast at home
• Lunch at Tim's

Oxford University Press © 2007 • Permission granted to reproduce for classroom use.
Step Forward Multilevel Grammar Exercises CD-ROM 1
Frequency expressions and adverbs of frequency; *How often*

How does *Step Forward* meet learners' needs?

Step Forward's framework supports the creation of effective, learner-centered classes. Researchers and teachers alike know that learners have a variety of learning styles and preferences; therefore the activities in the *Step Forward* program derive from a number of approaches and techniques.[2] Each lesson includes the visual and aural material, practice exercises, communication tasks, and evaluation activities that are key elements of an effective lesson. No matter what your teaching style, *Step Forward* will make it easier to respond to your learners' language needs.

The Step Forward Framework

Step Forward Student Book 1 has 12 thematic units based on these life-skill topics:

1. School
2. Time
3. Family and Friends
4. Home
5. The Community
6. Daily Routines
7. Clothing
8. Food
9. Health
10. Job Search
11. Safety
12. Recreation

Each unit is divided into six lessons. The first five lessons focus on objectives related to the unit theme and develop specific language skills within the context of the topic. The sixth lesson provides opportunities to review and expand upon the previous lessons' language and information.

In addition to its main objective, each lesson works with the support skills students will need in order to achieve the objective (vocabulary, grammar, pronunciation, computation, etc.) In each of the lessons, learners accomplish the following general objectives:

Lesson 1 Vocabulary: express thoughts and opinions about a topic using thematically linked vocabulary.

Lesson 2 Life stories: use the new vocabulary to tell and write personal stories and accomplish a life-skill competency related to the lesson topic.

Lesson 3 Grammar: learn and accurately use grammar in order to effectively interact and write on the lesson topic.

Lesson 4 Everyday conversation: use an authentic exchange as the basis for conversations on the lesson topic while developing listening and pronunciation skills and fluency.

---

2. C. Van Duzer and M. Florez Cunningham, *Adult English Language Instruction in the 21st Century* (Washington, D.C.: National Center for ESL Literacy Education/Center for Applied Linguistics, 2003):13.

Lesson 5 Real-life reading: increase comprehension of both narrative and life-skill reading materials while developing the skills required for both types of reading experiences.

Review and expand: integrate the language learned in the previous five lessons in order to accomplish a variety of communication tasks.

What are *Step Forward's* principles of effective lesson-plan design?

Lessons in the *Student Book* follow four principles of effective lesson-plan design:

- Successful learning is anchored to objectives that connect to learners' needs outside the classroom;
- Learners need listening, speaking, reading, and writing, plus math and critical-thinking skill development within each lesson. The lesson's skill focus always relates to the skills that support the objective;
- A staged and sequential lesson helps learners move from knowing about and

understanding new language and concepts to putting the new language and concepts to use in their daily lives; and

- A variety of processing and practice activities help learners integrate new information with their prior knowledge in order to achieve the lesson objectives.

Step-by-Step Lesson Plans employs these principles in the easy-access, detailed lesson-teaching notes and multilevel strategies for each of the 72 lessons in the *Student Book*.

The Stages of the *Step Forward* Lesson

A typical *Step Forward* lesson includes seven basic stages, as shown in the chart below. Multiple presentation and practice stages may occur in a lesson, depending on the complexity of the objectives.

Math Extension, Pronunciation Extension, and Problem Solving are self-contained mini-lessons that occur throughout the book. Each provides presentation and practice activities.

STEP FORWARD LESSON STAGES	
Warm-up and Review	Learners typically engage with the whole class and prepare for the upcoming lesson. Missing this stage does not penalize learners who have arrived late.
Introduction	The instructor focuses learners' attention on the lesson objective, relating it to their lives outside the classroom.
Presentation	New information, language, and content is presented and developed to ensure comprehension. Comprehension is carefully checked before proceeding to the next stage.
Guided Practice (controlled practice)	Learners work on developing their accuracy through various exercises and activities, which may be interactive. The activities are tightly structured to support learners' use of the lesson's grammar and vocabulary.
Communicative Practice (less-controlled practice)	Learners apply their skills to build their fluency. Team tasks, pair interviews, and role-plays are all examples of communicative practice.
Application	This stage is often merged with the communicative practice stage. In Lesson 5, however, learners "Bring It To Life" by finding print materials on the life skill or narrative reading topic outside of the classroom.
Evaluation	This stage assesses learners' achievement of the objective. Instructors use informal assessments, such as observations, and more formal evaluation tasks or tests.

How do I use this book?

Planning daily lessons with *Step Forward* and the *Step-by-Step Lesson Plans* is as easy as opening this book, making a couple of notes, and heading to class. Before you begin your daily planning though, it's wise to do a bit of "big picture" planning.

Step One

Reflect

The first step in planning effective lessons is to determine which learning objectives match the needs of your learners. Because the objectives in *Step Forward* are based on the CASAS competencies and the curriculum of some of the best adult programs across the country, it's a pretty safe bet that most of the objectives will match your students' communication needs. Nevertheless, it's important to determine what experience learners already have with the lesson topic, and what they already know. Before starting a unit, read through the topics (labeled *Focus on*) on the first *Student Book* page in the unit and ask yourself the following questions:

- What level of experience do my learners have with each of these topics?
- What is their command of the support skills needed to communicate about these topics?
- How will I determine what my learners already know about this topic? (Possible answers include using the opening exercises in each lesson, using the warm-up activity from the Lesson Plans, and using the Round Table Label activity from the *Multilevel Activity Book*.)

Step Two

Preview

Once you have an overview of the unit, preview the *Student Book* page of the first lesson and read through the lesson plan objectives. If you have a single-level class, you may choose to work from the on-level objective, or (as is so often the case) if you have an unidentified multilevel class, you may want to identify which learners will be working toward which objectives.

Step Three

Scan

Next, read through each stage of the lesson plan and the matching sections of the *Student Book* page. The lettered and numbered sections in the lesson plan correlate to the lettered and numbered exercises on the *Student Book* page.

Step Four

Gather

Be sure you have the tools you need. Ask yourself:

- Would any authentic materials help with the presentation of any of the lesson content? (For example, are coins needed for a lesson on money?)
- Will I use the audio CD or cassette tapes for the listening practice or read from the audio script (pages 148–158)?
- Which pages of *The Oxford Picture Dictionary* will be helpful in building comprehension?
- Which *Workbook* pages can learners use while waiting for other learners to complete a lesson task?

Step Five

Calculate

As you read through each stage of the lesson, be sure to notice the suggested time frames and use the compression and extension tips to adjust the lesson to your instructional time period.

Planning for Closing

Many teachers, new and experienced alike, commonly forget to provide a closing activity. Formally bringing the class back together to emphasize what has been accomplished gives learners a chance to assess what they liked and learned in the lesson. Closing activities can be as simple as a class brainstorm of all the words and ideas covered in the lesson or a chain drill that completes the sentence, "Today, I learned ...." The closing is also an opportunity for you to share your positive reflections on the lesson and send everyone out into the world a little more lighthearted.

How does *Step Forward* address the multilevel classroom?

Step Forward's multilevel framework addresses a common classroom reality that most instructors face: Even though learners share a classroom and an instructor, they may be working at different competency levels.

Two of the key concepts of successful multilevel instruction are:

1) learners need to feel that they are all part of the same class community; and
2) learners at different levels can work in the same general topic area while achieving different objectives.[3]

---

3. Jill Bell, *Teaching Multilevel Classes in ESL* (San Diego: Dominie Press, 1991): 36–38.

Using *Step Forward's* Multilevel Framework

Multilevel experts recommend that instructors begin their lesson planning by identifying a common theme for students at all levels. Instructors can then create level-specific objectives that relate to that theme. All the lessons within a *Step Forward* unit link to a common theme, with each lesson exploring a facet of that theme. In addition, each lesson plan in *Step-by-Step Lesson Plans* has a set of objectives for three sequenced levels:

Pre-level objectives are for those students who place below the level of the selected student book.

On-level objectives are for those learners who place at the level of the selected student book.

Higher-level objectives are for those learners who place above the level of the selected student book.

By planning a lesson around these three objectives, the teacher can use the *Student Book* and ancillary materials to support instruction across three sequential levels of learners.

Working with Broad Spectrum Multilevel Classes

Experts in multilevel instruction suggest that even broad spectrum classes, those with learners ranging from low-beginning to advanced and having a wide array of skill levels, can be divided into three general groups during each lesson. Because not all learners have the same proficiency level in the same skill areas, learners in multilevel classes may be placed in different groups depending on the skill focus. For example, a student may be in the beginning group in speaking but the intermediate group in writing. Also, depending on the span of levels, an instructor may want to use two levels of *Step Forward* to help meet the needs of learners at either end of the spectrum. (For more information, see the *Step Forward Professional Development Program*).

Learners may move between groups based on the type of lesson being taught. In a lesson where learners' listening and speaking skills are the focus, you might create one group of beginners, a second group of intermediate learners, and a third group of advanced learners. Of course, the formation of these groups would also depend on the number of learners at each level.

For more information, see the Multilevel Troubleshooting Chart on pg T-180 for more tips and resources for resolving multilevel instruction challenges.

How do I use the Multilevel Strategies to plan multilevel lessons?

Planning a multilevel lesson incorporates the same five steps from page T-x with three variations:

1. Base the lesson on two or three of the multilevel objectives (identified at the top of the lesson page), depending on the abilities of students in your class.
2. In preparing for the presentation stage, consider correlating materials from the *Basic Oxford Picture Dictionary* program for your pre-literacy learners.
3. Incorporate the multilevel grouping and instructional strategies in each lesson.

Grouping students in the multilevel classroom maximizes learner involvement and minimizes teacher stress. Putting learners in same-level groups during guided practice activities allows them to move at the right pace for their level. Creating different-level groups for communicative practice allows learners to increase their fluency. Assigning roles and tasks based on learners' proficiency level allows all learners to participate and succeed. The multilevel instructional strategies in this book are fairly consistent within each lesson type. Once a strategy is mastered, it can easily be applied to future lessons or activities.

How is *Step Forward* a complete program?

In addition to the *Student Book* and the *Step-by-Step Lesson Plans*, the *Step Forward* program also includes ancillary materials that support communicative language instruction. Each of the following ancillary materials is correlated to the units and topics of each *Student Book*:

- *Audio Program*
- *Workbook*.
- *Multilevel Activity Book*
- *Test Generator*
- *Professional Development Program*

The *Step Forward* team created these materials and this *Step-by-Step Lesson Plans* with one goal in mind: to help *you* help *your learners*. Please write to us at **Stepforwardteam.us@oup.com** with your comments, questions, and ideas.

Jayme Adelson-Goldstein, Series Director

TABLE OF CONTENTS

Listening & Speaking	CASAS Life Skills Competencies	Standardized Student Syllabi/ LCPs	SCANS Competencies	EFF Content Standards
• Listen to basic classroom directions • Say and spell names • Listen and say numbers, phone numbers, and addresses	0.1.2, 0.1.4, 0.1.6, 6.0.1, 6.0.2	22.01, 25.01	• Listening • Speaking • Sociability	• Speaking so others can understand • Listening actively
• Give classroom directions • Listen for and give personal information • Talk about the classroom • Practice social conversations • Interview a partner to fill out an application **Pronunciation:** • Listen for contractions and use them in conversations	**L1:** 0.1.2, 0.1.5, 7.4.5, 7.4.7 **L2:** 0.1.2, 0.2.1, 0.2.2, 2.5.5, 6.0.1, 7.4.7 **L3:** 0.1.2, 7.4.7 **L4:** 0.1.2, 0.1.4, 0.2.1, 7.4.7 **L5:** 0.1.2, 0.2.2, 2.5.5, 7.4.7 **RE:** 0.1.2, 0.1.4, 0.1.5, 0.2.1, 0.2.2, 4.8.1, 7.2.5–7.2.7, 7.3.1	**L1:** 32.01, 33.06 **L2:** 22.01, 25.01, 31.02, 32.01, 32.02, 32.13 **L3:** 22.01, 32.01, 33.02, 33.06, 33.09 **L4:** 22.01–22.03, 32.01, 32.02, 32.13, 33.09, 34.01, 34.02 **L5:** 22.01, 31.02, 32.01, 32.03, 32.04, 32.13 **RE:** 22.01–22.03, 32.01, 32.02, 32.05, 32.13, 33.02, 33.06, 33.07, 33.09	Most SCANS are incorporated into this unit, with an emphasis on: • Seeing things in the mind's eye • Self-management • Participating as a member of a team	Most EFFs are incorporated into this unit, with an emphasis on: • Observing critically • Cooperating with others • Reflecting and evaluating • Solving problems and making decisions
• Ask and answer questions with time and calendar words • Talk about a calendar • Listen for information about people • Listen for information about ID cards • Ask and answer personal information questions • Listen for information on an extended form	**L1:** 0.1.2, 2.3.1, 2.3.2, 6.0.1, 7.1.4, 7.4.5, 7.4.7 **L2:** 0.1.2, 0.1.4, 0.2.1, 6.01, 7.4.7 **L3:** 0.1.1, 0.1.2, 0.2.1, 7.4.7 **L4:** 0.1.2, 0.1.3, 0.2.1, 0.2.2, 6.0.1, 7.4.7 **L5:** 0.1.2, 0.2.1, 1.1.3, 2.7.2, 5.2.4, 5.2.5, 5.5.1, 6.0.1, 6.7.1, 6.7.2, 6.9.2 **RE:** 0.1.2, 0.1.5, 0.2.1, 2.3.2, 4.8.1, 6.0.1, 7.2.5–7.2.7, 7.3.1	**L1:** 25.01–25.03, 32.01, 33.07 **L2:** 22.01, 22.02, 25.01, 25.04, 32.01, 32.02, 32.13, 33.07 **L3:** 22.01, 32.01, 33.02 **L4:** 22.01, 22.03, 25.01, 32.01, 32.02, 33.02, 33.07 **L5:** 22.01, 25.01, 32.01, 32.02–32.05, 32.06, 32.13 **RE:** 22.01, 25.01, 25.03, 32.01, 32.13, 33.02, 33.07	Most SCANS are incorporated into this unit, with an emphasis on: • Seeing things in the mind's eye • Self-management • Acquiring and evaluating information • Interpreting and communicating information	Most EFFs are incorporated into this unit, with an emphasis on: • Observing critically • Using math to solve problems and communicate • Cooperating with others
• Listen for and talk about physical descriptions • Listen to phone messages • Talk about names and birthdays **Pronunciation:** • Ordinal numbers	**L1:** 0.1.2, 7.4.5, 7.4.7 **L2:** 0.1.2, 0.2.1, 7.4.7 **L3:** 0.1.2, 0.2.1, 7.4.7 **L4:** 0.1.2, 2.1.7, 2.3.2, 6.0.1, 6.0.2, 7.4.7 **L5:** 0.1.2, 0.2.1, 6.0.1, 6.0.2, 6.4.2, 6.7.4 **RE:** 0.1.2, 0.2.1, 4.8.1, 6.0.1, 7.2.5–7.2.7, 7.3.1, 7.3.2, 7.3.3, 7.3.4	**L1:** 22.01, 25.03, 31.01, 32.01, 32.02, 33.05 **L2:** 22.01, 31.01, 32.01, 32.02, 33.03 **L3:** 22.01, 31.01, 32.01, 32.13, 33.03, 33.07 **L4:** 22.03, 23.02, 25.01, 25.03, 31.01, 32.01, 32.02, 32.13, 34.01, 34.02 **L5:** 22.01, 25.01, 31.01, 32.01, 32.03–32.06, 33.03 **RE:** 22.01, 25.01, 25.03, 25.04, 31.01, 32.01, 32.02, 32.05, 33.02, 33.03, 33.05, 33.07	Most SCANS are incorporated into this unit, with an emphasis on: • Seeing things in the mind's eye • Self-management • Acquiring and evaluating information • Participating as a member of a team • Organizing and maintaining information	Most EFFs are incorporated into this unit, with an emphasis on: • Observing critically • Using math to solve problems and communicate • Cooperating with others • Solving problems and making decisions • Reflecting and evaluating

Unit	Life Skills & Civics Competencies	Vocabulary	Grammar	Critical Thinking & Math Concepts	Reading & Writing
Unit 4 **At Home** **page 40**	• Identify colors • Identify places and things in the home • State the location of things in the home • State common activities in the home • Ask a friend for help • Save money by conserving resources • Pay bills and address envelopes	• Rooms and other areas in the home • Furniture and appliances • Things to do at home • Items on a bill • Items on an envelope	• *This* and *that* • The present continuous • Present continuous *Yes/No* questions • Subject and object pronouns	• Describe objects in rooms • Analyze personal activity times • Decide when to pay bills **Real-life math:** • Add utility bill totals **Problem solving:** • Delegate responsibility	• Read about a day at home • Write a story about places and activities at home • Read about things to do in the home • Read about paying bills • Read about saving money • Read addresses on envelopes • Write about objects in rooms
Unit 5 **In the Neighborhood** **page 52**	• Identify neighborhood places and modes of transportation • Read a neighborhood map • Ask for and give directions • Respond to emergencies • Use an emergency exit map	• Places in a neighborhood • Things in a neighborhood • Descriptions of locations • Directions • Emergencies	• Prepositions of location • *There is* and *There are* • Questions and answers with *There is* and *There are* • *How many*	• Interpret information from a map • Label a map • Ask for and give directions • Make an emergency exit map **Real-life math:** • Determine distance between points on a map **Problem solving:** • Determine what to do when lost	• Read and write about a neighborhood • Write questions with *Is there* and *Are there* • Write a list of home emergencies • Read about home emergencies • Read emergency exit maps
Unit 6 **Daily Routines** **page 64**	• Identify and discuss daily routines • Make a schedule • State ways to relax • Follow directions to operate office machines • Interpret personal, family, and work responsibilities	• Everyday activities • Ways to relax • Office machines and equipment • Housework	• The simple present • Contractions of *do* • Questions and answers using the simple present • *Have* • *A little* or *a lot*	• Differentiate between daily and special activities • Analyze problems and ask for help with an office machine • Estimate duration of various activities **Problem solving:** • Determine how to solve problems and ask for help in the workplace	• Read and write about a work schedule • Read about office machines and equipment • Read and write about daily routines in the U.S.

Listening & Speaking	CASAS Life Skills Competencies	Standardized Student Syllabi/ LCPs	SCANS Competencies	EFF Content Standards
• Talk about objects in the home • Listen for appliances and furniture • Talk about paying bills • Listen for bill totals • Talk about activities done in the home	**L1:** 0.1.2, 1.4.1, 7.4.5 **L2:** 0.1.2, 1.4.1, 7.4.7, 8.2.5 **L3:** 0.1.2, 0.2.4, 7.4.7, 8.2.3 **L4:** 0.1.2, 0.1.3, 0.2.3, 1.2.4, 1.5.3, 2.1.4, 6.0.1–6.0.4, 6.1.1, 7.1.3, 7.4.7 **L5:** 0.1.2, 1.5.3, 2.1.4, 2.4.1, 6.0.1, 7.1.3 **RE:** 0.1.2, 1.4.1, 4.8.1, 7.2.5–7.2.7, 7.3.1	**L1:** 32.01, 33.03 **L2:** 32.01, 32.02, 32.13, 33.03 **L3:** 32.01, 33.02, 33.07 **L4:** 22.03, 23.03, 25.01, 28.05, 29.01, 32.01, 32.02, 33.01 **L5:** 23.03, 25.01, 28.05, 29.01, 32.01–32.04, 32.12, 32.13 **RE:** 28.05, 32.01, 32.02, 32.05, 32.13, 33.01, 33.02	Most SCANS are incorporated into this unit, with an emphasis on: • Seeing things in the mind's eye • Self-management • Participating as a member of a team	Most EFFs are incorporated into this unit, with an emphasis on: • Observing critically • Cooperating with others • Using math to solve problems and communicate • Solving problems and making decisions
• Talk about transportation and places • Listen for places and things on a map • Listen for neighborhood information • Ask and answer questions with *There is* and *There are* • Listen for and give directions **Pronunciation:** • Stressed words in descriptions	**L1:** 0.1.2, 1.1.3, 2.2.1, 2.2.3, 2.2.5, 2.5.1, 2.5.3, 2.5.5, 7.4.5, 7.4.7 **L2:** 0.1.2, 1.1.3, 2.2.1, 2.5.1, 2.5.3, 7.4.7 **L3:** 0.1.2, 2.2.1, 2.6.1, 6.0.1, 7.4.7 **L4:** 0.1.2, 0.1.3, 1.1.3, 1.1.4, 1.9.4, 2.2.1, 6.0.1, 7.4.7 **L5:** 0.1.2, 1.1.3, 1.4.8, 2.1.2, 2.5.1 **RE:** 0.1.2, 4.8.1, 7.2.5–7.2.7, 7.3.1	**L1:** 26.01, 26.03, 32.01, 32.13 **L2:** 26.03, 32.01, 32.02, 32.13, 33.04 **L3:** 26.03, 32.01, 32.05, 32.13 **L4:** 22.03, 25.01, 26.03, 30.02, 32.01, 32.02, 34.02 **L5:** 26.03, 27.01, 32.01–32.04, 32.06, 32.16 **RE:** 26.03, 32.01, 32.02, 32.05, 33.04	Most SCANS are incorporated into this unit, with an emphasis on: • Seeing things in the mind's eye • Self-management • Participating as a member of a team • Acquiring and evaluating information • Interpreting and communicating information	Most EFFs are incorporated into this unit, with an emphasis on: • Observing critically • Cooperating with others • Using math to solve problems and communicate • Reflecting and evaluating
• Talk about daily routines • Talk about times for daily routines • Listen for information about a work schedule • Talk about a work schedule • Ask and answer questions about daily routines **Pronunciation:** • Verbs ending in -*s*	**L1:** 0.1.2, 0.2.4, 6.0.1, 7.4.5, 7.4.7 **L2:** 0.1.2, 0.2.4, 6.0.1, 7.4.7, 8.2.3 **L3:** 0.1.2, 0.2.4, 3.5.4, 3.5.5, 6.0.1, 7.4.7, 8.1.1 **L4:** 0.1.2, 0.1.3, 0.2.4, 1.7.3, 4.5.1, 4.5.4, 4.5.7, 4.6.1 **L5:** 0.1.2, 0.2.4, 1.1.3, 7.2.5, 7.2.6, 8.2.3 **RE:** 0.1.2, 0.2.4, 1.7.3, 4.5.1, 4.5.4, 4.5.7, 4.6.1, 4.8.1, 6.0.1, 7.2.6, 7.2.7, 7.3.1	**L1:** 32.01 **L2:** 32.01, 32.02, 32.13 **L3:** 32.01, 32.13, 33.02 **L4:** 19.02, 21.01, 22.03, 32.01–32.03, 34.01, 34.02, 34.03 **L5:** 32.01, 32.02, 32.04–32.06, 32.13 **RE:** 19.02, 21.01, 32.01, 32.02, 32.05, 32.13, 33.02	Most SCANS are incorporated into this unit, with an emphasis on: • Seeing things in the mind's eye • Self-management • Time • Participating as a member of a team • Acquiring and evaluating information • Interpreting and communicating information	Most EFFs are incorporated into this unit, with an emphasis on: • Observing critically • Using math to solve problems and communicate • Cooperating with others

Listening & Speaking	CASAS Life Skills Competencies	Standardized Student Syllabi/ LCPs	SCANS Competencies	EFF Content Standards
• Listen and talk about currency • Listen and talk about clothing items • Talk about clothing for different occasions • Request specific clothing from a salesperson • Listen for sizes and prices of clothing • Talk about purchases **Pronunciation:** • Differentiate between -*teen* and -*ty* numbers	**L1:** 0.1.2, 1.1.6, 1.2.1, 1.2.4, 1.3.9, 6.0.1–6.0.4, 6.1.1, 7.4.5, 7.4.7 **L2:** 0.1.2, 1.3.1, 1.3.3, 1.3.9, 4.4.1, 6.0.1, 7.4.7 **L3:** 0.1.2, 1.3.9, 7.4.7 **L4:** 0.1.2, 1.1.6, 1.1.9, 1.2.1, 1.2.4, 1.2.5, 1.3.9, 1.6.4, 4.4.1, 6.0.1–6.0.4, 6.1.1, 6.1.2, 7.4.7 **L5:** 0.1.2, 1.1.6, 1.3.1, 1.3.3, 1.8.1, 1.8.2, 6.0.1 **RE:** 0.1.2, 0.1.3, 1.1.6, 1.3.1, 1.3.3, 1.3.9, 1.8.1, 1.8.2, 4.8.1, 4.8.6, 6.0.1–6.0.4, 6.1.2, 7.2.5–7.2.7, 7.3.1	**L1:** 25.01, 25.05, 25.06, 28.02, 32.01, 32.02 **L2:** 28.02, 32.01, 32.02, 32.13 **L3:** 28.02, 32.01, 33.02 **L4:** 25.01, 25.05, 25.06, 28.02, 28.03, 32.01, 32.02, 32.13, 34.01, 34.02, 34.03 **L5:** 25.01, 25.06, 32.01, 32.03–32.07, 32.13 **RE:** 25.01, 25.06, 28.02, 32.01, 32.02, 32.05, 32.13, 33.02	Most SCANS are incorporated into this unit, with an emphasis on: • Seeing things in the mind's eye • Self-management • Participating as a member of a team	Most EFFs are incorporated into this unit, with an emphasis on: • Observing critically • Using math to solve problems and communicate • Cooperating with others • Reflecting and evaluating
• Talk about food shopping • Listen for food items on a shopping list • Talk about routines • Order in a restaurant • Listen for restaurant orders • Talk about food labels **Pronunciation:** • Question and statement intonation patterns	**L1:** 0.1.2, 1.3.8, 7.4.5, 7.4.7 **L2:** 0.1.2, 0.2.4, 1.1.6, 1.2.1, 1.2.5, 1.3.8, 6.0.1, 7.4.7, 8.2.1 **L3:** 0.2.4, 2.3.2, 7.4.7 **L4:** 0.1.2, 0.1.3, 0.1.6, 1.1.6, 1.2.1, 1.2.4, 1.3.8, 2.6.4, 6.0.1–6.0.4, 6.1.1, 7.4.7 **L5:** 0.1.2, 1.3.8, 1.6.1, 3.5.1, 3.5.2 **RE:** 0.2.4, 1.3.8, 4.8.1, 6.0.1, 7.2.5–7.2.7, 7.3.1	**L1:** 28.01, 32.01 **L2:** 28.01, 32.01, 32.02, 32.13 **L3:** 25.03, 32.01, 32.08, 33.08 **L4:** 22.03, 25.01, 28.01, 29.03, 32.01, 32.02, 32.13 **L5:** 27.02, 28.01, 32.01, 32.02–32.06, 32.13 **RE:** 28.01, 31.03, 32.01, 32.02, 32.05, 32.13, 33.08	Most SCANS are incorporated into this unit, with an emphasis on: • Seeing things in the mind's eye • Self-management • Participating as a member of a team • Interpreting and communicating information	Most EFFs are incorporated into this unit, with an emphasis on: • Observing critically • Using math to solve problems and communicate • Cooperating with others • Reflecting and evaluating
• Ask and answer questions about a doctor's office • Listen and talk about a visit to the doctor • Talk about ways to get well and to stay healthy • Listen for medical advice • Listen for information to complete an appointment card • Ask and answer questions about obligations **Pronunciation:** • Listen for forms of *have* and *have to*	**L1:** 0.1.2, 3.1.1, 7.4.5, 7.4.7 **L2:** 0.1.2, 3.1.1, 3.2.3, 7.4.7 **L3:** 3.1.1, 7.1.1–7.1.3, 7.4.7 **L4:** 0.1.2, 2.3.2, 3.1.1–3.1.3, 4.8.3, 6.0.1, 7.4.7 **L5:** 3.3.1, 3.3.3, 3.4.1, 3.5.8, 3.5.9 **RE:** 0.1.2, 3.1.1, 4.8.1, 6.0.1, 7.2.5–7.2.7, 7.3.1	**L1:** 24.01–24.03, 32.01 **L2:** 24.01–24.03, 32.01, 32.02, 32.07 **L3:** 24.02, 32.01, 32.13, 33.02, 33.07 **L4:** 22.03, 24.02, 24.03, 25.01, 25.03, 32.01, 32.02, 32.13, 33.04, 33.07 **L5:** 24.02–24.04, 27.02, 32.01–32.06, 32.13 **RE:** 24.01–24.03, 32.01, 32.02, 32.05, 32.13, 33.04, 33.06, 33.07	Most SCANS are incorporated into this unit, with an emphasis on: • Seeing things in the mind's eye • Self-management • Participating as a member of a team • Acquiring and evaluating information	Most EFFs are incorporated into this unit, with an emphasis on: • Observing critically • Cooperating with others • Reflecting and evaluating • Solving problems and making decisions • Planning

A Word or Two About Reading Introductions to Textbooks

Teaching professionals rarely read a book's introduction. Instead, we flip through the book's pages, using the pictures, topics, and exercises to determine whether the book matches our learners' needs and our teaching style. We scan the reading passages, conversations, writing tasks, and grammar charts to judge the authenticity and accuracy of the text. At a glance, we assess how easy it would be to manage the pair work, group activities, evaluations, and application tasks.

This Introduction, however, also offers valuable information for the teacher. Because you've read this far, I encourage you to read a little further to learn how *Step Forward's* key concepts, components, and multilevel applications will help you help your learners.

Step Forward's Key Concepts

Step Forward is...

- the instructional backbone for single-level and multilevel classrooms.
- a standards-based, performance-based, and topic-based series for low-beginning through high-intermediate learners.
- a source for ready-made, four-skill lesson plans that address the skills our learners need in their workplace, civic, personal, and academic lives.
- a collection of learner-centered, communicative English-language practice activities.

The classroom is a remarkable place. *Step Forward* respects the depth of experience and knowledge that learners bring to the learning process. At the same time, *Step Forward* recognizes that learners' varied proficiencies, goals, interests, and educational backgrounds create instructional challenges for teachers.

To ensure that our learners leave each class having made progress toward their language and life goals, *Step Forward* works from these key concepts:

- **The wide spectrum of learners' needs makes using materials that support multilevel instruction essential.** *Step Forward* works with single-level and multilevel classes.
- **Learners' prior knowledge is a valuable teaching tool.** Prior knowledge questions appear in every *Step Forward* lesson.

- **Learning objectives are the cornerstone of instruction.** Each *Step Forward* lesson focuses on an objective that derives from identified learner needs, correlates to state and federal standards, and connects to a meaningful communication task. Progress toward the objective is evaluated at the end of the lesson.
- **Vocabulary, grammar and pronunciation skills play an essential role in language learning. They provide learners with the tools needed to achieve life skill, civics, workplace, and academic competencies.** *Step Forward* includes strong vocabulary and grammar strands and features pronunciation and math lesson extensions in each unit.
- **Effective instruction requires a variety of instructional techniques and strategies to engage learners.** Techniques such as Early Production Questioning, Focused Listening, Total Physical Response (TPR), Cooperative Learning, and Problem Solving are embedded in the *Step Forward* series, along with grouping and classroom management strategies.

The *Step Forward* Program Components

The *Step Forward* program has four levels:

- Book 1: low-beginning
- Book 2: high-beginning
- Book 3: low-intermediate
- Book 4: intermediate to high-intermediate

Each level of *Step Forward* correlates to *The Oxford Picture Dictionary*. For pre-literacy learners, *The Basic Oxford Picture Dictionary Literacy Program* provides a flexible, needs-based approach to literacy instruction. Once learners develop strong literacy skills, they will be able to transition seamlessly into *Step Forward Student Book 1*.

Each *Step Forward* level includes the following components:

Step Forward Student Book

A collection of clear, engaging, four-skill lessons based on meaningful learning objectives.

Step Forward Audio Program

The recorded vocabulary, focused listening, conversations, pronunciation, and reading materials from the *Step Forward Student Book*.

Step Forward Step-By-Step Lesson Plans with Multilevel Grammar Exercises CD-ROM

An instructional planning resource with interleaved *Step Forward Student Book* pages, detailed lesson plans featuring multilevel teaching strategies and teaching tips, and a CD-ROM of printable multilevel grammar practice for the structures presented in the *Step Forward Student Book*.

Step Forward Workbook

Practice exercises for independent work in the classroom or as homework.

Step Forward Multilevel Activity Book

More than 100 photocopiable communicative practice activities and 72 picture cards; lesson materials that work equally well in single-level or multilevel settings.

Step Forward Test Generator CD-ROM with ExamView® Assessment Suite

Hundreds of multiple choice and life-skill oriented test items for each *Step Forward Student Book*.

Multilevel Applications of *Step Forward*

All the *Step Forward* program components support multilevel instruction.

Step Forward is so named because it helps learners "step forward" toward their language and life goals, no matter where they start. Our learners often start from very different places and language abilities within the same class.

Regardless of level, all learners need materials that bolster comprehension while providing an appropriate amount of challenge. This makes multilevel materials an instructional necessity in most classrooms.

Each *Step Forward* lesson provides the following multilevel elements:

• **a general topic or competency area** that works across levels. This supports the concept that members of the class community need to feel connected, despite their differing abilities.

• **clear, colorful visuals and realia** that provide pre-level and on-level support during introduction, presentation and practice exercises, as well as prompts for higher-level questions and exercises.

In addition, *Step Forward* correlates to *The Oxford Picture Dictionary* so that teachers can use the visuals and vocabulary from *The Oxford Picture Dictionary* to support and expand upon each lesson.

• **learner-centered practice exercises** that can be used with same-level or mixed-level pairs or small groups. *Step Forward* exercises are broken down to their simplest steps. Once the exercise has been modeled, learners can usually conduct the exercises themselves.

• **pre-level, on-level, and higher-level objectives for each lesson and the multilevel strategies** necessary to carry out the lesson. These objectives are featured in the *Step-By-Step Lesson Plans*.

• **Grammar Boost pages in the Step Forward Workbook that provide excellent "wait time" activities** for learners who complete an exercise early, thus solving a real issue in the multilevel class.

• **a variety of pair, whole class, and small group activities** in the *Step Forward Multilevel Activity Book*. These activities are perfect for same-level and mixed-level grouping.

• **customizable grammar and evaluation exercises** in the *Step Forward Test Generator CD-ROM with ExamView® Assessment Suite*. These exercises make it possible to create evaluations specific to each level in the class.

Professional Development

As instructors, we need to reflect on second language acquisition in order to build a repertoire of effective instructional strategies. The *Step Forward Professional Development Program* provides research-based teaching strategies, tasks, and activities for single- and multilevel classes.

About Writing an ESL Series

It's collaborative! *Step Forward* is the product of dialogs with hundreds of teachers and learners. The dynamic quality of language instruction makes it important to keep this dialog alive. As you use this book in your classes, I invite you to contact me or any member of the *Step Forward* authorial team with your questions or comments.

Jayme Adelson-Goldstein, Series Director
Stepforwardteam.us@oup.com

GUIDE TO THE *STEP FORWARD* SERIES

Step Forward: All you need to ensure your learners' success. All the *Step Forward Student Books* follow this format.

LESSON 1: VOCABULARY teaches key words and phrases relevant to the unit topic, and provides conversation practice using the target vocabulary.

New vocabulary is introduced through vibrant art and high-interest listening texts.

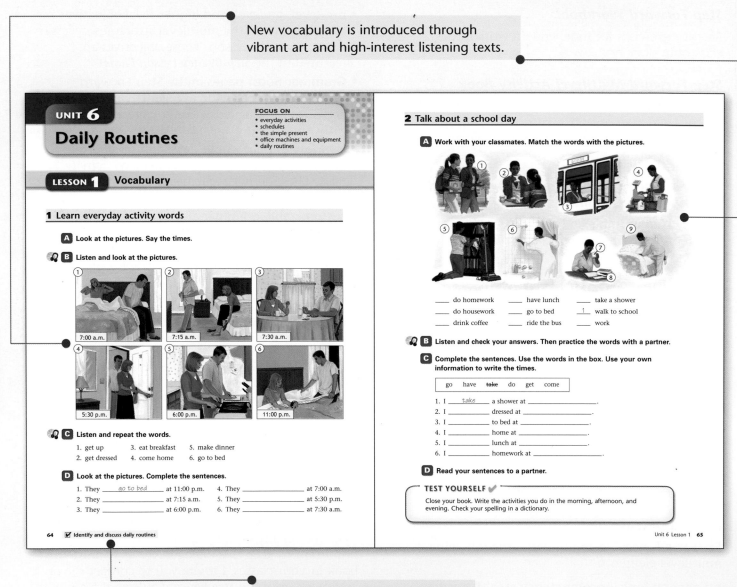

Standards-based objectives are identified at the beginning of every lesson for quick reference.

LESSON 2: LIFE STORIES expands on vocabulary learned in Lesson 1 and furthers learners' understanding through reading and writing about a life skills topic.

Life skills readings help learners practice the vocabulary in natural contexts.

Learners apply the vocabulary to their own lives by writing about their personal experiences.

LESSON 2   Life stories

1 Read about a work schedule

A Look at the pictures. Listen.

Good morning. Doctor's office.

B Listen again. Read the sentences.
1. My name is Tina Aziz. I work in a doctor's office.
2. This is my work schedule. I work from 9 a.m. to 5 p.m., Monday to Thursday.
3. I turn on the computer and copy machine at 9:00. I answer the phone all day.
4. At noon, I meet my friend. We have lunch and talk.
5. On Fridays, I don't work. I relax. I take my kids to the park.
6. I like my job and my schedule a lot, but Fridays are my favorite day.

C Check your understanding. Circle *a* or *b*.
1. Tina works ____.
   a. four days a week
   b. on Saturday
2. She answers the phone ____.
   a. at 9 a.m.
   b. all day
3. Tina and her friend have lunch ____.
   a. at 11 a.m.
   b. at 12 p.m.
4. She likes her job ____.
   a. a lot
   b. a little

66   ☑ Describe and report on schedules

2 Write about your schedule

A Write about your schedule. Complete the sentences.
I go to school from _____ to _____.
I study _____ at school.
On _____, I relax.
I _____.

B Read your story to a partner.

> **Need help?**
>
> **Ways to relax**
> go to the park
> watch TV
> listen to music
> talk to friends and family
> take a walk

3 Talk about a work schedule

A Listen and check (✔) the activities you hear.
____ 1. mop the floor
____ 2. vacuum the rug
____ 3. answer the phone
____ 4. wash the windows
____ 5. turn on the copy machine
____ 6. help the manager

Mel at work

B Listen again. Complete Mel's work schedule.

MORNING 10 A.M.–12 P.M.	AFTERNOON 12 P.M.–3 P.M.
1. _mop the floor_	3. _____
2. _____	4. _____

C Listen and repeat.
A: I work on Saturday and Sunday. How about you?
B: I don't work.
A: I go to school from Monday to Friday. How about you?
B: I go to school on Monday and Wednesday.

D Work with a partner. Practice the conversation. Use your own information.

> **TEST YOURSELF** ✔
>
> Close your book. Listen to your partner's schedule for the week. Write the schedule you hear.

Unit 6 Lesson 2   **67**

Test Yourself, at the end of every lesson, provides learners with ongoing self-assessment.

LESSON 3: GRAMMAR provides clear, simple presentation of the target structure followed by thorough, meaningful practice of it.

Clear grammar charts and exercises help learners develop language confidence and accuracy.

Learners work together to increase fluency and accuracy, using the grammar point to talk about themselves.

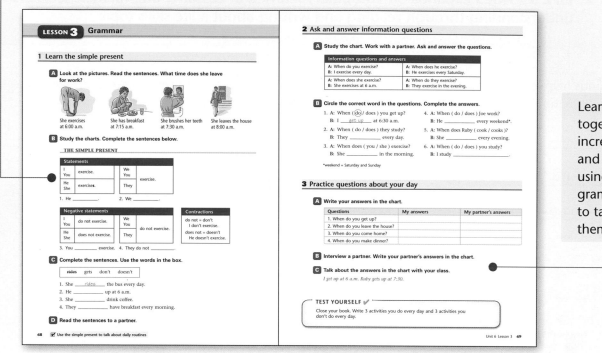

LESSON 4: EVERYDAY CONVERSATION provides learners with fluent, authentic conversations to increase familiarity with natural English.

Pronunciation activities focus on common areas of difficulty.

Listening activities build listening skills.

Model dialogs feature authentic examples of everyday conversation.

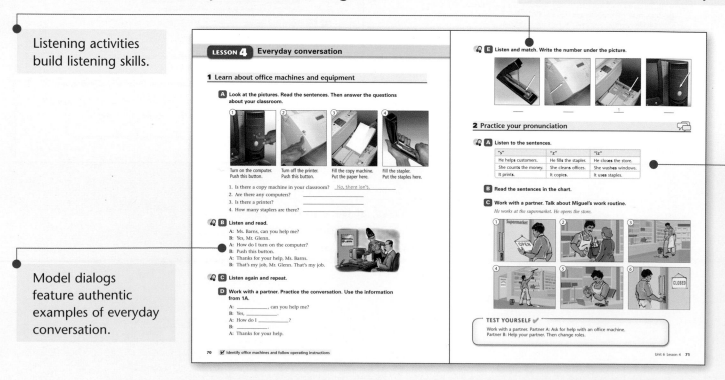

LESSON 5: REAL-LIFE READING develops essential reading skills and offers both life skill and pre-academic reading materials.

High-interest readings recycle vocabulary and grammar.

Chart literacy is increased through practice reading and understanding different types of charts.

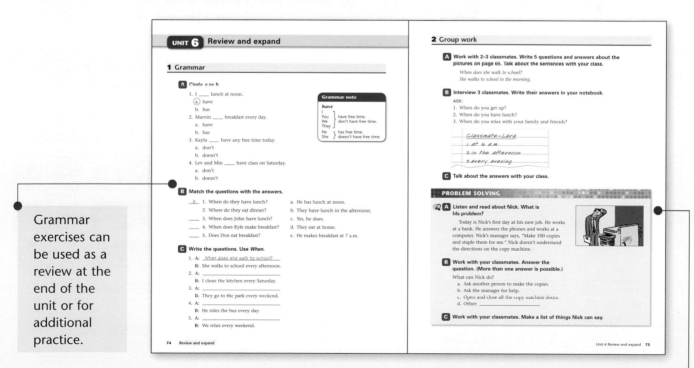

REVIEW AND EXPAND includes additional grammar practice and communicative group tasks to ensure your learners' progress.

Grammar exercises can be used as a review at the end of the unit or for additional practice.

Problem solving tasks encourage learners to use critical thinking skills and meaningful discussion to find solutions to common problems.

Step Forward offers many different components.

Step-By-Step Lesson Plans

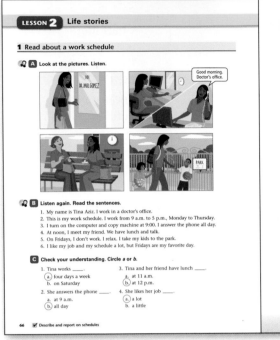

The *Step-By-Step Lesson Plans* provide tips and strategies for conducting *Student Book* activities and applying the lesson to the multilevel classroom.

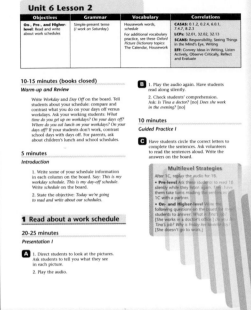

Multilevel Strategies

After 1C, replay the audio for 1B.

- **Pre-level** Ask these students to read 1B silently while they listen again. Then have them take turns reading the sentences in 1C with a partner.
- **On- and Higher-level** Write the following questions on the board for these students to answer: What is Tina's job? [She works in a doctor's office.] Do you like Tina's job? Why is Friday her favorite day? [She doesn't go to work.]

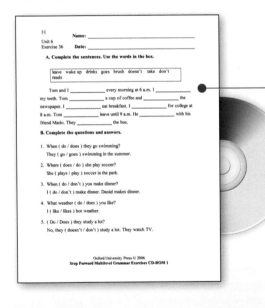

The *Multilevel Grammar Exercises CD-ROM*, a free CD-ROM included with the *Step-By-Step Lesson Plans*, offers additional exercises for pre-level, on-level, and higher-level learners for each grammar point in the *Student Book*.

Workbook

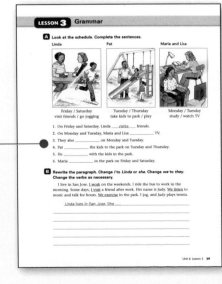

The *Workbook* offers additional exercises ideal for independent practice, homework, or review.

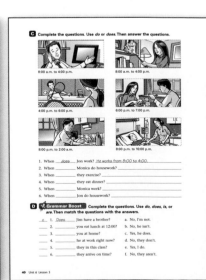

Multilevel Activity Book

The *Multilevel Activity Book* features over 100 reproducible communication activities to complement the multilevel classroom through a variety of pair, small group, and whole-class activities.

There are over 140 picture cards in the *Multilevel Activity Book* that are perfect for practicing key vocabulary and grammar.

Audio Program

Audio CDs and Cassettes feature the listening exercises from the *Student Book* as well as conversations, pronunciation, and readings.

Test Generator

ExamView®
Assessment Suite

The *Test Generator CD-ROM with ExamView® Assessment Suite* offers hundreds of test items for each *Student Book*. Teachers can print out ready-made tests or create their own tests.

Professional Development

Professional Development Task 8
Imagine you want your learners to practice listening carefully during a group task. One behavior you could demonstrate would be leaning forward. Make a list of at least three other behaviors or expressions that careful listeners use.

The *Professional Development Program* offers instructors research-based teaching strategies and activities for single- and multilevel classes, plus Professional Development Tasks like this one.

The First Step

Names and Numbers

1 Spell your name

A Listen and look at the pictures.

1. Point to a letter.

ABCDEFGHI

2. Say your name. Tom.

ABCDEFGH

3. Spell your name. T-O-M.

ABCDEFGH

B Listen and repeat.

The Alphabet

A	B	C	D	E	F	G	H	I
a	b	c	d	e	f	g	h	i
J	K	L	M	N	O	P	Q	R
j	k	l	m	n	o	p	q	r
S	T	U	V	W	X	Y	Z	
s	t	u	v	w	x	y	z	

C Listen and spell the names.

1. M a r i a
2. L e e
3. T o m

4. R e b e c c a
5. K u m a r
6. D a v i d

D Work with 2–3 classmates. Say and spell your name.

A: *I'm Jack.*
B: *Please spell that.*
A: *J-A-C-K.*

A: *I'm Carmen.*
B: *Excuse me. I don't understand.*
A: *I'm Carmen. C-A-R-M-E-N.*

✓ Identify letters of the alphabet; spell words; identify numbers

The First Step

Objectives	Grammar	Vocabulary	Correlations
On- and Higher-level: Identify letters and numbers **Pre-level:** Recognize letters and numbers	I'm (*I'm Jack.*)	Letters and numbers For additional vocabulary practice, see this **Oxford Picture Dictionary** topic: Numbers and Measurements	**CASAS:** 0.1.2, 0.1.4, 0.1.6, 6.0.1, 6.0.2 **LCPs:** 22.01, 25.01 **SCANS:** Listening, Seeing things in the mind's eye, Speaking **EFF:** Listen actively, Observe critically, Speak so others can understand, Use math to solve problems and communicate

Warm-up

10–15 minutes (books closed)

Write *Hi. I'm* (your name). on the board. Walk around the room introducing yourself to the students with these sentences. Repeat the students' names when they respond, and have classmates repeat the name as well.

Introduction

5 minutes

1. Point to the letters of your name on the board, and say them. Count the number of students in the room aloud, and write it on the board. *Forty-two students*

2. State the objective: *Today we're going to learn to pronounce the alphabet and numbers.*

1 Spell your name

Presentation I

15–20 minutes

A Direct students to look at the pictures. Act out the actions. Read and have students repeat the words.

B 1. Have students listen to the audio. Ask them to point to each letter as they listen. Circulate and monitor.

2. Check comprehension. Write various letters on the board, and ask students to say them.

> **TIP**
> Students often forget how to pronounce the alphabet because it's not a part of everyday conversation. It is, however, very important for them to be able to spell words aloud when they are not understood. Make a habit of having students spell aloud some of the words that you write on the board.

Guided Practice

5 minutes

C Ask students to listen and complete the names.

Communicative Practice

15–20 minutes

D 1. Read and have students repeat the conversations. Have volunteers model each conversation with you. Then switch roles and model again.

2. Group students and demonstrate how everyone in the group should take turns being A or B. Assign a time limit (three minutes).

> **Multilevel Strategies**
> Target 1D to the level of your students.
> • **Pre- and On-level** If these students are having difficulty spelling their names aloud, allow them extra time to practice. Tell them to practice spelling their names aloud until they come out relatively smoothly.
> • **Higher-level** If these students can spell their names easily, have them walk around the class practicing the conversations in 2D with as many students as they can.

2 Learn numbers

Presentation II
15–20 minutes

 1. Introduce the new topic: *Now let's say numbers*. Write *numbers* on the board. Say: *One, two, three, four, five are <u>numbers</u>.*

2. Play the audio. Have students listen and repeat. Check comprehension. Write numbers on the board out of order, and call on students to say them.

Guided Practice I
30–35 minutes

 1. Demonstrate the exercise. Say a phone number, and tell students to write it. Circulate and check their work. If necessary, say another number and have students try again.

2. Before students work with their partners, write a phone number on the board, and indicate the appropriate places to pause. Show with pantomime that Partner B is not to look in the book.

3. Have students practice with a partner. Circulate and monitor.

C Demonstrate the exercise. Say an address and tell students to write it. Circulate and check their work. If necessary, say another address and have students try again. Have students practice with a partner. Circulate and monitor.

> ### Multilevel Strategies
> Use 2C to help you determine the speaking level of your students.
>
> • **Pre-level** If these students have difficulty with this exercise, have them look at the addresses with their partners and practice saying them together instead of doing the pair dictation.
>
> • **Higher-level** If these students find this exercise easy, challenge them to invent new addresses, and dictate them to their partners.
>
> Monitor and make a note of which students will need extra help or extra challenges.

3 Learn more numbers

Guided Practice II
15–20 minutes

 Play the audio. Have students listen and repeat.

 Play the audio. Have students listen and count by tens.

> **TIP**
> Students have difficulty distinguishing between 13 and 30, 14 and 40, etc. Show the difference in the stress pattern by writing *thir<u>teen</u>* and *<u>thir</u>ty* on the board and exaggerating the stressed syllable. Write *13–19* on the board in a vertical column and *30–90* in a parallel column. Label the columns *A* and *B*. Pass out *A/B* cards (see page T-175). Say numbers randomly, and have students hold up their cards to indicate whether the number is in column A or B.

C Play the audio. Have students listen and write the numbers. Ask volunteers to write the numbers on the board.

Evaluation
10–15 minutes

Dictate two or three phone numbers. Then dictate two or three numbers by spelling them: *E-I-G-H-T, N-I-N-E-T-E-E-N, S-E-V-E-N-T-Y.* Don't say the numbers, just the letters. Collect the work to check students' listening accuracy.

To compress this lesson: Have students practice 1D with only one partner.

To extend this lesson: Ask students to tell you the names of streets in the area. Write the street names on the board, and have students practice pronouncing and spelling them.

And/Or have students complete **Multilevel Activity Book 1 pages 15–16.**

2 Learn numbers

A Listen and say the numbers.

1	2	3	4	5
one	two	three	four	five
6	**7**	**8**	**9**	**10**
six	seven	eight	nine	ten
11	**12**	**13**	**14**	**15**
eleven	twelve	thirteen	fourteen	fifteen
16	**17**	**18**	**19**	**20**
sixteen	seventeen	eighteen	nineteen	twenty

> **Need help?**
>
> **0 = zero**
> You can say "O" instead of "zero" in phone numbers and addresses.

B Work with a partner. Partner A: Say a phone number. Partner B: Listen and write the phone number.

1. 555-3611
2. 555-1468
3. (213) 555-8837
4. (714) 555-9592

5-5-5-4-3-2-1

phone number

C Work with a partner. Partner A: Say an address. Partner B: Listen and write the address.

1. 1711 G Street
2. 1214 B Street
3. 613 K Street
4. 1516 Q Street

address

3 Learn more numbers

A Listen and count from 20 to 30.

20 21 22 23 24 25 26 27 28 29 30

B Listen and count by tens.

10	20	30	40	50
ten	twenty	thirty	forty	fifty
60	**70**	**80**	**90**	**100**
sixty	seventy	eighty	ninety	one hundred

C Listen and write the numbers.

1. _____20_____
2. _____40_____
3. _____90_____
4. _____100_____

In the Classroom

FOCUS ON
- classroom English
- personal information
- the verb *be*
- meeting people
- study goals

LESSON **1**   Vocabulary

1 Learn classroom directions

A   Look at the pictures. Say the letters.

B   Listen and look at the pictures.

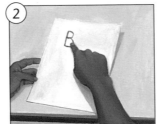
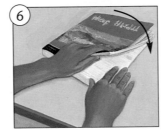

C   Listen and repeat the words.

1. listen to	3. say	5. open	7. sit down
2. point to	4. repeat	6. close	8. stand up

D   Look at the pictures. Complete the sentences.
Use the words in the box.

Point   Sit   Say   Close   Listen to   Stand   ~~Open~~   Repeat

1. *Open* the notebook.
2. *Repeat* the letter D.
3. *Close* the book, please.
4. *Point* to the letter B.

5. *Sit* down, please.
6. *Stand* up, please.
7. *Say* the letter C.
8. *Listen to* the letter A.

  ☑ Identify classroom items; respond to simple commands

Unit 1 Lesson 1

Objectives	Grammar	Vocabulary	Correlations
On-level: Identify classroom directions and classroom objects **Pre-level:** Recognize classroom directions and classroom objects **Higher-level:** Talk and write about classroom directions and classroom objects	Regular singular and plural nouns (*a pen, pens*)	Classroom directions, classroom words For additional vocabulary practice, see this **Oxford Picture Dictionary** topic: A Classroom	**CASAS:** 0.1.2, 0.1.5, 7.4.5, 7.4.7 **LCPs:** 32.01, 33.06 **SCANS:** Listening, Seeing things in the mind's eye, Self-management, Participates as member of a team **EFF:** Cooperate with others, Listen actively, Observe critically, Reflect and evaluate, Speak so others can understand

Warm-up and Review

10 minutes (books closed)

Ask *What's this?* as you point to a table, a desk, a chair, and a clock and as you hold up a book, a pen, and a pencil. If a student calls out the answer, write it on the board. Spell the words aloud, pointing to each letter as you say it, and have students repeat chorally. Repeat problem letters. Call on volunteers to spell each word aloud. Say: *Can you spell* book, *please?*

Introduction

5 minutes

1. Above the words on the board, write *classroom.* Ask: *Can you name other things in a classroom?* Point to additional items students might be able to name.

2. State the objective: *Today we're going to talk about a classroom.*

1 Learn classroom directions

Presentation

20–25 minutes

A Direct students to look at the pictures. Ask: *Is she a teacher or a student?* [a student]

B 1. Have students listen to the audio. Ask them to point to the correct picture as they listen. Circulate and monitor.

2. Check comprehension. Pass out *yes/no* cards (see page T-175), or have students hold up one finger for *yes* and two for *no* in order to get a nonverbal response. Play the audio and mime

each action. Tell students to hold up the *yes* card if your action matches the audio and the *no* card if it doesn't.

TIP

A nonverbal comprehension check, like the one in 1B, allows you to see at a glance who understands and who doesn't. It also allows students to respond without the pressure of having to speak up.

C Ask students to listen and repeat the words.

Guided Practice I

15–20 minutes

D 1. Have students complete the sentences using the new vocabulary.

2. Encourage students to take turns reading the completed sentences in pairs.

Multilevel Strategies

For 1D, pair same-level students together. After they complete the exercise, provide more vocabulary practice targeted to the level of your students.

• **Pre-level** Ask these students to practice together by pointing to the pictures in 1B and saying the correct words.

• **On-level** Ask these students to work in pairs, covering the words and testing each other on the vocabulary. Have one student point to the pictures while the other student says the correct word.

• **Higher-level** Ask these students to dictate the words to each other.

2 Talk about a classroom

Guided Practice II
35–40 minutes

 A 1. Ask students to repeat the words from the warm-up. Introduce the new topic: *Now let's talk about a classroom.*

2. Group students and assign roles: leader, fact checker, recorder, and reporter. Write the roles on the board. As you explain each role, pantomime the duties you expect that person taking the role to perform. Explain that students work with their groups to match the words and pictures in 2A.

3. Check comprehension of the exercise. Pantomime the duties of each role again as you ask about it. Ask students to raise their hands when you say their roles. *Who looks up the words in the picture dictionary?* [fact checker] *Who writes the numbers in the book?* [recorder] *Who tells the class your answers?* [reporter] *Who helps everyone?* [leader]

4. Set a time limit (three minutes). Ask the groups to work together to complete the task. While students are working, copy the wordlist on the board.

5. Call "time" and have the reporters from each group take turns calling out the numbers for the wordlist. Record students' answers on the board. If groups disagree, write each group's choice next to the word.

B 1. Ask students to listen and check their answers.

2. Have students correct the wordlist on the board and then write the correct numbers in their books.

3. Tell the groups from 2A to break into pairs to practice the words. Set a time limit (two minutes).

C 1. Point out the *Grammar note.* Have students repeat the singular and plural forms.

2. Have students complete their charts. As they work, copy the chart on the board.

3. Ask volunteers to complete the chart on the board as their classmates dictate the answers.

Communicative Practice and Application
10–15 minutes

 D 1. Model the example with a volunteer. Then model it again with new directions. Say: *Point to the clock. Open the notebook.*

2. Set a time limit (five minutes). Ask students to practice the classroom directions with several partners.

Multilevel Strategies

For 2D, use mixed-level pairs.

• **Pre-level** Pair these students with on- or higher-level students. Direct them to listen to their partners and follow their commands.

Evaluation
10–15 minutes (books closed)

TEST YOURSELF

1. Make a two-column chart on the board with the headings *Directions* and *Classroom Words.* Have students close their books and give you an example for each column.

2. Have students copy the chart into their notebooks.

3. Give students five to ten minutes to test themselves by writing the words they recall from the lesson.

4. Call "time" and have students check their spelling in *The Oxford Picture Dictionary* or another dictionary. Circulate and monitor students' progress.

Multilevel Strategies

Target the *Test Yourself* to the level of your students.

• **Pre-level** Have these students work with their books open.

• **Higher-level** Have these students complete the chart and then write three directions by combining words from both columns. *Point to the pens.*

To compress this lesson: Conduct 2A as a whole-class activity. Have students practice 2D with only one partner.

To extend this lesson: Dictate short sentences using the lesson vocabulary. For example, *Point to the chair.* Allow students to look in the book for spelling help.

And/Or have students complete **Workbook 1 page 2** and **Multilevel Activity Book 1 page 18.**

2 Talk about a classroom

A Work with your classmates. Match the words with the picture.

__1__ board __10__ chairs __8__ desk __6__ notebooks __4__ students

__9__ books __3__ clock __5__ dictionary __7__ pens __2__ teacher

B Listen and check your answers. Then practice the words with a partner.

C Complete the chart.

Singular	Plural
a desk	desks
a chair	chairs
a teacher	teachers
a board	boards
a notebook	notebooks

Grammar note

Singular (1)	Plural (2, 3, 4 . . .)
a pen	pens
a book	books
a student	students

D Work with a partner. Give classroom directions.

A: *Say "book."*

B: *Book.*

TEST YOURSELF ✔

Close your book. Write 3 classroom directions. Write 3 words for things or people in the classroom. Check your spelling in a dictionary.

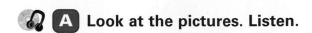

LESSON 2 | Life stories

1 Read about school forms

🎧 **A** **Look at the pictures. Listen.**

> Jim. S-a-n-t-o-s.

Welcome
to
School

School Registration Form

Name:

1. <u>Jim</u>   <u>Santos</u>
   (first)   (last)

Address:

2. <u>27 Lima Street, Apartment 3</u>
   (street)

   <u>Dallas,</u>   <u>Texas</u>   <u>75202</u>
   (city)   (state)   (zip code)

Telephone:

3. <u>(214) 555-1204</u>
   (area code)

Email:

4. <u>jsantos@work.net</u>

Signature:

5. <u>Jim Santos</u>

🎧 **B** **Listen. Read the sentences.**

1. Tell me your first name. Please spell your last name.
2. Complete the form. Please print your address.
3. Write your telephone number with the area code.
   Then write your email address.
4. Sign your name on line five.
5. Please give me the form. Welcome to school.

C **Check your understanding. Match the numbers with the letters.**

<u>b</u> 1. tell   a. (J-I-M.)

<u>a</u> 2. spell   b. (Jim.)

<u>d</u> 3. print   c. *Jim Santos*

<u>c</u> 4. sign   d. Jim Santos

6   ✔ Complete personal information forms

Unit 1 Lesson 2

Objectives	Grammar	Vocabulary	Correlations
On-, Pre-, and Higher-level: Read and write about school forms	Imperative (*Tell me your name.*)	*Complete, form, print, registration, signature* For additional vocabulary practice, see this **Oxford Picture Dictionary** topic: Personal Information	**CASAS:** 0.1.2, 0.2.1, 0.2.2, 2.5.5, 6.0.1, 7.4.7 **LCPs:** 22.01, 25.01, 31.02, 32.01, 32.02, 32.13 **SCANS:** Listening, Reading, Self-management, Speaking, Writing **EFF:** Convey ideas in writing, Listen actively, Reflect and evaluate, Speak so others can understand

Warm-up and Review

10–15 minutes (books closed)

Divide your class into two teams, and have them line up at opposite sides of the board. Have one pair from each side approach the board. Tell them: *One person writes; the other person helps.* Dictate words from Lesson 1: *pen, desk, chairs, say, repeat, listen to, students, board, books, open.* Have a new pair from the team approach the board for each word. Give each pair about ten seconds to write the word and correct their work. When you finish, have students sit down and compare the two lists. If one side has more correct words, declare that team the winner. If both sides are 100 percent correct, declare them all winners.

Introduction

5 minutes

1. Hold up a registration form for your school. Ask and mime the question: *Did you complete this form? Did you write your name on the form?*

2. Write the word *form* on the board. State the objective: *This paper is a form. Today we'll read and write about forms.*

1 Read about school forms

Presentation I

20–25 minutes

 1. Direct students to look at the pictures. Ask: *Where is he?* [at school] *What's his name?* [Jim Santos] *What's his phone number?* [(214) 555-1204]

2. Play the audio.

B 1. Play the audio again. Have students read along silently.

2. Check comprehension. Ask: *Is his first name Santos?* [no] *Does he print his address?* [yes]

Multilevel Strategies

After the group comprehension check in 1B, challenge on- and higher-level students while working with pre-level students.

• **Pre-level** Reread the sentences in 1B with your pre-level students while on- and higher-level students practice independently.

• **On- and Higher-level** Ask these students to pair up and read the sentences to each other out of order. One partner should read, and the other partner should perform the action (print his/her address, sign his/her name, etc.).

Guided Practice I

10 minutes

C Have students match the numbers with the letters. Go over the answers as a class.

2 Complete a form

Guided Practice II

20–25 minutes

A 1. Copy the form on the board. Read it aloud with your own information.

2. Give students time to complete the form on their own. Circulate and assist.

> ### Multilevel Strategies
>
> For 2A, seat same-level students together.
>
> • **Pre-level** Assist these students individually as necessary.
>
> • **Higher-level** Give these students the personal-information section of a real form, and ask them to complete it. You can pick up registration forms and job applications in your school office or download tax forms, passport applications, etc., from the Internet. Copy only the section regarding personal information to give to the students.

B Ask students to read their information to a partner. Call on individuals. Ask: *What's your partner's first name? What's your partner's last name?*

3 Give personal information

Presentation II

20–25 minutes

A 1. Introduce the topic: *Now we're going to say our personal information.* Direct students to look at the ID card in 3A. Ask: *What's his last name?* [Ramirez] *Is his address 15 Elm Street?* [no]

2. Ask students to put their pencils down and listen and point to the correct answers when they hear them. Play the entire audio once.

3. Play the audio in segments. After each number, stop the audio and check answers with the students: *Did you circle* A *or* B*?* If necessary, replay the segment.

4. Check students' listening accuracy. Call out the numbers, and have students hold up one finger for *A* or two for *B*. Or pass out *A/B* cards (see page T-175).

Guided Practice

15–20 minutes

B Play the audio and have students follow the directions. Elicit answers from volunteers.

C Have students read along silently while they listen. Play the audio again, and have students repeat the conversation. Replay if necessary.

Communicative Practice and Application

10 minutes

D 1. Model the conversation with a volunteer. Then model it again, switching roles.

2. Set a time limit (five minutes). Ask students to practice the conversation with several partners Ask volunteers to present their conversation to the class.

> **TIP** To review spelling and numbers while protecting student privacy, give students a set of fake addresses and phone numbers. Have students practice using their real names but the made-up addresses and phone numbers.

Evaluation

10–15 minutes (books closed)

TEST YOURSELF

Have students close their books. Write the instruction on the board: *Write your address and your phone number.* Monitor and provide feedback.

To compress this lesson: Assign 1C as homework. Have students practice the conversation in 3D with only one partner.

To extend this lesson: Dictate sentences with letters and numbers: *My name is Julie. (J-U-L-I-E). My phone number is (547) 555-4628.* After students complete the dictation individually, have volunteers write the sentences (or just the names and numbers) on the board.

And/Or have students complete **Workbook 1 page 3** and **Multilevel Activity Book 1 page 19.**

2 Complete a form

A Write your information on the form. Sign your name on line 3. Answers will vary.

1. Name: _____
   (FIRST)   (LAST)

2. Telephone: (_____) _____
   (AREA CODE)

3. Signature: _____

B Read your information to a partner.

3 Give personal information

A Listen and circle *a* or *b*.

1. a. Elm Street
   b. Ramirez

2. a. 555-1242
   b. 16

3. a. (323)
   b. 90011

4. a. 16 Elm Street
   b. joseram@123.net

5. a. Jose
   b. Ramirez

6. a. Los Angeles
   b. Jose Ramirez

Jose Ramirez
16 Elm Street
Los Angeles, CA 90011
(323) 555-1242

B Listen and write. Answers will vary.

1. _____
2. _____
3. _____
4. _____
5. _____
6. _____

C Listen and repeat.

A: Tell me your first name.
B: Maria.

A: Please spell your last name.
B: G-O-N-Z-A-L-E-S.

D Work with a partner. Practice the conversation.
Use your own information.

TEST YOURSELF ✔
Close your book. Write your address and your phone number.

1 Learn the verb *be*

A Look at the pictures. Read the sentences. Count the students in each picture.

My Class

I am a student.
1 student

He is my teacher.
1 student

She is my partner.
2 students

They are
my classmates.
3 students

We are a group.
4 students

It is my classroom.
1 student

B Study the charts. Complete the sentences below.

STATEMENTS WITH *BE*

Statements						
I	am	a student.	We	are	students.
You	are		You		
He She	is		They		
It	is	my classroom.	They	are	my books.

1. I __am__ a student.   2. They __are__ students.

Negative statements						
I	am not	a student.	We	are not	students.
You	are not		You		
He She	is not		They		
It	is not	my classroom.	They	are not	my books.

3. He __is not__ a student.   4. They __are not__ my books.

C Work with your classmates. Talk about your classroom.

I am a student.   *They are my books.*
She is not a teacher.   *It is not my pen.*

☑ Use subject pronouns and the simple present with *be* to talk about the classroom

Unit 1 Lesson 3

DESCRIBE

Objectives	Grammar	Vocabulary	Correlations
On- and Higher-level: Use the verb *be* to talk about a classroom **Pre-level:** Recognize the verb *be*	The verb *be* (*I am a student. He is a teacher. They are books.*)	*Classmates, computer, contractions, door, group, window, Count,* For additional vocabulary practice, see this **Oxford Picture Dictionary** topic: A Classroom	**CASAS:** 0.1.2, 7.4.7 **LCPs:** 22.01, 32.01, 33.02, 33.06, 33.09 **SCANS:** Self-management, Speaking, Writing **EFF:** Convey ideas in writing, Reflect and evaluate, Speak so others can understand

Warm-up and Review

10 minutes (books closed)

Write classroom words from Lesson 1 on the board with the vowels missing: st__nd __p, d__sk, t__ __ch__r, b__ __k, p__ns, etc. Ask students to tell you the words and then spell them. Ask them to tell you if the words are singular or plural.

Introduction

5 minutes

1. Using the words from the warm-up, say and write sentences using the subject pronouns and the verb *be*: *I am a teacher. You are a student. He is a student. It is a pen.* Underline *am, is,* and *are.*

2. State the objective: *Today we're going to learn the verb* be.

1 Learn the verb *be*

Presentation I

20–25 minutes

A 1. Direct students to look at the pictures. Ask: *Are they at work or school?* [school]

2. Read each sentence aloud. Point to people and things in the classroom, and have your students call out the appropriate pronouns. For *they* and *we*, have a group of students stand up. Point to the students for *they*, and stand among them for *we*.

B 1. Demonstrate how to read the grammar charts as complete sentences. Read the chart through sentence by sentence. Then read it again, and have students repeat after you.

2. Use the pictures in 1A to illustrate points in the grammar chart. Say only the pronoun + verb portion of the sentence: *I am; she is.*

3. As a class, complete the sentences under the charts. Ask volunteers to write the sentences on the board. Have other students read the sentences aloud.

4. Give students time to silently review the charts and, if they haven't already done so, fill in the blanks.

5. Assess students' understanding of the charts. Say: *I am a teacher.* Then point to a student, and say: *She _____ a teacher* to elicit the negative. (Hum or clap to indicate the blank.) Repeat for all the pronouns.

Guided Practice

15–20 minutes

C Read the sentences and point around the room to demonstrate their meaning. Call on individuals to tell you about the classroom.

Multilevel Strategies

After initial practice in 1C, challenge on- and higher-level students while allowing pre-level students to review the grammar.

• **Pre-level** While you are calling on individuals to tell you about the classroom, have pre-level students copy the sentences from 1B into their notebooks. While on- and higher-level students complete the follow-up activity below, have pre-level students read the sentences aloud to you.

• **On- and Higher-level** Have these students draw pictures of classroom objects and write sentences to describe their pictures. *They are pens. They are not clocks.* Display their creations in the classroom if possible.

2 Contractions with *be*

Presentation II

15–20 minutes

1. Write *I am = I'm* and *I am not = I'm not* on the board. Show students how the apostrophe replaces a letter in contractions by erasing the *a* in *am* and writing the apostrophe. Read and have students repeat the long and the contracted forms in the chart.

2. Have students work individually to circle the answers. Go over the answers as a class. Have students repeat the sentences, pronouncing the contracted form.

Guided Practice

5–10 minutes

Assign a time limit (three minutes), and ask students to work with a partner. Monitor pairs and provide feedback to the class on their use of the contracted forms. If students aren't pronouncing the contractions, repeat the sentences in the chart in 2A again.

3 Practice statements with *be*

Communicative Practice and Application

20–25 minutes

1. Read the words under the pictures, and have students repeat.

2. Elicit a sentence for each picture. *They're windows.* Emphasize pronunciation of the contraction and of the *s* on the plural nouns.

B
1. Model the exercise with a volunteer. Use negative as well as affirmative sentences in your demonstration: *It isn't a radio. It's a computer.*

2. Set a time limit (three minutes) for students to practice with their partners. Circulate and monitor.

Multilevel Strategies

For 3B, seat same-level students together.

• **Pre-level** Have these students copy the words under the pictures in 3A. Assist them with adding *It's, They're, He's,* or *She's* to make complete sentences orally and in writing.

• **On- and Higher-level** While you work with the pre-level students, have the rest of the class create sentences based on picture prompts. Group these students. Give each group pictures of classroom items or use the picture cards on page 24 of *Multilevel Activity Book 1*. Have one student hold up the picture and another say an appropriate negative or affirmative sentence. When they finish the activity, have students write some of their sentences on the board or hold up the pictures and say sentences for the class.

Evaluation

10–15 minutes (books closed)

TEST YOURSELF

Ask students to write the sentences independently before they read them to a partner. Collect and correct their writing.

Multilevel Strategies

Target the *Test Yourself* to the level of your students.

• **Pre-level** Allow these students to work with their books open. Provide skeleton sentences for these students to complete. _____ *a teacher.* _____ *students.* _____ *a computer.*

• **Higher-level** Have these students write three negative and three affirmative sentences.

To compress this lesson: Conduct 1C and 3B as whole-class activities rather than partner practice.

To extend this lesson: Have students look at the pictures of classrooms in *The Oxford Picture Dictionary,* or another picture dictionary, and say *It's/They're* sentences about the items in the picture.

Or have students complete **Workbook 1 pages 4–5** and **Multilevel Activity Book 1 page 20.**

2 Contractions with *be*

A Study the chart. Circle the correct words below.

Contractions			
I am	= I'm	I am not	= I'm not
you are	= you're	you are not	= you're not / you aren't
he is	= he's	he is not	= he's not / he isn't
she is	= she's	she is not	= she's not / she isn't
it is	= it's	it is not	= it's not / it isn't
we are	= we're	we are not	= we're not / we aren't
they are	= they're	they are not	= they're not / they aren't

1. (**I'm** / They're) a student.
2. (**She's** / It's) a teacher.
3. (He's / **It's**) a pen.
4. (**He's** / I'm) my partner.
5. (It isn't / **They aren't**) my books.
6. He (**isn't** / aren't) a teacher.

B Work with a partner. Talk about your classroom. Use contractions.

A: *He's a student.*
B: *They're books.*

3 Practice statements with *be*

A Read the words.

  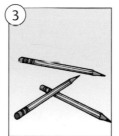   

| windows | a computer | pencils | a door | a new student | a teacher |

B Work with a partner. Talk about the pictures.

A: *They're windows.*
B: *It's a computer.*

TEST YOURSELF ✔

Close your book. Write 5 sentences about your classroom. Read your sentences to a partner.

1 Learn how to meet new people

🎧 **A** Listen and read the conversations.

B Complete the conversations.

1. **A:** Hi, I'm Li. What is your name?
   B: My ___name___ is Neela.

2. **A:** It's nice to meet ___you___, Neela.
   B: It's nice to meet you, ___too___.

3. **A:** ___Hi___, Neela.
   B: Good morning, Li.

4. **A:** ___How___ are ___you___?
   B: ___Fine___, thanks. And you?
   A: Fine.

5. **A:** ___Good___ evening, Neela.
   B: Hello, Li.

6. **A:** See you ___later___, Neela.
   B: ___Goodbye___, Li.

🎧 **C** Listen and read.

A: Hi, I'm Tim. What is your name?
B: My name is Asha. This is my friend Sara.
A: Can you repeat that, please?
B: Yes. I'm Asha, and this is Sara. It's nice to meet you.
A: Nice to meet you, too. Who is your teacher?
B: Ms. Simpson.
A: Oh! She's my teacher, too.

🎧 **D** Listen again and repeat.

✔ Begin and end social conversations

Unit 1 Lesson 4

Objectives	Grammar	Vocabulary	Correlations
On- and Higher-level: Introduce self and others **Pre-level:** Introduce self	Contractions with *be* (*I'm Maria. Who's your teacher?*)	*Nice to meet you, see you later* For additional vocabulary practice, see this **Oxford Picture Dictionary** topic: Everyday Conversation	**CASAS:** 0.1.2, 0.1.4, 0.2.1, 7.4.7 **LCPs:** 22.01–22.03, 32.01, 32.02, 32.13, 33.09, 34.01, 34.02 **SCANS:** Acquires and evaluates information, Interprets and communicates information, Listening, Self-management, Sociability, Speaking **EFF:** Speaks so others can understand

Warm-up and Review

10 minutes (books closed)

Write *I, you, he, she, it, we,* and *they* on the board. Point to the pronouns, and have students call out the correct form of *be*. Point to objects and people in the class, and have students call out sentences: *It's a desk. She's a student.* Remind them to use contractions when they speak. Point to objects, beginning negative sentences and calling on individuals to complete them. For example, point to a pen, and say: *It isn't a _____.* (pencil)

Introduction

5 minutes

1. Referring to the pronouns on the board, say: *I'm the teacher. My name is _____.* Indicate a student and say: *This is _____. She's my student.* Look at the student, and say: *Good morning/afternoon/evening!*

2. State the objective: *Today we'll learn to say hello and goodbye, and to introduce ourselves.*

1 Learn how to meet new people

Presentation

20–30 minutes

A 1. Direct students to look at the pictures. Ask questions: *Are they in a classroom? Where are they?*

2. Play the audio and have students read along silently. Read the sentences in 1–6, and pantomime shaking hands and waving where appropriate. Have students repeat the sentences.

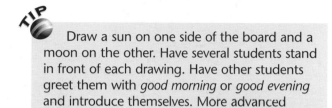

TIP Draw a sun on one side of the board and a moon on the other. Have several students stand in front of each drawing. Have other students greet them with *good morning* or *good evening* and introduce themselves. More advanced students can introduce a partner as well.

Guided Practice I

20–25 minutes

B 1. Using number 1 as an example, show students how they can find the word in 1A to fill in the blank.

2. Have students work individually to complete the conversations. Ask pairs of students to read the conversations aloud. Write the answers on the board.

Multilevel Strategies

For 1B, pair same-level students.

• **Pre-level** While other students are completing 1B, have these students read the sentences in 1A to each other. Give them time to copy the answers from the board.

• **On- and Higher-level** After these students have completed 1B, have them practice the conversations with only one partner looking in the book.

C Play the audio. Ask students to read along silently.

D Play the audio again, and have students repeat the conversation. Replay if necessary.

TIP Do a choral reading of the conversation in 1C. Split the class in half. Have one side be A and one side be B, and then have the sides switch roles.

Guided Practice I

10–15 minutes

E 1. Model the conversation with a volunteer. Then switch roles and model it with another volunteer.

2. Set a time limit (five minutes). Ask students to practice the conversation with several partners.

Multilevel Strategies

For 1E, adapt the oral practice to the level of your students.

• **Pre-level** While on- and higher-level students are practicing, assist these students by sitting with them in a group and modeling the conversation with several individuals.

2 Practice your pronunciation

Pronunciation Extension

15–20 minutes

A Direct students to look at the chart. Play the audio. Have students repeat the contracted forms.

B 1. Write *What is* and *What's* on the board. Play the audio for number 1. Ask students which they heard. [*What is*—no contraction]

2. Play the audio one segment at a time. Replay each segment if necessary. Go over the answers as a class.

3. Play the audio again, and have students repeat the statements or questions.

C Pair students and have them practice the questions and answers.

 It's easy to give intensive practice with introductions and to help students learn each other's names. Have the class watch as you shake hands with a student and greet him/her: *Good morning/evening/afternoon. I'm _____.* Have the student introduce him/herself and the student next to him/her. Move to the second student and repeat the process. After you have done this a few times, call on one of your more-verbal students to take on the "greeter" role. After a few more introductions, call on other students to be greeters. Instruct greeters to walk all around the room, introducing themselves and being introduced to a third party. Assign approximately a third of your students (the most verbal) to be greeters. When you wrap up the activity, provide feedback about pronunciation and common mistakes.

Evaluation

15–20 minutes

TEST YOURSELF

1. Model the role-play with a volunteer. Then switch roles.

2. Pair students. Have one pair model the conversation.

3. Set a time limit (five minutes), and have the partners say the conversation in both roles.

4. Circulate and monitor. Encourage students to shake hands.

5. Provide feedback.

Multilevel Strategies

Target the *Test Yourself* to the level of your students.

• **Pre-level** Have these students read the questions and answers in 1C in pairs.

• **Higher-level** Encourage these students to greet and say goodbye without looking in the book and to include other questions from the lesson. *Who's your teacher? How are you?*

To compress this lesson: Have students practice the conversation in 1E with only one partner.

To extend this lesson: Teach students more everyday expressions.
1. Write on the board: *See you tomorrow/later/Monday. Have a nice day/evening/weekend. You, too!*
2. Show students how to use the expressions in a conversation. Have them practice in pairs.
And/Or have students complete **Workbook 1 page 6** and **Multilevel Activity Book 1 page 21**.

E **Work with a partner. Practice the conversation. Use your own information.**

A: Hi, I'm _____. What is your name?

B: My name is _____.

A: Can you repeat that, please?

B: I'm _____. It's nice to meet you, _____.

A: Nice to meet you, too. Who is your teacher?

B: _____.

A: Oh! _____ my teacher, too.

2 Practice your pronunciation

A **Study the chart. Listen for the contractions.**

No contraction	Contraction
What is your name?	What**'s** your name?
I am Maria.	I**'m** Maria.
Who is your teacher?	Who**'s** your teacher?

B **Listen and check (✔) *no contraction* or *contraction*.**

	No contraction	Contraction
1.	✔	
2.		✔
3.		✔
4.	✔	
5.		✔

C **Work with your classmates. Ask and answer the questions.**

1. A: What's your name?

   B: My name is _____.

2. A: How are you?

   B: I'm _____.

3. A: Who's your teacher?

   B: My teacher is _____.

TEST YOURSELF ✔

Work with a partner. Partner A: Say hello to your partner and say your name. Ask your partner's name. Partner B: Answer the question and say goodbye. Then change roles.

1 Get ready to read

A Look at the pictures. Read the sentences.

☐ Read English. ☐ Go to school. ☐ Speak English. ☐ Ask for help.

I'm a student.

B How do you study English? Check (✔) the boxes in 1A. Answers will vary.

2 Read about studying English

A Read the poster.

Learn more English.

Study every day.

Good morning.

Speak English at home.

Go to school.

Today in the news…

Listen to English on the radio.

?

Ask your classmates and teacher for help.

B Listen and read the poster again.

Unit 1 Lesson 5

Objectives	Grammar	Vocabulary	Correlations
On- and Higher-level: Read about and discuss studying English and stating goals **Pre-level:** Read about studying English and stating goals	Imperative (*Learn more English.*)	*Ask for help, conversation, citizenship, health, fun* For additional vocabulary practice, see this **Oxford Picture Dictionary** topic: Studying	**CASAS:** 0.1.2, 0.2.2, 2.5.5, 7.4.7 **LCPs:** 22.01, 31.02, 32.01, 32.03, 32.04, 32.13 **SCANS:** Knowing how to learn, Listening, Participates as member of a team, Reading, Responsibility, Seeing things in the mind's eye **EFF:** Listening actively, Observe critically, Read with understanding

Warm-up and Review

10 minutes (books closed)

Have your students introduce themselves in a "chain": *1. Hi. I'm Ruben. 2. Hello. I'm Nasrin. This is Ruben. 3. Hi. I'm Orane. This is Ruben. This is Nasrin,* etc. If you have a small class, the entire group can stand in a circle for this activity. If you have a large class, call on students from around the room to stand, and have the standing group be the chain while the rest of the class helps them remember the names.

Introduction

5 minutes

1. Write *Learn English* on the board, and ask: *How can you learn English?* Write some of the students' ideas.

2. State the objective: *Today we'll read about good ways to study English.*

1 Get ready to read

Presentation

15–20 minutes

A Direct students to look at the pictures and read the captions. Have students repeat the captions after you.

B Give students time to read and check the boxes. Ask volunteers to tell which ones they checked.

TIP After 1B, ask students about more ways to practice English (watch TV, go to the library, go to the language lab, listen to/sing English songs). Put their advice and the advice from the poster in 2A on sentence strips and post them around the room. Every week, ask students to discuss which of the things they did. Congratulate the students who share.

Pre-Reading

Direct students to look at the poster in 2A. Say: *Look at the man. Do you think he's a good student?*

2 Read about studying English

Guided Practice I

25–30 minutes

A 1. Ask students to read the poster silently.

2. Ask if there are any questions about the reading.

B Play the audio. Have students read along silently.

Multilevel Strategies

For 2A–B, seat same-level students together.

• **Pre-level** Assist these students with the reading by saying each sentence aloud slowly while they follow along.

• **On- and Higher-level** While you are working with pre-level students, ask these students to read the poster to a partner.

C Have students work individually to circle the correct answers. Ask volunteers to read the completed sentences.

D 1. Have students work individually to complete the sentences. Ask volunteers to read the completed sentences.

2. Check comprehension by saying sentences from the poster with blanks in them (hum or clap to indicate the blanks): *Speak _____ at home. Ask your teacher for _____.*

> ## Multilevel Strategies
>
> After the group comprehension check in 2D, call on individuals and tailor your questions to the level of your students.
>
> • **Pre-level** Ask *yes/no* questions. *Can you listen to English on the radio?*
>
> • **On-level** Make fill-in-the-blank statements. *_____ to English on the radio.*
>
> • **Higher-level** Ask open-ended questions. *What's one way to learn English?*

3 Name your goals

Guided Practice II

15–20 minutes

A 1. Write *goal* on the board. Say: *A goal is what we want. My goal is to be a good teacher. Your goal is to learn English. Different people have different goals.*

2. Read the captions on the form. Say: *These are goals. I want to know your English-learning goals. Please complete the form and check three goals.* Emphasize that they should check only three.

> ## Multilevel Strategies
>
> For 3A, seat pre-level students together.
>
> • **Pre-level** Assist these students with the form by reading each goal aloud again and giving them time to choose three. Write your name on the board as a model for how to fill out the name part of the form, and provide individual assistance with the *first name/last name* section as necessary.
>
> • **On- and Higher-level** While you are working with pre-level students, ask these students to read their three goals to several partners.

Communicative Practice

10–15 minutes

B Read each goal and ask for a show of hands to find out which goals were the most popular.

Application

5–10 minutes

BRING IT TO LIFE

Ask each student to write down the name of the person or people with whom they are going to speak English. Ask for a show of hands of people who have no one to speak English with at home, and help them make an "appointment" with each other to speak English for five minutes after class or before the next class.

To compress this lesson: Assign 2D as homework.

To extend this lesson: Have students illustrate commands.

1. Review classroom directions or have students look at the Studying topic in *The Oxford Picture Dictionary*. Demonstrate any new vocabulary.

2. Put students in groups, and give each group a large sheet of paper. Explain that you will give a command and students will show the meaning of the command on their papers. For example, if you say *Fill in the blank*, the group should write a sentence with a blank in it and then write in the blank.

3. Do a "practice run" with each group to help them think of ideas for illustrating the commands. Make it a competitive game by setting a timer (30 seconds) and awarding a point to the group that finishes first.

4. Have students pass the paper around the group after each round so that one strong student doesn't dominate.

And/Or have students complete **Workbook 1 page 7** and **Multilevel Activity Book 1 page 22**.

C Circle *a* or *b*.

1. Ask your _____ for help.
   - (a.) teacher
   - b. pencil

2. _____ to English on the radio.
   - a. Speak
   - (b.) Listen

D Complete the sentences. Use the words in the box.

| English   school   help   ~~study~~ |

1. _Study_ every day.
2. Learn more _English_.
3. Go to _school_.
4. Ask your classmates for _help_.

3 Name your goals

A Complete the form. Answers will vary.

_____ (first name)   _____ (last name)   _____ (name of teacher)

Please check (✔) three pictures to complete the sentence.

I study English for _____.

☐ school and children   ☐ work   ☐ conversation and fun

☐ United States citizenship   ☐ health   ☐ money and shopping

B Work with your classmates. Count the checks (✔) for each picture.

BRING IT TO LIFE

Speak English at home or with your friends for 5 minutes today.

1 Grammar

A Circle *a* or *b*.

1. What are they?
   a. It's a pen.
   b. They're notebooks.

2. Who is he?
   a. It's a window.
   b. He's my teacher.

3. What are they?
   a. They're desks.
   b. She's a student.

4. Who is your friend?
   a. He's Mark.
   b. It's my pen.

Grammar note

For people: *Who*

A: Who is she?   A: Who are they?
B: She's my teacher.   B: They're my friends.

For things: *What*

A: What is it?   A: What are they?
B: It's my book.   B: They're my books.

B Complete the chart.

Singular	Plural
a book	books
a pencil	pencils
a desk	desks
a window	windows
a teacher	teachers

C Complete the sentences. Use the words in the box.

| I   My books   ~~Maria~~   We |

1. __Maria_____ is a teacher.
2. __I_____ am a good student.

3. __We_____ are students.
4. __My books_____ are open.

D Write new sentences. Use contractions.

1. We are students. __We're students._____
2. She is at work. __She's at work._____
3. They are not new computers. __They're not (They aren't) new computers.__
4. It is a window. __It's a window._____

Unit 1 Review and expand

Objectives	Grammar	Vocabulary	Correlations
On-, Pre-, and Higher-level: Expand upon and review unit grammar and life skills	Questions with *who* and *what*, the verb *be* (*Who is she? What are they?*)	*First, friend, new* For additional vocabulary practice, see these **Oxford Picture Dictionary** topics: A Classroom, Personal Information, Everyday Conversation	**CASAS:** 0.1.2, 0.1.4, 0.1.5, 0.2.1, 0.2.2, 4.8.1, 7.2.5–7.2.7, 7.3.1 **LCPs:** 22.01–22.03, 32.01, 32.02, 32.05, 32.13, 33.02, 33.06, 33.07, 33.09 **SCANS:** Participates as member of a team, Problem solving, Seeing things in the mind's eye, Writing **EFF:** Convey ideas in writing, Solve problems and make decisions

Warm-up and Review

10–15 minutes (books closed)

1. Review the *Bring It to Life* assignment from Lesson 5.

2. Have students who did the exercise discuss what they talked about. Have other students tell you what they can say in English. Encourage them to try the assignment after class today.

3. As students relate their experiences, write their sentences on the board.

Introduction and Presentation

5 minutes

1. Write *What is it?* on the board, and hold up a pen. Ask the question and then write the answer: *It's a pen*. Write *Who is she?* and point to a student. Accept *She's Maria* or *She's a student*, and write it on the board. Repeat with *Who is he?* and *Who are they?*

2. State the objective: *Today we're going to review questions and answers with the verb* be.

1 Grammar

Guided Practice

40–45 minutes

A 1. Direct students to look at the *Grammar note*. Read aloud and have students repeat the questions and answers.

2. Have students work individually to circle the correct answers. Ask volunteers to read the questions and answers.

B 1. Write *Singular* and *Plural* on the board. Ask: *What is the singular form of* student? Then write *student* under *Singular*. Ask: *What's the plural?* Write *students* under *Plural*.

2. Have students work individually to complete the chart. Ask a volunteer to copy the completed chart on the board.

C Have students work individually to complete the sentences. Have them check their answers with a partner.

D Have students work individually to rewrite the sentences with contractions. Ask volunteers to write the sentences on the board.

Multilevel Strategies

For 1C and 1D, seat same-level students together.

• **Pre-level** Read the sentences (hum or clap to indicate blanks), and have these students dictate their answers. Write them on the board, and tell students to copy them into their notebooks.

• **On- and Higher-level** While you are working with pre-level students, ask the remaining students to write three or four more sentences with contractions like the ones in 1D. Have students put one of their sentences on the board.

2 Group work

Communicative Practice

20–35 minutes

A 1. Direct students, in groups of three or four, to focus on the picture on page 5. Ask: *What do you see in the classroom?*

2. Set a time limit (five minutes) to complete the exercise. Circulate and answer any questions. Have a reporter from each group read the group's sentences to the class.

Multilevel Strategies

For 2A and 2B, use same-level groups.

• **Pre-level** For 2A, ask these students to write three vocabulary words and one complete sentence. For 2B, allow pre-level students to ask and answer the questions without writing.

• **Higher-level** For 2A, ask these students to write two additional sentences about the picture. For 2B, have them ask and answer these questions: *How are you? Can you spell your name? Who's your teacher? Who's your friend?*

B 1. Have students work in the same groups from 2A, taking turns interviewing each other in pairs. Set a time limit (five minutes) to complete the exercise.

2. Tell students to make a note of their partners' answers but not to worry about writing complete sentences.

TIP

To review and have fun, play the "flyswatter" game. Draw or find pictures of the classroom items studied in the unit. You need singular and plural pictures of the same objects—for example, a picture of one book and a picture of several books. Put them on the board in a grid, or draw them in a grid and project them. Divide the class into two teams. Have one member of each team approach the board. Say *They're books* or *It's a book.* The student who swats the correct picture first wins a point. Teammates will want to yell out help, so teach them *top, middle,* and *bottom.* Tell them they can only help in English using those words. To keep it challenging, change some of the pictures throughout the game.

PROBLEM SOLVING

20–25 minutes

A 1. Direct students to look at the picture. Say: *Point to the teacher.* Tell students they will read a story about a new student. Direct students to read Jose's story silently. Then play the audio, and have them read along silently.

2. Check comprehension. Ask: *Is it the first day of school?* [yes] *Who is the student?* [Jose Ortiz]

B 1. Read the question and identify the problem. Read the possible solutions.

2. Elicit student ideas for other solutions. Write each one on the board.

3. Discuss whether the statements are appropriate.

4. Ask for a show of hands to see which solution the class likes best.

Evaluation

30–35 minutes

To test students' understanding of the unit grammar and life skills, have students take the Unit 1 Test in the *Step Forward Test Generator CD-ROM with ExamView® Assessment Suite.*

Learning Log

To help students record and discuss their progress, use the *Learning Log* on page T-176.

To extend this review: Have students complete **Workbook 1 page 8, Multilevel Activity Book 1 pages 23–26,** and the **Unit 1 Grammar Exercises** on the **Multilevel Grammar Exercises CD-ROM 1.**

2 Group work

A Work with 2–3 classmates. Look at the picture on page 5.
Write 5 sentences about the picture in your notebook.
Talk about the sentences with your class. Answers will vary.

They are pens.   He's a student.   It's a book.
It's a desk.   She's a teacher.

B Interview a partner. Write your partner's answers in your notebook.

ASK OR SAY:
1. What is your first name?
2. What is your last name?
3. Please sign your name here.

	1. Dora
	2. Sanchez
	3. Dora Sanchez

PROBLEM SOLVING

A Listen and read. Look at the picture.
What is the problem? Jose doesn't know what to say.

Today is the first day of class at Pass Street
Adult School. The teacher is Nora Jackson.
Jose Ortiz is a student.

B Work with your classmates. Answer the
question.

What can Jose say to Nora Jackson?
    a. Good morning.
    (b.) Good evening. I'm Jose Ortiz.
    c. See you later, Nora.

UNIT **2**
My Classmates

FOCUS ON
- time and dates
- personal information
- *yes/no* questions with *be*
- completing a form
- countries and population

LESSON 1 **Vocabulary**

---

1 Learn the time

A Look at the pictures. Count the clocks. 6 clocks

B Listen and look at the pictures.

1. Good morning. 8:00 a.m.
2. 9:15 a.m.
3. 12:00 p.m.
4. Good evening. 8:30 p.m.
5. 9:45 p.m.
6. Good night. 12:00 a.m.

C Listen and repeat the words.

1. eight o'clock
2. nine fifteen a.m.
3. noon
4. eight thirty p.m.
5. nine forty-five p.m.
6. midnight

D Match the sentences with the times.

_e_ 1. It's eight o'clock in the morning.
_c_ 2. It's midnight.
_a_ 3. It's eight thirty in the evening.
_b_ 4. It's nine forty-five in the evening.
_d_ 5. It's noon.

a. 8:30 p.m.
b. 9:45 p.m.
c. 12:00 a.m.
d. 12:00 p.m.
e. 8:00 a.m.

Need help?

8:00 a.m. *or*
    8:00 in the morning

12:00 p.m. *or* noon

8:30 p.m. *or*
    8:30 in the evening

12:00 a.m. *or* midnight

16   ☑ Interpret clock time; identify days, months, and dates

Unit 2 Lesson 1

Objectives	Grammar	Vocabulary	Correlations
On-level: Identify time, days, and months **Pre-level:** Recognize time, days, and months **Higher-level:** Talk and write about time, days, and months	The verb *be* (*It's 9:00. What month is it?*)	Time and calendar words For additional vocabulary practice, see these **Oxford Picture Dictionary** topics: Time, The Calendar, Everyday Conversation	**CASAS:** 0.1.2, 2.3.1, 2.3.2, 6.0.1, 7.1.4, 7.4.5, 7.4.7 **LCPs:** 25.01–25.03, 32.01, 33.07 **SCANS:** Listening, Participates as member of a team, Seeing things in the mind's eye, Self-management, Speaking **EFF:** Cooperate with others, Use math to solve problems and communicate

Warm-up and Review

10 minutes (books closed)

Draw a clock with no hands on the board, and elicit the numbers 1–12. Point to the clock in the room, and ask if anyone can tell you the time. Using the wrong time of day, ask: *Is it morning/afternoon/evening?* Write those three words on the board. Ask students what day it is using the wrong day: *Is today Saturday?* Repeat with the wrong month: *Is it January?* Write the correct day, month, and clock time on the board.

Introduction

5 minutes

1. Pointing to the words on the board, state the correct time, day, and month. *Today is Monday. It's September. It's 6:30 in the evening.*

2. State the objective: *Today we'll learn about time, days, and months.*

1 Learn the time

Presentation

20–25 minutes

A Direct students to look at the pictures. Say and have students repeat *good morning, good evening,* and *good night.* Ask: *How many clocks do you see?* [six]

TIP
Use pantomime to show students that *good night* cannot be used for *hello.* (It means either *goodbye* or *I'm going to bed.*) Say *Good night* and walk out the door. Say *Good night* and pretend to go to sleep. On the board, write *good evening = hello* and *good night = goodbye.*

B 1. Have students listen to the audio. Ask them to point to the correct picture as they listen. Circulate and monitor.

2. Check comprehension by asking *yes/no* questions. Pass out *yes/no* cards (see page T-175), or have students hold up one finger for *yes* and two for *no* in order to get a nonverbal response. Pointing to picture number 2, ask: *Is it 8:15 in the evening?* [no] Pointing to picture number 5, ask: *Is it 8:45 in the morning?* [no]

C Ask students to listen and repeat the words.

TIP
For more practice with time, draw four clock faces on the board showing 8:00, 3:30, 6:15, and 10:45. Write the times under the clocks, and have students repeat. Invite volunteers to the board to change the hands of the clocks and change the times below. Have everyone say the new times. Put a sun on the board, and discuss whether the times are a.m. or p.m. Draw students' attention to the fact that p.m. is not always night. Change the sun to a moon, and add p.m. to the times.

Guided Practice I

15–20 minutes

D 1. Have students match the sentences with the times.

2. Go over the answers as a class.

2 Talk about a calendar

Guided Practice II

35–40 minutes

 1. Ask students to repeat the words from the warm-up. Introduce the new topic: *Now let's talk about the calendar.*

2. Group students and assign roles: leader, fact checker, recorder, and reporter. Write the roles on the board. As you explain each role, pantomime the duties you expect that person taking the role to perform. Explain that students work with their groups to match the words and pictures in 1A.

3. Check comprehension of the exercise. Pantomime the duties of each role again as you ask about it. Ask students to raise their hands when you say their roles. *Who looks up the words in the picture dictionary?* [fact checker] *Who writes the numbers in the book?* [recorder] *Who tells the class your answers?* [reporter] *Who helps everyone?* [leader]

4. Set a time limit (three minutes). Ask the groups to work together to complete the task. While students are working, copy the wordlist on the board.

5. Call "time" and have the reporters from each group take turns calling out the numbers for the wordlist. Record students' answers on the board. If groups disagree, write each group's choice next to the word.

Multilevel Strategies

For 2A, use mixed-level groups.

- **On-level** Assign these students as recorders and reporters.
- **Pre-level** Assign a role of timekeeper (one who lets the group know when the three minutes are up) to allow these students an active role in the group.
- **Higher-level** Assign these students as leaders.

---

 1. Ask students to listen and check their answers.

2. Have students correct the wordlist on the board and then write the correct numbers in their books.

3. Tell the groups from 2A to break into pairs to practice the words. Set a time limit (two minutes).

 1. Have students work individually to complete their charts.

2. Go over the answers as a class.

3. Say and have students repeat each column.

Communicative Practice and Application

10–15 minutes

D 1. Model the interview with a volunteer. Have students repeat the questions after you.

2. Set a time limit (five minutes). Ask students to interview several partners.

Evaluation

10–15 minutes (books closed)

TEST YOURSELF

1. Make a two-column chart on the board with the headings *Time* and *Calendar*. Have students close their books and give you an example for each column.

2. Have students copy the chart into their notebooks.

3. Give students five to ten minutes to test themselves by writing the words they recall from the lesson.

4. Call "time" and have students check their spelling in *The Oxford Picture Dictionary* or another dictionary. Circulate and monitor students' progress.

Multilevel Strategies

Target the *Test Yourself* to the level of your students.

- **Pre-level** Have these students work with their books open.
- **Higher-level** Ask these students to write all the days and months under the *Calendar* heading.

To compress this lesson: Conduct 2A as a whole-class activity. Have students practice 2D with only one partner.

To extend this lesson: Draw pictures of clocks showing different times on the board, or have students look at the clocks in *The Oxford Picture Dictionary*. Have pairs ask each other *What time is it?* and answer based on the pictures. And/Or have students complete **Workbook 1 page 9** and **Multilevel Activity Book 1 page 28.**

2 Talk about a calendar

A Work with your classmates. Match the words with the pictures.

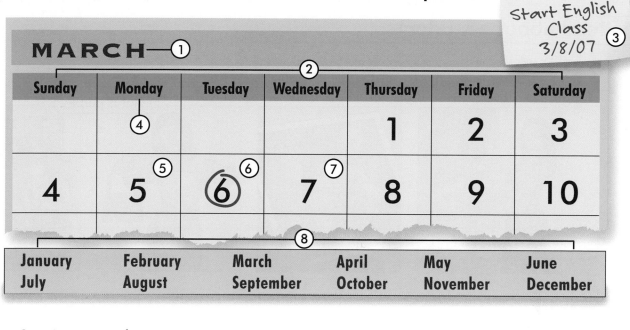

Start English Class 3/8/07 ③

MARCH — ①

②

Sunday	Monday	Tuesday	Wednesday	Thursday	Friday	Saturday
	④			1	2	3
4	5 ⑤	⑥ 6 ⑥	7 ⑦	8	9	10

⑧

January	February	March	April	May	June
July	August	September	October	November	December

___3___ date   ___1___ month   ___7___ tomorrow   ___8___ year

___2___ day   ___6___ today   ___4___ week   ___5___ yesterday

B Listen and check your answers. Then practice the words with a partner.

C Complete the chart. Use the words in the box.

Years	~~Times~~	Days	Months

Times	Days	Months	Years
5:00	Monday	January	1870
7:30	Wednesday	March	1999
12:10	Friday	September	2015

D Work with a partner. Ask and answer the questions.

1. What time is it? Answers will vary.
2. What are the days of the week? Sunday, Monday, Tuesday, Wednesday, Thursday, Friday, Saturday
3. What day is today? Answers will vary.
4. What day is tomorrow? Answers will vary.
5. What are the months of the year? January, February, March, April, May, June, July, August, September, October, November, December

TEST YOURSELF ✔

Close your book. Write 4 time words and 4 calendar words. Check your spelling in a dictionary.

1 Read about a student

A **Look at the pictures. Listen.**

My favorite color is purple.

CLASS 1A

B **Listen again. Read the sentences.**

1. My name is Irma Chavez.
2. I live in California.
3. I'm from Mexico.
4. My date of birth is January 7th, 1988.
5. My favorite color is purple.
6. I'm a student at City Community College.

C **Check your understanding. Circle the correct words.**

1. Irma is a ((student) / teacher).
2. She is from (California / (Mexico)).
3. She lives in ((California) / Mexico).
4. Irma's favorite color is ((purple) / green).

2 Write about your life

A **Write your story. Complete the sentences.** Answers will vary.

My name is _____.

I live in _____.

I am from _____.

My date of birth is _____.

My favorite color is _____.

Need help?

Colors

■ red	■ orange	□ tan	
■ blue	■ purple	■ gray	
□ yellow	■ pink	□ white	
■ green	■ brown	■ black	

B **Read your story to a partner.**

Unit 2 Lesson 2

Objectives	Grammar	Vocabulary	Correlations
On-, Pre-, and Higher-level: Read and write life stories	The verb *be* (*My favorite color is red.*)	Colors, *date of birth, favorite* For additional vocabulary practice, see these **Oxford Picture Dictionary** topics: Colors, North America and Central America, World Map	**CASAS:** 0.1.2, 0.1.4, 0.2.1, 6.01, 7.4.7 **LCPs:** 22.01, 22.02, 25.01, 25.04, 32.01, 32.02, 32.13, 33.07 **SCANS:** Acquires and evaluates information, Interprets and communicates information, Listening, Sociability, Speaking, Writing **EFF:** Convey ideas in writing, Listen actively

Warm-up and Review

10 minutes (books closed)

Review previously learned questions and answers. In one column, write: *What day is it? What's your last name? Who is she? What time is it? How are you?* In another column, write: *My last name is Lee. She's the teacher. It's Monday. It's 3:15. I'm fine.* Ask volunteers to match the questions and answers. Then have students repeat them.

Introduction

5 minutes

1. Write your name, your birthplace, the state where you live, your date of birth, your favorite color, and the name of your school on the board. Use the information to tell students about yourself: *My name is _____. I live in _____,* etc.

2. State the objective: *Today we'll read and write about our lives.*

1 Read about a student

Presentation I

20–25 minutes

A 1. Direct students to look at the first picture. Ask: *Is she pointing to a clock or a map?* [map]

2. Play the audio.

B 1. Play the audio again. Have students read along silently.

2. Check comprehension. Ask: *Is she from New York?* [no] *Was she born in 2004?* [no] *Is her favorite color purple?* [yes]

Guided Practice I

10 minutes

C Have students circle the correct words to complete the sentences. Ask volunteers to write the sentences on the board.

Multilevel Strategies

For 1C, seat pre-level students together.

• **Pre-level** Reread the sentences in 1B with your pre-level students while on- and higher-level students complete 1C. After the 1C sentences are written on the board, read them with the class so that pre-level students have time to circle the answers.

• **On- and Higher-level** After these students work individually to circle the correct words in 1C, have volunteers write the sentences on the board.

2 Write about your life

Guided Practice II

20–25 minutes

A 1. Pronounce and clarify the colors in the *Need help?* box. Have students point to items in the room that are examples of each color.

2. Copy the sentences on the board. Read them aloud with your own information.

3. Have students complete the sentences independently. Circulate and assist.

B Ask students to read their sentences to a partner.

3 Get to know your classmates

Presentation II
20–25 minutes

1. Introduce the topic: *Now we'll ask our classmates for information.* Direct students to look at the ID cards in 3A. Ask: *Where is Linda Perez from?* [Mexico]

2. Ask students to put their pencils down and listen for the answer to this question: *Do they spell their names?* Play the entire audio once.

3. Play the audio again, and have students repeat the questions.

Guided Practice
10–15 minutes

1. Pronounce and have students repeat the sentences in the *Grammar note.*

2. Play the audio again, and have students fill in the blanks in the questions.

3. Ask volunteers to write the completed questions on the board.

4. Direct the questions to different students.

C 1. Have students read along silently while they listen.

2. Play the audio again, and have students repeat the conversation. Replay if necessary.

Communicative Practice and Application
10 minutes

D 1. Model the conversation with a volunteer. Then model it again playing the other role.

2. Set a time limit (five minutes). Ask students to practice the conversation with several partners.

3. Ask volunteers to present their conversations to the class.

TIP Provide intensive practice with self-introduction. Put students in mixed-level groups of four. Assign each group member a different letter, A–D (see A–D cards, page 175). Tell students to introduce themselves to the group. Write skeleton sentences on the board for the students to follow. *My name is _____. I'm from _____. I live in _____. My favorite color is _____.* Then tell students to re-group with two or three partners who have the same letter and practice again. Monitor and provide feedback.

Evaluation
10–15 minutes

TEST YOURSELF

Assign a time limit (five minutes), and have students ask and answer the questions with their partners. Circulate and provide feedback.

Multilevel Strategies

Target the *Test Yourself* to the level of your students.

• **Pre-level** Allow pre-level students to ask and answer the questions with just one partner.

• **Higher-level** Write these questions on the board, and have students ask and answer them as well: *What's your favorite color? Who's your teacher? What's your phone number? How are you today?*

To compress this lesson: Assign 1C as homework. Have students practice the conversation in 3D with only one partner.

To extend this lesson: Write questions and answers on different slips of paper, or scrambled on the board, and have students work in groups to match them.

What's your name?	I'm from India.
What's your date of birth?	5804 Santos Street.
Where are you from?	My teacher's name is Mr. Ortiz.
What's your favorite color?	My date of birth is 4/19/74.
What's your address?	My favorite color is red.
Who's your teacher?	My name is Nora.

And/Or have students complete **Workbook 1 page 10** and **Multilevel Activity Book 1 page 29.**

3 Get to know your classmates

A Listen and number the ID cards.

③
First Name: Linda
Last Name: Perez
Place of Birth: Mexico
Identification Card

①
Student Identification Card
First Name: James
Last Name: Lee
Place of Birth: China
STATE COLLEGE

②
Student Identification
First Name: Lan
Last Name: Le
Place of Birth: Vietnam
CITY UNIVERSITY HUSKIES!

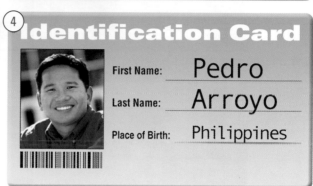

④
Identification Card
First Name: Pedro
Last Name: Arroyo
Place of Birth: Philippines

B Listen and complete the questions.

1. What's your ____name____?
2. ____Where____ are you from?
3. What's your ___date___ of birth?
4. What's your favorite ___color___?

C Listen and repeat.

A: What's your name?
B: My name is Tara. What's your name?
A: My name is Jun Sook. Where are you from?
B: I'm from India. Where are you from?
A: I'm from Korea.

D Work with a partner. Practice the conversation. Use your own information.

> **Grammar note**
>
> **Information questions with *be***
>
> What's { your name?
>   { your address?
>   { your favorite color?
> Where are you from?

TEST YOURSELF ✔

Ask 3 classmates:

What's your name?   What's your date of birth?   What's your place of birth?

1 Learn *Yes/No* questions and answers

A Look at the pictures. Read the questions and answers.
Then answer the question: How do *you* feel? Answers will vary.

1

A: Is Trang happy?
B: Yes, he is.

2

A: Is Maria worried?
B: Yes, she is.

3

A: Is the dog hungry?
B: Yes, it is.

4

A: Are Raj and Padma worried?
B: No, they aren't. They're proud.

5

A: Is Jake happy?
B: No, he isn't. He's angry.

6

A: Is Paul angry?
B: No, he isn't. He's tired.

B Study the charts. Complete the questions and answers below.

YES/NO QUESTIONS WITH BE

Questions		
Are	you	
Is	he she it	hungry?
Are	you they	

Answers				
	I am.			I'm not.
Yes,	he is. she is. it is.	No,	he isn't. she isn't. it isn't.
	we are. they are.		we aren't. they aren't.

1. **A:** __Is__ she hungry?
   B: __Yes__ , she is.

2. **A:** __Are__ they hungry?
   B: No, they __aren't__ .

C Look at the pictures in 1A. Ask and answer the questions.

A: *Is Trang happy?*
B: *Yes, he is.*

Unit 2 Lesson 3

Objectives	Grammar	Vocabulary	Correlations
On- and Higher-level: Use *yes/no* questions to ask about feelings **Pre-level:** Recognize *yes/no* questions to ask about feelings	*Yes/no* questions with *be* (*Is he happy? Are you hungry?*)	Feelings For additional vocabulary practice, see this **Oxford Picture Dictionary** topic: Feelings	**CASAS:** 0.1.1, 0.1.2, 0.2.1, 7.4.7 **LCPs:** 22.01, 32.01, 33.02 **SCANS:** Acquires and evaluates information, Interprets and communicates information, Knowing how to learn, Seeing things in the mind's eye, Self-management, Writing **EFF:** Convey ideas in writing, Reflect and evaluate

Warm-up and Review

10–15 minutes (books closed)

Write: *My name is _____. I live in _____. I'm from _____. I'm a _____. My date of birth is _____. I'm _____ today.* Say the sentences with your own information, completing the last sentence with *happy*. Call on volunteers to say the sentences with their own information.

Introduction

3 minutes

1. Indicate the last sentence on the board. Say: *I feel happy today. Sometimes I'm not happy.*

2. State the objective: *Today we're going to ask and answer questions about our feelings.*

1 Learn *Yes/No* questions and answers

Presentation I

20–25 minutes

A 1. Direct students to look at the pictures. Ask: *Are they all happy?*

2. Read the questions and answers. Have students repeat *worried, hungry,* and *angry.* Help with the initial sounds until most students can pronounce the words comfortably.

3. Ask students: *Are you worried? Are you hungry? Are you angry?*

B 1. Demonstrate how to read the grammar charts as complete questions and answers. Read the chart through sentence by sentence. Then read it again, and have students repeat after you.

2. Use the pictures in 1A to illustrate points in the grammar chart. Ask the questions using *he/she/it/they* instead of the names.

3. As a class, complete the questions and answers. Ask volunteers to write the questions and answers on the board. Have other students read the questions and answers aloud.

4. Give students time to silently review the charts and, if they haven't already, fill in the blanks.

5. Assess their understanding of the charts. Ask different questions about the pictures in 1A: *Is Jake worried?* [no] *Is Maria angry?* [no]

Guided Practice I

15–20 minutes

C 1. Model questions and answers with a volunteer. Demonstrate original questions. *Is Trang worried? No, he isn't.*

2. Have students practice with a partner.

Multilevel Strategies

For 1C, seat same-level students together.

• **Pre-level** While other students are completing 1C, ask pre-level students to read the questions and answers in 1A together.

• **On- and Higher-level** Have these students write four original *yes/no* questions about the pictures. Ask volunteers to write their questions on the board. Elicit the answers.

2 Ask and answer *Yes/No* questions

Guided Practice II

25–30 minutes

A 1. Have students work individually to match the questions and answers.

2. Ask volunteers to read the questions and answers. Write the number-letter match on the board.

B 1. Direct students to read the chart. Read the questions and elicit the answers for each person: *Are you a teacher? Is Trang a teacher?* [no] *Is Maria a teacher?* [yes] *Is Paul a teacher?* [yes]

2. Have students work individually to write the short answers. Ask volunteers to write the answers on the board.

> ### Multilevel Strategies
>
> For 2B, seat same-level students together.
>
> • **Pre-level** After they have copied the answers from the board, help these students read the questions and answers to each other.
>
> • **On- and Higher-level** Have these students ask and answer more questions about the chart. Ask volunteers to say their new questions and answers for the class.

3 Practice *Yes/No* questions

Communicative Practice and Application

20–25 minutes

A 1. Draw the chart on the board, and elicit suggestions to finish the questions.

2. Show students that they should write answers only in the first column.

3. Give students time (three minutes) to fill in their own information.

B 1. Model the interview with a volunteer, and on the board, show where to chart the answers.

2. Check comprehension. Ask: *How many students do you talk to?* [two]

3. Set a time limit (five minutes) for students to interview two partners. Circulate and monitor.

> ### Multilevel Strategies
>
> For 3B, seat pre-level students together.
>
> • **Pre-level** Write completions for the questions on the board: *1. student, 2. China, 3. happy.* While on- and higher-level students interview each other, allow pre-level students to ask the questions without writing.

C Discuss the class's answers. Call on volunteers to talk about their classmates using the information in their charts.

Evaluation

10–15 minutes (books closed)

TEST YOURSELF

Ask students to write the *yes/no* questions independently. Assign a time limit (two minutes), and have them ask and answer the questions with a partner. Collect and correct their writing.

> ### Multilevel Strategies
>
> Target the *Test Yourself* to the level of your students.
>
> • **Pre-level** Allow these students to work with their books open. Provide skeleton sentences for them to complete. *Are you _____ today? Are you a _____? Are you from _____?*

To compress this lesson: Conduct 2B as a whole-class activity.

To extend this lesson: Review *yes/no* answers with pronouns.
1. Make cards that say: *Yes, he is. No, she isn't. No, I'm not. No, it isn't.* and *Yes, they are.*
2. Group students and give each group member one of the cards. Call out questions with pronouns: *Are they happy today? Is she a student? Is he angry?* The group member with the correct card should hold it up.

And/Or have students complete **Workbook 1 pages 11–12** and **Multilevel Activity Book 1 page 30.**

2 Ask and answer *Yes/No* questions

A Match the questions with the answers.

  _b_   1. Is Jake happy?   a. Yes, I am.

  _d_   2. Is Maria happy?   b. No, he isn't. He's angry.

  _a_   3. Are you a student?   c. Yes, it is.

  _e_   4. Are Raj and Padma angry?   d. No, she isn't. She's worried.

  _c_   5. Is the dog hungry?   e. No, they aren't. They're proud.

B Look at the chart. Answer the questions about Trang, Maria, and Paul.

Questions	Trang	Maria	Paul
Are you a teacher?	No	Yes	Yes
Are you from Mexico?	No	Yes	No
Are you hungry?	Yes	No	Yes

1. Is Paul a teacher? _Yes, he is._

2. Is Maria hungry? _No, she isn't._

3. Are Trang and Paul from Mexico? _No, they aren't._

4. Is Maria a teacher? _Yes, she is._

5. Are Trang and Paul hungry? _Yes, they are._

3 Practice *Yes/No* questions

A Complete the questions with your own ideas. Write your answers.

Questions	You	Classmate 1	Classmate 2
1. Are you a ___student___ ?			yes
2. Are you from _____ ?			
3. Are you _____ today?			

B Interview 2 classmates. Write your classmates' answers in the chart.

C Talk about the answers in the chart with your class.

Rafael is a student. He's from Brazil. He's happy today.

TEST YOURSELF ✔

Close your book. Write 3 *Yes/No* questions. Ask and answer the questions with a partner.

1 Learn to talk about marital status

A Look at the pictures. Read the sentences. Then answer the questions below.

Answers will vary.

I'm single.

Ms. Garcia is a single woman. She isn't married.

I'm single.

Mr. Moloto is a single man. He isn't married.

We're married.

Mr. and Mrs. Kim are a married couple. They aren't single.

1. Are you single? _____

2. Are you married? _____

B Listen and read.

A: Can you help me with this form?
B: Sure. Write your first name here.
A: OK.
B: Are you married or single?
A: I'm married.
B: OK, Mrs. Lee. Fill in the "married" bubble.
A: Thank you.

First name:
_____

Last name:
Lee
_____

Title: ○ Mr. ○ Ms. ○ Mrs.
Marital status: ○ married
                 ○ single

Place of birth: *China* _____

Phone: *(213) 555-2178*

C Listen again and repeat.

D Work with a partner. Practice the conversation. Use your own information.

A: Can you help me with this form?
B: Sure. Write your first name here.
A: OK.
B: Are you married or single?
A: I'm _____.
B: OK, _____. Fill in the _____ bubble.

Need help?

Mrs. = a married woman
Miss = a single woman
Ms. = a married or single woman

Mr. = a married or single man

Unit 2 Lesson 4

Objectives	Grammar	Vocabulary	Correlations
On- and Higher-level: Ask and answer questions about personal information **Pre-level:** Ask questions about personal information	Questions with *be* (*Are you married or single?*)	*Married, marital status, Mr., Miss, Ms., Mrs., single* For additional vocabulary practice, see this **Oxford Picture Dictionary** topic: Personal Information	**CASAS:** 0.1.2, 0.1.3, 0.2.1, 0.2.2, 6.0.1, 7.4.7 **LCPs:** 22.01, 22.03, 25.01, 32.01, 32.02, 33.02, 33.07 **SCANS:** Acquires and evaluates information, Interprets and communicates information, Self-management, Speaking **EFF:** Observe critically, Speak so others can understand

Warm-up and Review

10 minutes (books closed)

Review personal information questions. Write on the board: *What's your _____?* Provide possible answers: *555-2346, (304), Gonzalez, 90815, Maria, red.* Elicit the ways to end the question in order to match the answer. Ask individuals the questions.

Introduction

5 minutes

1. Indicating the information on the board, say: *This is personal information.*

2. State the objective: *Today we'll learn more ways to give personal information.*

1 Learn to talk about marital status

Presentation

20–30 minutes

A 1. Direct students to look at the pictures. Ask: *Is Ms. Garcia married?* [no] *Is Mr. Moloto married?* [no] *Are Mr. and Mrs. Kim married?* [yes]

2. Give students a minute to answer the questions. Go over the answers as a class. Encourage students to use the complete short answer: *Yes, I am. No, I'm not.* Call on various individuals to answer the questions.

TIP Sometimes divorced or widowed students don't know what to say. Teach them *I'm divorced* and *I'm a widow (widower),* but tell them it's OK to say *I'm single,* if they are more comfortable with that. Also clarify to students that these questions are asked in official situations but are not always appropriate for casual conversation.

Guided Practice

20–25 minutes

B Play the audio. Ask students to read along silently.

C Play the audio again, and have students repeat the conversation. Replay if necessary.

Communicative Practice and Application

15–20 minutes

D 1. Read the titles in the *Need help?* box and practice their pronunciation.

2. Model the conversation with a volunteer. Elicit other ways to complete the conversation.

3. Set a time limit (five minutes). Ask students to practice the conversation with several partners.

Multilevel Strategies

For 1D, adapt the oral practice to the level of your students.

• **Pre-level** Tell these students to skip the last three lines of the conversation.

• **On- and Higher-level** Encourage these students to practice the conversation with their own information and with several partners.

E 1. Ask students to put their pencils down and listen for the answer to this question: *Is Terry Farmer a teacher?* [yes]

2. Play the audio in segments. After each number, stop the audio and check answers with the students. If necessary, replay the segment.

3. Ask volunteers to write the answers on the board. Practice the pronunciation.

Multilevel Strategies

After the answers are on the board, replay 1E to challenge on- and higher-level students while allowing pre-level students to catch up.

• **Pre-level** Have these students copy the answers from the board and read along as they listen.

• **On- and Higher-level** Write these questions on the board: *Who are the teachers? What does Ms. Silver say? Where is Mr. Gold?* Discuss the answers as a class. Write Ms. Silver's expression on the board, and discuss the use of first names.

2 More questions with *be*

Grammar Extension

15–20 minutes

A Direct students to look at the charts. Play the audio and have students repeat the questions.

TIP

Students often have difficulty differentiating among *Mr., Miss, Ms.,* and *Mrs.* After they listen to the questions and answers in 2A, provide additional practice with these titles. Have students introduce themselves to each other using their formal title. *Hi, I'm Mrs. Kim. Nice to meet you, Mrs. Kim. I'm Mr. Lopez.* Walk around the class asking students third-person questions about their partners. *Is Mrs. Kim a student? Is Mr. Lopez from Korea?*

B 1. Direct students to read the form before they listen. Tell them they will hear a man talking to a woman. Have them put down their pencils and listen for the answer to this question: *Whose information is on the form? The man's or the woman's?* Play the entire audio once.

2. Play the audio in segments, stopping after each piece of information. Ask for a show of hands to see if students caught the answer. Replay the segment if necessary.

3. Write the categories on the board, and ask volunteers to fill in the answers.

C Have students work individually to match the questions and answers. Ask volunteers to read the questions and answers aloud. Write the number-letter match on the board.

Evaluation

10–15 minutes

TEST YOURSELF

1. Model the questions and answers with a volunteer. Then switch roles.

2. Pair students. Check comprehension by asking: *How many questions do you ask?* [six] *Do you read the answers from 1C?* [no]

3. Set a time limit (five minutes), and have the partners take turns asking and answering.

4. Circulate and monitor. Provide feedback.

Multilevel Strategies

Target the *Test Yourself* to the level of your students. Pair same-level students.

• **Pre-level** Allow these students to write their answers before they speak.

• **Higher-level** When these students finish the first-person questions, tell them to ask third-person questions about the form in 2B: *What's his first name? What's his last name? Is he married or single?* Write *you → he* and *your → his* on the board to help them make the transformation.

To compress this lesson: Have students practice the conversation in 1D with only one partner.

To extend this lesson: Give students more practice with identification forms.
1. Draw a large identification form on the board. Label spaces for date, first name, last name, title, marital status, date of birth, address, place of birth, and phone number.
2. Write pieces of information on strips of paper. Sample information could include: 3/04/08; Maria/Kennedy; 115 River St., Los Angeles, CA 90506; Ireland; (808); 555-9087; Ms.; single; 10/17/84.
3. Distribute the strips. Have students tape their pieces of information in the correct spots on the board.

And/Or have students complete **Workbook 1 page 13** and **Multilevel Activity Book 1 page 31.**

E Listen and write the correct title for each name.

1. <u>Mrs.</u>   Pat Tyson
2. <u>Mr.</u>   Pat Song
3. <u>Ms.</u>   Terry Miller
4. <u>Mrs.</u>   Terry Farmer
5. <u>Ms.</u>   Jean Silver
6. <u>Mr.</u>   Gene Gold

2 More questions with *be*

A Study the charts. Listen and repeat the questions.

Information questions
Where is Mrs. Lee from?
What's your name?

Yes/No questions
Is she a student?
Are you a student?

Or questions
Is she married or single?
Are you married or single?

B Listen and complete the missing information.

REGISTRATION FORM

Date: <u>10 / 26 / 07</u>

First name: <u>Sasha</u>   Last name: <u>Milovich</u>

Title: ☑ Mr.   ☐ Ms.   ☐ Mrs.

Marital status: ☐ married   ☑ single

Date of birth: <u>06 / 10 / 71</u>   Place of birth: <u>Russia</u>

Address: <u>1769 Rose Ave.</u>   Phone: <u>(312) 555-1669</u>
<u>Chicago, IL 60601</u>

C Match the questions with the answers.

<u>c</u> 1. What's your first name?   a. (213) 555-3954
<u>f</u> 2. What's your last name?   b. 198 Second St.
<u>d</u> 3. Are you married or single?   c. Pat
<u>a</u> 4. What's your phone number?   d. married
<u>b</u> 5. What's your address?   e. Singapore
<u>e</u> 6. Where are you from?   f. Miller

TEST YOURSELF ✔

Work with a partner. Partner A: Ask the questions from 2C. Partner B: Answer the questions. Use the information on the form in 2B or your information. Then change roles.

1 Get ready to read

A Look at the pictures. Read the words.

countries

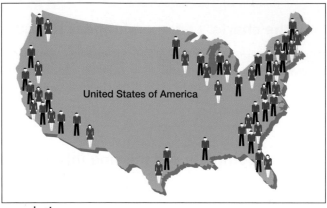

population

B Find your home country on a map. What countries are your classmates from?

2 Read about the population in the U.S.

A Read the article.

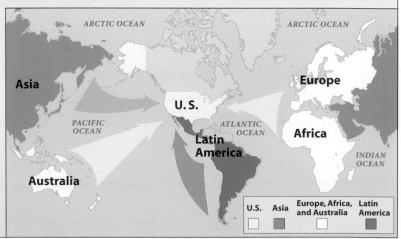

People in the United States: Where are they from?

The population of the United States is about 295 million[1] people. Today, 32.5 million people in the U.S. are from other countries. Where are they from?

- Seventeen million are from Latin America.
- Eight million are from Asia.
- Seven million are from Europe, Africa, and Australia.

[1] million = 1,000,000

Source: *U.S. Department of Commerce*

B Listen and read the article again.

✓ Interpret information on U.S. population and immigration

Unit 2 Lesson 5

Objectives	Grammar	Vocabulary	Correlations
On- and Higher-level: Read about and discuss the population in the U.S. **Pre-level:** Read about the population in the U.S.	Questions with *be* (*Where are you from?*)	*Country, population, million* For additional vocabulary practice, see this **Oxford Picture Dictionary** topic: North America and Central America	**CASAS:** 0.1.2, 0.2.1, 1.1.3, 2.7.2, 5.2.4, 5.2.5, 5.5.1, 6.0.1, 6.7.1, 6.7.2, 6.9.2 **LCPs:** 22.01, 25.01, 32.01–32.06, 32.13 **SCANS:** Arithmetic/Mathematics, Listening, Organizes and maintains information, Reading, Sociability **EFF:** Learn through research, Read with understanding

Warm-up and Review

10–15 minutes (books closed)

Write *3; 13; 30; 300; 3,000* on the board to illustrate differences in place value. Have students repeat these numbers after you. Dictate one- and two-digit numbers, and ask volunteers to write them on the board in numeral form. Have the class repeat them. Write the numbers in word form, and have volunteers read them aloud.

Introduction

5–10 minutes

1. Say: *How many people are in this classroom? How many people are in this city? How many people are in this state?* (Students probably won't know the answers to the second and third questions, so come prepared with the answers.)

2. Write *New York's population = eight million, Los Angeles's population = four million, Chicago's population = three million* on the board. Say: *The population of a place is the number of people who live there.* Write *1,000,000 = one million* on the board.

3. If possible, give students examples of approximate populations from your area. If you can, also look up population statistics for major cities in your students' native countries and share those. (*Mexico City = nine million, Seoul = ten million, Moscow = eight million*)

4. State the objective: *Today we're going to read about the population of the U.S.*

1 Get ready to read

Presentation

15–20 minutes

A Direct students to look at the first picture. Say: *Mexico is a country. The U.S. is a country. What country are you from?* Direct students to look at the second picture. Ask: *Are there many people in Florida?* [yes] *Are there many people in Montana?* [no]

B Display a world map, and ask students to come up and point to their native countries. If several countries are represented by your class, have students write their names on a small sticky-note and place it on the map.

Pre-Reading

Direct students to look at the world map in 2A. Have students repeat the names of the continents where people in the U.S. are from.

2 Read about the population in the U.S.

Guided Practice I

25–30 minutes

A Ask students to read the article silently. Ask if there are any questions about the reading.

B Play the audio. Have students read along silently.

C 1. Have students work individually to mark the sentences *true* or *false*.

2. Ask additional comprehension questions. *Are many people in the U.S. from other countries?* [yes] *How many?* [32.5 million]

Multilevel Strategies

After the group comprehension check in 2C, call on individuals and tailor your questions to the level of your students.

• **Pre-level** Ask *or* questions. *Are there seven million people from Latin America or seventeen million?*

• **On-level** Ask information questions. *How many people in the U.S. are from Asia?*

• **Higher-level** Ask students to generalize. *Where are many people in the U.S. from? Is it the same in our class?*

D Have students work individually to complete the sentences. Ask volunteers to read the sentences aloud. Write the answers on the board.

TIP
Before doing 3A, have students practice *Where are you from?* using a world map (see *The Oxford Picture Dictionary* for a world map). Group students, if possible from different countries, and give each student a letter card *A–D* (see page T-175). Have Student A (with *A* card) ask Student B (with *B* card): *Where are you from?* After Student B answers and points to the country on the map, have Student C (with *C* card) tell Student D (with *D* card): *He/She is from _____.* Student D points to the country on the map. The groups will repeat the activity until everyone has had a turn asking the question, answering, making the third-person statement, and pointing to the map. Have a group of more-advanced students model an entire round for the class. When you begin the practice, put these students in different groups, and assign them the role of Student A.

3 Real-life math

Math Extension

15–20 minutes

A 1. Write the word *graph* on the board. Say and have students repeat it. Direct their attention to the graph in 3A.

2. Read and have students repeat the names of the countries. Ask: *How many people in the U.S. are from Mexico?* [ten million] *How many are from China?* [1.6 million]

Communicative Practice

10–15 minutes

B 1. Copy the blank graph on the board. Elicit from students the names of the countries that will need to appear on the graph. Ask for a show of hands to determine how many students are from each country. Have students count the raised hands and tell you the appropriate number for your graph.

2. When the graph on the board is completed, have students copy it into their books.

C 1. Put two skeleton sentences on the board: _____ *students in my class are from* _____. *One student in my class is from* _____.

2. Ask students to work individually to write sentences about the graph.

5–10 minutes

Application

BRING IT TO LIFE

1. Discuss where students could ask these questions, and write the ideas on the board: *school, children's school*, etc.

2. Make a two-column chart on the board with the headings *Name* and *Place*. Tell students to ask as many people as they can.

To compress this lesson: Assign 2D as homework.

To extend this lesson: Extend 2C by having students rewrite the false sentences so that they are true. Or look up demographic information for your school, district, or city, and write it on the board in graphic form. Have students write sentences about the information.

And/Or have students complete **Workbook 1 page 14** and the **Multilevel Activity Book 1 page 32**.

C Mark the sentences T (true) or F (false).

___F___ 1. 295 million people in the U.S. are from other countries.

___T___ 2. Seventeen million people in the U.S. are from Latin America.

___F___ 3. Seventy-eight million people in the U.S. are from Europe.

D Complete the sentences. Use the words in the box.

> million   population   countries

1. Many people in the U.S. are from other ___countries___ .
2. Eight ___million___ people in the U.S. are from Asia.
3. The U.S. ___population___ from Latin America is seventeen million.

3 Real-life math

A Look at the graph. What countries are people in the U.S. from?

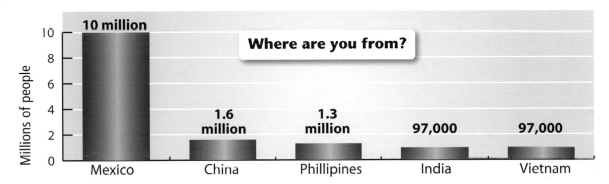

B Work with your classmates. Make a graph about your class.

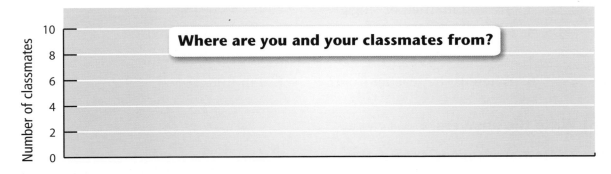

C Write sentences about your graph.

Seven students in my class are from Korea.

BRING IT TO LIFE

Ask a person NOT in your class: What's your name?   Where are you from?
Write the answers in your notebook. Talk about the answers with your classmates.

1 Grammar

A Circle *a* or *b*.

1. _____ she a student?
   a. (Is)
   b. Are

2. _____ they worried?
   a. Is
   b. (Are)

3. Are _____ from Japan?
   a. Li
   b. (you)

4. Is _____ at school today?
   a. (Ms. Baker)
   b. Mr. and Mrs. Jones

B Complete the questions. Use the words in the box.

What	Where	~~Who~~	Are

1. _Who_ is she?
2. _Where_ are you from?
3. _Are_ you married or single?
4. _What_ is your name?

C Match the questions with the answers.

_d_ 1. Where are you from?
_c_ 2. What is your phone number?
_a_ 3. Are you married or single?
_f_ 4. How are you?
_b_ 5. Are you hungry?
_e_ 6. Where is the teacher from?

a. I'm married.
b. Yes, I am.
c. It's 555-9134.
d. I'm from Mexico.
e. She's from Miami.
f. I'm fine.

D Write the answers. Answers will vary.

1. Are you a student? _Yes, I am._
2. What is your first name? _____
3. What time is it? _____
4. Is today Monday? _____
5. What is your date of birth? _____

Unit 2 Review and expand

Objectives	Grammar	Vocabulary	Correlations
On-, Pre-, and Higher-level: Expand upon and review unit grammar and life skills	Questions with *be* (*Is she a student? Where are you from?*)	Personal information For additional vocabulary practice, see this **Oxford Picture Dictionary** topic: Personal Information	**CASAS:** 0.1.2, 0.1.5, 0.2.1, 2.3.2, 4.8.1, 6.0.1, 7.2.5–7.2.7, 7.3.1 **LCPs:** 22.01, 25.01, 25.03, 32.01, 32.13, 33.02, 33.07 **SCANS:** Creative thinking, Participates as member of a team, Problem solving, Seeing things in the mind's eye **EFF:** Solve problems and make decisions

Warm-up and Review

10–15 minutes (books closed)

1. Review the *Bring It to Life* assignment from Lesson 5.

2. Have students who did the exercise share how many people they talked to and where they were from. Ask students who didn't do the exercise to ask their classmates the *Bring It to Life* questions.

Introduction and Presentation

5 minutes

1. Write the questions from the warm-up on the board: *Where are they from? Where is he from? Where is she from?* Underline the verb in each question, and ask: *What is this verb?*

2. State the objective: *Today we'll practice more questions with the verb* be.

1 Grammar

Guided Practice

40–45 minutes

A Have students work individually to circle the answers. Ask volunteers to read the completed questions aloud. Write the answers on the board.

B Have students work individually to complete the sentences. Ask volunteers to read the completed sentences aloud. Write the answers on the board.

C Have students work individually to match the questions and answers. Ask pairs of students to read the matching questions and answers aloud. Write the number-letter match on the board.

TIP For more practice with questions after 1C, write questions and answers on cards or slips of colored paper: *What's your date of birth? What's your telephone number? How are you? Who is she?* etc. Put the questions on one colored paper and the answers on another. It's OK if there are different possible matches, as long as every question has an answer. Give questions to half the class and answers to the other half. Make extras and keep them in reserve. Direct students to circulate and read their questions and answers aloud to each other. When they think they have a match, the pairs should line up at your desk. Listen to their matches. If they have a match, give each of them a new question or answer and send them back to look for another partner. When you run out of questions, have pairs sit down after they've reported to you. To make this game more challenging, insist that students not show each other their questions or answers.

D Have students work individually to write the answers. Ask volunteers to write the answers on the board.

Multilevel Strategies

For 1A–D, seat same-level students together.

• **Pre-level** Give these students time to copy the answers from the board. As other students move on to the next exercise, assist these students with reading the questions and answers from the exercise they have completed.

• **On- and Higher-level** When these students have finished all of the exercises, have them ask a partner the questions in 1C and 1D and answer with their own information.

2 Group work

Communicative Practice

20–35 minutes

 A 1. Direct students, in groups of three to four, to focus on the picture on page 17. Ask: *What month is this calendar page?* [March]

2. Set a time limit (five minutes) to complete the exercise. Circulate and answer any questions.

3. Have a reporter from each group read his/her group's sentences to the class.

Multilevel Strategies

For 2A and 2B, use same-level groups.

• **Pre-level** For 2A, ask these students to write the names of three days and three months. For 2B, allow pre-level students to ask and answer the questions without writing.

• **Higher-level** For 2A, ask these students to write two additional sentences about the picture. For 2B, have students ask and answer these questions: *What's your date of birth? How are you today?*

B 1. Have students work in the same groups from 2A to take turns interviewing each other in pairs.

2. Set a time limit (five minutes) to complete the exercise.

3. Tell students to make a note of their partners' answers but not to worry about writing complete sentences.

C Call on individuals to share what they learned about their partners.

🌐 **TIP** Use the 1C report-back to provide intensive practice with third-person sentences. Have each pair of students tell the other pair (from the original groups in 2A) about their partners. Then direct one pair from each group to stand up and move to a new group. In the new group, they should repeat the process. Monitor and provide feedback.

PROBLEM SOLVING

20–25 minutes

A Direct students to look at the picture. Ask: *Is she happy?* [no] *Where is Bella?* [at school, in the classroom] *Is her form OK?* [no]

B 1. Identify the problem. Read the question. Read the possible solutions.

2. Elicit student ideas for other solutions. Write each one on the board.

3. Discuss whether the statements are appropriate.

4. Ask for a show of hands to see which solution the class likes best.

🌐 **TIP** Bring in the personal-information section of several real forms—the registration form for your school, a job application, and a medical form. Make a transparency of the form, and have students take turns coming up and filling out one section of the form. You will end up with a "composite person" (one student's last name, another's first name, another's address). With the class, correct any information that is not in the right place.

You can also do this as group work by giving one transparency to each group and having the group present its completed form to the class.

Evaluation

30–35 minutes

To test students' understanding of the unit grammar and life skills, have them take the Unit 2 Test in the *Step Forward Test Generator CD-ROM with ExamView® Assessment Suite*.

Learning Log

To help students record and discuss their progress, use the *Learning Log* on page T-176.

To extend this review: Have students complete **Workbook 1 page 15, Multilevel Activity Book 1 pages 33–36,** and the **Unit 2 Grammar Exercises** on the **Multilevel Grammar Exercises CD-ROM 1.**

2 Group work

A Work with your classmates. Write 5 sentences about the calendar on page 17. Talk about the sentences with your class. Answers will vary.

It's Tuesday.	Today is Tuesday.	It's March 6.
The month is March.	Tomorrow is Wednesday.	

B Interview 3 classmates. Write their answers in your notebook.

ASK:

1. Where are you from?
2. Are you married or single?
3. What's your favorite color?

> Classmate—Javier
> 1. He's from Chile.
> 2. He's married.
> 3. It's green.

C Talk about the answers with your class.

PROBLEM SOLVING

A Look at the picture. What is the problem?
Her form is dirty.

B Work with your classmates. Answer the question. (More than one answer is possible.)

What can Bella do?
  a. Give the form to the teacher.
  b. Read the form to the teacher.
  c. Ask for a new form.
  d. Other: _Answers will vary._

OH, NO!

Please give me your form.

UNIT 3

Family and Friends

FOCUS ON
- family members
- descriptions of people
- possessives
- dates and phone messages
- families in the U.S.

LESSON 1 Vocabulary

---

1 Learn about family members

A Look at the pictures. Read and say the names and the dates.

B Listen and look at the pictures.

The Martinez Family

Carlos and Anita are married! 6/22/97   Carlos and baby Eric 11/15/99

Anita and baby Robin 4/20/03

Carlos, Anita, Eric, and Robin 6/30/06

C Listen and repeat the words.

1. wife   3. father   5. mother   7. parents
2. husband   4. son   6. daughter   8. children*   *one child / two children

D Look at the pictures. Complete the sentences.

1. Anita is a ___wife___ and ___mother___.   4. Carlos is a ___husband___ and ___father___.
2. Eric is a ___son (child)___.   5. Carlos and Anita are ___parents___.
3. Eric and Robin are ___children___.   6. Robin is a ___daughter (child)___.

☑ Identify family members

Unit 3 Lesson 1

Objectives	Grammar	Vocabulary	Correlations
On-level: Identify vocabulary about family members **Pre-level:** Recognize vocabulary about family members **Higher-level:** Talk and write about family members	Sentences with *be* (*I'm a mother. He's my son.*)	Family For additional vocabulary practice, see this **Oxford Picture Dictionary** topic: Families	**CASAS:** 0.1.2, 7.4.5, 7.4.7 **LCPs:** 22.01, 25.03, 31.01, 32.01, 32.02, 33.05 **SCANS:** Listening, Participates as member of a team, Seeing things in the mind's eye, Self-management, Speaking **EFF:** Cooperate with others, Listen actively, Observe critically, Reflect and evaluate

Warm-up

10 minutes (books closed)

Draw your family in stick figures on the board. Tell the students about your family members. *Her name is Carmen. She's my daughter. She's married. She lives in California. She has two children.* Say the sentences as you point to each picture. After you finish, point to the pictures, and ask students to tell you what they remember. Write the relationship words under each person: *daughter, husband, father, mother.*

Introduction

5 minutes

1. Point to the people on the board, and say: *This is my family.*

2. State the objective: *Today we'll learn words to talk about families.*

1 Learn about family members

Presentation

20–25 minutes

A 1. Direct students to look at the pictures. Say: *Look at the Martinez family. Are they happy?* [yes]

2. Read the captions in 1B, and have students repeat after you.

B 1. Have students listen to the audio. Ask them to point to the correct picture as they listen. Circulate and monitor.

2. Check comprehension by asking *yes/no* questions. Pass out *yes/no* cards (see page T-175), or have students hold up one finger for *yes* and two for *no* in order to get a nonverbal response. Ask: *Is Anita a mother?* [yes] *Is Carlos a wife?* [no] *How many children do Carlos and Anita have?* [two]

Multilevel Strategies

After the group comprehension check in 1B, call on individuals and tailor your questions to the level of your students.

• **Pre-level** Ask *yes/no* questions. *Is Robin a father?* [no]

• **On-level** Ask information questions. *Who is Eric?* [son/baby/child]

• **Higher-level** Ask these students to use the vocabulary. *Tell me about Carlos and Eric.* [They are father and son.]

C Ask students to listen and repeat the words.

Guided Practice I

15–20 minutes

D 1. Have students complete the sentences using the new vocabulary.

2. Encourage students to take turns reading the completed sentences in pairs.

2 Talk about a family

Guided Practice II

35–40 minutes

 1. Ask: *Do you have a big family or a small family?* Introduce the new topic: *Now let's talk about other family members.*

2. Group students and assign roles: leader, fact checker, recorder, and reporter. Explain that students work with their groups to match the words and pictures.

3. Check comprehension of the exercise. *Who looks up the words in the picture dictionary?* [fact checker] *Who writes the numbers in the book?* [recorder] *Who tells the class your answers?* [reporter] *Who helps everyone and manages the group?* [leader]

4. Set a time limit (three minutes), and have students work together to complete the task. While students are working, copy the wordlist on the board.

5. Call "time" and have the reporters from each group take turns calling out the numbers for the wordlist. Record students' answers on the board. If groups disagree, write each group's choice next to the word.

Multilevel Strategies

For 2A, use mixed-level groups.

• **On-level** Assign these students as recorders and reporters.

• **Pre-level** Assign these students the role of timekeeper (letting the group know when the three minutes are up) to allow these students an active role in the group.

• **Higher-level** Assign these students as leaders.

B 1. Ask students to listen and check their answers. Then have them correct the wordlist on the board and write the correct numbers in their books.

2. Tell the groups from 2A to break into pairs to practice the words. Set a time limit (two minutes).

 1. Have students complete the sentences.

2. Ask students to take turns reading the completed sentences in the same pairs from 2B.

Communicative Practice and Application

10–15 minutes

D 1. Point out the *Grammar note.* Copy it on the board, and draw a link from *an* to *aunt.* Write *a sister* under *a father,* and write *an uncle* under *an aunt.* Write the vowels on the board, and explain that we use *an* before a vowel sound. Put up a few more words with which students will be familiar, and have students tell you whether to use *a* or *an.*

2. Model the conversation with a volunteer. Then model it again, switching roles. Model it a third time with your own information.

3. Set a time limit (five minutes). Ask students to practice the conversation with several partners.

Evaluation

10–15 minutes (books closed)

TEST YOURSELF

1. Make a three-column chart on the board with the headings *Man, Woman,* and *Both.* Have students close their books and give you an example for each column. Have students copy the chart into their notebooks.

2. Give students five to ten minutes to test themselves by writing the words they recall from the lesson.

3. Call "time" and have students check their spelling in *The Oxford Picture Dictionary* or another dictionary. Circulate and monitor students' progress.

To compress this lesson: Conduct 2A as a whole-class activity. Have students practice 2D with only one partner.

To extend this lesson: Use lesson vocabulary to tell a story, and have students repeat back what they remember.
1. Make transparencies of pictures with people and families in them or use pictures big enough to show to the class (see page 44 of *Multilevel Activity Book 1* for pictures of family members).
2. As you hold up or project one picture at a time, tell a story about it. *He's my son. He lives in Alaska. He's married.*
3. Ask students to report what they heard. Repeat the sentences. (Hum or clap to indicate the blank.) *He's my* _____. *He lives in* _____. *He's* _____. Write the sentences on the board as the students complete them.

And/Or have students complete **Workbook 1 page 16** and **Multilevel Activity Book 1 page 38.**

2 Talk about a family

A Work with your classmates. Number the people in Eric's family.

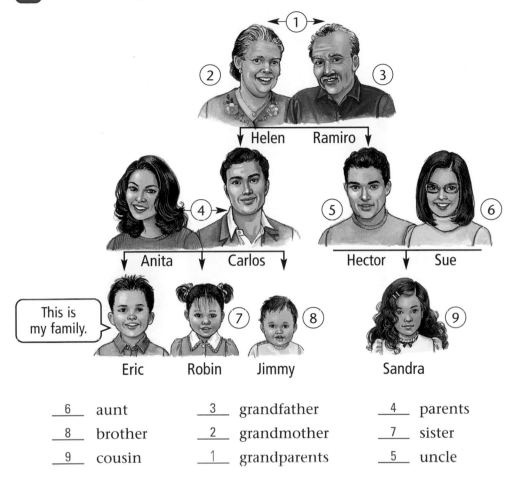

__6__	aunt	__3__	grandfather	__4__	parents
__8__	brother	__2__	grandmother	__7__	sister
__9__	cousin	__1__	grandparents	__5__	uncle

B Listen and check your answers. Then practice the words with a partner.

C Look at the picture. Complete the sentences.

1. I'm Eric's uncle. Carlos is my brother. I'm _____Hector_____.
2. Eric and Jimmy are my brothers. I'm __Robin_____.
3. Anita is my aunt. Sue is my mother. I'm ___Sandra_____.
4. Eric is my grandson. Ramiro is my husband. I'm __Helen_____.

D Work with a partner. Tell your partner 2 things about yourself.

A: I'm a mother and an aunt. How about you?
B: I'm a grandfather and a husband.

Grammar note

a or *an*?

a father   an aunt

TEST YOURSELF ✔

Close your book. Write 10 words for family members. Write *M* (man), *W* (woman), or *B* (both) next to each. Check your spelling in a dictionary.

1 Read about a family

🎧 **A** **Look at the pictures. Listen.**

Sam

Karina

Simon

🎧 **B** **Listen again. Read the sentences.**

1. My name is Paulina Gutman. These are photos of my family.
2. Sam is my son. He is the tall boy with blond hair.
3. Karina is my daughter. She is the girl with brown hair and big blue eyes.
4. My husband is the short man with beautiful gray hair. His name is Simon.
5. They are all very special to me.

C **Check your understanding. Match the numbers with the letters.**

_d_ 1. Paulina   a. brown hair and blue eyes

_a_ 2. Karina   b. short with gray hair

_b_ 3. Simon   c. tall with blond hair

_c_ 4. Sam   d. blond hair and blue eyes

Unit 3 Lesson 2

Objectives	Grammar	Vocabulary	Correlations
On-, Pre-, and Higher-level: Read and write about a family	Sentences with *be*, possessive adjectives (*His name is Simon. My eyes are brown.*)	Words to describe hair and eyes For additional vocabulary practice, see these **Oxford Picture Dictionary** topics: Describing People, Describing Hair	**CASAS:** 0.1.2, 0.2.1, 7.4.7 **LCPs:** 22.01, 31.01, 32.01, 32.02, 33.03 **SCANS:** Acquires and evaluates information, Listening, Seeing things in the mind's eye, Self-management, Sociability, Speaking, Writing **EFF:** Convey ideas in writing, Read with understanding, Reflect and evaluate

Warm-up and Review

10–15 minutes (books closed)

Review the colors. Hold up colored cards or objects of different colors, and ask: *What color is it?* Put the color words on the board scrambled: *thwie* [white], *wbonr* [brown], *ragy* [gray], *lyelow* [yellow], *ulbe* [blue], *enegr* [green], *dre* [red], *rpulep* [purple], *ckabl* [black]. Give students time to complete the activity individually. Ask volunteers to come to the board and write the unscrambled words.

Introduction

5 minutes

1. Point to your hair, and say: *What color is my hair?* (If your hair is blond, use a student's hair.) Talk about your students' hair colors and underline the appropriate words. Say: *Is hair purple? Is hair blue?* Erase the words that do not relate to hair color from the board except *yellow*. If you have a blond student, say: *Sara's hair is not yellow. It's blond.* Erase *yellow* and write *blond* on the board. If you don't have a blond in the room, introduce the word when students look at the pictures in 1A.

2. State the objective: *Today we'll read about a family and how to describe people in writing.*

1 Read about a family

Presentation I

20–25 minutes

A 1. Direct students to look at the pictures. Say: *Point to the man with gray hair. Point to the boy with blond hair.*

2. Play the audio.

B 1. Play the audio again. Have students read along silently.

2. Check comprehension. Ask: *Is Paulina married or single?* [married] *Is Simon her husband or her son?* [husband]

Guided Practice I

10 minutes

C Have students match the names with the descriptions. Ask a volunteer to read the description for each name and write the number-letter match on the board.

Multilevel Strategies

After 3C, challenge on- and higher-level students while working with pre-level students.

• **Pre-level** Reread the sentences in 1B with your pre-level students while on- and higher-level students complete additional work.

• **On- and Higher-level** On the board, post pictures or write the names of five famous people with whom your students will be familiar. While you are working with pre-level students, ask on- and higher-level students to copy the names into their notebooks and list each person's hair and eye color. When they are finished, ask volunteers to write this information on the board.

2 Write about yourself

Guided Practice II

20–25 minutes

A 1. Pronounce and clarify the *Need help?* words.

2. Copy the sentences on the board. Read them aloud with your own information.

3. Have students complete the sentences independently. Circulate and assist.

> **Multilevel Strategies**
>
> Seat same-level students together for 2A.
>
> • **Higher-level** Ask these students to add these sentences as well: *I'm from _____. I live in _____. My favorite color is _____. I'm _____ today.*

B Ask students to read their sentences to a partner.

3 Describe family members

Presentation II

20–25 minutes

A 1. Introduce the topic: *We're going to listen to a description of Paulina's family and fill in the chart.* Direct students to look at the chart in 3A. Read the column heads. Point out that a word is missing after the word *Paulina's* in rows 2 and 3.

2. Ask students to put their pencils down and listen for the answer to this question: *Who are the family members?* Play the entire audio once.

3. Play the audio in segments. After each number, stop the audio and ask for a show of hands: *Did you get the answer?* If necessary, replay the segment.

4. Copy the chart on the board, and ask volunteers to come up and complete the information.

Guided Practice

10–15 minutes

B 1. Direct students to look at the pictures. Talk about picture 1: *Do they look good or bad? They look good. They are attractive.* Have students repeat the words under the pictures. Clarify as necessary.

2. Model the conversation with a volunteer. Then model it again with different ideas from the pictures in 1A.

C 1. Have students read along silently while they listen.

2. Play the audio again, and have students repeat the conversation. Replay if necessary.

Communicative Practice and Application

10 minutes

D 1. Model the conversations with a volunteer. Then model them again, switching roles.

2. Set a time limit (five minutes). Ask students to practice the conversations with several partners. Ask volunteers to present their conversations to the class.

Evaluation

10–15 minutes (books closed)

TEST YOURSELF

1. Make a model chart on the board, showing three of your friends or family members and writing their descriptions.

2. Erase the information and ask students to copy the blank chart into their notebooks. Have students work individually to complete their charts.

To compress this lesson: Assign 1C as homework. Have students practice the conversations in 3D with only one partner.

To extend this lesson: Have students write descriptions of people in magazine pictures. Bring in magazines. Group students. Tell each group to cut out pictures of as many different-looking people as they can. Have each group make a poster with the pictures. Direct group members to write a description of each picture on the poster. Have a reporter from each group show the posters to the class and read the descriptions. As groups share their work, elicit corrections from the rest of the class.

And/Or have students complete **Workbook 1 page 17** and **Multilevel Activity Book 1 page 39.**

2 Write about yourself

A Write your story. Complete the sentences. Answers will vary.

My name is _____.

My eyes are _____.

My hair is _____.

B Read your story to a partner.

Need help?

Colors for eyes

| ■ black | ■ brown |
| ■ blue | ■ green |

Colors for hair

■ black	■ brown
☐ blond	■ gray
■ red	☐ white

3 Describe family members

A Listen to the sentences. Then complete the chart.

Names	Family members	Hair	Eyes
1. Simon	Paulina's husband	gray	brown
2. Karina	Paulina's daughter	brown	blue
3. Sam	Paulina's son	blond	brown

B Work with a partner. Talk about the pictures in 1A. Tell your partner *Point to…*.

A: Point to the thin man with gray hair.

B: Point to the attractive girl with blue eyes.

More words to describe people

attractive   young   heavy   average   thin

C Listen and repeat.

A: What color are your eyes?   A: What color is your hair?

B: My eyes are blue.   B: My hair is brown.

D Work with a partner. Practice the conversations. Use your own information.

TEST YOURSELF ✔

Close your book. Make a chart about 3 people you know. Write their names, hair color, and eye color.

1 Learn possessives

A Listen and read Joe's story. Complete the sentences below.

> My name is Joe. This is my daughter. Her name is Grace. This is my grandson. He is a great kid. His name is Charlie. Charlie's eyes are brown. His hair is blond. My eyes are green, but brown eyes are my favorite.

1. Charlie's eyes are __brown__ .   2. His hair is __blond__ .

B Study the chart. Then complete the sentences below. Use the words in parentheses.

POSSESSIVE ADJECTIVES

Pronouns	Possessive adjectives	Examples
I	my	My eyes are green.
you	your	Your eyes are blue.
he	his	His eyes are brown.
she	her	Her eyes are blue.
it	its	Its eyes are yellow.
we	our	Our eyes are blue.
you	your	Your eyes are brown.
they	their	Their eyes are green.

1. __My__ eyes are green. (I)   3. __Our__ eyes are blue. (we)
2. __His__ eyes are brown. (he)   4. __Their__ eyes are green. (they)

C Look at the pictures in 1A. Circle the correct words.

1. ((Her)/ Their) name is Grace.
2. ((His)/ Her) name is Charlie. His hair ((is)/ are) blond.
3. ((Their)/ Your) names (is /(are)) Grace and Charlie.
4. Grace is a mother. Charlie is (his /(her)) son.

Unit 3 Lesson 3

Objectives	Grammar	Vocabulary	Correlations
On- and Higher-level: Use possessive adjectives to describe people **Pre-level:** Recognize possessive adjectives to describe people	Possessive adjectives (*Her name is Grace.*)	Possessive adjectives For additional vocabulary practice, see this **Oxford Picture Dictionary** topic: Describing People	**CASAS:** 0.1.2, 0.2.1, 7.4.7 **LCPs:** 22.01, 31.01, 32.01, 32.13, 33.03, 33.07 **SCANS:** Knowing how to learn, Listening, Self-management, Speaking, Writing **EFF:** Convey ideas in writing, Listen actively, Read with understanding, Reflect and evaluate

Warm-up and Review

10–15 minutes (books closed)

Bring in pictures of people who have different-colored hair. You can cut them from magazines or find them on the Internet. Give each student one picture. Write hair colors on the board, and have students come up and tape their pictures under the right color. Say and write sentences about the pictures: *His hair is blond. Her hair is red. His hair is gray.*

Introduction

5–10 minutes

1. Underline the possessive adjectives on the board.

2. State the objective: *Today we'll use possessives to describe people.*

1 Learn possessives

Presentation I

20–25 minutes

 1. Direct students to look at the picture. Point to people in the picture, and ask: *Is her hair blond?* [yes] *Is his hair brown?* [no]

2. Play the audio and have students read along silently. Say: *Point to Grace. Point to Charlie. Point to the person with green eyes.* [Joe]

3. Have students complete the sentences individually. Ask a volunteer to read the completed sentences aloud.

 1. Read each row of the chart. Have students repeat the sentences after you.

2. Use the pictures in 1A and your students to illustrate the use of the possessive. *His hair is blond.*

3. As a class, complete the sentences under the chart. Ask volunteers to write the sentences on the board. Have other students read the sentences aloud.

4. Give students time to silently review the chart and, if they haven't already, fill in the blanks.

5. Assess students' understanding of the chart. Point to students and groups of students to elicit the proper possessive adjective.

Guided Practice

15–20 minutes

C Have students work individually to circle the correct answers. Ask volunteers to write the completed sentences on the board.

Multilevel Strategies

For 1C, seat same-level students together.

• **Pre-level** While other students are completing 1C, ask pre-level students to copy the sentences from 1B into their notebooks. Give them time to copy the answers to 1C after they are written on the board.

• **On- and Higher-level** Have these students write three to five additional sentences using different possessive adjectives.

2 Ask and answer information questions with possessives

Presentation II

20–25 minutes

1. Copy the chart on the board. Read and have students repeat the phrases. Demonstrate the possessive *s* by picking up objects that belong to the students and saying *Juliana's book; Mohammed's paper.* Be sure to emphasize the possessive *s*.

2. Read and have students repeat the questions and answers in the chart.

3. Check comprehension by asking similar questions about your students: *What color is Lupe's hair?* Have students respond with complete sentences.

Guided Practice

10–15 minutes

1. Have students work individually to complete the answers. Ask volunteers to write the completed answers on the board.

2. Conduct a choral practice of the questions and answers.

C Have students work individually to write sentences. Ask volunteers to write the answers on the board.

3 Practice possessives

Communicative Practice and Application

20–25 minutes

A 1. Draw the chart on the board, and fill in your own information. Elicit other possible answers.

2. Give students time (three minutes) to fill in their own information.

Multilevel Strategies

Use mixed-level pairs for 3B.

• **Pre-level** Have these students answer questions first, so they can watch their on- or higher-level partners charting the answers before doing it themselves.

B 1. Model the interview with a volunteer, and, on the board, show where to chart the answers.

2. Check comprehension. Ask: *How many students do you talk to?* [one] Set a time limit (three minutes) for students to interview their partners. Circulate and monitor.

TIP

To prepare students for 3C, write these questions on the board: *What color is your _____'s hair? What color are your _____'s eyes?* Elicit possible completions. Write these skeleton answers on the board: *My _____'s hair is _____. His/Her eyes are _____. His/her name is _____.* Elicit possible completions. Ask students to talk to at least two partners about their family members or friends. As a follow-up, have volunteers write a sentence about a family member or friend on the board.

C Call on individuals to describe themselves and their partners.

Evaluation

10–15 minutes (books closed)

TEST YOURSELF

Ask students to write the sentences independently. Collect and correct their writing.

Multilevel Strategies

Target the *Test Yourself* to the level of your students.

• **Pre-level** Put up a picture of a man and a picture of a woman along with sentence skeletons: *_____ hair is blond. _____ hair is brown.* Ask pre-level students to copy and complete the skeletons.

To compress this lesson: Conduct 2B as a whole-class activity. Assign 2C as homework.

To extend this lesson: Put up a picture of a family, and ask your students for help writing a story about its members.
1. Elicit names for the people, where the family is from, relationships, marital status, and hair and eye color.
2. Write the story on the board as the students compose it, and have students copy it into their notebooks.

And/Or have students complete **Workbook 1 pages 18–19** and the **Multilevel Activity Book 1 page 40**.

2 Ask and answer information questions with possessives

A Study the chart. Listen and repeat the questions and answers.

Information questions and answers with possessives		Notes:
A: What color is Charlie's hair? B: His hair is blond.	A: What color is Grace's hair? B: Her hair is blond.	Use **'s** after a name for the possessive.
A: What color are Charlie's eyes? B: His eyes are brown.	A: What color are Grace's eyes? B: Her eyes are blue.	Charlie's eyes = his eyes Mary's book = her book Mr. Smith's pen = his pen

B Complete the answers.

1. A: Who is Charlie's grandfather?
   B: _His_ name is Joe.

2. A: Who is Joe's grandson?
   B: Charlie is _his_ grandson.

3. A: What is his daughter's name?
   B: _Her_ name is Grace.

4. A: What is your teacher's name?
   B: _My_ teacher's name is _Answers will vary._

C Underline the possessive names. Write new sentences.

1. <u>Grace's</u> hair is blond.   Her hair is blond.
2. <u>Joe's</u> eyes are green.   His eyes are green.
3. <u>Paulina's</u> children are tall.   Her children are tall.
4. <u>Grace and Charlie's</u> dog is brown.   Their dog is brown.

3 Practice possessives

A Read the questions. Write your answers in the chart. Answers will vary.

Questions	My answers	My partner's answers
1. What's your name?		
2. What color are your eyes?		
3. What color is your hair?		

B Interview a partner. Write your partner's answers in the chart.

C Talk about the answers in the chart with your class.

His name is Asim. Asim's eyes are green. His hair is black.

TEST YOURSELF ✔

Close your book. Write 4 sentences. Describe your classmates and your teacher.
My teacher's hair is brown.

1 Learn to read and say dates

 **A** **Listen and read the calendar. Then complete the sentences below.**

March

Sun.	Mon.	Tues.	Wed.	Thurs.	Fri.	Sat.
		1st	2nd Ashley	3rd	4th	5th
6th	7th	8th	9th	10th	11th	12th
13th	14th	15th	16th	17th	18th	19th
20th The first day of spring	21st	22nd	23rd Julie	24th	25th	26th
27th	28th	29th	30th	31st		

Need help?

Months of the year

January	July
February	August
March	September
April	October
May	November
June	December

Dates

1st = first
2nd = second
3rd = third
4th = fourth
5th = fifth
20th = twentieth
21st = twenty-first

1. Ashley's birthday is on <u>March 2nd</u> .
2. The first day of spring is on <u>March 20th</u> .

 **B** **Listen and read.**

Ashley: Hello, Ed. It's Ashley. What's the date today?
Ed: It's March 2nd.
Ashley: Well, what day is today? Is it a special day?
Ed: It's Wednesday.
Ashley: Wednesday, March 2nd?
Ed: Yes, that's right. Oh! Happy birthday, Ashley!

C **Listen again and repeat.**

D **Work with a partner. Practice the conversation.
Talk about today.**

A: What's the _____ today?
B: It's _____.
A: What _____ is today?
B: It's _____.
A: _____, _____?
B: Yes, that's right.

Unit 3 Lesson 4

Objectives	Grammar	Vocabulary	Correlations
On- and Higher-level: Ask and answer questions about the calendar **Pre-level:** Ask questions about the calendar	Questions and answers with *be* (*What's the date today? It's April 25.*)	Ordinal numbers For additional vocabulary practice, see this **Oxford Picture Dictionary** topic: The Calendar	**CASAS:** 0.1.2, 2.1.7, 2.3.2, 6.0.1, 6.0.2, 7.4.7 **LCPs:** 22.03, 23.02, 25.01, 25.03, 31.01, 32.01, 32.02, 32.13, 34.01, 34.02 **SCANS:** Listening, Organizes and maintains information, Reading, Responsibility, Self-management, Sociability, Speaking **EFF:** Speak so others can understand

Warm-up and Review

10–15 minutes (books closed)

Call out a number and have students tell you what month goes with that number. Continue until you have elicited all twelve months. Then write the numbers on the board, and call on volunteers to come up and write the name of the month next to the correct number. Have students repeat the months.

Introduction

5 minutes

1. Erase the months, leaving the numbers on the board, and write the rest of the numbers up to 31. Circle the number that represents today's date, and say: *This number is three, but when we say the date, we use special numbers. We say: Today is October third.*

2. State the objective: *Today we're going to learn how to read and say the date, and practice taking phone messages.*

1 Learn to read and say dates

Presentation

20–30 minutes

 A 1. Direct students to look at the calendar. Ask: *What month is it?* [March]

2. Say and have students repeat the ordinal numbers under *Dates*.

3. Give students a minute to complete sentences 1 and 2. Go over the answers as a class.

Guided Practice

20–25 minutes

B Play the audio. Ask students to read along silently.

C Play the audio again, and have students repeat the conversation. Replay if necessary.

Communicative Practice and Application

15–20 minutes

D 1. Model the conversation with a volunteer. Then model it again with another month and day.

2. Elicit other ways to complete the conversation.

3. Set a time limit (five minutes). Ask students to practice the conversation with several partners.

Multilevel Strategies

For 1D, adapt the oral practice to the level of your students.

• **Pre-level** Write a completed version of the conversation on the board, and have students read it as written.

• **On-level** Encourage these students to practice the conversation with different months and days.

• **Higher-level** Ask these students to ask and answer this question in their conversation: *Is it your birthday?*

2 Practice taking phone messages

Presentation

5 minutes

 1. Ask: *Do you like talking on the phone in English?* Introduce the new topic: *Now we're going to practice taking phone messages.*

2. Read the question. Ask students to put their pencils down and listen for the answer to the question. Play the entire audio once.

Guided Practice

5–10 minutes

 1. Play the audio in segments. After each message, stop the audio and check answers with the students: *Raise your hand if you wrote the date, time, and phone number.* If necessary, replay the segment.

2. Check students' listening accuracy: *What's Jackie's phone number? Who is message three from?*

3 Practice your pronunciation

Pronunciation Extension

10–15 minutes

Play the audio. Have students repeat the words in the chart.

B Play the audio. Have students work individually to circle the correct answers. Say the answers and have students repeat.

 1. Direct students to look at the calendar on page 34. Model the exercise with a volunteer. Model it again, switching roles.

2. Set a time limit (three minutes), and have students practice saying the dates with a partner. Circulate and provide feedback on pronunciation. Make a note of common problems and conduct choral practice with problem sounds.

4 Real-life math

Math Extension

5–10 minutes

1. Direct students to look at the picture. Ask: *What month is it? Is today Julie's birthday?*

2. Have students work individually to complete the sentence. Ask a volunteer to read the completed sentence.

Evaluation

10–15 minutes

TEST YOURSELF

1. Tell the class the names and birthdays of three of your friends or family members. Then have a volunteer tell you the names and birthdays of three of his/her friends or family members.

2. Pair students. Check comprehension by asking: *How many birthdays are you telling about?* [three]

3. Set a time limit (five minutes). Circulate and monitor. Provide feedback.

To compress this lesson: Have students practice the conversation in 1D with only one partner.

To extend this lesson: Play a dice game to practice saying dates.
1. Group students and give each group a set of dice. If you have different-colored dice, give each group a mismatched set.
2. Have students take turns throwing the dice and saying a date, using one die as the month (from January to June) and the other as the day. For example, a student who throws a six and a two would say *June 2.* Monitor and provide feedback.
3. After every group member has thrown the dice, give each group an additional die. Tell students to roll two dice and say the month. They should add the first two dice together for the month (a "three" plus a "four" equals July). Then they should roll the third die and say the complete date (if they roll a six, the date would be July 6).

And/Or have students complete **Workbook 1 page 20** and the **Multilevel Activity Book 1 page 41.**

2 Practice taking phone messages

A Listen to the phone messages. Which call is in the evening?

B Listen again. Then complete the phone messages.

1
phone messages
Date: 10/5
Time: 3:00
From: Tim
Phone number: 555-9241
          Please call

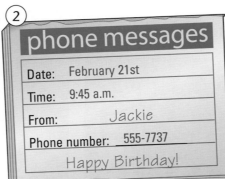

2
phone messages
Date: February 21st
Time: 9:45 a.m.
From: Jackie
Phone number: 555-7737
          Happy Birthday!

3
phone messages
Date: May 18th
Time: 7:30 p.m.
From: Jim
Phone number: 555-1089
   See you Monday

3 Practice your pronunciation

A Listen and repeat the numbers in the chart.

-st	-nd	-rd	-th
first	second	third	fourth
twenty-first	twenty-second	twenty-third	twenty-fourth

B Listen and circle *a* or *b*.

1. a. 1st
   b. 3rd

2. a. 23rd
   b. 26th

3. a. 7th
   b. 2nd

4. a. 4th
   b. 14th

5. a. 1st
   b. 21st

6. a. 3rd
   b. 23rd

C Work with a partner. Look at the calendar on page 34.
Partner A: Say a date. Partner B: Point to the date on the calendar.

4 Real-life math

Complete the sentences about Julie.

The date is March 10th.
Julie's birthday is on March 23rd.
Her birthday is __13__ days from today.

Julie

TEST YOURSELF ✔

Tell a partner the names and birthdays of 3 friends or family members.
Write your partner's information.

1 Get ready to read

A Look at the pictures. Read the words.

adult children

large family

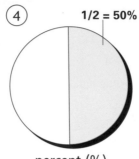

small family

1/2 = 50%

percent (%)

B Work with classmates. Answer the questions.

1. How many children are in a large family?
2. How many children are in a small family?

2 Read about U.S. families

A Read the article.

Families—Large and Small

Do you know that in the United States, three percent of families are large, with four or more children? Twenty-two percent of families are small, with only one child.

Surprise! In fifty percent of American families, there are no children at home. These are families with adult children or no children.

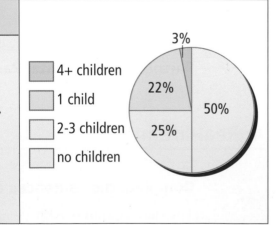

4+ children
1 child
2-3 children
no children

3%
22%
50%
25%

Source: *U.S. Census Bureau*

B Listen and read the article again.

Unit 3 Lesson 5

Objectives	Grammar	Vocabulary	Correlations
On- and Higher-level: Read about and discuss U.S. families **Pre-level:** Read about U.S. families	Statements with *be* (*Three percent of families are large.*)	*Percent, surprise, adult* For additional vocabulary practice, see this **Oxford Picture Dictionary** topic: Families	**CASAS:** 0.1.2, 0.2.1, 6.0.1, 6.0.2, 6.4.2, 6.7.4 **LCPs:** 22.01, 25.01, 31.01, 32.01, 32.03–32.06, 33.03 **SCANS:** Arithmetic/Mathematics, Interprets and communicates information, Reading, Uses computers to process information **EFF:** Learn through research, Read with understanding

Warm-up and Review

10–15 minutes (books closed)

Write the number of your children or siblings on the board—for example, *one daughter, one son,* or *three sisters.* Say: *I have a small/large family.* Ask your students: *Is your family small or large? How many children do you have? How many brothers and sisters?* Call on volunteers to share information about their families.

Introduction

5 minutes

1. Using the information from the warm-up, make some observations about the class. *Many of us have large families,* or *Most of us have two or three children.*

2. State the objective: *Today we'll read about families in the U.S.*

1 Get ready to read

Presentation

15–20 minutes

A 1. Direct students to look at the pictures. Ask questions about each picture: *Are they children or adults? Is this a large family or a small family?*

2. Say and have students repeat the captions. Indicate half of the class, and say: *This is 50 percent of the class.*

B Read the questions aloud, and elicit your students' ideas.

Pre-Reading

Direct students to read the title and then look at the pie chart. Ask: *What percentage of families have no children?*

2 Read about U.S. families

Guided Practice I

25–30 minutes

A 1. Ask students to read the article silently. Direct students to circle words they don't know.

2. Monitor students and discuss the words that were difficult.

B Play the audio. Have students read along silently.

Multilevel Strategies

For 2A–B, seat same-level students together.

• **Pre-level** Ask these students to copy the pie chart into their notebooks.

• **On- and Higher-level** Have these students make a pie chart representing your class. Ask them to guess the percentages of large families, small families, and families with no children in your classroom. Tell them to keep the chart, so they can check the accuracy of their guesses at the end of the lesson.

C 1. Have students work individually to complete the sentences. Ask volunteers to write the answers on the board. Read the sentences to the class.

2. Ask additional comprehension questions. *How many children are in a large family? How many are in a small family?*

Multilevel Strategies

After the group comprehension check in 2C, call on individuals and tailor your questions to the level of your students.

• **Pre-level** Ask *yes/no* questions. *Are 22 percent of the families large?* [no]

• **On-level** Ask information questions: *What percentage of families have no children at home?* [50]

• **Higher-level** Ask these students to expand on the reading. *Do you think your country is the same or different?*

D Read the percentages in the pie chart. Use number 1 to show students how to find the answers in the article.

Multilevel Strategies

For 2D, seat pre-level students together.

• **Pre-level** While other students are completing 2D, help pre-level students copy the percentages into the correct spots on the pie chart in their notebooks. Assist them with reading the chart.

 Put up signs around the room: *0, 1, 2, 3, 4, 5, 6+* and have students stand next to the sign that represents the number of children, siblings, or roommates in their houses.

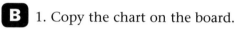
3 Think about family size

Guided Practice II

15–20 minutes

A 1. Say: *Now let's talk about family size.*

2. Ask students to work individually to answer the questions. Call on volunteers to discuss their answers.

Communicative Practice

10–15 minutes

B 1. Copy the chart on the board.

2. Ask for a show of hands for each column, and have a student count for you. Have another student write the numbers in the chart on the board.

C Call on volunteers to discuss the chart with the class.

Application

5–10 minutes

BRING IT TO LIFE

Students can easily find pictures of families by typing *family* into an Internet image search engine. You can also tell them to look through any magazines or newspapers they have at home.

To compress this lesson: Assign 2D as homework.

To extend this lesson: Have students help you figure out the percentages of family sizes for your class. Make a pie chart on the board. Compare the class pie chart with the U.S. pie chart.

And/Or have students complete **Workbook 1 page 21** and **Multilevel Activity Book 1 page 42.**

C **Complete the sentences. Use the words in the box.**

> at home   ~~large~~   small   families

1. Three percent of families in the U.S. are __large__.
2. Twenty-two percent of families in the U.S. are __small__.
3. In fifty percent of families, there are no children __at home__.
4. In twenty-five percent of __families__, there are two or three children.

D **Match the letters in the chart with the sentences. Look at the article in 2A for help.**

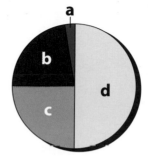

__b__ 1. families with one child

__c__ 2. families with two or three children

__a__ 3. families with four or more children

__d__ 4. families with no children at home

3 Think about family size

A **Think about your family. Answer the questions.** Answers will vary.

1. How many children are there in your home? _____
2. How many adults are there in your home? _____
3. Is your family large or small? _____

B **Work with your classmates. Complete the chart.**

	Number of children at home			
	1 child	2–3 children	4 or more children	no children
Number of classmates with:				

C **Talk about the answers in the chart with your class.**

Five people have one child.

BRING IT TO LIFE

Find pictures of families in newspapers, in magazines, or on the Internet. Bring the pictures to class. Talk about the pictures with your classmates.

1 Grammar

A Complete the sentences. Use *a* or *an*.

1. It's __a__ new computer.
2. It's __an__ old computer.
3. She's __an__ attractive child.
4. He's __a__ tall man.
5. It's __an__ easy exercise.
6. It's __a__ difficult exercise.

new

old

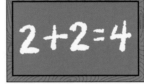
easy

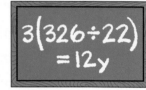
difficult

B Match the questions with the answers.

__c__ 1. What color are Mr. Smith's eyes?   a. Her name is Jan.

__f__ 2. What color are his mother's eyes?   b. My class is at 8:00.

__a__ 3. What is your cousin's name?   c. His eyes are brown.

__b__ 4. What time is your class?   d. His class is at 10:00.

__d__ 5. What time is her brother's class?   e. Her hair is brown.

__e__ 6. What color is Marta's hair?   f. Her eyes are blue.

C Work with a partner. Complete the chart. Then say the dates.

11/2	November 2nd
1/11	January 11th
6/3	June 3rd
10 / 1	October 1st

D Complete the story. Use the words in the box.

a	are	her	is	our	an	he	his	~~my~~	~~she~~

____My____ name is Jack. Dora is my wife. ___She___ is ___an___ attractive
      1   2   3

woman. Her eyes ___are___ green. ___Her___ hair is black. ___Our___ son's
                          4   5   6

name ___is___ Chris. ___His___ hair and eyes are brown. ___He___ is
              7   8   9

___a___ good little boy.
    10

Unit 3 Review and expand

Objectives	Grammar	Vocabulary	Correlations
On-, Pre-, and Higher-level: Expand upon and review unit grammar and life skills	Questions and answers with *be*, possessive adjectives (*What's her name? Her name is Jean.*)	*Easy, difficult, new, old* For additional vocabulary practice, see this **Oxford Picture Dictionary** topic: Describing Hair	**CASAS:** 0.1.2, 0.2.1, 4.8.1, 6.0.1, 7.2.5–7.2.7, 7.3.1–7.3.4 **LCPs:** 22.01, 25.01, 25.03, 25.04, 31.01, 32.01, 32.02, 32.05, 33.02, 33.03, 33.05, 33.07 **SCANS:** Creative thinking, Problem solving **EFF:** Solve problems and make decisions, Use math to solve problems and communicate

Warm-up and Review

10–15 minutes (books closed)

1. Review the *Bring It to Life* assignment from Lesson 5.

2. Write these questions on the board: *Who is he? Who is she? How many children are in the family? How many adults are in the family?*

3. Have students who brought in pictures answer the questions about the people in their pictures. Have magazines or pictures of families available for students who didn't bring pictures.

4. As students talk about their pictures, write some of their answers to the questions on the board.

Introduction and Presentation

5 minutes

1. Have the class repeat the sentences written on the board. Choose one of the family pictures, and say additional sentences about the people: *Her hair is brown. He's attractive.*

2. State the objective: *Today we're going to review how to talk about people.*

1 Grammar

Guided Practice

40–45 minutes

A 1. Direct students to look at the pictures. Say and have them repeat the words in the captions. Ask them to point to something old and something new in the classroom. Ask: *Is English easy or is it difficult?*

2. Write the vowels on the board, and review the rule for using *an* before a vowel sound.

3. Have students work individually to complete the sentences. Ask volunteers to read the sentences aloud. Write the answers on the board.

B 1. Read all of the questions and then all of the answers. Read the example question and answer together.

2. Have students work individually to match the questions and answers. Ask volunteers to read the matching questions and answers. Write the number-letter match on the board.

C Have students work with a partner to complete the chart. Ask them to take turns reading the dates aloud.

D 1. Read the words in the box. Read the first two sentences aloud. Read the third sentence, and elicit the answer.

2. Have students work individually to complete the paragraph. Ask volunteers to put the answers on the board.

Multilevel Strategies

For 1A–D, seat same-level students together.

• **Pre-level** Assist these students individually with the exercises, and give them time to copy the answers from the board while other students move on to the next exercise. After they have copied the answers, read the sentences and questions aloud for them as they read along.

• **On-level** Ask these students to read all of the exercises aloud with a partner.

• **Higher-level** Ask these students to compose a paragraph about their family like the one in 1D. Collect and correct their writing.

2 Group work

Communicative Practice

25–35 minutes

 A 1. Direct students, in groups of three to four, to focus on the picture on page 29. Ask: *Who is Helen?* [Eric's grandmother]

2. Read the directions and check comprehension of the exercise: *How many sentences are you going to write?* [five]

3. Set a time limit (five minutes) to complete the exercise. Circulate and answer any questions.

4. Have a reporter from each group read his/her group's sentences to the class.

Multilevel Strategies

For 2A and 2B, use same-level groups.

• **Pre-level** For 2A, ask these students to write three vocabulary words and one complete sentence. For 2B, allow them to ask and answer the questions without writing.

• **Higher-level** For 2A, ask these students to write two additional sentences about the picture. For 2B, have them ask and answer these questions: *Who is he/she? Is he/she an adult or a child?*

B 1. Have students work in the same groups from 2A to take turns interviewing each other in pairs.

2. Set a time limit (five minutes) to complete the exercise.

3. Tell students to make a note of their partners' answers but not to worry about writing complete sentences.

C Have a reporter from each group share the group's work.

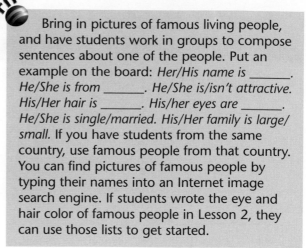

TIP Bring in pictures of famous living people, and have students work in groups to compose sentences about one of the people. Put an example on the board: *Her/His name is _____. He/She is from _____. He/She is/isn't attractive. His/Her hair is _____. His/her eyes are _____. He/She is single/married. His/Her family is large/small.* If you have students from the same country, use famous people from that country. You can find pictures of famous people by typing their names into an Internet image search engine. If students wrote the eye and hair color of famous people in Lesson 2, they can use those lists to get started.

PROBLEM SOLVING

20–25 minutes

A Direct students to look at the picture of Miguel. Ask: *What color is Miguel's hair?* [brown] Tell students they will read a story about a problem with an ID card. Direct students to read Miguel's story silently. Then play the audio, and have them read along silently. Ask: *What's his date of birth?* [11/09/82]

B 1. Identify the problem. Read the question and the possible solutions. Elicit student ideas for other solutions. Write each one on the board.

2. Discuss whether the statements are appropriate. Ask for a show of hands to see which solution the class likes best.

Evaluation

30–35 minutes

To test students' understanding of the unit grammar and life skills, have them take the Unit 3 Test in the *Step Forward Test Generator CD-ROM with ExamView® Assessment Suite*.

Learning Log

To help students record and discuss their progress, use the *Learning Log* on page T-176.

To extend this review: Have students complete **Workbook 1 page 22, Multilevel Activity Book 1 pages 43–46,** and the **Unit 3 Grammar Exercises** on the **Multilevel Grammar Exercises CD-ROM 1.**

2 Group work

A Work with 2–3 classmates. Write 5 sentences about the family on page 29. Talk about the sentences with your class. Answers will vary.

His name is Hector. He is Eric's uncle.   Her name is Helen.   Her husband is Ramiro.
She is Eric's grandmother.

B Interview 3 classmates. Write their answers in your notebook.

ASK OR SAY:
1. Name a friend or family member.
2. What color is his or her hair?
3. What color are his or her eyes?

```
Classmate—Alan
1. Raisa—sister
2. Her hair is red.
3. Her eyes are green.
```

C Talk about the answers with your class.

PROBLEM SOLVING

A Listen and read about Miguel.
What is the problem? His hair is not blond.

Today is Miguel's first day of school. This is his new student ID card. Miguel is not happy with the card. There's a problem.

B Work with your classmates. Answer the question. (More than one answer is possible.)

What can Miguel do?
a. Go to the school office.
b. Tell the teacher.
c. Say nothing about it.
d. Other: <u>Answers will vary.</u>

STUDENT ID CARD

Miguel Ramirez
123 First Street
Big City, CA 91100

Eyes: brown
Hair: blond
Date of birth: 11/09/82

Fall

Miguel Ramirez

UNIT 4

At Home

FOCUS ON
• places and things in the home
• things to do at home
• the present continuous
• paying bills
• addressing an envelope

LESSON 1   Vocabulary

1 Learn about places in the home

A Look at the picture. Name the colors. 1. pink 2. blue 3. gray 4. green 5. yellow 6. white

🎧 **B** Listen and look at the picture.

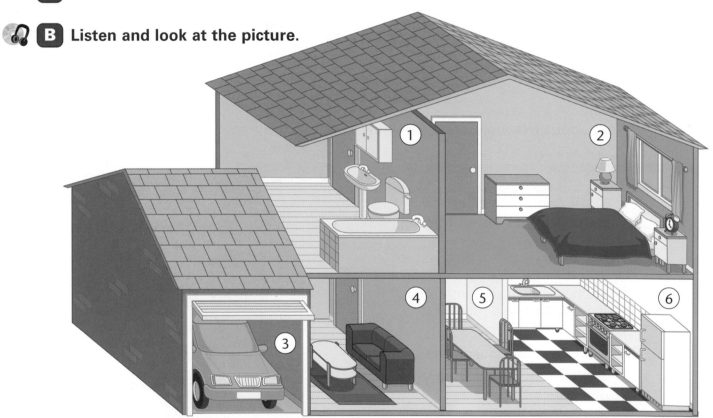

🎧 **C** Listen and repeat the words.

1. bathroom   3. garage   5. dining area
2. bedroom   4. living room   6. kitchen

D Look at the picture. Complete the sentences.

1. The _____kitchen_____ is white.
2. The __bathroom_____ is pink.
3. The __living room_____ is green.
4. The _garage_____ is gray.
5. The _dining area_____ is yellow.
6. The _bedroom_____ is blue.

Unit 4 Lesson 1

Objectives	Grammar	Vocabulary	Correlations
On-level: Identify places and things in the home **Pre-level:** Recognize places and things in the home **Higher-level:** Talk and write about places and things in the home	Questions with *be* (*Where is the bed? Is the sofa in the living room?*)	Rooms in the house, furniture For additional vocabulary practice, see these **Oxford Picture Dictionary** topics: A Home, A Bathroom, A Bedroom, Colors, A Dining Area, A Kitchen, A Living Room	**CASAS:** 0.1.2, 1.4.1, 7.4.5 **LCPs:** 32.01, 33.03 **SCANS:** Listening, Participates as member of a team, Seeing things in the mind's eye, Speaking **EFF:** Cooperate with others, Listen actively, Observe critically, Speak so others can understand

Warm-up and Review

10–15 minutes (books closed)

1. Draw a chair, a table, a desk, a door, and a window on the board. Ask volunteers to write the correct word under your pictures.

2. Repeat the words and ask students to point to the correct objects in the classroom. Ask: *Is there a window in this class? How many? Is there a chair? How many? What about your home? How many chairs are in your home? Is there a board in your home? A TV?*

3. Write *TV* on the board, and encourage students to name more items in their homes. Write the ideas on the board. Leave these words on the board.

Introduction

5 minutes

1. Say and have students repeat the words on the board. Say: *These things are in your home.*

2. State the objective: *Today we're going to learn places in the home and things in the home.*

1 Learn about places in the home

Presentation

20–25 minutes

A 1. Direct students to look at the picture of the house. Ask: *Is this a small house? Is this a big house?*

2. Ask: *What colors are there in the house?* Write the colors on the board.

B 1. Have students listen to the audio. Ask them to point to the correct part of the picture as they listen. Circulate and monitor.

2. Check comprehension by asking *yes/no* questions. Pass out *yes/no* cards to the students (see page T-175), or have them hold up one finger for *yes* and two for *no* in order to get a nonverbal response. Point to each room, and ask: *Is this the (kitchen)?*

C Ask students to listen and repeat the words.

TIP After completing 1C, tell students about your house, including the color of the various rooms. Then ask: *What color is your kitchen? What color is your bedroom?*

Guided Practice I

15–20 minutes

D 1. Have students complete the sentences using the new vocabulary.

2. Encourage students to take turns reading the completed sentences in pairs.

Multilevel Strategies

After completing 1D, seat same-level students together and provide vocabulary practice targeted to the level of your students.

• **Pre-level** Ask these students to practice together by pointing to the picture in 1B and saying the correct words.

• **On-level** Ask these students to cover 1C and 1D and practice saying the room and its color. *The kitchen is white.*

• **Higher-level** Have these students dictate the sentences in 1D to each other.

2 Talk about things in the home

Guided Practice II

35–40 minutes

A 1. Point to one of the words from the warm-up (*TV*), and ask: *Is your TV in the bathroom? Is it in the kitchen?* Introduce the new topic: *Now let's talk about things in our homes.*

2. Group students and assign roles: leader, fact checker, recorder, and reporter. Explain that students work with their groups to match the words and pictures.

3. Check comprehension of the exercise: *Who looks up the words in the picture dictionary?* [fact checker] *Who writes the numbers in the book?* [recorder] *Who tells the class your answers?* [reporter] *Who helps everyone and manages the group?* [leader]

4. Set a time limit (three minutes), and have students work together to complete the task. While students are working, copy the wordlist on the board.

5. Call "time" and have the reporters from each group take turns calling out the numbers for the wordlist. Record students' answers on the board. If groups disagree, write each group's choice next to the word.

B 1. Ask students to listen and check their answers.

2. Have students correct the wordlist on the board and then write the correct numbers in their books.

3. Tell the groups from 2A to break into pairs to practice the words. Set a time limit (two minutes).

C 1. Copy the first line on the board. Do not cross out *sink* yet. Say: *Is the sofa in the living room? Is the TV in the living room? Is the sink in the living room? The sink is not in the living room.* Sink *is different.*

2. Cross out *sink* and direct students to complete the exercise independently.

3. Go over the answers as a class.

Communicative Practice and Application

10–15 minutes

D 1. Write these skeleton questions on the board: *Where is the _____? Is the _____ in the _____?*

2. Model the first question, and answer with several volunteers. Use the items in 2A. Write their answers on the board. Then model the second question and answer with several volunteers to elicit negative and affirmative answers. Write *Yes, it is.* and *No, it isn't.* on the board.

3. Have several more-advanced pairs model the questions and answers for the class.

4. Set a time limit (five minutes). Ask students to practice the conversation with a partner.

Evaluation

10–15 minutes (books closed)

TEST YOURSELF

1. Make a two-column chart on the board with the headings *Places in the Home* and *Things in the Home*. Have students close their books and give you an example for each column.

2. Have students copy the chart into their notebooks.

3. Give students five to ten minutes to test themselves by writing the words they recall from the lesson.

4. Call "time" and have students check their spelling in *The Oxford Picture Dictionary* or another dictionary. Circulate and monitor students' progress.

To compress this lesson: Conduct 2A as a whole-class activity.

To extend this lesson: Have students ask and answer questions about pictures of furniture.
1. Group students. Provide each group with pictures of furniture or use the picture cards on page 54 of *Multilevel Activity Book 1*.
2. Have each group draw a simple housing outline with the rooms labeled and place the cards in the correct room.
3. Direct them to ask and answer questions about the cards: *Where is the _____? Is the _____ in the _____?*
And/Or have students complete **Workbook 1 page 23** and **Multilevel Activity Book 1 page 48**.

2 Talk about things in the home

A Work with your classmates. Match the words with the picture.

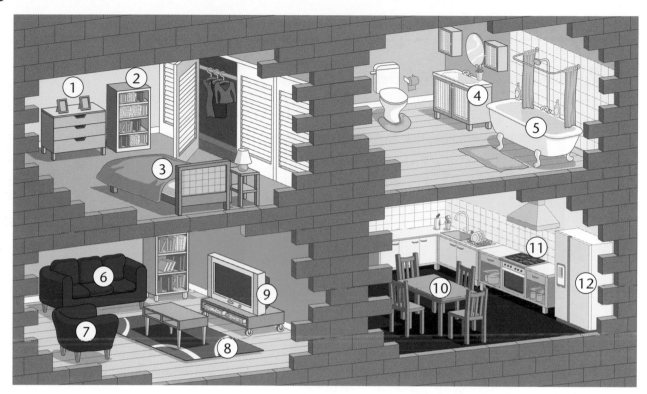

_5_	bathtub	_7_	chair	_8_	rug	_11_	stove
_3_	bed	_1_	dresser	_4_	sink	_10_	table
_2_	bookcase	_12_	refrigerator	_6_	sofa	_9_	TV (television)

B Listen and check your answers. Then practice the words with a partner.

C Cross out (X) the thing that is NOT usually in these rooms.

1. living room: sofa   TV   si̶n̶k̶
2. bedroom: dresser   st̶o̶v̶e̶   bed
3. kitchen: stove   refrigerator boo̶k̶case
4. bathroom: be̶d̶   sink   bathtub

D Work with a partner. Ask and answer questions. Use the picture in 2A.

A: Where is the sofa?
B: It's in the living room.

A: Is the stove in the living room?
B: No, it isn't. It's in the kitchen.

TEST YOURSELF ✔

Close your book. Write 4 places and 6 things in the home. Check your spelling in a dictionary.

1 Read about things to do at home

🎧 **A**   Look at the pictures. Listen.

Sunday at Our Place

🎧 **B**   Listen again. Read the sentences.

1. My roommates and I go to Lake City College. We are at home today.
2. Robert is in the yard. He's cutting the grass.
3. Simon is watching TV in the living room.
4. Julio and Luis are in the bedroom. They are playing a video game.
5. And me? I'm cooking dinner and listening to music with my friend.
6. Sundays are great at our place.

C   Check your understanding. Mark the sentences T (true) or F (false).

  __T__ 1. Robert is in the yard.

  __F__ 2. Simon is cooking in the kitchen.

  __T__ 3. Julio and Luis are in the bedroom.

  __F__ 4. Robert is studying.

  __F__ 5. My friend and I are listening to music in the living room.

Unit 4 Lesson 2

Objectives	Grammar	Vocabulary	Correlations
On-, Pre-, and Higher-level: Read and write about things to do at home	Present continuous (*He is cooking in the kitchen.*)	Activities in the home For additional vocabulary practice, see these **Oxford Picture Dictionary** topics: A Bedroom, A Kitchen, A Living Room, A House and Yard	**CASAS:** 0.1.2, 1.4.1, 7.4.7, 8.2.5 **LCPs:** 32.01, 32.02, 32.13, 33.03 **SCANS:** Knowing how to learn, Listening, Reading, Responsibility, Seeing things in the mind's eye, Self-management, Writing **EFF:** Convey ideas in writing, Use math to solve problems and communicate

Warm-up and Review

10–15 minutes (books closed)

Write the places in the home on the board as column heads: *Living Room, Dining Area, Kitchen, Bathroom, Bedroom, Garage.* Have students line up at the board. Name an item from the home, and have the student in the front of the line write it in the correct place. Many items will have more than one correct answer. Allow students to approach the board with a partner if it makes them more comfortable.

Introduction

3 minutes

1. Point to the word *stove* on the board, and say: *The stove is in the kitchen. I cook in the kitchen.* Point to *bed* and say: *The bed is in the bedroom. I sleep in the bedroom.*

2. State the objective: *Today we'll read and write about things to do at home.*

1 Read about things to do at home

Presentation I

20–25 minutes

 A 1. Direct students to look at the pictures. Ask students to name the things they see in the

pictures. Point to each picture, and ask: *Where is he? Where are they?*

2. Play the audio.

B 1. Play the audio again. Have students read along silently.

2. Check comprehension. Ask: *Is this a family?* [no]

Multilevel Strategies

For 1B and 1C, seat pre-level students together.

• **Pre-level** Reread the sentences in 1B with your pre-level students while on- and higher-level students complete 1C. Ask these students to copy the answers to 1C when you go over them as a class.

• **On- and Higher-level** After these students finish 1C, ask them to write two more sentences about the picture in 1A. *The computer is in the bedroom. The sofa is in the living room.*

Guided Practice I

10 minutes

C 1. Have students mark the sentences *true* or *false*.

2. Go over the answers as a class.

T-42

2 Write about your home

Guided Practice II

20–25 minutes

A 1. Pronounce and clarify the *Need help?* words.

2. Draw an outline of a house on the board with stick figures of you and your family. Have students complete their own drawings.

B 1. Copy the sentence skeletons on the board. Read them aloud with your own information.

2. Have students complete the sentences independently. Circulate and assist.

> ### Multilevel Strategies
>
> Adapt 2A–B to the level of your students.
>
> • **Pre-level** Draw a new picture on the board, and work with these students to create sentences for it. Have students complete the sentences in their books.
>
> • **Higher-level** Ask these students to copy the sentences from 2B into their notebooks and add more sentences about what the people in their house are doing.

C 1. Ask students to read their sentences to a partner.

2. Call on individuals to share what they learned about their partners.

3 Talk about your home

Presentation II

20–25 minutes

A 1. Introduce the topic: *Now we're going to talk about things in our homes.* Direct students to look at the charts in 3A. Repeat the words on the charts. Demonstrate *near* and *far* by pointing to items in the classroom and providing example sentences.

2. Ask students to put their pencils down and listen for the answer to this question: *What color chairs does Sally like?* Play the entire audio once. Ask students to identify Sally in the pictures.

3. Play the audio in segments. After each conversation, stop the audio and check answers with the students: *Who likes the green chairs?* If necessary, replay the segment.

4. Check students' listening accuracy. Point to the small TV in the picture, and say: *This TV or that TV?*

Guided Practice

5–10 minutes

B Have students work independently to complete the sentences. Ask volunteers to write the answers on the board.

Communicative Practice and Application

10 minutes

C 1. Make a quick drawing of your home on the board.

2. Have students repeat the questions and answers. Have a volunteer ask you the questions about your drawing.

3. Ask a volunteer to draw his/her home on the board. Encourage classmates to ask him/her questions about the drawing. If you have board space, have several students draw their homes, and have other students ask them questions. Monitor the use of *this* and *that, these* and *those.*

Evaluation

10–15 minutes (books closed)

TEST YOURSELF

Have students work independently to write their sentences. Collect and correct their writing.

To compress this lesson: Conduct 1C and 3B as whole-class activities.

To extend this lesson: Have students draw pictures of their homes on scratch paper. Put them in groups, and have them take turns asking about the pictures. *What's that? Where's the stove? Is that the kitchen?*

And/Or have students complete **Workbook 1 page 24** and the **Multilevel Activity Book 1 page 49.**

2 Write about your home

A Look at the pictures on page 42. In your notebook, draw yourself and your family or friends in the rooms of your home.

B Use your picture to write your story. Answers will vary.

My _____ and I are at home.

I am in the _____.

_____ is in the _____.

It's a _____ day at our home.

C Read your story to a partner.

3 Talk about your home

A Listen and look at the pictures.

Singular	
Near	this
Far	that

This TV?

No, that TV!

Plural	
Near	these
Far	those

These chairs?

No, those chairs.

B Study the charts and the pictures in 3A. Complete the sentences.

1. __This__ is a small TV.
2. __That__ is a large TV.
3. __These__ are brown chairs.
4. __Those__ are green chairs.

C Draw your home on the board. Ask and answer questions with your classmates.

A: *What's that?*
B: *This is my kitchen.*

A: *What are those?*
B: *These are my chairs.*

What's that?

TEST YOURSELF ✔

Close your book. Write 3 sentences about things in your home.
My sofa is in the living room.

1 Learn the present continuous

A Look at the pictures. Read the sentences. Who is working? Tina is working. Mark is working.

1 Tina is cleaning her home.

2 Mark is washing the windows.

3 Jean and Pam are eating lunch.

B Study the charts. Complete the sentences below.

THE PRESENT CONTINUOUS

Statements		
I	am	
You	are	eating.
He She It	is	

We		
You	are	eating.
They		

Contractions
I am = I'm
I'm eating.
We are = We're
We're eating.

1. I __am__ eating.

2. They are __eating__.

Negative statements		
I	am not	
You	are not	eating.
He She It	is not	

We		
You	are not	eating.
They		

Contractions
is not = isn't
He isn't eating.
are not = aren't
They aren't eating.

3. He __is__ not eating.

4. We are __not__ eating.

C Look at the pictures. Complete the sentences.

1. He __is mopping__ the floor.

2. She __is vacuuming__ the rug.

3. They __are dusting__ the furniture.

4. The cat __is sleeping__ on the rug.

D Read the sentences to a partner.

mopping vacuuming dusting   sleeping

  ☑ Use the present continuous to describe daily activities

Unit 4 Lesson 3

Objectives	Grammar	Vocabulary	Correlations
On- and Higher-level: Use the present continuous to talk about household activities **Pre-level:** Recognize the present continuous	Present continuous (*He is eating. They are sleeping.*)	Housework words For additional vocabulary practice, see these **Oxford Picture Dictionary** topics: Daily Routines, Describing Things, Housework	**CASAS:** 0.1.2, 0.2.4, 7.4.7, 8.2.3 **LCPs:** 32.01, 33.02, 33.07 **SCANS:** Acquires and evaluates information, Listening, Participates as member of a team, Seeing things in the mind's eye, Self-management, Speaking, Writing **EFF:** Convey ideas in writing, Cooperate with others

Warm-up and Review

10–15 minutes (books closed)

Pantomime activities you do at home. Ask: *Where am I?* Use these activities: taking a shower [bathroom], sleeping [bedroom], eating [dining area], cooking [kitchen], watching TV [living room], fixing or washing a car [garage]. Write the rooms on the board as students guess them correctly. Write a sentence with a present continuous verb for each of your activities under the correct room. *I am taking a shower.*

Introduction

5–10 minutes

1. Underline the verb in the sentences on the board, and say: *These verbs are in the present continuous.*

2. State the objective: *Today we'll use the present continuous to talk about things people are doing at home.*

1 Learn the present continuous

Presentation I

20–25 minutes

A 1. Direct students to look at the pictures. Ask: *Where is she?* [living room] *Where are they?* [work?]

2. Read and have students repeat the sentences under the pictures.

B 1. Demonstrate how to read the grammar charts as complete sentences. Read the charts through sentence by sentence. Then read them again, and have students repeat after you.

2. Use the pictures in 1A to illustrate points in the grammar charts. Point out that the pronoun *she* substitutes for *Tina* and uses *is + ing*. The pronoun *they* substitutes for *Jean and Pam* and uses *are + ing*.

3. As a class, complete the sentences under the charts. Ask volunteers to write the sentences on the board. Have other students read the sentences aloud.

4. Give students time to silently review the charts and, if they haven't already, fill in the blanks.

5. Assess students' understanding of the charts. Refer to verbs in the warm-up, and elicit sentences with different subjects: *I _____ taking a shower. Tony _____ sleeping.*

Guided Practice

15–20 minutes

C 1. Direct students to look at the pictures. Pronounce and clarify the words.

2. Have students complete the sentences individually. Go over the answers as a class.

> ### Multilevel Strategies
>
> After 1C is corrected, group same-level students together.
>
> • **Pre-level** Have these students copy the sentences under the grammar chart into their notebooks.
>
> • **On- and Higher-level** Ask these students to say or write three additional sentences in the present continuous using the verbs from the warm-up or other verbs.

D Ask students to read their sentences to a partner.

2 Ask and answer information questions

Presentation II

20–25 minutes

 1. Direct students to look at the chart. Play the audio and ask students to listen without repeating the questions and answers.

2. Play the audio again, and have students repeat.

3. Assess their understanding of the chart. Point to different students in the class, and ask: *What is he/she doing?*

Guided Practice

10–15 minutes

 1. Have students work individually to complete the answers.

2. Call on volunteers to read the questions and answers aloud. Have different volunteers write the answers on the board.

Multilevel Strategies

For 2B and 2C, seat same-level students together. Challenge on- and higher-level students while providing extra assistance to pre-level students.

• **Pre-level** Allow these students to copy answers from the board. Read the questions and answers in each exercise aloud with them.

• **On- and Higher-level** Ask these students to draw a quick picture of a house, or use the one they drew previously, and draw people (stick figures) in every room. Direct them to practice asking and answering about the people in their pictures: *What _____ he/she/they doing?* Tell higher-level students to also ask questions with *where*: *Where _____ he/she/they?*

C Have students work individually to complete the answers. Ask volunteers to write the completed sentences on the board.

3 Practice the present continuous

Communicative Practice and Application

20–25 minutes

1. Pantomime one of the words, and ask the class to guess what you are doing.

2. Ask volunteers to choose one of the words and act it out for the class.

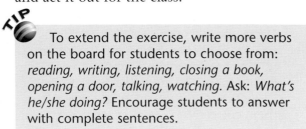

To extend the exercise, write more verbs on the board for students to choose from: *reading, writing, listening, closing a book, opening a door, talking, watching.* Ask: *What's he/she doing?* Encourage students to answer with complete sentences.

Evaluation

10–15 minutes (books closed)

TEST YOURSELF

Ask students to write the answers independently. Collect and correct their writing.

Multilevel Strategies

Target the *Test Yourself* to the level of your students.

• **Pre-level** Allow these students to answer only the first question.

• **Higher-level** Ask these students to think about a friend or family member and write what he/she is doing.

To compress this lesson: Conduct 2B as a whole-class activity.

To extend this lesson: Give students more practice asking and answering questions with the present continuous.
1. Provide students with a picture of people working in a house. You can use the pictures of housework in *The Oxford Picture Dictionary* or another dictionary.
2. Teach any unfamiliar vocabulary, and write the *–ing* form on the board. Have students practice asking *What is he/she doing/What are they doing?* and answering with the present continuous.

And/Or have students complete **Workbook 1 pages 25–26** and **Multilevel Activity Book 1 page 50.**

2 Ask and answer information questions

A Study the chart. Listen and repeat the questions and answers.

Information questions and answers	
A: What are you doing? **B:** I'm studying.	**A:** What are you doing? **B:** We're studying.
A: What is he doing? **B:** He's studying.	**A:** What are they doing? **B:** They're studying.

B Match the questions with the answers.

_c_ 1. What are Jean and Pam doing?   a. I'm studying.

_e_ 2. What is Tina doing?   b. It's sleeping.

_d_ 3. What is Mark doing?   c. They're eating.

_b_ 4. What is the cat doing?   d. He's washing the windows.

_a_ 5. What are you doing?   e. She's cleaning.

C Work with a partner. Complete the sentences with the words in the box.

am writing	~~is reading~~	is playing	are listening	are studying	is sleeping

1. **A:** What is Maria doing?

   B: She _____is reading_____ a book.

2. **A:** What are Janet and Nancy doing?

   B: They ___are listening___ to music.

3. **A:** What is Neil doing?

   B: He ___is playing___ a video game.

4. **A:** What are you doing?

   B: I ___am writing___ sentences.

5. **A:** What is the cat doing?

   B: It ___is sleeping___ .

6. **A:** What am I doing?

   B: You ___are studying___ English.

3 Practice the present continuous

Work with your classmates. Follow the directions.

Student A: Act out an activity in the box. Don't talk.
Classmates: Guess the activity.

mopping	dusting	cooking	sleeping	vacuuming	studying	eating

TEST YOURSELF ✔

Close your book. Write the answers to the questions: What are you doing?
What is your teacher doing? What are you and your classmates studying?

1 Learn about utility bills

A Look at the utility bills. Complete the sentences below with the due dates.

Acme Electric Company	Atlantic Phone Service	Globe Gas Company	West Water Company
PAYMENT DUE DATE: 10/01	PAYMENT DUE DATE: 10/01	PAYMENT DUE DATE: 10/15	PAYMENT DUE DATE: 10/15

electric bill   phone bill   gas bill   water bill

1. Pay the electric bill and phone bill by <u>10/01</u>.
2. Pay the gas bill and water bill by <u>10/15</u>.

B Listen and write the totals for the utility bills.

1. The gas bill total is $<u>17.00</u>.
2. The phone bill total is $<u>26.00</u>.
3. The electric bill total is $<u>82.00</u>.
4. The water bill total is $<u>14.50</u>.

C Listen and read.

A: Can you help me?
B: Sure. What are you doing?
A: I'm writing a note to my roommate. He's not here.
B: OK. Read the note to me.
A: Please pay the gas bill. Tomorrow is the 31st.
B: That sounds good to me.

D Listen again and repeat.

E Work with a partner. Practice the conversation. Use your own information.

A: Can you help me?
B: Sure. What are you _____?
A: I'm writing a note to _____. _____ not here.
B: OK. Read the note to me.
A: Please pay the _____. Tomorrow is the _____.
B: That sounds good to me.

Unit 4 Lesson 4

Objectives	Grammar	Vocabulary	Correlations
On- and Higher-level: Ask and answer questions about utility bills **Pre-level:** Ask questions about utility bills	Subject and object pronouns (*She is talking to him.*)	*Electric bill, gas bill, phone bill, utility, water bill* For additional vocabulary practice, see this **Oxford Picture Dictionary** topic: Money	**CASAS:** 0.1.2, 0.1.3, 0.2.3, 1.2.4, 1.5.3, 2.1.4, 6.0.1–6.0.4, 6.1.1, 7.1.3, 7.4.7 **LCPs:** 22.03, 23.03, 25.01, 28.05, 29.01, 32.01, 32.02, 33.01 **SCANS:** Arithmetic/Mathematics, Listening, Responsibility, Self-management, Speaking, Writing **EFF:** Speak so others can understand

Warm-up and Review

10–15 minutes (books closed)

Put up some pictures of things in the house (a sofa, a TV, a table, chairs, a phone, bookshelves, a lamp, windows, a stove, a sink, a shower). Mix singular and plural objects. You can cut pictures out of magazines, or find them on the Internet. Ask *What's this? What are these?* and elicit responses with *that's* and *those.* Invite volunteers up to ask the questions.

Introduction

5 minutes

1. Circle the items on the board that require electricity, and say: *To use a lamp, I have to pay the electric bill.* Do the same with the *gas, phone,* and *water.* Erase the non-utility items. Say: *Electricity, gas, phones and water are utilities.* Write the word *utilities* on the board.

2. State the objective: *Today we're learning about utility bills.*

1 Learn about utility bills

Presentation

20–30 minutes

A 1. Direct students to look at the utility bills. Say: *The payment due date is the last day to pay the bill. When is the due date for the gas bill?* [10/15]

2. Give students a minute to fill in the sentences. Go over the answers as a class.

Guided Practice

20–25 minutes

B 1. Play the audio. Ask students to listen for the answer to this question: *Which bill is a lot of money?* [the electric bill]

2. Play the audio again, and have students fill in the amounts. Go over the answers as a class.

C Play the audio. Have students read the conversation silently.

D Play the audio again, and have students repeat. Replay if necessary.

Communicative Practice and Application

15–20 minutes

E 1. Model the conversation with a volunteer. Then model it again with other information.

2. Elicit other ways to complete the conversation.

3. Set a time limit (five minutes). Ask students to practice the conversation with several partners.

Multilevel Strategies

For 1E, adapt the oral practice to the level of your students.

• **Pre-level** Have these students read the conversation in 1C.

• **Higher-level** Ask these students to add this exchange to the conversation after *That sounds good to me: B: How much is the bill? A: It's _____. B: That's a lot of money!* or *That's not bad!*

2 Learn subject and object pronouns

Grammar Extension

15–20 minutes

A 1. Direct students to look at the pictures. Ask: *What is he doing?* [talking] *What is she doing?* [listening and paying a bill]

2. Read the sentences. Tell students to point to the man or the woman when you refer to them. Demonstrate with number 1.

B 1. Read and have students repeat the pronouns in the chart.

2. Check comprehension. Point to various students, saying sentences and pausing for students to supply the missing object pronoun: *I'm looking at _____. She's looking at _____.*

C Write the first sentence on the board. Cross out *Martin* and elicit *He*; cross out *Sara* and elicit *her*. Have students work individually to rewrite the sentences with pronouns. Ask volunteers to write the new sentences on the board.

> ### Multilevel Strategies
>
> Group pre-level students for 2C.
>
> • **Pre-level** While other students are working on extra sentences, work with these students in a group to complete 2C.
>
> • **On- and Higher-level** Ask these students to write two or three original sentences with names and then with subject and object pronouns. *Tom is listening to the radio. He is listening to it.* Have students share their sentences after 2C is corrected.

3 Real-life math

Math Extension

10–15 minutes

1. Direct students to look at the utilities bills in 1B.

2. Have them work individually to complete the sentences. Go over the answers as a class.

> **TIP**
> For more practice identifying totals, bring in real utility bills from your area. Cut off the personal information. Have students look at the bills and answer these questions: *What is the due date? What is the total due?*

Evaluation

10–15 minutes

TEST YOURSELF

Write *Please _____.* on the board. Elicit ways to complete the note. Have students work individually to write their notes. Then ask them to read their notes to a partner.

> ### Multilevel Strategies
>
> Target the *Test Yourself* to the level of your students.
>
> • **Pre-level** Put these skeleton sentences on the board for these students to complete. *Please pay the _____. Tomorrow is the _____.*

To compress this lesson: Have students practice the conversation in 1E with only one partner.

To extend this lesson: Have students write captions using pronouns.
1. Group students and supply each group with some magazines.
2. Tell them to look for pictures of people or animals doing the following things: talking to, listening to, looking at, reading, watching, and paying.
3. Have students write sentences about the pictures using subject and object pronouns.
4. Have a reporter from each group present the group's pictures and sentences.

And/Or have students complete **Workbook 1 page 27** and **Multilevel Activity Book 1 page 51.**

2 Learn subject and object pronouns

A Look at the pictures. Read the sentences.

1. <u>Joe</u> is talking to <u>Mary</u>.
   <u>He</u> is talking to <u>her</u>.

2. <u>Mary</u> is listening to <u>Joe</u>.
   <u>She</u> is listening to <u>him</u>.

3. <u>Mary</u> is paying <u>the bill</u>.
   <u>She</u> is paying <u>it</u>.

B Study the charts.

Subject pronouns	Object pronouns	Subject pronouns	Object pronouns
I	me	we	us
you	you	you	you
he	him	they	them
she	her		
it	it		

C Change the sentences. Use the pronouns in the chart.

1. <u>Martin</u> is writing to <u>Sara</u>. <u>He is writing to her.</u>
2. <u>Jean and Pat</u> are listening to <u>Mark</u>. <u>They are listening to him.</u>
3. <u>Tina</u> is talking to <u>you and me</u>. <u>She is talking to us.</u>
4. <u>You and I</u> are listening to <u>our teacher</u>. <u>We are listening to him/her.</u>
5. <u>My sister</u> is talking to <u>Simon and Jack</u>. <u>She is talking to them.</u>
6. I am looking at <u>my book</u>. <u>I am looking at it.</u>

3 Real-life math

Look at exercise 1B. Add the utility bills. Complete the sentences.

1. The total for the electric bill and the phone bill is $ <u>108.00</u> .
2. The total for the gas bill and water bill is $ <u>31.50</u> .
3. The total for all of the utility bills is $ <u>139.50</u> .

TEST YOURSELF ✔

Write a note to a friend about a utility bill. Read the note to a partner.
Listen to your partner's note.

LESSON 5 Real-life reading

1 Get ready to read

A Look at the pictures. Read the words. What are the people doing?

She is taking a shower.

He is calling long distance.

He is turning off the lights.

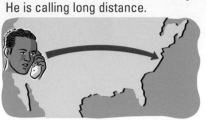

taking a shower

calling long distance

turning off the lights

B Think about the questions. Check (✔) your answers. Answers will vary.

1. How long are your showers?
   - ☐ five minutes
   - ☐ ten minutes
   - ☐ fifteen minutes
   - ☐ twenty minutes

2. How long are your phone calls?
   - ☐ five minutes
   - ☐ ten minutes
   - ☐ twenty minutes
   - ☐ one hour

2 Read about saving money

A Read the website.

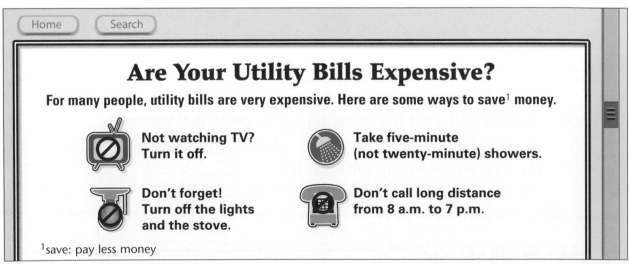

| Home | Search |

Are Your Utility Bills Expensive?

For many people, utility bills are very expensive. Here are some ways to save[1] money.

Not watching TV?
Turn it off.

Take five-minute
(not twenty-minute) showers.

Don't forget!
Turn off the lights
and the stove.

Don't call long distance
from 8 a.m. to 7 p.m.

[1]save: pay less money

Source: *Oregon Department of Energy*

B Listen and read the website again.

48   ✔ Identify ways to conserve resources; address envelopes

Unit 4 Lesson 5

Objectives	Grammar	Vocabulary	Correlations
On- and Higher-level: Read about and discuss saving money and addressing an envelope **Pre-level:** Read about saving money and addressing an envelope	Present continuous (*Who is paying the bill?*)	*Taking a shower, calling long distance, turning off the lights/TV, expensive, forget* For additional vocabulary practice, see these **Oxford Picture Dictionary** topics: Energy and Conservation, Money	**CASAS:** 0.1.2, 1.5.3, 2.1.4, 2.4.1, 6.0.1, 7.1.3 **LCPs:** 23.03, 25.01, 28.05, 29.01, 32.01–32.04, 32.12, 32.13 **SCANS:** Acquires and evaluates information, Interprets and communicates information, Reading **EFF:** Read with understanding, Use math to solve problems and communicate

Warm-up and Review

10–15 minutes (books closed)

Write *Utilities* on the board, and elicit: *Gas, Electric, Phone, Water.* Have students brainstorm words they associate with these utility bills, for example: *sink, shower, cell phone, stove, dryer, TV, radio.* Write these words on the board.

Introduction

5 minutes

1. Using the items on the board, pantomime examples of high-energy use. Do and say the following with exaggerated slowness: *I'm turning on the water. I'm opening the toothpaste. I'm putting the toothpaste on the toothbrush. I'm brushing my teeth. The water is running and running. I'm talking to my husband. I'm looking at my face in the mirror. Finally, I'm turning off the water. Is my water bill a lot of money or a little money?* Say: *My water bill will be expensive.* Write *expensive* on the board. Say: *Expensive means a lot of money.* Act out the same scenario with efficient water use: *I'm putting the toothpaste on the toothbrush. I'm brushing my teeth. I'm turning on the water, rinsing my mouth and my brush. I'm turning off the water. I'm saving money!* Write *save money* on the board.

2. State the objective: *Today we're going to read about saving money.*

1 Get ready to read

Presentation

15–20 minutes

A Direct students to look at the pictures. Read and have students repeat the captions. Write

turn off/turn on on the board and demonstrate with the classroom lights. Ask: *Do you call long distance? Where do you call?*

B Read the questions aloud, and ask students to work individually to check the boxes. Ask for a show of hands for each alternative.

Pre-Reading

Direct students to look at the website in 2A. Ask: *Is this an article in the newspaper?* [no] *What are the pictures of?* [TV, light, shower, phone]

2 Read about saving money

Guided Practice I

25–30 minutes

A 1. Ask students to read the article silently.

2. Ask if there are any questions about the reading.

B Play the audio. Have students read along silently.

Multilevel Strategies

After 2B, seat same-level students together.

• **Pre-level** Work with this group. Point to each picture, and read the advice in 2A, stopping to clarify when necessary.

• **On- and Higher-level** While you are working with pre-level students, ask these students to work in pairs to look at the pictures and cover the text in 2A, and then see if their partners remember the advice.

C 1. Have students work individually to mark the sentences *true* or *false*. Go over the answers as a class.

2. Ask additional comprehension questions: *To save money, do I turn on the lights?* [no] *Do I turn off the TV?* [yes]

> ### Multilevel Strategies
>
> After the group comprehension check in 2C, call on individuals and tailor your questions to the level of your students.
>
> • **Pre-level** Ask *yes/no* questions. *To save money, do I take 20-minute showers?*
>
> • **On-level** Ask information questions. *How do I save money on the phone bill?*
>
> • **Higher-level** Ask these students for additional ideas. *What are other ways to save money on utility bills?*

D Have students work individually to circle the correct answers. Ask volunteers to read the completed sentences aloud.

3 Addressing an envelope

Guided Practice II

15–20 minutes

A 1. Draw an envelope on the board with lines for the mailing address and the return address and a square for the stamp. Elicit the related words, and label the envelope. Give students time to copy your example.

2. Ask: *When you pay your gas bill, do you go to the gas company? Or do you pay by mail?*

3. Have students read the directions, look at the phone bill and envelope, and answer the question.

B Have students work individually to choose the correct answers. Go over the answers as a class.

Communicative Practice

10–15 minutes

C 1. Review the questions.

2. Set a time limit (three minutes). Allow students to think about the questions and then write their answers individually.

3. Ask various volunteers for their answers to question 1. Discuss the answer to question 2. Pantomime what would happen if the letter were lost at the post office: *Who sent this letter? Where do we return it? I don't know. Oh, well.* Teach students the word *lost*.

Application

5–10 minutes

BRING IT TO LIFE

If possible, distribute envelopes to your students to help them complete this assignment. Review the placement of address, return address, and stamp: *Where is your address? Where is the utility address?*

> Explain to students why it is important to neatly address an envelope. Tell students that the post office uses machines to sort the letters. Therefore, they should always format the addresses like Ms. Mavis Clark did (name on first line; street on second line; city, proper state abbreviation, and zip code on the third line). It is also important to place the address in the center of the envelope, use dark blue or black ink, and print neatly. Put a badly addressed envelope on the board, and ask students to correct the problems.

To compress this lesson: Conduct 2D as a whole-class activity.

To extend this lesson: Have a class discussion about other ways to save money on utility bills.

1. Use items that students brainstormed in the warm-up. For example: explain that you can save money if you:
   • don't dry very small loads in your dryer or hang clothes outside on sunny days
   • turn off water while washing dishes
   • keep the top of your refrigerator uncovered and vacuum the back of it
   • turn your heater off or down when you're in bed
   • set your air conditioner thermostat higher

2. As a class, make a poster like the one in 2A.

And/Or have students complete **Workbook 1 page 28** and **Multilevel Activity Book 1 page 52.**

C Mark the sentences T (true) or F (false).

___T___ 1. Save money. Turn the TV off.

___F___ 2. Save money. Take twenty-minute showers.

___F___ 3. Save money. Call long distance from 8 a.m. to 7 p.m.

D Circle the correct words.

1. Some utility bills are ((expensive) / five-minute).
2. You can ((save) / turn off) money on your bills.
3. Don't forget! Turn off the (phone / (lights)).

3 Addressing an envelope

A Look at the envelope. What kind of utility bill is this? It's a phone bill.

Ms. Mavis Clark
24 Oak Street
Greene, TX 75268

Atlantic Phone Services
P.O. Box 24
Dallas, TX 75220

Atlantic Phone Services

Ms. Mavis Clark
24 Oak Street
Greene, TX 75268

Billing date: 3/09
Payment due date: 3/28
Amount due: $22.50

B Look at the envelope. Circle the correct answers.

1. Who is paying the bill?
   a. Atlantic Phone Services
   (b.) Mavis Clark
   c. Greene, Texas

2. What is the city in the mailing address?
   a. Greene
   b. Clark
   (c.) Dallas

C Think about the questions. Talk about the answers with your class.

1. When do you pay your utility bills?
2. Why is a return address on an envelope important?

BRING IT TO LIFE

Look at a utility bill at home. Address an envelope for the bill or address an envelope for the phone company in 3A. Bring the envelope to class.

1 Grammar

A Circle the correct words.

1. A: (Is /(Are)) Ed and Sue eating?
   B: Yes, (we /(they)) are.
2. A: Is Tom ((cooking)/ cook)?
   B: No, he ((isn't)/ aren't).
3. A: Is the (rug /(girl)) sleeping?
   B: No, (it /(she)) isn't.
4. A: (Is /(Are)) you and Sam studying?
   B: Yes, (I /(we)) are.

> **Grammar note**
>
> **_Yes/No questions and answers_**
>
> A: Are you working?
> B: Yes, I am. *or*
>   No, I'm not.
>
> A: Is Mark cooking?
> B: Yes, he is. *or*
>   No, he isn't.
>
> A: Are you working?
> B: Yes, we are. *or*
>   No, we aren't.
>
> A: Are they playing?
> B: Yes, they are. *or*
>   No, they aren't.

B Write answers for these questions.

1. Are you studying English? _Yes, I am._
2. Are you mopping the floor? _No, I'm not._
3. Is your teacher eating lunch? _No, he / she isn't._
4. Are your classmates writing the answers? _Yes, they are._
5. Are you working with a partner? _No, I'm not._

C Write new sentences. Use object pronouns.

1. Janet is talking to <u>Joe</u>.
   Janet is talking to him.
2. Jeff is writing to <u>Maria</u>.
   Jeff is writing to her.
3. Paul is listening to <u>his friends</u>.
   Paul is listening to them.
4. Ingrid is talking to <u>Jane and me</u>.
   Ingrid is talking to us.

D Match the questions with the answers.

_b_ 1. Where is she?   a. Yes, he is.
_d_ 2. What's he doing?   b. She's in the living room.
_a_ 3. Is he studying English?   c. No, they aren't.
_e_ 4. What time is it?   d. He's studying.
_c_ 5. Are Mr. and Mrs. Li at home?   e. It's 6:00.

Unit 4 Review and expand

Objectives	Grammar	Vocabulary	Correlations
On-, Pre-, and Higher-level: Expand upon and review unit grammar and life skills	Use the present continuous to talk about daily activities (*She is cooking dinner.*) Object pronouns (*Janet is talking to him.*)	Present continuous verbs For additional vocabulary practice, see this **Oxford Picture Dictionary** topic: Housework	**CASAS:** 0.1.2, 1.4.1, 4.8.1, 7.2.5–7.2.7, 7.3.1 **LCPs:** 28.05, 32.01, 32.02, 32.05, 32.13, 33.01, 33.02 **SCANS:** Creative thinking, Listening, Participates as member of a team, Problem solving, Speaking, Writing **EFF:** Cooperate with others, Solve problems and make decisions

Warm-up and Review

10–15 minutes (books closed)

1. Review the *Bring It to Life* assignment from Lesson 5.

2. Have students who did the exercise show their envelopes to their classmates. Ask students who didn't do the exercise to identify the stamp, return address, and mailing address on their classmates' envelopes

3. Elicit the names of the utility companies that students chose.

Introduction and Presentation

5 minutes

1. Show a picture of someone doing a familiar activity (eating, talking, reading, etc.). Ask: *What is he/she doing?* Write the question and the answer on the board. Ask, using the correct activity: *Is he/she _____ing?* Write the question and *Yes, he/she is.* on the board. Ask the question again using the wrong activity. Write *No, he/she isn't.* on the board.

2. State the objective: *Today we'll review using present continuous to talk about daily activities.*

1 Grammar

Guided Practice

40–45 minutes

A 1. Read the questions and answers in the *Grammar note*. Check comprehension by asking questions about them and their classmates: *Are you studying English? Are you sleeping? Is Chung playing? Is Francisca listening to me?*

2. Have students work individually to circle the correct answers. Ask volunteers to read the completed questions and answers aloud.

B Have students work individually to write the answers. Ask volunteers to write them on the board.

C 1. Remind students of the object pronouns. Write: *I am looking at _____* on the board, and ask the question *looking at* a man, a woman, and a group to elicit *him, her,* and *them.* Write *She is looking at _____,* and get a female student to look at you alone to model *me.* Have the student look at you with a group to model *us.* Write the object pronouns on the board.

2. Have students work individually to write new sentences. Ask volunteers to put them on the board. Ask other volunteers to read them aloud.

D Have students work individually to match the questions and answers. Ask volunteers to read the matching questions and answers aloud. Write the number-letter match on the board.

Multilevel Strategies

For 1D, seat same-level students together.

• **Pre-level** Read the questions aloud, and ask these students to respond chorally with the correct answers. After they have completed the exercise, ask individuals to read the question-answer combination.

• **On- and Higher-level** While you are working with pre-level students, direct these students to look at the picture in 1A on page 42. Ask them to write questions and answers, like those in 1D, to go with it. Ask volunteers to share their questions and answers with the class.

2 Group work

Communicative Practice

20–35 minutes

 1. Direct students, in groups of three or four, to focus on the picture on page 41. Ask: *Where is the refrigerator? Is the dresser in the dining area?*

2. Set a time limit (five minutes) to complete the exercise. Circulate and answer any questions.

3. Have a reporter from each group read the group's sentences to the class.

> ### Multilevel Strategies
>
> For 2A and 2B, use same-level groups.
>
> • **Pre-level** For 2A, ask these students to write one question and one answer with *Where*. For 2B, allow them to ask and answer the questions without writing.
>
> • **Higher-level** For 2A, ask these students to write two additional sentences about the picture. For 2B, have them talk about these ideas as well: *Tell me where you watch TV. Tell me where you read. Tell me where you listen to music.*

B 1. Have students work in the same groups from 2A to take turns interviewing each other in pairs.

2. Set a time limit (five minutes) to complete the exercise.

3. Tell students to make a note of their partners' answers but not to worry about writing complete sentences.

TIP For more practice with questions about furniture, provide students with furniture catalogs or furniture store advertisements. Assign each student a particular piece of furniture. Draw a large house outline on butcher paper with the rooms labeled. Have students put their pictures in the correct rooms. Ask questions about the furniture: *Is the _____ in the _____? What is this? Where is it? What color is it? Is it a _____?* If your class has access to the Internet, have students find their pieces of furniture on an Internet shopping site.

C Have a reporter from each group share the group's work.

15–25 minutes

 1. Direct students to look at the picture. Ask: *Where are they? What is the mother doing? What are the children doing?* Tell students they will read a story about a woman with a housework problem. Direct students to read Mrs. Simms's story silently. Then play the audio, and have them read along silently.

2. Ask: *What is Jack doing?* [listening to music] *What are Judy and Joni doing?* [watching TV] *What is Mrs. Simms's problem?*

 1. Read the question. Read the possible solutions.

2. Elicit student ideas for other solutions. Write each one on the board.

3. Discuss whether the statements are appropriate.

4. Ask for a show of hands to see which solution the class likes best.

Evaluation

30–35 minutes

To test students' understanding of the unit grammar and life skills, have them take the Unit 4 Test in the *Step Forward Test Generator CD-ROM with ExamView® Assessment Suite.*

Learning Log

To help students record and discuss their progress, use the *Learning Log* on page T-177.

To extend this review: Have students complete **Workbook 1 page 29, Multilevel Activity Book 1 pages 53–56,** and the **Unit 4 Grammar Exercises** on the **Multilevel Grammar Exercises CD-ROM 1.**

2 Group work

A Work with 2–3 classmates. Write 5 questions and answers about the picture on page 41. Talk about the sentences with your class. Answers will vary.

A: *Where is the sofa?*
B: *It's in the living room.*

A: *Is the sink in the kitchen?*
B: *Yes, it is.*

Is the TV in the bedroom?
No, it isn't.

B Interview 3 classmates. Write their answers in your notebook.

SAY:

1. Tell me where you study.
2. Tell me where you eat.
3. Tell me where you pay your bills.

Classmate—Nancy
1. in the living room
2. in the kitchen
3. in the living room

C Talk about the answers with your class.

PROBLEM SOLVING

A Listen and read about Mrs. Simms. **What is the problem?** The children aren't helping Mrs. Simms.

The Simms family is at home today. Mrs. Simms is cleaning the house. Her son, Jack, is listening to music. Her daughters, Judy and Joni, are watching TV. Mrs. Simms is tired. She's doing all the work.

B Work with your classmates. Answer the question. (More than one answer is possible.)

What can Mrs. Simms do?
  a. Play video games.
  (b.) Tell the children to help.
  (c.) Pay the children to help.
  (d.) Other: ___Answers will vary.___

UNIT 5

In the Neighborhood

FOCUS ON
- places and transportation
- describing locations
- *there is/there are*
- maps and directions
- preparing for emergencies

LESSON 1 **Vocabulary**

1 Learn neighborhood words

A Look at the map. Say the names of the streets.

B Listen and look at the map.

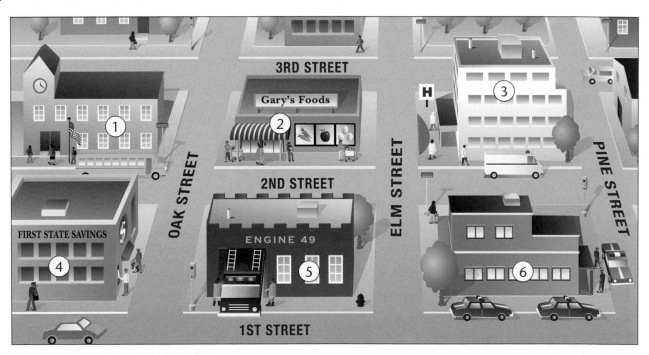

C Listen and repeat the words.

1. school 3. hospital 5. fire station
2. supermarket 4. bank 6. police station

D Look at the map. Complete the sentences.

1. The ___supermarket___ is on 2nd Street.
2. The ___hospital___ is on Elm Street.
3. The ___fire station___ is on 1st Street.
4. The ___bank___ is on Oak Street.
5. The ___police station___ is on Pine Street.
6. The ___school / supermarket___ is on 2nd Street.

☑ Identify common neighborhood places and modes of transportation

Unit 5 Lesson 1

Objectives	Grammar	Vocabulary	Correlations
On-level: Identify neighborhood places and transportation words **Pre-level:** Recognize neighborhood places and transportation words **Higher-level:** Talk and write about neighborhood places and transportation	Present continuous (*The boy is riding a bicycle.*)	Neighborhood places and transportation For additional vocabulary practice, see these **Oxford Picture Dictionary** topics: City Streets, An Intersection	**CASAS:** 0.1.2, 1.1.3, 2.2.1, 2.2.3, 2.2.5, 2.5.1, 2.5.3, 2.5.5, 7.4.5, 7.4.7 **LCPs:** 26.01, 26.03, 32.01, 32.13 **SCANS:** Listening, Participates as member of a team, Seeing things in the mind's eye, Self-management, Speaking **EFF:** Cooperate with others, Observe critically

Warm-up and Review

10–15 minutes (books closed)

Review different kinds of questions. Show students pictures of people doing things, and ask: *Where is he/she?* (or *Where are they?*) *What's he/she doing? Is he/she _____–ing? What's this? What's that? What are these?* Include pictures of people who are in familiar places but not at home (in the street or at a restaurant, school, or park). Elicit complete sentences. Choose one of the pictures, and write the entire set of questions and answers.

Introduction

5 minutes

1. Referring to the warm-up pictures, say: *He/She is at the park/school/restaurant. He/She's not at home. He/She's in the neighborhood. What's in our neighborhood?* Elicit names of places near the school. Write *neighborhood* on the board, and have students repeat it.

2. State the objective: *Today we'll learn how to talk about neighborhoods.*

1 Learn neighborhood words

Presentation

20–25 minutes

A Direct students to look at the map. Ask: *Where is the supermarket?* [Second Street]

B 1. Have students listen to the audio. Ask them to point to the correct place as they listen. Circulate and monitor.

2. Check comprehension by asking *yes/no* questions. Pass out *yes/no* cards to the students (see page T-175), or have them hold up one finger for *yes* and two for *no* in order to get a nonverbal response. Ask: *Is the bank on Elm Street?* [no]

C Ask students to listen and repeat the words.

Guided Practice I

15–20 minutes

D 1. Have students complete the sentences using the new vocabulary.

2. Encourage students to take turns reading the completed sentences in pairs.

Multilevel Strategies

After completing 1D, seat same-level students together and provide vocabulary practice targeted to the level of your students.

• **Pre-level** Ask these students to practice together by pointing to the pictures and saying the correct words.

• **On-level** Ask these students to work in pairs, covering the words and testing each other on the vocabulary. Have one student point to the pictures while the other student says the correct word.

• **Higher-level** Ask these students to dictate the words to each other.

2 Talk about transportation and places

Guided Practice II
35–40 minutes

A 1. Ask: *Do you come to school in a car? On a bus? On a bicycle? That's your transportation.* Write *transportation* on the board. Introduce the new topic: *Now let's talk about more places and transportation.*

2. Group students and assign roles: leader, fact checker, recorder, and reporter. Explain that students work with their groups to match the words and pictures.

3. Check comprehension of the exercise. Ask: *Who looks up the words in the picture dictionary?* [fact checker] *Who writes the numbers in the book?* [recorder] *Who tells the class your answers?* [reporter] *Who helps everyone and manages the group?* [leader]

4. Set a time limit (three minutes), and have students work together to complete the task. While students are working, copy the wordlist on the board.

5. Call "time" and have the reporters from each group take turns calling out the numbers for the wordlist. Record students' answers on the board. If groups disagree, write each group's choice next to the word.

Multilevel Strategies

For 2A, use mixed-level groups.

• **On-level** Assign these students as recorders and reporters.

• **Pre-level** Assign these students as timekeepers (to let the group know when the three minutes are up) to allow them an active role in the group.

• **Higher-level** Assign these students as leaders.

B 1. Ask students to listen and check their answers.

2. Have students correct the wordlist on the board and then write the correct numbers in their books.

3. Tell the groups from 2A to break into pairs to practice the words. Set a time limit (two minutes).

C 1. Have students circle the correct words to complete the sentences.

2. Ask students to take turns reading the completed sentences in the same pairs from 2B.

Communicative Practice and Application
10–15 minutes

D 1. Model the conversations with a volunteer. Then model them again with information from the picture in 2A and then with information from the picture in 1A.

2. Set a time limit (five minutes). Ask students to practice the conversations with several partners.

Evaluation
10–15 minutes (books closed)

TEST YOURSELF

1. Make a two-column chart on the board with the headings *Neighborhood Places* and *Transportation Words*. Have students close their books and give you an example for each column.

2. Have students copy the chart into their notebooks.

3. Give students five to ten minutes to test themselves by writing in the chart the words they recall from the lesson.

4. Call "time" and have students check their spelling in *The Oxford Picture Dictionary* or another dictionary. Circulate and monitor students' progress.

To compress this lesson: Conduct 2A as a whole-class activity. Have students practice 2D with only one partner.

To extend this lesson: Ask students about places close to the school. *Where's a bank?* Use the information they provide to write sentences about the locations of real places. Ask students to copy the sentences into their notebooks.

And/Or have students complete **Workbook 1 page 30** and **Multilevel Activity Book 1 page 58.**

2 Talk about transportation and places

A Work with your classmates. Match the words with the picture.

__11__ bank	__7__ bus stop	__10__ parking lot	__8__ restaurant
__12__ bicycle	__4__ car	__3__ movie theater	__5__ stop sign
__6__ bus	__9__ gas station	__2__ pharmacy	__1__ supermarket

B Listen and check your answers. Then practice the words with a partner.

C Look at the picture in 2A. Circle the correct words.

1. The boy is riding ((a bicycle) / a car).
2. The children are riding (a bicycle / (the bus)).
3. The woman is going to (the pharmacy / (the supermarket)).
4. The man is driving ((a car) / a bicycle).
5. The girl is standing at ((the bus stop) / the stop sign).

D Work with a partner. Practice the conversations. Use the pictures in 1A and 2A.

A: Where is the school?
B: It's on 2nd Street.

A: What's the woman doing?
B: She's going to the supermarket.

TEST YOURSELF ✔

Close your book. Write 5 neighborhood places and 3 transportation words. Check your spelling in a dictionary.

1 Read about a neighborhood

 A Look at the pictures. Listen.

My Neighborhood

My apartment

My favorite movie theater

My supermarket

Me

B Listen again. Read the sentences.

1. Let me tell you about my new neighborhood.
2. My apartment building is on 6th Street. It's next to a little library.
3. There is a big park behind the library.
4. My favorite movie theater is near my home. It's across from the post office.
5. My supermarket is on Main Street between the bank and the clinic.
6. There is a bus stop in front of my apartment. That's me. I'm waiting for the bus.

next to

behind

in front of

across from

between

C Check your understanding. Mark the sentences T (true) or F (false).

__T__ 1. His apartment is next to the library.

__F__ 2. There is a bank behind the library.

__T__ 3. The supermarket is on Main Street.

__F__ 4. The bus stop is in front of the clinic.

Unit 5 Lesson 2

Objectives	Grammar	Vocabulary	Correlations
On-, Pre-, and Higher-level: Read and write about a neighborhood	Prepositions of location (*across from, behind, between, in front of, near, next to, on*)	Neighborhood places For additional vocabulary practice, see these **Oxford Picture Dictionary** topics: City Streets, Prepositions	**CASAS:** 0.1.2, 1.1.3, 2.2.1, 2.5.1, 2.5.3, 7.4.7 **LCPs:** 26.03, 32.01, 32.02, 32.13, 33.04 **SCANS:** Acquires and evaluates information, Listening, Seeing things in the mind's eye, Self-management, Speaking, Writing **EFF:** Convey ideas in writing, Listen actively, Observe critically

Warm-up and Review

10–15 minutes (books closed)

Draw a street on the board with squares on either side to represent buildings. Put a symbol in each building representing what it is—for example, a dollar sign ($) for a bank, prescription sign (RX) for a pharmacy, a shopping cart for a supermarket, a hamburger for a restaurant, etc. Elicit the names of the buildings: *What's this?* Write the names. Draw a parking lot behind the hospital. To elicit the labels for your drawing, ask: *What's this?* Give your street a name (First Street), and have the students repeat: *The bank is on First Street.*

Introduction

5 minutes

1. Describe the location of the buildings in your drawing, pointing to indicate the relationships. *The bank is next to the hospital. The parking lot is behind the hospital. The restaurant is across from the bank.*

2. State the objective: *Today we'll read and write about a neighborhood and talk about locations.*

1 Read about a neighborhood

Presentation I

20–25 minutes

A 1. Direct students to look at the pictures. Ask: *Where is the apartment?* [Sixth Street] *Where is the supermarket?* [Main Street]

2. Play the audio. Ask students to repeat the captions.

B 1. Draw students' attention to the pictures. State the relationship in each picture: *The pink house is next to the blue house. The pink house is behind the blue house.*

2. Play the audio again. Have students read along silently.

3. Check comprehension. Ask: *Is the apartment next to a library?* [yes] *Is the movie theater across from the apartment?* [no]

Multilevel Strategies

After the group comprehension check in 1B, challenge on- and higher-level students while working with pre-level students.

• **Pre-level** Reread the sentences in 1B with your pre-level students while on- and higher-level students answer additional questions.

• **On- and Higher-level** Write these questions on the board: *Where is the library?* [on Sixth Street] *What is across from the post office?* [the movie theater] *Where is he?* [at the bus stop] *What is he doing?* [waiting for the bus] While you are working with the pre-level students, ask the on- and higher-level students to individually answer the questions. Have volunteers write the answers on the board.

Guided Practice I

10 minutes

C Have students work independently to mark the sentences *true* or *false*. Go over the answers as a class.

T-54

2 Write about your neighborhood

Guided Practice II

20–25 minutes

1. Copy the sentences on the board. Read them aloud with your own information.

2. Have students complete the sentences independently. Circulate and assist.

> ### Multilevel Strategies
>
> Adapt 2A to the level of your students.
>
> • **Pre-level** Group these students. Brainstorm and write on the board possibilities for each blank, and have students select one to write in their books.
>
> • **Higher-level** Tell these students to write the sentences in their notebooks and add a sentence with *near*. Ask each student to make an illustration (a map) to go with his/her sentence.

Ask students to read their sentences to a partner. Call on individuals to share what they learned about their partners.

3 Talk about locations

Presentation II

20–25 minutes

1. Introduce the topic: *Now we're going to look at a map and talk about locations.* Direct students to look at the map in 3A. Ask: *What's in front of the apartment building?* [a supermarket]

2. Ask students to put their pencils down and point to each location as they hear it mentioned. Play the entire audio once.

3. Play the audio in segments. After each interchange, stop the audio and check answers with the students: *Did you write the answer?* If necessary, replay the segment.

4. Check students' listening accuracy: *Where is the hospital? Where is the fire station?*

Guided Practice

10 minutes

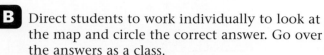

Direct students to work individually to look at the map and circle the correct answer. Go over the answers as a class.

Communicative Practice and Application

10 minutes

1. Have students read along silently while they listen.

2. Play the audio again, and have students repeat the conversations. Replay if necessary.

3. Model the conversations with a volunteer. Then model them again with your own information

4. Set a time limit (five minutes). Ask students to practice the conversations with several partners. Ask volunteers to present their conversations to the class.

Evaluation

10–15 minutes (books closed)

TEST YOURSELF

Have students tell a partner about three places in their neighborhood. Ask them to listen to their partners and write what they hear without showing their partners the paper. When they finish, ask them to read back what they wrote to their partners to check accuracy.

> ### Multilevel Strategies
>
> For the *Test Yourself*, pair same-level students.
>
> • **Pre-level** Allow these students to talk to a partner without writing.
>
> • **Higher-level** Tell these students to talk and write about five places.

To compress this lesson: Have students practice the conversation in 3D with only one partner.

To extend this lesson: Have groups draw a map of an imaginary neighborhood and write sentences about it. And/Or have students complete **Workbook 1 page 31** and **Multilevel Activity Book 1 page 59**.

2 Write about your neighborhood

A Write about your neighborhood. Complete the sentences. Answers will vary.

Let me tell you about my neighborhood.

My apartment/house is across from _____ .

There is a/an _____ next to my home.

There is a/an _____ behind my home.

B Read your sentences to a partner.

3 Talk about locations

A Listen to the directions. Label the map with the words in the box.

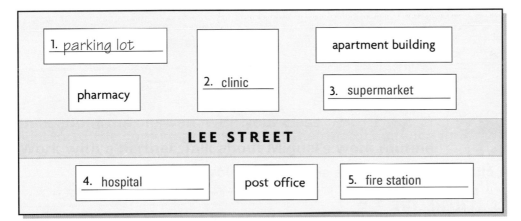

1. parking lot		apartment building
pharmacy	2. clinic	3. supermarket

LEE STREET

4. hospital	post office	5. fire station

clinic
fire station
hospital
supermarket
~~parking lot~~

B Look at the map. Circle the correct word.

1. The parking lot is (between /(behind)) the pharmacy.
2. The supermarket is ((in front of)/ on) the apartment building.
3. The pharmacy is (in front of /(across from)) the hospital.
4. The clinic is (across from /(next to)) the supermarket.
5. The post office is ((between)/ behind) the hospital and the fire station.

C Listen. Then practice the conversations with a partner. Use your own information.

A: Where is your favorite supermarket?

B: It's on Main Street next to the bank.

A: Where is your favorite restaurant?

B: It's on 1st Street across from the park.

TEST YOURSELF ✔

Close your book. Ask a partner to give the location of 3 places in his or her neighborhood. Write what you hear.

1 Learn *There is* and *There are*

A Listen and look at the picture. Read the story. Find Dave in the picture.

I'm Dave. I live on 4th Street. There are two restaurants on my street. One restaurant is next to my apartment building. There is a nice park across the street. Right now I'm sitting on a bench in the park. It's my favorite place to have lunch.

B Study the charts. Complete the sentences below.

THERE IS / THERE ARE

Statements
There is a supermarket on 4th Street. There are two restaurants.

Negative statements
There isn't a post office. There aren't any schools.

1. There __is__ a supermarket on 4th Street.

2. There __are__ two restaurants.

3. There __isn't__ a post office.

4. There __aren't__ any schools.

C Look at the picture in 1A. Change the sentences from false to true.

1. There is one restaurant. _There are two restaurants._

2. There's a movie theater. _There isn't a movie theater._

3. There are two mailboxes. _There aren't two mailboxes. or There is one mailbox._

4. There are two gas stations. _There aren't two gas stations. or There's one / a gas station_

D Work with a partner. Use *There is* and *There are* to talk about your classroom.

There are ten students in the classroom. There's a green notebook on my desk.

Unit 5 Lesson 3

Objectives	Grammar	Vocabulary	Correlations
On- and Higher-level: Use *There is* and *There are* to describe location **Pre-level:** Recognize *There is* and *There are*	*There is* and *There are* statements (*There's a park across the street. There are two schools.*) *Yes/no* questions with *there is* and *there are* (*Is there a pharmacy on Fourth Street? Yes, there is.*)	Places in the neighborhood, *bench* For additional vocabulary practice, see these **Oxford Picture Dictionary** topics: The Bank, City Streets, An Intersection, A Restaurant	**CASAS:** 0.1.2, 2.2.1, 2.6.1, 6.0.1, 7.4.7 **LCPs:** 26.03, 32.01, 32.05, 32.13 **SCANS:** Interprets and communicates information, Listening, Seeing things in the mind's eye, Self-management, Speaking, Writing **EFF:** Convey ideas in writing, Cooperate with others, Reflect and evaluate

Warm-up and Review

10–15 minutes (books closed)

1. Write scrambled sentences on the board: *gas supermarket The is from station. the across* [The supermarket is across from the gas station.] *post The to next park. the office is* [The post office is next to the park.] *parking The front library. of the in is lot* [The parking lot is in front of the library.] Include the capital letters and periods, so students can determine the order of the words.

2. Give students a few minutes to work out the sentences. Ask volunteers to come to the board and write the unscrambled sentences.

Introduction

5–10 minutes

1. Tell students there is another way to say the ideas on the board. Rewrite the sentences with *There is: There is a supermarket next to the post office.* Have students repeat the new sentences.

2. State the objective: *Today we'll talk about our neighborhoods using* There is *and* There are.

1 Learn *There is* and *There are*

Presentation I

20–25 minutes

A 1. Direct students to look at the picture. Ask: *How many people are there in the park?* [four] *What are they doing?* [eating, having a picnic]

2. Have students read the paragraph silently and look at the picture. Play the audio and have students read along silently.

3. Check comprehension. Ask: *Where is Dave?* [in the park] *Where is his apartment building?* [Fourth Street] *How many restaurants are there on his street?* [two]

B 1. Read the charts through sentence by sentence. Then read them again, and have students repeat after you.

2. Ask students to reread the paragraph in 1A and circle *There is* and *There are.*

3. As a class, complete the sentences under the chart. Ask volunteers to write the sentences on the board. Have other students read the sentences aloud.

4. Give students time to silently review the charts and, if they haven't already, fill in the blanks.

5. Assess students' understanding of the charts. Point to items in the picture in 1A and elicit sentences. *There is a post office. There are people.*

Guided Practice

15–20 minutes

C Have students work individually to write true sentences. Ask volunteers to write the answers on the board.

Communicative Practice and Application

10–15 minutes

D 1. Read the example sentences. Then say additional sentences about your classroom.

2. Set a time limit (five minutes). Ask students to practice talking about the classroom with several partners.

3. Ask volunteers to present their sentences to the class.

2 Ask and answer *Yes/No* questions with *there is* and *there are*

Presentation II

20–25 minutes

 1. Play the audio and have students read the questions and answers in the chart. Play the audio again, and have students repeat.

2. Check comprehension of the chart by asking questions about the neighborhood where your school is located.

Guided Practice

10–15 minutes

B Have students work individually to write the questions. Ask volunteers to write their questions on the board.

> ### Multilevel Strategies
>
> Group pre-level students for 2B.
>
> • **Pre-level** Read the sentences in 2A with these students while other students are completing 2B. Give them time to copy the answers to 2B off the board and to read the questions and answers together.

3 Practice *Yes/No* questions with *there is* and *there are*

Communicative Practice and Application

20–25 minutes

 1. Draw the chart on the board. Elicit how to fill in the blanks in the first column. Put your own answers in the second column, and elicit other possible answers.

2. Give students time (three minutes) to fill in their own information.

B 1. Model the interview with a volunteer, and on the board, show where to chart the answers.

2. Check comprehension. Ask: *How many partners do you talk to?* [one] *Do you write your partner's answers in the chart?* [yes]

3. Set a time limit (two minutes) for students to interview their partners. Circulate and monitor.

> ### Multilevel Strategies
>
> Use mixed-level pairs for 3B.
>
> • **Pre-level** Have these students answer questions first, so they watch their partners charting the answers before they do it themselves.

C Discuss the class's answers. Ask for a show of hands: *How many people have a library in their neighborhood? How many have good restaurants?*

Evaluation

10–15 minutes (books closed)

TEST YOURSELF

Ask students to write the sentences independently. Collect and correct their writing.

To compress this lesson: Conduct 2B as a whole-class activity.

To extend this lesson: Have students create a poster about their "dream neighborhood."
1. Group students. Have them talk about what they would like to have in their dream neighborhood. A pool? A spa?
2. Ask each group to draw an intersection on poster paper to represent this dream neighborhood. Have each group member choose one place to put on the map. Then have them find an image or draw a picture of their place.
3. Tell students to glue each picture into its place on the map. Under the map, have them describe the neighborhood using sentences with *There is/There are*. *There is a park across from my house. There is a pool next to the park. There aren't any fast-food restaurants.* Have a reporter from each group present the poster and tell the class about the group's dream neighborhood.

And/Or have students complete **Workbook 1 pages 32–33** and **Multilevel Activity Book 1 page 60.**

2 Ask and answer *Yes/No* questions with *there is* and *there are*

A Study the chart. Listen and repeat the questions and answers.

Yes/No questions and answers with *there is* and *there are*	
A: Is there a park on 4th Street? **B:** Yes, there is.	**A:** Are there any restaurants on 4th Street? **B:** Yes, there are.
A: Is there a clinic on 4th Street? **B:** No, there isn't.	**A:** Are there any schools on 4th Street? **B:** No, there aren't.

B Write the questions. Use *Is there* or *Are there*.

1. **A:** _Is there a park on 4th Street?_

   B: Yes, there's a park on 4th Street.

2. **A:** _Is there a supermarket on 4th Street?_

   B: Yes, there is. There's a supermarket on 4th Street.

3. **A:** _Are there many people in the park?_

   B: Yes, there are many people in the park.

4. **A:** _Is there a pharmacy on 4th Street?_

   B: No, there isn't. There isn't a pharmacy on 4th Street.

3 Practice *Yes/No* questions with *there is* and *there are*

A Think about your neighborhood. Complete the questions in the chart.
Then write the answers.

Questions	My answers	My partner's answers
1. _Is there_ a library?		
2. _Is there_ a good restaurant?		
3. _Are there_ any bus stops?		

B Interview a partner. Write your partner's answers in the chart.

C Talk about the answers in the chart with your class.

There's a library in my neighborhood. There isn't a library in Ivan's neighborhood.

TEST YOURSELF ✔

Close your book. Write 3 sentences about your school's neighborhood.
Use *there is* and *there are*.

1 Learn directions

A Look at the pictures. Read the directions.

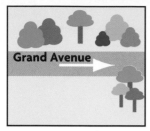
Grand Avenue

Go straight.

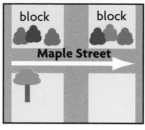
block   block
Maple Street

Go two blocks.

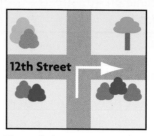
12th Street

Turn right.

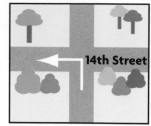
14th Street

Turn left.

B Listen. Complete the directions to the clinic.

1. Go __straight__ on Grand Avenue.
2. Turn __right__ on 12th Street.
3. Go two __blocks__ on Maple Street.
4. Turn __left__ on 14th Street.
5. It's __across from__ the park.
6. It's __next__ to the pharmacy.

C Listen and read.

A: Excuse me. Is there a bank near here?
B: Yes, there is. Go one block on Main Street and turn left on 6th Avenue. The bank is on the corner, next to the clinic.
A: Thanks for your help.
B: No problem. Have a nice day.

D Listen again and repeat each line.

E Work with a partner. Practice the conversation. Use the map.

A: Excuse me. Is there a _____ near here?
B: Yes, there is. Go _____ on _____ and turn _____ on _____. It's on the corner, next to the _____.
A: Thanks for your help.
B: No problem. Have a nice day.

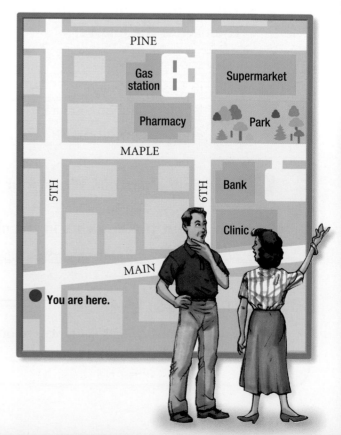

PINE
Gas station   Supermarket
Pharmacy   Park
MAPLE
5TH   6TH   Bank
Clinic
MAIN
You are here.

Unit 5 Lesson 4

Objectives	Grammar	Vocabulary	Correlations
On- and Higher-level: Ask for and give directions **Pre-level:** Ask for directions	Imperative (*Go straight. Turn right.*)	Direction words For additional vocabulary practice, see these **Oxford Picture Dictionary** topics: Directions and Maps, Traffic Signs, City Streets, An Intersection	**CASAS:** 0.1.2, 0.1.3, 1.1.3, 1.1.4, 1.9.4, 2.2.1, 6.0.1, 7.4.7 **LCPs:** 22.03, 25.01, 26.03, 30.02, 32.01, 32.02, 34.02 **SCANS:** Arithmetic/Mathematics, Knowing how to learn, Sociability, Speaking **EFF:** Speak so others can understand, Use math to solve problems and communicate

Warm-up and Review

10–15 minutes (books closed)

Draw an intersection on the board with several labeled buildings. Label the streets. Ask *where* questions and have students respond with prepositions of location. *Where is the bank? The bank is across from the post office.* Then ask volunteers to describe the neighborhood to you with *There is* and *There are.*

Introduction

5 minutes

1. Draw an X on the intersection, and say: *I want to go to the (bank). How? I have to go straight and turn left.* Draw your route. Say: *These are directions.* Write *directions* on the board.

2. State the objective: *Today we're going to learn directions.*

1 Learn directions

Presentation

5–10 minutes

 1. Direct students to look at the pictures. Read the captions aloud.

2. Have volunteers read the captions while you act out the directions *go straight, turn right,* and *turn left.*

 For more practice with directions, separate your students' desks/tables to create "streets" in your classroom. Ask students for directions *to the window* or *to Maria,* and have them call out directions to you as you walk down the streets.

Guided Practice

20–25 minutes

 B 1. Play the audio. Ask students to read along silently.

2. Replay the audio, and have students fill in the correct answers. Go over the answers as a class.

C Play the audio. Have students read the conversation silently.

D Have students listen again and repeat each line.

Communicative Practice and Application

15–20 minutes

E 1. Model the conversation with a volunteer. Then model it again with other information from the map.

2. Elicit other ways to complete the conversation.

3. Set a time limit (five minutes). Ask students to practice the conversation with several partners.

Multilevel Strategies

For 1E, adapt the oral practice to the level of your students.

• **Pre-level** Have these students read the conversation as written in 1C.

• **Higher-level** When these students finish practicing with information from the map, ask them to talk about directions to real places.

T-58

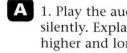

2 Practice your pronunciation

Pronunciation Extension

10–15 minutes

 1. Play the audio and have students read along silently. Explain that stressed words are said higher and longer. Demonstrate both aspects of stress by saying the sentence, exaggerating length, and then exaggerating pitch.

2. Play the audio again, and tell students to listen for the stressed words.

B Have students listen and underline the stressed words. Go over the answers as a class.

3 Real-life math

Math Extension

10–15 minutes

A 1. Direct students to look at the map. Ask: *What state is this?* [Florida]

2. Have students work individually to complete the sentences. Ask volunteers to share their answers.

 Model the sentence, filling it in with information from the map. Ask students to take turns saying sentences about the map with a partner.

Evaluation

10–15 minutes

TEST YOURSELF

1. Model the role-play with a volunteer. Then switch roles.

2. Pair students. Write *Is there a _____ near here?* on the board for Partner A. Check comprehension. Ask: *Are you asking about Florida or about a place near the school?*

3. Set a time limit (five minutes), and have the partners act out the role-play in both roles.

4. Circulate and monitor. Encourage pantomime and improvisation.

5. Provide feedback.

Multilevel Strategies

Target the *Test Yourself* to the level of your students.

• **Pre-level** Allow these students to answer the question with locations rather than directions.

• **Higher-level** Ask these students to prepare their role-play for presentation to the class.

To compress this lesson: Have students practice the conversation in 1E with only one partner.

To extend this lesson: Have students practice writing directions.
1. Put students in mixed-level groups. Assign each group a location from the map in 1E.
2. Have each group write directions to their location on poster or butcher paper. Tell them not to write the name of the location.
3. Have a group reporter read the directions aloud. Ask the class to guess the location.
4. If your students are likely to be familiar with a number of locations near the school, do this activity again using real places instead of the map in 1E.
And/Or have students complete **Workbook 1 page 34** and **Multilevel Activity Book 1 page 61**.

2 Practice your pronunciation

A Listen to the sentences. Listen for the stressed words.

1. The **police** **station** is in **front** of the **park**.
2. It's **across** from the **library**.
3. There's a **restaurant** **next** to the **movie** **theater**.
4. It's **behind** the **parking** **lot**.

B Listen and <u>underline</u> the stressed words. Read the sentences to a partner.

1. There's a <u>park</u> <u>behind</u> the <u>fire</u> <u>station</u>.
2. The bank is next to the post office. The <u>bank</u> is <u>next</u> to the <u>post office</u>.
3. There are two restaurants on the street. There are two <u>restaurants</u> on the <u>street</u>.
4. The bus stop is in front of the restaurant. The <u>bus stop</u> is in <u>front</u> of the <u>restaurant</u>.

3 Real-life math

A Complete the sentences. How far is it?

1. It's ___235___ miles* from Miami to Orlando.
2. It's ___85___ miles from Orlando to Tampa.
3. It's ___140___ miles from Tampa to Daytona Beach.
4. It's ___290___ miles from Miami to Daytona Beach.

*1 mile = 1.61 kilometers

B Work with a partner. Make sentences about the map.

It's _____ miles from _____
to _____.

TEST YOURSELF ✔

Work with a partner. Partner A: Ask for directions to a place near your school. Partner B: Give the directions. Then change roles.

1 Get ready to read

A Look at the pictures. Read the words.

Home Emergencies

1

Fire

2

Power outage

3

Accident

B Work with your classmates. Make a list of other home emergencies. Ask your teacher for the words you need in English, or use a dictionary.

2 Read about home emergencies

A Read the poster.

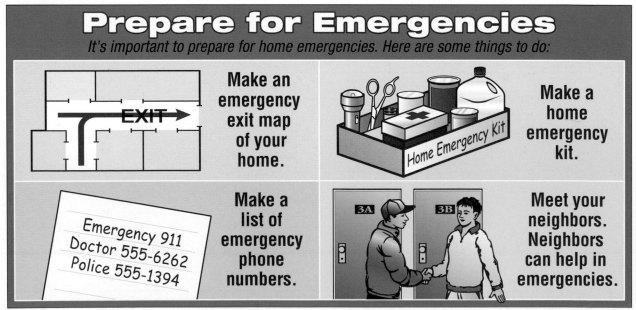

Prepare for Emergencies

It's important to prepare for home emergencies. Here are some things to do:

EXIT →

Make an emergency exit map of your home.

Home Emergency Kit

Make a home emergency kit.

Emergency 911
Doctor 555-6262
Police 555-1394

Make a list of emergency phone numbers.

3A   3B

Meet your neighbors. Neighbors can help in emergencies.

Source: *www.fema.gov*

B Listen and read the poster again.

Unit 5 Lesson 5

Objectives	Grammar	Vocabulary	Correlations
On- and Higher-level: Read about and discuss emergencies **Pre-level:** Read about emergencies	Imperative (*Make an exit plan.*)	*Fire, power outage, accident, exit, kit, neighbors, prepare, fire extinguisher* For additional vocabulary practice, see this **Oxford Picture Dictionary** topic: Emergencies and Natural Disasters	**CASAS:** 0.1.2, 1.1.3, 1.4.8, 2.1.2, 2.5.1 **LCPs:** 26.03, 27.01, 32.01–32.04, 32.06, 32.16 **SCANS:** Creative thinking, Listening, Organizes and maintains information, Reading **EFF:** Learn through research, Read with understanding, Reflect and evaluate, Take responsibility for learning

Warm-up and Review

10–15 minutes (books closed)

Write the alphabet on the board. Say each letter and ask students if they can name something in their house that starts with that letter. Accept any English word that might be in the house or part of a home. If you're sure students know a word but aren't thinking of it, pantomime it or give another hint. When you finish, repeat all the words and congratulate students on how much English they have learned.

Introduction

5 minutes

1. Write *911* on the board, and say: *What is this number? When do I call it?* Write the word *emergency*. Say: *Many emergencies happen in our homes.*

2. State the objective: *Today we'll read about home emergencies.*

1 Get ready to read

Presentation

15–20 minutes

A Direct students to look at the pictures. Read the captions aloud.

B 1. Brainstorm a list of emergencies on the board. If students know an emergency but can't remember the English word, ask them to pantomime it.

2. Give students time to copy the words from the board.

 Have students look at pictures of emergencies and natural disasters (see the topic Emergencies and Disasters in *The Oxford Picture Dictionary*) and practice this conversation.
A: *What's the emergency?*
B: *Fire! (flood, etc.)*

Pre-Reading

1. Show students any emergency preparedness items you have in your classroom. Say: *At school, we are prepared for an emergency.*

2. Direct students to look at the poster in 2A. Read the title and subtitle. Ask: *Is it important to prepare for emergencies?*

2 Read about home emergencies

Guided Practice I

25–30 minutes

A Ask students to read the poster silently. Ask if there are any questions about the reading.

Multilevel Strategies

For 2A–B, seat same-level students together.

• **Pre-level** Assist these students by grouping them and reading the four sections of the poster.

• **On- and Higher-level** While you are working with pre-level students, ask these students to list some of the items in the emergency kit. Allow them to consult their dictionaries. Go over their ideas as a class.

B Play the audio. Have students read along silently.

C 1. Have students work individually to mark the sentences *true* or *false*.

2. Go over the answers as a class.

3. Ask an additional comprehension question: *To prepare for an emergency, do you call 911?* [no]

Multilevel Strategies

Group pre-level students for 2C and 2D.

• **Pre-level** While other students are completing 2D, help these students with 2C by reading the sentences in 2C and then reading the corresponding sentences in 2A. When the 2C sentence is false, ask students to identify the difference.

• **On- and Higher-level** While you are working with the pre-level students, ask these students to first complete 2D and then write an additional idea for preparing for an emergency.

D Have students work individually to complete the sentences. Go over the answers as a class.

 Ask for a show of hands about each item on the poster in 2A: *Do you have an emergency exit map/a list of numbers/an emergency kit? Do you know your neighbors?*

3 Read an emergency exit map

Guided Practice II

15–20 minutes

A 1. Say: *Now we're going to look at an emergency map.* Direct students to look at the map in 3A. Ask: *Is this a map of a house?* [no]

2. Have students work individually to answer the questions. Go over the answers as a class.

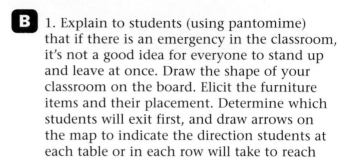 Show students the emergency exit plan for your school. Have them identify your classroom on the map and discuss the route they are to take.

Communicative Practice

10–15 minutes

B 1. Explain to students (using pantomime) that if there is an emergency in the classroom, it's not a good idea for everyone to stand up and leave at once. Draw the shape of your classroom on the board. Elicit the furniture items and their placement. Determine which students will exit first, and draw arrows on the map to indicate the direction students at each table or in each row will take to reach the door.

2. Practice the exit strategy, and determine if the map needs to be revised.

Application

5–10 minutes

BRING IT TO LIFE

Draw a simple emergency exit map on the board, like the one in 2A. Leave open spaces for doors, and draw rectangles for windows. Tell students to indicate where the doors and windows are when they make their home map and to mark a meeting place outside with an X.

To compress this lesson: Assign 2D as homework.

To extend this lesson: Have students use a simple map to create conversations about emergencies.
1. Provide students with a simple city map, like the one on page 58.
2. Have them work with a partner to practice telling each other the locations of emergencies. *A: What's your emergency? B: There's a fire at the bank!* or *There's an accident in front of the post office!* Ask partner A to mark the correct spot on the map.
3. Make the task more challenging by having partner A write the name of the emergency in the correct location, by using more emergencies, or by telling students to name the street as well as the building.

And/Or have students complete **Workbook 1 page 35** and **Multilevel Activity Book 1 page 62.**

C Mark the sentences T (true) or F (false).

To prepare for home emergencies:

   _T_ 1. Make an exit map for your home.

   _F_ 2. Make an emergency kit for your teacher.

   _F_ 3. Call the doctor.

   _T_ 4. Make a list of emergency phone numbers.

D Complete the sentences. Use the words in the box.

exit	~~prepare~~	neighbors	kit

1. It's important to ___prepare___ for home emergencies.
2. Make an emergency _exit_____ map.
3. Make a home emergency _kit_____.
4. Meet your _neighbors_____.

3 Read an emergency exit map

A Look at the emergency exit map. Answer the questions below.

Emergency Map for Blue Valley School

Office	201	203	205

stairs — elevator

| 202 | 204 | 206 |

LEGEND
Fire Extinguisher   Meeting Place: SE
Emergency Exit   corner of parking lot

X Meeting Place

1. Is there an emergency exit in the building? _Yes, there is._____
2. Are there any fire extinguishers in the classrooms? _No, there aren't._____

B Work with a your classmates. Draw an emergency exit map for your classroom.

BRING IT TO LIFE

Work with your family or roommates at home. Make a home emergency exit map.
Bring your map to class.

1 Grammar

A Complete the questions. Then answer the questions. Use your own information.

1. A: How many parks are ____there____ near your school?

   B: There __Answers will vary__ near our school.

2. A: How many good restaurants __are__ there near your school?

   B: There __Answers will vary__ near our school.

3. A: How __many__ students are there in class today?

   B: __Answers will vary__ in class today.

4. A: __How__ many computers are there in your classroom?

   B: There __Answers will vary__ in my classroom.

5. A: How __many__ books are there on your desk?

   B: There __Answers will vary__ on my desk.

> **Grammar note**
>
> ***How many?***
> A: How many banks are there on Elm Street?
> B: There is one bank on Elm Street.
> A: How many people are there in the park?
> B: There are four people in the park.

B Complete the sentences. Use the words in the box.

~~to~~   from   of   in   on

1. The parking lot is next ____to____ the supermarket.
2. The school is across __from__ the hospital.
3. The bus stop is __in__ front __of__ the apartment building.
4. The park is __on__ the corner.

C Unscramble the sentences.

1. a / theater / on / 1st / movie / There's / Avenue __There's a movie theater on 1st Avenue__.
2. on / the / The / is / park / corner __The park is on the corner__.
3. here / Is / near / there / clinic / a __Is there a clinic near here__?
4. the / people / many / in / How / are / park __How many people are in the park__?
5. street / two / There / gas / my / stations / are / on __There are two gas stations on my street__.

Unit 5 Review and expand

Objectives	Grammar	Vocabulary	Correlations
On-, Pre-, and Higher-level: Expand upon and review unit grammar and life skills	*There is/There are* and prepositions of location (*There's a park across from the bank.*)	Community places For additional vocabulary practice, see these **Oxford Picture Dictionary** topics: Directions and Maps, Traffic Signs, City Streets, An Intersection, Prepositions	**CASAS:** 0.1.2, 4.8.1, 7.2.5–7.2.7, 7.3.1 **LCPs:** 26.03, 32.01, 32.02, 32.05, 33.04 **SCANS:** Creative thinking, Listening, Participates as member of a team, Problem solving, Speaking, Writing **EFF:** Cooperate with others, Listen actively, Solve problems and make decisions

Warm-up and Review

10–15 minutes (books closed)

1. Review the *Bring It to Life* assignment from Lesson 5.

2. Have students who did the exercise show their emergency exit maps.

3. Have students who didn't make a map ask a question about the maps: *Is this a door? What's this?* Encourage them to complete the assignment when they go home.

Introduction and Presentation

5 minutes

1. Use the students' emergency exit maps, or one of your own, to ask *How many* questions. *How many rooms are there in the house? How many doors are there?*

2. State the objective: *Today we'll use questions with* How many *and answers with* There *to talk about the community.*

1 Grammar

Guided Practice

40–45 minutes

A 1. Read and have students repeat the questions and answers in the *Grammar note*.

2. Have students work individually to complete the questions and answers.

3. Ask volunteers to write the questions and answers on the board.

Multilevel Strategies

For 1A and 1B, seat pre-level students together.

• **Pre-level** While the other students are completing 1A, have these students work on 1B, helping them as necessary. Give pre-level students time to copy the answers to 1A from the board.

B 1. Have students work individually to complete the sentences.

2. Ask volunteers to read the sentences aloud.

C 1. Draw students' attention to the capitalized word in the first sentence (*There's*). Point out that finding the capitalized word will help them find the first word.

2. Ask students to work individually to unscramble the sentences and then compare their answers with a partner.

3. Ask volunteers to write the sentences on the board. Read them aloud and have students repeat them.

Multilevel Strategies

For 1C, seat pre-level students together.

• **Pre-level** Have these students read the questions and answers in 1A with a partner while other students are completing 1C.

Give all students time to copy the answers in 1C from the board.

2 Group work

Communicative Practice

20–35 minutes

 A 1. Direct students, in groups of three to four, to focus on the picture on page 53. Read the two sample questions, and point out to students that they can ask questions with *Where* or with *Is there?*

2. Set a time limit (five minutes) to complete the exercise. Circulate and answer any questions.

3. Have a reporter from each group read the group's questions to the class.

Multilevel Strategies

For 2A–B, use same-level groups.

• **Pre-level** For 2A, ask these students to write three building names and one question. For 2B, allow pre-level students to ask and answer the questions without writing.

• **Higher-level** For 2A, ask these students to write two additional questions about the picture. For 2B, have them ask and answer these questions: *Is there a hospital near your house? Is there a nice park in your neighborhood? Is there a pharmacy near your house?*

B 1. Have students work in the same groups from 2A to take turns interviewing each other in pairs.

2. Set a time limit (five minutes) to complete the exercise.

3. Tell students to write their partners' answers.

C Have a reporter from each group share the group's work.

15–25 minutes

 A 1. Direct students to look at the picture. Ask: *Where is he?* [on Orange Street] *Is he happy?* [No, he's lost.] Tell students they will read a story about a man who is confused. Write *confused* on the board, and clarify its meaning. Direct students to read Jim's story silently. Then play the audio, and have them read along silently while listening.

2. Ask: *Is Jim in a new neighborhood?* [yes] *What is he looking for?* [a supermarket] *What's the problem?* [wrong directions]

 B 1. Read the question. Read the possible solutions.

2. Elicit student ideas for other solutions. Write each one on the board.

3. Discuss whether the statements are appropriate.

4. Ask for a show of hands to see which solution the class likes best.

Evaluation

30–35 minutes

To test students' understanding of the unit grammar and life skills, have them take the Unit 5 Test in the *Step Forward Test Generator CD-ROM with ExamView® Assessment Suite*.

Learning Log

To help students record and discuss their progress, use the *Learning Log* on page T-177.

To extend this review: Have students complete **Workbook 1 page 36, Multilevel Activity Book 1 pages 63–66,** and the **Unit 5 Grammar Exercises** on the **Multilevel Grammar Exercises CD-ROM 1.**

2 Group work

A Work with 2–3 classmates. Write 5 questions about the pictures on page 53. Talk about the questions with your class. Answers will vary.

Where is the supermarket?   Is there a restaurant on the street?   Is there a school?

Is there a bus on the street?   Where is the gas station?

B Interview 3 classmates. Write their answers in your notebook.

ASK:

1. Is there a gas station on your street?
2. Is there a new movie theater in your neighborhood?
3. Are there any schools in your neighborhood?
4. How many supermarkets are there in your neighborhood?

> Classmate–Malaya
> 1. Yes, there is.
> 2. No, there isn't.
> 3. Yes, there are.
> 4. There are two supermarkets.

C Talk about the answers with your class.

PROBLEM SOLVING

A Listen and read about Jim. What is his problem? Jim is lost.

Jim is new in the neighborhood. His apartment is on Green Street. He is looking for the supermarket, but there's a problem with the directions. Jim is confused.

B Work with your classmates. Answer the question. (More than one answer is possible.)

What can Jim do?
  a. Go to a restaurant and eat.
  (b.) Ask a neighbor for help.
  c. Go home.
  (d.) Other: ___Answers will vary.___

Daily Routines

FOCUS ON
- everyday activities
- schedules
- the simple present
- office machines and equipment
- daily routines

LESSON 1 Vocabulary

1 Learn everyday activity words

A Look at the pictures. Say the times.

B Listen and look at the pictures.

1 — 7:00 a.m.

2 — 7:15 a.m.

3 — 7:30 a.m.

4 — 5:30 p.m.

5 — 6:00 p.m.

6 — 11:00 p.m.

C Listen and repeat the words.

1. get up   3. eat breakfast   5. make dinner
2. get dressed   4. come home   6. go to bed

D Look at the pictures. Complete the sentences.

1. They ____go to bed____ at 11:00 p.m.
2. They ____get dressed____ at 7:15 a.m.
3. They ____make dinner____ at 6:00 p.m.
4. They ____get up____ at 7:00 a.m.
5. They ____come home____ at 5:30 p.m.
6. They ____eat breakfast____ at 7:30 a.m.

Unit 6 Lesson 1

Objectives	Grammar	Vocabulary	Correlations
On-level: Identify daily activities **Pre-level:** Recognize daily activities **Higher-level:** Talk and write about daily activities	Simple-present tense (*I take a shower at 7 a.m.*)	Everyday activities For additional vocabulary practice, see these **Oxford Picture Dictionary** topics: Daily Routines, Time	**CASAS:** 0.1.2, 0.2.4, 6.0.1, 7.4.5, 7.4.7 **LCP:** 32.01 **SCANS:** Participates as Member of a Team, Seeing Things in the Mind's Eye, Self-Management, Time **EFF:** Cooperate With Others, Listen Actively, Observe Critically, Use Math to Solve Problems and Communicate

10-15 minutes (books closed)

Warm-up and Review

1. Draw clocks with different times on the board. Have students call out the times. You can also use a wall clock, changing the time and having students call it out.

2. Write some times on the boards, and using words they have learned, tell students about your daily schedule. *I take a shower at 6:30 a.m. I come to school at 8 a.m. I eat lunch at 1 p.m.* Write only the times on the board. Then see what students remember. *What time do I eat lunch? What time do I take a shower?*

3 minutes

Introduction

1. Say: *In the morning, I take a shower; I read the newspaper; I come to school. Those are my daily activities.* Write *activities* on the board.

2. State the objective: *Today we'll talk about our daily activities.*

1 Learn everyday activity words

20-25 minutes

Presentation

A Direct students to look at the pictures and repeat the times.

B 1. Have students listen to the audio. Ask them to point to the correct picture as they listen. Circulate and monitor.

2. Check comprehension by asking *yes/no* questions. Pass out *yes/no* cards to the students (see page T-175), or have them hold up one finger for *yes* and two for *no* in order to get a nonverbal response. Ask: *Do they eat breakfast at 6 p.m.?* [no] *Do they get dressed at 11 p.m.?* [no]

C Ask students to listen and repeat the words.

15-20 minutes

Guided Practice I

D 1. Have students complete the sentences using the new vocabulary.

2. Encourage students to take turns reading the completed sentences in pairs.

Multilevel Strategies

After completing 1D, seat same-level students together and provide vocabulary practice targeted to the level of your students.

• **Pre-level** Ask these students to practice together by pointing at the pictures as you say the words.

• **On-level** Ask these students to cover the words and test each other on the vocabulary. Have one student point at the pictures while the other student says the correct word.

• **Higher-level** Ask these students to dictate the words to each other.

2 Talk about a school day

35-40 minutes
Guided Practice II

 A 1. Say: *You eat lunch every day. You take a shower every day.* Introduce the new topic: *Now let's talk about more things you do on school days.*

2. Group students and assign roles: leader, fact checker, recorder, and reporter. Explain that students work with their groups to match the words and pictures.

3. Check comprehension of the activity. Ask: *Who looks up the words in the picture dictionary?* [fact checker] *Who writes the numbers in the book?* [recorder] *Who tells the class your answers?* [reporter] *Who helps everyone and manages the group?* [leader]

4. Set a time limit (three minutes), and have students work together to complete the task. While students are working, copy the wordlist on the board.

5. Call "time" and have the reporters from each group take turns calling out the numbers for the wordlist. Record students' answers on the board. If groups disagree, write each group's choice next to the word.

Multilevel Strategies

For 2A, use mixed-level groups.

• **Pre-level** Assign these students as recorders or create a role of timekeeper (the one who lets the group know when the three minutes are up) to allow these students an active role in the group.

• **On-level** Assign these students as fact checkers and reporters.

• **Higher-level** Assign these students as leaders.

B 1. Ask students to listen and check their answers.

2. Have students correct the wordlist on the board and then write the correct numbers in their books.

3. Tell the groups from 2A to break into pairs to practice the words. Set a time limit (two minutes).

C Have students complete the sentences with the vocabulary words. Stress that they are to use their own times.

10-15 minutes
Communicative Practice and Application

D Say the sentences in 2C with your own information. Call on volunteers to say different sentences with their information. Ask students to read their sentences to a partner.

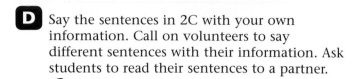

Before the *Test Yourself*, review *in the morning, in the afternoon,* and *in the evening.* Ask for a show of hands: *Who takes a shower in the morning? In the evening? Who drinks coffee in the morning? In the afternoon?*

10-15 minutes (books closed)
Evaluation

TEST YOURSELF

1. Make a three-column chart on the board with the headings *Morning, Afternoon, Evening.* Have students close their books and give you an example for each column. Have students copy the chart into their notebooks.

2. Give students five to ten minutes to test themselves by writing the words they recall.

3. Call "time" and have students check their spelling in *The Oxford Picture Dictionary* or another dictionary. Circulate and monitor.

Multilevel Strategies

Target the *Test Yourself* to the level of your students.

• **Pre-level** Have these students work with their books open.

• **Higher-level** Have these students complete the chart and then write three sentences about their daily activities.

To compress this lesson: Conduct 2A as a whole-class activity.

To extend this lesson: Pair students and have them look at the pictures in 1B and 2A. Ask them to tell their partners what time they do each of the activities.

Or have students complete **Workbook 1 page 37** and **Multilevel Activity Book 1 page 68**.

2 Talk about a school day

A Work with your classmates. Match the words with the pictures.

   8 do homework   **2** have lunch   **6** take a shower

   5 do housework   **9** go to bed   **1** walk to school

   7 drink coffee   **3** ride the bus   **4** work

B Listen and check your answers. Then practice the words with a partner.

C Complete the sentences. Use the words in the box. Use your own information to write the times.

go	have	~~take~~	do	get	come

1. I _____take_____ a shower at _Answers will vary_____.
2. I _get_____ dressed at _Answers will vary_____.
3. I _go_____ to bed at _Answers will vary_____.
4. I _come_____ home at _Answers will vary_____.
5. I _have_____ lunch at _Answers will vary_____.
6. I _do_____ homework at _Answers will vary_____.

D Read your sentences to a partner.

TEST YOURSELF ✔

Close your book. Write the activities you do in the morning, afternoon, and evening. Check your spelling in a dictionary.

LESSON 2 **LESSON 2** **Life stories**

1 Read about a work schedule

A Look at the pictures. Listen.

B Listen again. Read the sentences.

1. My name is Tina Aziz. I work in a doctor's office.
2. This is my work schedule. I work from 9 a.m. to 5 p.m., Monday to Thursday.
3. I turn on the computer and copy machine at 9:00. I answer the phone all day.
4. At noon, I meet my friend. We have lunch and talk.
5. On Fridays, I don't work. I relax. I take my kids to the park.
6. I like my job and my schedule a lot, but Fridays are my favorite day.

C Check your understanding. Circle *a* or *b*.

1. Tina works ___a___ .
   a. four days a week
   b. on Saturday

2. She answers the phone ___b___ .
   a. at 9 a.m.
   b. all day

3. Tina and her friend have lunch ___b___ .
   a. at 11 a.m.
   b. at 12 p.m.

4. She likes her job ___a___ .
   a. a lot
   b. a little

☑ Describe and report on schedules

Unit 6 Lesson 2

Objectives	Grammar	Vocabulary	Correlations
On-, Pre-, and Higher-level: Read and write about work schedules	Simple-present tense (*I work on Saturday.*)	Housework words, *schedule* For additional vocabulary practice, see these **Oxford Picture Dictionary** topics: The Calendar, Housework	**CASAS:** 0.1.2, 0.2.4, 6.0.1, 7.4.7, 8.2.3 **LCPs:** 32.01, 32.02, 32.13 **SCANS:** Responsibility, Seeing Things in the Mind's Eye, Writing **EFF:** Convey Ideas in Writing, Listen Actively, Observe Critically, Reflect and Evaluate

10-15 minutes (books closed)

Warm-up and Review

Write *Workday* and *Day Off* on the board. Tell students about your schedule: compare and contrast what you do on your days off versus workdays. Ask your working students: *What time do you get up on workdays? On your days off? Where do you eat lunch on your workdays? On your days off?* If your students don't work, contrast school days with days off. For parents, ask about children's lunch and school schedules.

5 minutes

Introduction

1. Write some of your schedule information in each column on the board. Say: *This is my workday schedule. This is my day-off schedule.* Write *schedule* on the board.

2. State the objective: *Today we're going to read and write about our schedules.*

1 Read about a work schedule

20-25 minutes

Presentation I

A 1. Direct students to look at the pictures. Ask students to tell you what they see in each picture.

2. Play the audio.

B 1. Play the audio again. Have students read along silently.

2. Check students' comprehension. Ask: *Is Tina a doctor?* [no] *Does she work in the evening?* [no]

10 minutes

Guided Practice I

C Have students circle the correct letters to complete the sentences. Ask volunteers to read the sentences aloud. Write the answers on the board.

Multilevel Strategies

After 1C, replay the audio for 1B.

• **Pre-level** Ask these students to read 1B silently while they listen again. Then have them take turns reading the sentences in 1C with a partner.

• **On- and Higher-level** Write the following questions on the board for these students to answer: *What is Tina's job?* [She works in a doctor's office.] *Do you like Tina's job? Why is Friday her favorite day?* [She doesn't go to work.]

2 Write about your schedule

20-25 minutes
Guided Practice II

 1. Pronounce and clarify the *Need help?* phrases. Ask for a show of hands about each activity. *Do you go to the park on your day off?*

2. Copy the sentences on the board. Read them aloud with your own information (change *study* to *teach*).

3. Have students complete the sentences independently. Circulate and assist.

> ### Multilevel Strategies
>
> Adapt 2A to the level of your students.
>
> • **Pre-level** Group these students and read the sentences one at a time. Elicit different answers from the group, and direct students to write in the completion. Assist before moving on to the next sentence.
>
> • **Higher-level** While you are working with the pre-level students, ask these students to copy the sentences into their notebooks. Ask them to include two or three more sentences about their work activities or their ways of relaxing.

B Ask students to read their sentences to a partner.

3 Talk about a work schedule

20-25 minutes
Presentation II

 1. Introduce the topic: *Now we're going to listen to a work schedule.* Direct students to look at the picture in 3A. Ask: *Where does Mel work?* [a supermarket]

2. Read and have students repeat the activities. Ask if there are questions about the vocabulary.

3. Ask students to put their pencils down and point to the activities as they hear them. Play the entire audio once.

3. Play the audio in segments. After the "morning" section, stop the audio and check answers with the students: *How many activities did you check?* If necessary, repeat that segment of the audio before moving on.

4. Check students' listening accuracy: *Does Mel mop the floor?* [yes] *Does he vacuum?* [no]

10–15 minutes
Guided Practice

B Play the audio again, and have students complete Mel's work schedule.

C Have students read along silently while they listen. Play the audio again, and have students repeat the conversation. Replay if necessary.

10 minutes
Communicative Practice and Application

D 1. Model the conversation with a volunteer. Then model it again with your own information.

2. Set a time limit (five minutes). Ask students to practice the conversation with several partners. Ask volunteers to present their conversations to the class.

10-15 minutes (books closed)
Evaluation

TEST YOURSELF

Ask a volunteer to tell you his/her schedule. Write it on the board as a model. Erase the model before students begin.

> ### Multilevel Strategies
>
> Target the *Test Yourself* to the level of your students.
>
> • **Pre-level** Allow these students to write about their own schedules rather than listening to a partner.

To compress this lesson: Have students practice the conversation in 3D with only one partner.

To extend this lesson: Brainstorm additional work activities and write them on a poster for students to refer to during the rest of the unit.

Or have students complete **Workbook 1 page 38** and **Multilevel Activity Book 1 page 69**.

2 Write about your schedule

A Write about your schedule. Complete the sentences.

I go to school from _____ to _____.

I study _____ at school.

On _____, I relax.

I _____.

Need help?

Ways to relax
go to the park
watch TV
listen to music
talk to friends and family
take a walk

B Read your story to a partner.

3 Talk about a work schedule

A Listen and check (✔) the activities you hear.

✔ 1. mop the floor

____ 2. vacuum the rug

✔ 3. answer the phone

✔ 4. wash the windows

____ 5. turn on the copy machine

✔ 6. help the manager

Mel at work

B Listen again. Complete Mel's work schedule.

MORNING 10 A.M.–12 P.M.	AFTERNOON 12 P.M.–3 P.M.
1. _mop the floor_	3. _help the manager_
2. _wash the windows_	4. _answer the phone_

C Listen and repeat.

A: I work on Saturday and Sunday. How about you?

B: I don't work.

A: I go to school from Monday to Friday. How about you?

B: I go to school on Monday and Wednesday.

D Work with a partner. Practice the conversation. Use your own information.

TEST YOURSELF ✔

Close your book. Listen to your partner's schedule for the week. Write the schedule you hear.

1 Learn the simple present

A Look at the pictures. Read the sentences. What time does she leave for work? She leaves for work at 8:00 a.m.

She exercises
at 6:00 a.m.

She has breakfast
at 7:15 a.m.

She brushes her teeth
at 7:30 a.m.

She leaves the house
at 8:00 a.m.

B Study the charts. Complete the sentences below.

THE SIMPLE PRESENT

Statements			
I You	exercise.	We You	exercise.
He She	exercise**s**.	They	

1. He ___exercises___ .   2. We ___exercise___ .

Negative statements				Contractions

I
You
	do not exercise.	We
		You
			do not exercise.	do not = don't
				  I don't exercise.
				does not = doesn't
				  He doesn't exercise.

He She	does not exercise.	They		

3. You ___do not___ exercise.   4. They do not ___exercise___ .

C Complete the sentences. Use the words in the box.

~~rides~~   gets   don't   doesn't

1. She _____rides_____ the bus every day.
2. He __gets_____ up at 6 a.m.
3. She __doesn't_____ drink coffee.
4. They __don't_____ have breakfast every morning.

D Read the sentences to a partner.

☑ Use the simple present to talk about daily routines

Unit 6 Lesson 3

Objectives	Grammar	Vocabulary	Correlations
On- and Higher-level: Use the simple present to talk about daily activities **Pre-level:** Recognize the simple present in statements about daily activities	Simple-present tense (*She gets up at 7:00. He doesn't work.*)	Everyday activities For additional vocabulary practice, see these **Oxford Picture Dictionary** topics: Daily Routines, Time	**CASAS:** 0.1.2, 0.2.4, 3.5.4, 3.5.5, 6.0.1, 7.4.7, 8.1.1 **LCPs:** 32.01, 32.13, 33.02 **SCANS:** Self-Management, Speaking **EFF:** Speak So Others Can Understand, Reflect and Evaluate

10-15 minutes (books closed)

Warm-up and Review

Write different times on cards: *7 a.m., 10 a.m., 12 p.m., 3 p.m., 5 p.m., 7 p.m., 9 p.m., 11 p.m.* Pass out the cards to eight students. Ask the students to stand and put themselves in order. Then ask them to make a statement about what they do every day at that time. Model with 7 a.m. After each student speaks, ask a student in the "audience": *What does he/she do at 7 a.m.?*

5-10 minutes

Introduction

1. Write the names of the students from the warm-up on the board. Elicit the correct activity and time to go with each student and write a third-person sentence.

2. State the objective: *Today we'll learn to use the simple-present tense to talk about our daily activities.*

1 Learn the simple present

20-25 minutes

Presentation I

A Direct students to look at the pictures. Read and have students repeat the captions. Elicit the answer to the question.

B 1. Demonstrate how to read the grammar charts as complete sentences. Read the chart through sentence by sentence. Then read it again, and have students repeat after you.

2. Use the pictures in 1A to illustrate points in the grammar charts. Ask students what happens if you change the subject to *I*. Demonstrate how to make the sentences negative.

3. As a class, complete the sentences under the charts. Ask volunteers to write the sentences on the board. Have other students read the sentences aloud.

4. Give students time to silently review the charts and, if they haven't already, fill in the blanks.

5. Assess students' understanding of the charts. Elicit negatives of the sentences from the warm-up by asking other students for information. Ask students to help you write a negative sentence. Point to the verb. Ask: *Do I use the s form with* doesn't?

15-20 minutes

Guided Practice

C Have students work individually to complete the sentences with the words in the box.

Multilevel Strategies

For 1C, seat same-level students together.

• **Pre-level** While other students are completing 1C, ask pre-level students to copy the sentences from 1B into their notebooks. Give them time to copy the answers to 1C after they are written on the board in 1D.

• **On- and Higher-level** Have these students write three to five additional sentences using the phrases from the Warm-up.

D Ask students to read their sentences to a partner. Call on individuals to write the completed sentences on the board.

2 Ask and answer information questions

5 minutes

Presentation II

A Have students repeat the questions and answers in the chart with a partner.

10-15 minutes

Guided Practice

B Have students work individually to complete the questions and answers.

> ### Multilevel Strategies
>
> Group pre-level students for 2A and 2B.
>
> • **Pre-level** While other students are completing 2B, read the questions in the chart in 2A to pre-level students and have them respond by reading the answers. Then have students cover their charts. Ask the questions with *I, he,* and *she,* and have students respond without looking in the book.
>
> • **On- and Higher-level** While you are working with the pre-level students, have these students complete 2B and take turns reading the questions and answers with a partner. Ask students to write an original question and answer. Have volunteers write the answers to 2B and their own creations on the board.

3 Practice questions about your day

20-25 minutes

Communicative Practice and Application

A 1. Draw the chart on the board and fill in your own information.

2. Elicit other possible answers.

3. Give students time (three minutes) to fill in their own information.

B 1. Model the interview with a volunteer. On the board, show where to chart the answers.

2. Check comprehension. Ask: *Do you write your partner's answers?* [yes]

3. Set a time limit (five minutes) for students to interview their partners. Circulate and monitor.

C Discuss the class's answers. Ask volunteers to share information about themselves and their partners.

> ### Multilevel Strategies
>
> After 3C, provide more practice with third-person sentences. Have students look again at the pictures in Lesson 1 or use the pictures on page 74 of *Multilevel Activity Book 1.*
>
> • **Pre-level** Have these students use the pictures to say first-person sentences.
>
> • **On-level** Have students say third-person sentences about the pictures.
>
> • **Higher-level** Have students ask and answer third-person questions about the pictures.

10-15 minutes (books closed)

Evaluation

TEST YOURSELF

Write these skeleton sentences on the board: *I _____ every day. I don't _____ every day.* Ask students to write the sentences independently. Collect and correct their writing.

To compress this lesson: Conduct 2B as a whole-class activity.

To extend this lesson: Give students more practice talking about daily routines using the simple present.
1. Pair students. Have them look at the pictures of daily routines (see the topic Daily Routines in *The Oxford Picture Dictionary*). Teach any new vocabulary.
2. Tell partners to take turns making statements about the pictures. Have more advanced students ask and answer questions using *What time does he/she _____?* and *What time do they _____?*
Or have students complete **Workbook 1 pages 39–40** and **Multilevel Activity Book 1 page 70**.

2 Ask and answer information questions

A Study the chart. Work with a partner. Ask and answer the questions.

Information questions and answers	
A: When do you exercise? **B:** I exercise every day.	**A:** When does he exercise? **B:** He exercises every Saturday.
A: When does she exercise? **B:** She exercises at 6 a.m.	**A:** When do they exercise? **B:** They exercise in the evening.

B Circle the correct word in the questions. Complete the answers.

1. **A:** When ((do)/ does) you get up?

   B: I ___get up___ at 6:30 a.m.

2. **A:** When ((do)/ does) they study?

   B: They ___study___ every day.

3. **A:** When does (you /(she)) exercise?

   B: She ___exercises___ in the morning.

4. **A:** When (do /(does)) Joe work?

   B: He ___works___ every weekend*.

5. **A:** When does Ruby ((cook)/ cooks)?

   B: She ___cooks___ every evening.

6. **A:** When ((do)/ does) you study?

   B: I study ___Answers will vary___.

*weekend = Saturday and Sunday

3 Practice questions about your day

A Write your answers in the chart.

Questions	My answers	My partner's answers
1. When do you get up?		
2. When do you leave the house?		
3. When do you come home?		
4. When do you make dinner?		

B Interview a partner. Write your partner's answers in the chart.

C Talk about the answers in the chart with your class.

I get up at 6 a.m. Ruby gets up at 7:30.

TEST YOURSELF ✔

Close your book. Write 3 activities you do every day and 3 activities you don't do every day.

1 Learn about office machines and equipment

A Look at the pictures. Read the sentences. Then answer the questions about your classroom. Answers will vary.

1

Turn on the computer.
Push this button.

2

Turn off the printer.
Push this button.

3

Fill the copy machine.
Put the paper here.

4

Fill the stapler.
Put the staples here.

1. Is there a copy machine in your classroom? <u>No, there isn't.</u>

2. Are there any computers? _____

3. Is there a printer? _____

4. How many staplers are there? _____

B Listen and read.

A: Ms. Barns, can you help me?
B: Yes, Mr. Glenn.
A: How do I turn on the computer?
B: Push this button.
A: Thanks for your help, Ms. Barns.
B: That's my job, Mr. Glenn. That's my job.

PRINCIPAL GLENN

C Listen again and repeat.

D Work with a partner. Practice the conversation. Use the information from 1A.

A: _____, can you help me?
B: Yes, _____.
A: How do I _____?
B: _____.
A: Thanks for your help.

Unit 6 Lesson 4

Objectives	Grammar	Vocabulary	Correlations
On- and Higher-level: Ask and answer questions about using office machines and equipment **Pre-level:** Ask questions about using office machines and equipment	Simple-present tense (*He mops the floor.*)	Office equipment For additional vocabulary practice, see these **Oxford Picture Dictionary** topics: Housework, An Office	**CASAS:** 0.1.2, 0.1.3, 0.2.4, 1.7.3, 4.5.1, 4.5.4, 4.5.7, 4.6.1 **LCPs:** 19.02, 21.01, 22.03, 32.01, 32.02, 32.03, 34.01, 34.02, 34.03 **SCANS:** Acquires and Evaluates Information, Speaking, Sociability **EFF:** Cooperate With Others, Listen Actively, Speak So Others Can Understand

10-15 minutes (books closed)

Warm-up and Review

Divide the class into two teams. Write *In the Classroom* on the board. Ask students to approach the board one at a time and write the name of one item in the classroom. The next person must write a different item. Allow students to approach with a partner if they feel more comfortable. Assign a time limit (two minutes). When time is up, the team with the most items is the winner. Read that list aloud and have students repeat the words. Look at the list from the other team. If there is anything not mentioned by the winning team, read those words aloud. Correct spelling.

5 minutes

Introduction

1. Referring to the words from the warm-up, say: *These things are in the classroom. Which ones are in an office, too?* Go through the items, and erase anything that you would probably not find in an office.

2. State the objective: *Today we'll learn about more things in an office.*

1 Learn about office machines and equipment

20-30 minutes

Presentation

A Direct students to look at the pictures. Read and have students repeat the captions. Give students a minute to answer the questions. Go over the answers as a class.

20-25 minutes

Guided Practice

B 1. Direct students to look at the picture. Ask: *Where are they?*

2. Play the audio, and ask students to read along silently.

C Play the audio again, and have students repeat the conversation. Replay if necessary.

15-20 minutes

Communicative Practice and Application

D 1. Model the conversation with a volunteer, using information from 1A. Then model it again with different information from 1A.

2. Elicit other ways to complete the conversation.

3. Set a time limit (five minutes). Ask students to practice the conversation with several partners.

Multilevel Strategies

For 1D, adapt the oral practice to the level of your students.

• **Pre-level** Have these students read the conversation as written in 1B.

• **Higher-level** Ask these students to create an original conversation. Have volunteers act out the conversation using items in the classroom. For example, *How do I use the pencil sharpener? How do I turn on the projector? How do I turn on the calculator/translator? How do I open the file cabinet?* Allow them to be silly, *How do I use the pen?*

1. Direct students to look at the pictures and name the items.

2. Play the audio, and have students write the correct number under each picture. Go over the answers as a class.

TIP

Write your own activities on the board (*I come to school. I make copies. I write on the board. I open the door. I teach my class.*). Have the students help you change the sentences to third person. Ask volunteers to read the sentences. Correct pronunciation of the *s* form.

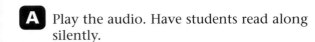

2 Practice your pronunciation

10-15 minutes

Pronunciation Extension

A Play the audio. Have students read along silently.

Read and have students repeat the sentences in the chart.

TIP

Point out that the words in the *"iz"* column have an extra syllable. Write the simple form of each verb alongside the *s* form on the board: *close, closes.* Pronounce each form, clapping for the syllables. Contrast this with *help/helps* and *fill/fills.* Write *watch, watches* and *push, pushes,* and have students clap out the syllables.

C 1. Direct students to look at the pictures. Elicit a sentence for each picture.

2. Have students take turns talking about the pictures with a partner. Tell them to listen for their partners' pronunciation of the *s.*

10-15 minutes

Evaluation

TEST YOURSELF

1. Model the role-play with a volunteer. Then change roles.

2. Pair students. Check comprehension. Ask all Partner A's to raise their hands. Ask: *Are you asking for help?* [yes]

3. Set a time limit (five minutes), and have the partners act out the role-play in both roles.

4. Circulate and monitor. Encourage pantomime and improvisation.

5. Provide feedback.

Multilevel Strategies

Target the *Test Yourself* to the level of your students.

• **Pre-level** While other students are practicing the role-play, have these students read sentences you have written on the board. For example, they can use the sentences from the Tip above.

To compress this lesson: Have students practice the conversation in 1D with only one partner.

To extend this lesson: Have students order scrambled work routines for various professions.
1. Put a job title and a list of activities on the board. An example is:
   Waitress
   A. *She gives the order to the cook.*
   B. *She takes the money.*
   C. *She talks to the customers.*
   D. *She writes the order.*
   E. *She brings the food.*
2. Pantomime the sentences and clarify as necessary.
3. Ask students to put the sentences in order.
4. Elicit the order and number the sentences. [C=1, D=2, A=3, E=4, B=5]
5. Tell students to copy the sentences into their notebooks in the correct order.

Or have students complete **Workbook 1 page 41** and **Multilevel Activity Book 1 page 71**.

E Listen and match. Write the number under the picture.

_3_

_2_

_1_

_4_

2 Practice your pronunciation

A Listen to the sentences.

"s"	"z"	"iz"
He help**s** customers.	He fill**s** the stapler.	He clos**es** the store.
She count**s** the money.	She clean**s** offices.	She wash**es** windows.
It print**s**.	It copi**es**.	It us**es** staples.

B Read the sentences in the chart.

C Work with a partner. Talk about Miguel's work routine. Answers will vary.

He works at the supermarket. He opens the store.

1

2

3

4

5

6

TEST YOURSELF ✔

Work with a partner. Partner A: Ask for help with an office machine.
Partner B: Help your partner. Then change roles.

1 Get ready to read

A **Look at the pictures. Read the words.**

He sleeps <u>a little</u>.

He sleeps <u>a lot</u>.

B **Think about your daily routine. Check (✔) the boxes.**

	I work …	I study …	I sleep …	I relax …	I exercise …
a little					
a lot					

C **Talk about your daily routine with your classmates. Use the chart.**

I work a lot.

2 Read about daily routines in the U.S.

A **Read the article.**

WHERE DOES THE TIME GO?

Many people in the U.S. work a lot and relax a little. Here's what people say about their daily routines.

They sleep for seven or eight hours.

[1] get ready: the things you do before you leave home every day

They get ready[1] for work for one hour. They walk, drive, or ride to work for twenty-five minutes. They work for eight or nine hours. They do housework for one or two hours every day. Then they have free time. They relax for two or three hours. They read, spend time with family, or watch TV.

Where does the time go? Now you know!

Source: *The NPD Group, Inc.*

B **Listen and read the article again.**

✔ Identify personal, family, and work responsibilities; interpret graphs

Unit 6 Lesson 5

Objectives	Grammar	Vocabulary	Correlations
On- and Higher-level: Read about and discuss daily routines in the U.S. and interpret a graph on housework **Pre-level:** Read about daily routines in the U.S. and interpret a graph on housework	Simple-present tense (*I work a lot.*)	Routines, housework words, *get ready* For additional vocabulary practice, see these **Oxford Picture Dictionary** topics: Daily Routines, Housework, Time	**CASAS:** 0.1.2, 0.2.4, 1.1.3, 7.2.5, 7.2.6, 8.2.3 **LCPs:** 32.01, 32.02, 32.04, 32.05, 32.06, 32.13 **SCANS:** Arithmetic/Mathematics, Interprets and Communicates Information, Reading **EFF:** Listen Actively, Observe Critically, Read With Understanding

10-15 minutes (books closed)

Warm-up and Review

Write Me and *My Husband/Wife* (*Roommate, Partner, Daughter,* etc) on the board. Tell students about work you do around the house and work someone else does. (*I cook dinner. He/She washes the dishes. I take the children to school. He/She goes shopping. I wash the car. He/She cleans the living room.*) Write your sentences in the correct column. Ask volunteers to tell about who does what in their homes.

5 minutes

Introduction

1. Ask students to put a star next to the jobs on the board they like doing.

2. State the objective: *Today we're going to read about daily routines in the U.S.*

1 Get ready to read

15-20 minutes

Presentation

A 1. Direct students to look at the pictures. Ask about the first man: *Is he tired?* [yes]

2. Read the captions. Ask students: *Do you sleep a little? Do you sleep a lot?*

B 1. Copy the chart on the board, and check the boxes to represent your information. Tell students about yourself.

2. Give student a couple of minutes to check the boxes in their charts.

C Ask volunteers to discuss the information in their charts.

Pre-Reading

Direct students to look at the title and the picture in 2A. Pantomime someone running out of time. Have students repeat the title: *Where does the time go?*

2 Read about daily routines in the U.S.

25-30 minutes

Guided Practice I

A 1. Ask students to read the article silently.

2. Ask if there are any questions about the reading.

3. Draw students' attention to the footnote. Elicit examples of getting ready for work (taking a shower, brushing hair, etc.).

B Play the audio. Have students read along silently.

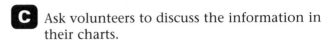

> Make a chart on the board with the verbs from the article. Elicit the correct number of hours to put next to each activity.
>
> *sleep* [seven to eight]
> *get ready for work* [one]
> *walk, drive, or ride to work* [25 minutes]
> *work* [eight to nine]
> *do housework* [one to two]
> *relax* [two to three]

C 1. Ask students to work individually to mark the sentences *true* or *false*.

2. Go over the answers as a class. Write them on the board. Note that students may have different opinions about whether relaxing two or three hours every day is a lot or a little.

Multilevel Strategies

Group pre-level students for 2C and 2D.

• **Pre-level** While other students are completing 2C and 2D, have these students read the article in 2A again and listen to the audio. Give them time to copy the answers to 2C and 2D from the board.

D Have students work individually to complete the sentences. Write the answers on the board.

3 Read about housework

15-20 minutes

Guided Practice II

A 1. Direct students to look at the graph. Ask: *Is red for women or men?* [women]

2. Show students how to read the bar graph: *Look at* cook *and* clean the kitchen. *Who cooks and cleans for seven hours?* [women] *Who cooks and cleans for three and a half hours?* [men]

3. Give students a minute to look at the graph and answer the questions. Go over the answers as a class.

TIP Make a transparency of the graph to help you demonstrate to students how to read it.

B 1. Read the questions and set a time limit (three minutes). Tell students to think about or write the answers.

2. Call on volunteers to share their answers.

5-10 minutes

Application

BRING IT TO LIFE

Students can find pictures of actions by typing the verbs into an Internet image search engine. If your students don't have magazines or computers at home, try to provide everyone with a magazine to take home and look through.

TIP Ask your doctor, dentist, and hairdresser/ barber if they'd be willing to donate their old waiting-room magazines to your classroom.

To compress this lesson: Assign 2D as homework.

To extend this lesson: Do a dictation.
1. Dictate first- and third-person sentences in the present tense. *I clean the bedroom. She cleans the living room. He makes lunch. I make dinner.*
2. Ask volunteers to write the sentences on the board. Ask other volunteers to read them aloud.

Or have students complete **Workbook 1 page 42** and **Multilevel Activity Book 1 page 72**.

C Mark the sentences T (true) or F (false).

__T__ 1. Many people do housework every day.

__F__ 2. People don't walk or drive to work.

__F__ 3. Many people get ready for work for two or three hours every day.

__T__ 4. Many people in the U.S. don't relax a lot.

D Complete the sentences. Use the words in the box.

do housework   relax   ~~sleep~~   work

1. People _____ sleep _____ for seven or eight hours every day.
2. People __work_____ for eight or nine hours every day.
3. People __relax_____ for two or three hours every day.
4. People __do housework_____ for one to two hours every day.

3 Read about housework

A Look at the graph. Complete the sentences.

1. __Women_____ cook and clean the kitchen for seven hours every week.
2. Men work in the yard for __3_____ hours every week.

B Think about the graph. Talk about the answers with your class.

1. What kinds of housework do men do a lot? What do they do a little?
2. What kinds of housework do women do a lot? What do women do a little?

BRING IT TO LIFE

Find pictures of everyday activities. Look in newspapers, magazines, or on the Internet. Bring the pictures to class. Talk about them with your classmates.

1 Grammar

A Circle *a* or *b*.

1. I _____ lunch at noon.
   a. have
   b. has

2. Marvin _____ breakfast every day.
   a. have
   b. has

3. Kayla _____ have any free time today.
   a. don't
   b. doesn't

4. Lev and Min _____ have class on Saturday.
   a. don't
   b. doesn't

Grammar note

have

I
You   have free time.
We   don't have free time.
They

He   has free time.
She   doesn't have free time.

B Match the questions with the answers.

_b_ 1. When do they have lunch?

_d_ 2. Where do they eat dinner?

_a_ 3. When does John have lunch?

_e_ 4. When does Kyle make breakfast?

_c_ 5. Does Don eat breakfast?

a. He has lunch at noon.

b. They have lunch in the afternoon.

c. Yes, he does.

d. They eat at home.

e. He makes breakfast at 7 a.m.

C Write the questions. Use *When*.

1. **A:** _When does she walk to school?_
   B: She walks to school every afternoon.

2. **A:** _When do you clean the kitchen?_
   B: I clean the kitchen every Saturday.

3. **A:** _When do they go to the park?_
   B: They go to the park every weekend.

4. **A:** _When does he ride the bus?_
   B: He rides the bus every day.

5. **A:** _When do you/we relax?_
   B: We relax every weekend.

Unit 6 Review and expand

Objectives	Grammar	Vocabulary	Correlations
On-, Pre-, and Higher-level: Expand upon and review unit grammar and life skills	Simple-present tense questions and answers *(When does he clean the house? He cleans the house on Saturday.)*	Daily activities For additional vocabulary practice, see this **Oxford Picture Dictionary** topic: Daily Routines	**CASAS:** 0.1.2, 0.2.4, 1.7.3, 4.5.1, 4.5.4, 4.5.7, 4.6.1, 4.8.1, 6.0.1, 7.2.6, 7.2.7, 7.3.1 **LCPs:** 19.02, 21.01, 32.01, 32.02, 32.05, 32.13, 33.02 **SCANS:** Creative Thinking, Cooperate With Others, Problem Solving **EFF:** Convey Ideas in Writing, Solve Problems and Make Decisions

10-15 minutes (books closed)

Warm-up and Review

1. Review the *Bring It to Life* assignment from Lesson 5.

2. Have students who collected pictures share them and talk about them. Bring extra pictures for students who didn't find their own.

3. Write any new verbs on the board. Use them in first-person and third-person sentences.

5-10 minutes

Introduction and Presentation

1. Choose one or two of the students' pictures, and put them on the board. Write third-person present-tense questions and sentences about the pictures. *When does he eat breakfast? He eats breakfast every morning.* Use a time marker, such as *every day* or *every Saturday,* to clarify the meaning of the present tense.

2. For every affirmative sentence on the board, write a negative sentence. *He doesn't eat eggs for breakfast.*

3. State the objective: *Today we're going to use present-tense questions and answers to talk about daily activities.*

1 Grammar

40-45 minutes

Guided Practice

A 1. Read the *Grammar note* aloud as complete sentences. Have students repeat.

2. Ask students to work individually to circle the correct choices to complete the sentences. Ask volunteers to read the completed sentences aloud.

B 1. Have students work individually to match the questions and answers.

2. Call on volunteers to read the matching questions and answers. Write the number-letter match on the board.

Multilevel Strategies

For 1B, seat same-level students together.

• **Pre-level** Read the questions in 1B, and have these students locate the correct answer. Have them repeat the question and answer.

• **On- and Higher-level** While you are working with the pre-level students, have these students complete 1C and write their questions on the board.

C Have students work individually to write the questions. Ask volunteers to write the questions on the board.

Multilevel Strategies

After 1C, leave same-level students together.

• **Pre-level** Have these students copy the answers to 1C from the board. Ask them to read the questions and answers with a partner.

• **On- and Higher-level** Ask these students to write two or three more questions and answers. Have them use the pictures from the warm-up. Post the pictures and sentences in the classroom.

2 Group work

20-35 minutes

Communicative Practice

 A 1. Direct students, in groups of three or four, to focus on the pictures on page 65. Ask: *Does she ride the bus?* [yes] *Does she walk to school in the evening?* [no]

2. Set a time limit (five minutes) to complete the activity. Circulate and answer any questions.

3. Have a reporter from each group read the group's sentences to the class.

> ## Multilevel Strategies
>
> For 2A and 2B, use same-level groups.
>
> • **Pre-level** For 2A, ask these students to write three vocabulary words and one complete sentence. After 2B, allow pre-level students to ask and answer the questions without writing.
>
> • **Higher-level** For 2A, ask these students to write two additional sentences about the picture. After 2B, have students ask and answer the following questions: *When do you clean the house? When do you do homework? When do you eat breakfast?*

B 1. Have students work in the same groups from 2A to take turns interviewing each other in pairs.

2. Set a time limit (five minutes) to complete the activity.

3. Tell students to make a note of their partners' answers but not to worry about writing complete sentences.

C Have a reporter from each group talk about the group's work.

20-25 minutes

 A 1. Direct students to look at the picture. Ask: *Where is he?* [in an office] *What's that?* [a copy machine] Tell students they will read a story about a man with a problem at work. Direct students to read Nick's story silently. Then play the audio, and have them read along silently.

2. Ask: *Is this a new job for Nick?* [yes] *Does Nick answer the phones?* [yes] *Does Nick understand the copy machine?* [no]

B 1. Read the question and identify the problem. Read the possible solutions.

2. Elicit student ideas for other solutions. Write each one on the board.

3. Discuss whether the statements are appropriate.

4. Ask for a show of hands to see which solution the class likes best.

C Elicit the students' ideas for what Nick can say, and write them on the board—for example, *Can you help me, please? I don't understand the copy machine.* Tell students to copy the expressions into their notebooks.

> Have students practice asking each other for help with class work. *Can you help me, please? I don't understand this exercise.*

10-15 minutes

Evaluation

To test students' understanding of the unit grammar and life skills, have them take the Unit 6 Test in the *Step Forward Test Generator CD-ROM with ExamView® Assessment Suite.*

Learning Log

To help students record and discuss their progress, use the Learning Log on page T-177.

To extend this review: Have students complete **Workbook 1 page 43** and **Multilevel Activity Book 1 pages 73–76**.

2 Group work

A Work with 2–3 classmates. Write 5 questions and answers about the pictures on page 65. Talk about the sentences with your class. Answers will vary.

When does she walk to school?
She walks to school in the morning.

When does she go to bed?
She goes to bed at night.

B Interview 3 classmates. Write their answers in your notebook.

ASK:

1. When do you get up?
2. When do you have lunch?
3. When do you relax with your family and friends?

> *Classmate—Lara*
> *1.at 6 a.m.*
> *2.in the afternoon*
> *3.every evening*

C Talk about the answers with your class.

PROBLEM SOLVING

A Listen and read about Nick. What is his problem? He doesn't know how to use the copy machine.

Today is Nick's first day at his new job. He works at a bank. He answers the phones and works at a computer. Nick's manager says, "Make 100 copies and staple them for me." Nick doesn't understand the directions on the copy machine.

B Work with your classmates. Answer the question. (More than one answer is possible.)

What can Nick do?
- (a.) Ask another person to make the copies.
- (b.) Ask the manager for help.
- c. Open and close all the copy machine doors.
- (d.) Other: Answers will vary.

C Work with your classmates. Make a list of things Nick can say.

UNIT 7

Shop and Spend

FOCUS ON
- money and shopping
- clothing
- simple present *yes/no* questions
- expressing needs and wants
- ATMs and personal checks

LESSON 1 **Vocabulary**

1 Learn money words

A **Look at the pictures. What's the total of the cash?** $6.41

B **Listen and look at the pictures.**

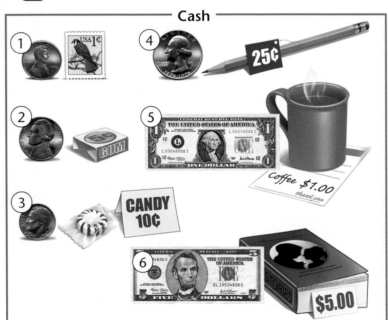

C **Listen and repeat the words.**

1. penny	3. dime	5. one-dollar bill	7. check
2. nickel	4. quarter	6. five-dollar bill	8. money order

D **Look at the pictures. Complete the sentences.**

1. The pencil is 25¢. Pay with a __quarter__.
2. The gum is 5¢. Pay with a __nickel__.
3. The candy is 10¢. Pay with a __dime__.
4. The stamp is 1¢. Pay with a __penny__.

5. The rent is $300. Pay with a __check/money__ order
6. The book is $5. Pay with a __five-dollar bill__.
7. The gas bill is $45. Pay with a __check/money__ order
8. The coffee is $1. Pay with a __one-dollar bill__.

76 ☑ Count and use currency; identify clothing items

Unit 7 Lesson 1

Objectives	Grammar	Vocabulary	Correlations
On-level: Identify currency and clothing items **Pre-level:** Recognize currency and clothing items **Higher-level:** Talk and write about currency and clothing items	How much, how many (*How much is the skirt? How many customers are there?*)	Currency and clothing For additional vocabulary practice, see these **Oxford Picture Dictionary** topics: Everyday Clothes, Casual, Work and Formal Clothing, Money, Shoes and Accessories	**CASAS:** 0.1.2, 1.1.6, 1.2.1, 1.2.4, 1.3.9, 6.0.1–6.0.4, 6.1.1, 7.4.5, 7.4.7 **LCPs:** 25.01, 25.05, 25.06, 28.02, 32.01, 32.02 **SCANS:** Arithmetic/Mathematics, Participates as member of a team, Self-management **EFF:** Cooperate with others, Use math to solve problems and communicate

Warm-up and Review

10–15 minutes (books closed)

Bring several clothing items to class, and display them in the front of the room. Include something inexpensive, like a pair of socks, and something more expensive, like a coat. Elicit the names of the items, and write them on the board. Ask students to guess prices of the items, or write prices on the board, and have students match the price with the correct item.

Introduction

5 minutes

A 1. Say and have students repeat the prices and the clothing words on the board.

2. State the objective: *Today we're going to learn words for money and clothing.*

1 Learn money words

Presentation

20–25 minutes

A Direct students to look at the pictures. Ask: *Which one is ten cents?* [three] *Which one is one cent?* [one]

B 1. Have students listen to the audio. Ask them to point to the correct picture as they listen. Circulate and monitor.

2. Check comprehension by asking *yes/no* questions. Pass out *yes/no* cards to the students (see page T-175), or have them hold up one finger for *yes* and two for *no* in order to get a nonverbal response. Point to the pictures, and ask: *Is this a penny? Is this a money order?*

C Ask students to listen and repeat the words.

TIP After 1C, refer to the clothing and prices from the warm-up, and have students raise their *yes/no* cards. *Do I pay for the socks with a money order? Do I pay for the socks with a five-dollar bill?*

Guided Practice I

15–20 minutes

D 1. Have students complete the sentences using the new vocabulary.

2. Encourage students to take turns reading the completed sentences in pairs.

Multilevel Strategies

After completing 1D, seat same-level students together, and provide vocabulary practice targeted to the level of your students.

• **Pre-level** Ask these students to practice together by pointing to the pictures in 1B and saying the correct words.

• **On-level** Ask these students to cover the words and test each other on the vocabulary. Have one student point to the pictures while the other student says the correct word.

• **Higher-level** Ask these students to dictate the words to each other.

2 Talk about clothes

Guided Practice II

35–40 minutes

 1. Review the clothing and prices from the warm-up. *How much is the coat? How much are the socks? Now let's talk about other clothes.*

2. Group students and assign roles: leader, fact checker, recorder, and reporter. Explain that students work with their groups to match the words and pictures.

3. Check comprehension of the exercise. Ask: *Who looks up the words in the picture dictionary?* [fact checker] *Who writes the numbers in the book?* [recorder] *Who tells the class your answers?* [reporter] *Who helps everyone and manages the group?* [leader]

4. Set a time limit (three minutes), and have students work together to complete the task. While students are working, copy the wordlist on the board.

5. Call "time" and have the reporters from each group take turns calling out the numbers for the wordlist. Record students' answers on the board. If groups disagree, write each group's choice next to the word.

B 1. Ask students to listen and check the answers.

2. Have students correct the wordlist on the board and then write the correct numbers in their books.

3. Tell the groups from 2A to break into pairs to practice the words. Set a time limit (two minutes).

C Have students work individually to match the questions and answers. Call on volunteers to read the matching questions and answers aloud. Write the number-letter match on the board.

Communicative Practice and Application

10–15 minutes

 1. Model the questions and answers with a volunteer. Then model them again with other items from 1A and 2A.

2. Set a time limit (five minutes). Ask students to practice the conversation with several partners.

Evaluation

10–15 minutes (books closed)

TEST YOURSELF

1. Make a two-column chart on the board with the headings *Clothing* and *Money*. Have students close their books and give you an example for each column.

2. Have students copy the chart into their notebooks.

3. Give students five to ten minutes to test themselves by writing the words they recall from the lesson on the chart.

4. Call "time" and have students check their spelling in *The Oxford Picture Dictionary* or another dictionary. Circulate and monitor students' progress.

> ## Multilevel Strategies
>
> Target the *Test Yourself* to the level of your students.
>
> • **Pre-level** Have these students work with their books open.
>
> • **Higher-level** Have these students complete the chart and then write sentences about the items in 2A. *The dress is $9.99.*

To compress this lesson: Conduct 2A as a whole-class activity. Have students practice 2D with only one partner.

To extend this lesson: Have students identify the colors of the clothing items in 2A. Give them a short conversation to practice using the color and the clothing item. *What color is the (dress)? It's (blue).*

And/Or have students complete **Workbook 1 page 44** and **Multilevel Activity Book 1 page 78**.

2 Talk about clothes

A Work with your classmates. Match the words with the picture.

_9_	blouse	_1_	customer	_12_	pants	_4_	shoes	_5_	socks	_8_ tie
_2_	change	_3_	dress	_7_	shirt	_10_	skirt	_6_	suit	_11_ T-shirt

B Listen and check your answers. Then practice the words with a partner.

C Look at the picture. Match the questions with the answers.

_d_ 1. How much is the dress?   a. $19.99

_c_ 2. What color are the shoes?   b. two

_a_ 3. How much is the shirt?   c. black

_e_ 4. How many customers are there?   d. $9.99

_b_ 5. How many people are working?   e. four

D Work with a partner. Ask and answer questions.
Use the pictures in 1A and 2A.

A: How much is the pencil?   A: How much are the pants?
B: It's 25¢.   B: They're $24.99.

TEST YOURSELF ✔

Close your book. Write 6 clothing words and 6 money words. Check your spelling in a dictionary.

1 Read about shopping at a mall

A Look at the pictures. Listen.

May I help you?

B Listen again. Read the sentences.

1. It's cold today. I need a new sweater. It's time to go to the mall!
2. I shop at Dan's Discount Store. The salespeople are friendly. The prices are good.
3. I want an inexpensive yellow sweater.
4. I don't like this one. It's yellow, but it's too expensive.
5. This sweater is perfect. It's beautiful, and it's on sale.
6. I usually pay with cash, but I have a new credit card. I'm using it today.

C Check your understanding. Mark the sentences T (true) or F (false).

___T___ 1. She's shopping at the mall.

___F___ 2. The salespeople at Dan's are not friendly.

___T___ 3. She wants a yellow sweater.

___T___ 4. She has a new credit card.

Unit 7 Lesson 2

Objectives	Grammar	Vocabulary	Correlations
On-, Pre-, and Higher-level: Read and write about shopping and what to wear	Simple present-tense questions and answers (*What does John wear? He wears jeans.*)	Clothing For additional vocabulary practice, see these **Oxford Picture Dictionary** topics: Describing Things, Colors, Shopping	**CASAS:** 0.1.2, 1.3.1, 1.3.3, 1.3.9, 4.4.1, 6.0.1, 7.4.7 **LCPs:** 28.02, 32.01, 32.02, 32.13 **SCANS:** Listening, Seeing things in the mind's eye, Self-management, Speaking, Writing **EFF:** Convey ideas in writing, Observe critically, Read with understanding, Reflect and evaluate

Warm-up and Review

10–15 minutes (books closed)

Display clothing items of different colors (or use pictures). Tell students the display is a clothing store. Ask for items using the color-clothing combination: *Do you have a pink blouse?* Have students say *yes* or *no*. When the answer is *yes*, say: *How much is it?* Call on a volunteer to give you a price. Invite volunteers up to be the "customers" and ask the questions. Invite other volunteers to be the "salespeople."

Introduction

5 minutes

1. Ask: *How many people like to go shopping? How many people don't like to go shopping?*

2. State the objective: *Today we're going to read about shopping for clothes and what to wear.*

1 Read about shopping at a mall

Presentation I

20–25 minutes

A 1. Direct students to look at the pictures. Ask: *Where is she?* [at a clothing store] *Is she wearing a yellow coat?* [no—a yellow sweater]

2. Play the audio.

B 1. Play the audio again. Have students read along silently.

2. Check comprehension. Ask: *What does she want?* [a yellow sweater] *Does she like the first sweater?* [no] *Why not?* [too expensive]

Multilevel Strategies

After the group comprehension check in 1B, challenge on- and higher-level students while working with pre-level students.

• **Pre-level** Reread the sentences in 1B with your pre-level students while on- and higher-level students complete 1C and answer additional questions.

• **On- and Higher-level** Have these students complete 1C. Write additional questions on the board. *Why does she want a new sweater? How does she usually pay?* After allowing students to individually answer the questions, have volunteers write the answers on the board.

Guided Practice I

10 minutes

C Have students work individually to mark the sentence *true* or *false*. Go over the answers as a class.

TIP

After 1C, review and teach more clothing words associated with the weather. Write *winter, spring, summer,* and *fall* on the board. Ask: *What do you need to wear in _____?* Allow students to look at pictures of clothing in *The Oxford Picture Dictionary* or another picture dictionary. Have volunteers write words in each category.

2 Write about shopping

Guided Practice II

20–25 minutes

A 1. Pronounce and clarify the *Need help?* phrases. Ask students how they prefer to pay for clothing.

2. Copy the sentences on the board. Read them aloud with your own information. Have students complete the sentences independently. Circulate and assist.

> ### Multilevel Strategies
>
> Adapt 2A to the level of your students.
>
> • **Pre-level** Go over each sentence with these students, writing possible completions on the board. Have them choose a completion before moving on.
>
> • **Higher-level** Ask these students to write about two or three things they need and to include the color.

B Ask students to read their sentences to a partner. Call on individuals to share what they learned about their partners.

3 Talk about what to wear

Presentation II

20–25 minutes

A 1. Introduce the topic: *Now we're going to talk about what to wear.* Direct students to look at the pictures in 3A. Ask: *Where is he?*

2. Ask students to put their pencils down and listen for the answer to this question: *Where is John today?* Play the entire audio once.

3. Play the audio in segments. After the clothing for each place is described, stop the audio and check answers with the students. If necessary, replay the segment.

4. Check students' listening accuracy. Elicit the clothing items mentioned for each place.

Guided Practice

10–15 minutes

B Model the conversation with a volunteer. Assign a time limit (three minutes), and have students practice with a partner.

C 1. Have students read along silently while they listen.

2. Play the audio again, and have students repeat the conversation. Replay if necessary.

Communicative Practice and Application

10 minutes

D 1. Model the conversation with a volunteer. Then model it again with your own information.

2. Set a time limit (five minutes). Ask students to practice the conversation with several partners.

3. Ask volunteers to present their conversations to the class.

Evaluation

10–15 minutes (books closed)

TEST YOURSELF

1. Write these sentence skeletons on the board: *I like to wear _____ at home. I usually wear _____ at work. I like to wear _____ on special occasions.*

2. Have students work independently to complete the sentences. Collect and correct their writing.

To compress this lesson: Have students practice the conversation in 3D with only one partner.

To extend this lesson: Give students more practice talking about clothing. Pair students. Distribute pictures of people wearing different kinds of clothing, or have students flip through magazines. Ask students to practice a conversation like the one in 3B with the pictures. *What does he wear at home? He wears a T-shirt.*

And/Or have students complete **Workbook 1 page 45** and **Multilevel Activity Book 1 page 79**.

2 Write about shopping

A Write about yourself. Complete the sentences. Answers will vary.

I (like / don't like) the mall.

I shop at _____.

I need _____.

I want _____.

I usually pay _____.

Need help?

Ways to pay
with cash
with a check
with a credit card

B Read your story to a partner.

3 Talk about what to wear

A Listen to John talk about his clothes. Write the words you hear.

1. T-shirt
2. jeans
3. sneakers

at home

4. hat
5. uniform
6. belt

at work

7. suit
8. tie
9. shoes

on special occasions

B Work with a partner. Look at the pictures. Talk about what John likes to wear.

A: What does John wear at home?

B: He wears a T-shirt and jeans.

C Listen and repeat.

A: What do you wear at home?

B: At home, I wear a T-shirt and jeans.

D Work with a partner. Practice the conversation. Use your own information.

TEST YOURSELF ✔

Close your book. Write 3 sentences about what you wear at home, at work, and on special occasions.

1 Learn simple present *Yes/No* questions

A Look at the pictures. Read the sentences. Who needs a jacket? Ann needs a jacket.

① Jim and Joe have new jackets.

② Ann doesn't have a jacket.
She needs a jacket.

③ Mario has a jacket.
He wants a new jacket.

B Study the charts. Complete the sentences below.

SIMPLE PRESENT *YES/NO* QUESTIONS

Questions			
Do	I you we they	need	a jacket?
			jackets?
Does	he she		a jacket?

Answers						
Yes,	I you we they	do.	No,	I you we they	don't.
	he she	does.		he she	doesn't.

1. **A:** __Does__ Ann __need__ a jacket?

   B: Yes, __she__ does.

2. **A:** Do Jim and Joe need __jackets__?

   B: No, they __don't__.

C Match the questions with the answers. Use the pictures in 1A.

__a__ 1. Does Mario have a jacket?   a. Yes, he does.

__c__ 2. Do Jim and Joe need new jackets?   b. No, he doesn't.

__b__ 3. Does Mario need a jacket?   c. No, they don't.

__d__ 4. Does Ann have a jacket?   d. No, she doesn't.

D Work with a partner. Ask and answer the questions. Look at the pictures in 1A.

A: Does Ann want a jacket?

B: Yes, she does.

A: Do Jim and Joe need new jackets?

B: No, they don't.

✓ Ask and answer simple present *Yes/No* questions to describe needs

Unit 7 Lesson 3

Objectives	Grammar	Vocabulary	Correlations
On- and Higher-level: Use simple-present questions to ask about clothing **Pre-level:** Recognize simple-present questions to ask about clothing	Simple-present yes/no questions and answers (*Does the woman need a jacket? Yes, she does.*)	Clothing words For additional vocabulary practice, see these **Oxford Picture Dictionary** topics: Everyday Clothes, Casual, Work and Formal Clothes, Seasonal Clothing, Shoes and Accessories	**CASAS:** 0.1.2, 1.3.9, 7.4.7 **LCPs:** 28.02, 32.01, 33.02 **SCANS:** Seeing things in the mind's eye, Self-management, Sociability, Speaking, Writing **EFF:** Convey ideas in writing, Observe critically, Speak so others can understand, Reflect and evaluate

Warm-up and Review

10–15 minutes (books closed)

Put up pictures of people wearing different kinds of clothes. Ask volunteers to come to the board and write the names of the clothes and their colors under the pictures.

Introduction

5–10 minutes

1. Write a sentence about one of the pictures using words on the board: *She has a blue sweater.* Ask a question that requires a negative answer: *Does she have a blue skirt?* When students say *no*, write: *She doesn't have a blue skirt. She has blue pants.* Write more sample sentences about the pictures, and ask additional questions.

2. State the objective: *Today we're going to use the simple present to ask and answer questions about clothes.*

1 Learn simple present *Yes/No* questions

Presentation

20–25 minutes

A Direct students to look at the pictures. Read the captions aloud. Ask: *Who needs a jacket? Who wants a jacket?*

B 1. Demonstrate how to read the grammar charts as complete questions and answers. Read the charts through sentence by sentence. Then read them again, and have students repeat after you.

2. Ask *yes/no* questions about the pictures in 1A. *Do they have jackets? Does she have a jacket?*

3. As a class, complete the questions and answers. Ask volunteers to write the questions and answers on the board. Have other students read the questions and answers aloud.

4. Give students time to silently review the charts and fill in the blanks. Assess their understanding of the charts. Have students ask and answer *yes/no* questions about the pictures from the warm-up.

Guided Practice I

15–20 minutes

C Have students work individually to match the questions and answers. Ask volunteers to write the number-letter match on the board.

Multilevel Strategies

For 1C, seat same-level students together.

• **Pre-level** While other students are completing 1C, ask pre-level students to copy the questions and answers from 1B into their notebooks. Give them time to copy the answers to 1C.

• **On- and Higher-level** Have these students write three to five additional questions and answers about the pictures from the warm-up.

Communicative Practice

15–20 minutes

D Model the conversation with a volunteer. Set a time limit (five minutes). Ask students to practice with several partners. Ask volunteers to present their conversations to the class.

2 Ask and answer simple present *Yes/No* questions

Guided Practice II

25–30 minutes

A Have students work individually to complete the answers. Ask volunteer pairs to read the conversations for the class.

B Have students work individually to write the questions. Ask volunteer pairs to read the conversations for the class.

C 1. Say the sentences, filling them in with your own information.

2. Give students a couple of minutes to work individually to complete the sentences.

3. Assign a time limit (three minutes), and have students read their sentences to a partner.

> ### Multilevel Strategies
>
> After 2C, group same-level students together.
>
> • **Pre-level** Group these students and assist them with completing 2B and 2C if they haven't already. Read the questions and answers in 2B with them. Have them read their 2C sentences to you.
>
> • **On- and Higher-level** Put the 2C pairs together in groups of four. While you are working with the pre-level students, have these students practice asking third-person questions. Tell students to talk to a new partner and ask questions about the original partner, using the ideas in 2C. *Does Maria want a jacket? Does Maria need a car? Does Maria have a dictionary?* Model this with several students before beginning work with the pre-level students.

3 Practice simple present *Yes/No* questions

Communicative Practice and Application

20–25 minutes

A Draw the chart on the board, and fill in your own information. Give students time (three minutes) to fill in their own information.

B 1. Model the interview with a volunteer, and on the board, show where to chart the answers.

2. Check comprehension. Ask: *Do you write your partner's answers?* [yes] Set a time limit (three minutes) for students to interview their partners. Circulate and monitor.

> ### Multilevel Strategies
>
> Use mixed-level pairs for 3B.
>
> • **Pre-level** Have these students answer questions first, so they watch their partners charting the answers before they do it themselves.

C Discuss the class's answers. Ask for a show of hands to find out how many people have new shoes, how many need a sweater, and how many want new clothes.

Evaluation

10–15 minutes

TEST YOURSELF

Ask students to write the sentences independently. Collect and correct their writing.

> ### Multilevel Strategies
>
> Target the *Test Yourself* to the level of your students.
>
> • **Pre-level** Have these students write first-person sentences about themselves.

To compress this lesson: Conduct 2A and 2B as a whole-class activities.

To extend this lesson: Have students ask each other about the clothes they have at home. Provide students with pictures of winter and summer clothing, or use the pictures in *The Oxford Picture Dictionary*. Teach any new vocabulary. Pair students and have them ask about the clothing items: *Do you have _____ at home? Yes, I do./No, I don't.*

And/Or have students complete **Workbook 1 pages 46–47** and **Multilevel Activity Book 1 page 80**.

2 Ask and answer simple present *Yes/No* questions

A Complete the answers.

1. A: Does the store have a bathroom?
   B: No, _____it doesn't_____.

2. A: Do the children have new jeans?
   B: Yes, __they do_____.

3. A: Do Ben and Rosa have a new car?
   B: No, __they don't_____.

4. A: Does Sue want a sweater?
   B: Yes, __she does_____.

B Write questions. Use *Do* or *Does.*

1. A: __Do you want new shoes?_____
   B: Yes, I do. I want new shoes.

2. A: __Do they need a computer?_____
   B: Yes, they do. They need a computer.

3. A: __Does he need a new suit?_____
   B: No, he doesn't need a new suit.

4. A: __Do they have new shoes?_____
   B: No, they don't have new shoes.

C Write about what you *have, need,* and *want.* Read your sentences with a partner. Answers will vary.

1. I ____want____ a new jacket.

2. I __don't need__ a new car.

3. I _____ a dictionary.

4. I _____ a job.

5. I _____ brown shoes.

6. I _____ a new _____.

3 Practice simple present *Yes/No* questions

A Read the questions. Write your answers in the chart. Answers will vary.

Questions	My answers	My partner's answers
1. Do you have new shoes?	Yes	
2. Do you need a sweater?		
3. Do you want new clothes?	Do	

B Interview a partner. Write your partner's answers in the chart.

C Talk about the answers in the chart with your class.

Maria has new shoes.

TEST YOURSELF ✔

Write 3 sentences about your partner's answers from 3B.

My partner has new shoes. He doesn't need a sweater. He wants new clothes.

---

1 Learn to buy clothes

A Look at the clothing ad. Complete the sentences.

SHOP & SAVE Labor Day Sale

School Uniforms All Colors - All Sizes

$9.99

$9.99 S M L XL

Also On Sale Now!

$14.99 $16.99

Men's sweatshirts 50% off S, M, L

$38.00 $19.99

$18.99

$16.00 $8.00

1. The ___yellow___ shirt is extra large (XL).
2. The _green_ shirt is medium (M).

3. The _red_ shirt is large (L).
4. The _brown_ shirt is small (S).

B Listen and read.

Customer A: Excuse me. How much is this blouse?

B: It's on sale for $16.99. What size do you need?

A: I need a medium.

B: Here's a medium in red.

A: I'll take it.

Here's a medium.

C Listen again and repeat.

D Work with a partner. Practice the conversation. Use the clothing ad in 1A.

A: Excuse me. How much is this _____?

B: It's on sale for _____. What size do you need?

A: I need _____.

B: Here's a/an ___blouse___ in ___purple___.

A: I'll take it.

☑ Select clothing based on sizes and prices

Unit 7 Lesson 4

Objectives	Grammar	Vocabulary	Correlations
On- and Higher-level: Ask and answer questions about buying clothing **Pre-level:** Ask questions about buying clothing	Simple-present tense (*How much is this? I need a small.*)	Clothing, colors, and sizes For additional vocabulary practice, see these **Oxford Picture Dictionary** topics: Describing Clothes, Money, Numbers, Measurements	**CASAS:** 0.1.2, 1.1.6, 1.1.9, 1.2.1, 1.2.4, 1.2.5, 1.3.9, 1.6.4, 4.4.1, 6.0.1–6.0.4, 6.1.1, 6.1.2, 7.4.7 **LCPs:** 25.01, 25.05, 25.06, 28.02, 28.03, 32.01, 32.02, 32.13, 34.01–34.03 **SCANS:** Knowing how to learn, Serves clients/customers, Speaking **EFF:** Speak so others can understand

Warm-up and Review

10–15 minutes (books closed)

Put scrambled clothing words on the board, and give students time to figure them out. Ask volunteers to come up and write the unscrambled word: *toca* [coat], *wseaert* [sweater], *tnspa* [pants], *rufomni* [uniform], *uelbso* [blouse], *jecakt* [jacket], *hssoe* [shoes]

Introduction

5 minutes

1. Ask students what they think are good prices for the items on the board. Write the prices.

2. State the objective: *Today we're going to talk about shopping for clothes.*

1 Learn to buy clothes

Presentation

5–10 minutes

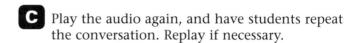 **A** 1. Direct students to look at the clothing ad. Read the headline. Elicit the meaning of *sale*. Elicit the meanings of the size abbreviations. Ask if they think this is a good sale.

2. Have students complete the sentences. Go over the answers as a class.

Guided Practice

10–15 minutes

B Play the audio. Have students read along silently.

C Play the audio again, and have students repeat the conversation. Replay if necessary.

Communicative Practice and Application

15–20 minutes

D 1. Model the conversation with a volunteer. Then model it again with ideas from the ad in 1A.

2. Elicit other ways to complete the conversation.

3. Set a time limit (five minutes). Ask students to practice the conversation with several partners.

Multilevel Strategies

For 1D, adapt the oral practice to the level of your students.

• **Pre-level** Have these students read the conversation as written in 1B.

• **Higher-level** Have these students ask and answer an additional question in their conversation. *Do you take checks/credit cards?*

 TIP Write the plural version of the conversation on the board. *A: Excuse me. How much are these _____? B: They're on sale for _____. What size do you need? A: I need a _____. B: Here's a/an _____ in _____. A: I'll take them.* Encourage your more-advanced students to use the plural version with *pants* and other plural items.

1. Direct students to look at the pictures. Ask them to name the clothing items.

2. Ask students to put down their pencils and listen for the answer to this question: *Which customer buys the clothing?* [the second one]

3. Play the audio in segments. Stop after each conversation, and ask students if they wrote the answers. Replay the segment as necessary.

4. Go over the answers as a class.

2 Practice your pronunciation

Pronunciation Extension

10–15 minutes

Play the audio. Have students point to each number as they hear it.

B Have students listen and repeat the numbers.

C 1. Play the audio. Have students work individually to circle the answers.

2. Ask students to compare their answers with a partner.

3. Ask volunteers to write the answers on the board. Play the audio again, and check the answers on the board. Stop and replay when necessary.

TIP After 2C, dictate sentences with clothing, colors, and prices. According to their ability, ask students to write the entire sentence, the clothing and price, or only the price.
1. *The red dress is $40.00.*
2. *The brown shoes are $50.00.*
3. *The blue T-shirt is $13.00.*
4. *The black pants are $17.00.*

3 Real-life math

Math Extension

10–15 minutes

1. Direct students to look at the receipt. Ask: *What's the total?* [$18.48]

2. Read the word problem aloud as students read along silently.

3. Give students time to answer the question. Ask a volunteer to put the math problem on the board.

Evaluation

10–15 minutes

TEST YOURSELF

1. Model the role-play with a volunteer. Then switch roles.

2. Pair students. Check comprehension. Ask "customers" to raise their hands. Elicit some examples of what they are going to say. Ask "salespeople" to raise their hands. Elicit some examples of what they're going to say.

3. Write *Customer* and *Salesperson* on the board. Write some appropriate expressions under each heading.

4. Set a time limit (five minutes), and have the partners act out the role-play in both roles.

5. Circulate and monitor. Encourage pantomime and improvisation.

6. Provide feedback.

Multilevel Strategies

Target the *Test Yourself* to the level of your students.

• **Pre-level** Have these students use the skeleton sentence in 1D.

To compress this lesson: Have students practice the conversation in 1D with only one partner.

To extend this lesson: Set up a "clothing store" in the class.
1. Put piles of clothing or pictures of clothing on different tables.
2. Assign a more-verbal student to be a "cashier" at each table. Have other students line up as "customers" and ask the questions in 1D. Have each customer take the clothing item back to his/her chair.
3. For follow-up, ask *What do you have?* as you collect the clothing.
And/Or have students complete **Workbook 1 page 48** and **Multilevel Activity Book 1 page 81**.

E Look at the pictures. Listen and write the sizes and the prices.

1. Size: large Price: $80.00
2. Size: small Price: $16.00
   Size: small Price: $17.00
3. Size: medium Price: $19.99
   Size: medium Price: $5.00

2 Practice your pronunciation

A Listen for the stress.

-teen	thir**teen**	four**teen**	fif**teen**	six**teen**	seven**teen**	eigh**teen**	nine**teen**
-ty	**thir**ty	**for**ty	**fif**ty	**six**ty	**seven**ty	**eigh**ty	**nine**ty

B Listen and repeat the numbers.

1. 40   3. 14   5. 90
2. 18   4. 13   6. 60

C Listen and circle the prices you hear. Compare answers with a partner.

1. $15.00   ($50.00)
2. $60.00   ($16.00)
3. ($40.28) $14.28
4. $12.16   ($12.60)
5. ($10.18) $10.80
6. $6.19   ($6.90)

3 Real-life math

Look at the receipt and read about Tanya. Then answer the question.

Tanya buys a sweater. The total is $18.48. She gives the salesperson a twenty-dollar bill. How much is her change? ___$1.52___

```
****SHOP AND SAVE****

SWEATER          $16.99
TAX               $1.49

TOTAL            $18.48
```

TEST YOURSELF ✔

Work with a partner. Partner A: You're the customer. Tell your partner what you want to buy. Partner B: You're the salesperson. Help the customer. Then change roles.

1 Get ready to read

A Look at the pictures. Read the sentences.

Put your ATM card in the machine.

Withdraw your cash.

Take your cash, card, and receipt.

Count your money.

B Work with your classmates. Put the steps in order.

__2__ Withdraw your cash.

__3__ Take your cash, card, and receipt.

__1__ Put your ATM card in the machine.

__4__ Count your money.

2 Read about ATMs

A Read the article.

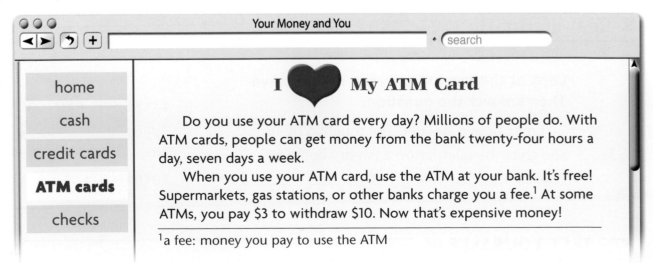

Your Money and You

search

home

cash

credit cards

ATM cards

checks

I ♥ My ATM Card

Do you use your ATM card every day? Millions of people do. With ATM cards, people can get money from the bank twenty-four hours a day, seven days a week.

When you use your ATM card, use the ATM at your bank. It's free! Supermarkets, gas stations, or other banks charge you a fee.[1] At some ATMs, you pay $3 to withdraw $10. Now that's expensive money!

[1] a fee: money you pay to use the ATM

Source: *www.fdic.gov*

B Listen and read the article again.

Unit 7 Lesson 5

Objectives	Grammar	Vocabulary	Correlations
On- and Higher-level: Read about and discuss ATMs and checks **Pre-level:** Read about ATMs and checks	Present continuous (*How much is she paying?*)	Banking words For additional vocabulary practice, see this **Oxford Picture Dictionary** topic: The Bank	**CASAS:** 0.1.2, 1.1.6, 1.3.1, 1.3.3, 1.8.1, 1.8.2, 6.0.1 **LCPs:** 25.01, 25.06, 32.01, 32.03–32.07, 32.13 **SCANS:** Acquires and evaluates information, Interprets and communicates information, Reading **EFF:** Listen actively, Read with understanding, Take responsibility for learning

Warm-up and Review

10–15 minutes (books closed)

Review ways to pay. Display the following items or pictures of them: a penny, a nickel, a dime, a quarter, a dollar bill, a five-dollar bill, a ten-dollar bill, a twenty-dollar bill, a check, a money order, a credit card, and an ATM card. Elicit the name of each item, and write it on the board. Call out items—for example, a pencil, a sweater, a sofa, dinner at a restaurant, the electric bill—and ask students how they would pay.

Introduction

5 minutes

1. Ask students how many use an ATM card every week.

2. State the objective: *Today we're going to read about ATM cards.*

1 Get ready to read

Presentation

15–20 minutes

A Direct students to look at the pictures. Read the captions.

B 1. Read each sentence. Ask students to raise their hands if they know which sentence is number 2.

2. When most students have their hands raised, call on someone to say the second sentence. Continue the process until all of the sentences are in order.

TIP After 2B, invite students up to pantomime one of the captions. Have the class guess the action.

Pre-Reading

Direct students to look at the web page headline in 2A. Ask what the heart means. Ask: *Do you love your ATM card? Why do people love their ATM cards? Where can you use an ATM card?*

2 Read about ATMs

Guided Practice I

25–30 minutes

A 1. Ask students to read the article silently.

2. Draw students' attention to the footnote. Say: *A fee is a price you pay for a service.* Ask if there are any questions about the reading.

B Play the audio. Have students read along silently.

Multilevel Strategies

For 2A–B, seat same-level students together.

• **Pre-level** Assist these students by reading the article aloud slowly, stopping after each sentence to clarify meaning.

• **On- and Higher-level** Before you work with the pre-level students, write *Sometimes, Usually,* and *Never* on the board, and review their meanings. While you are working with the pre-level students, ask on- and higher-level students to make a list of places they sometimes, never, and usually use an ATM card. Discuss their ideas as a class.

C 1. Have students work individually to mark the sentences *true* or *false*. Go over the answers together.

2. Ask additional comprehension questions. *Can you get money late at night from an ATM? Which ATMs charge a fee?*

D Have students work individually to complete the sentences. Go over the answers as a class.

Multilevel Strategies

Group pre-level students for 2C and 2D.

• **Pre-level** Help these students with 2C by reading each sentence and then reading the corresponding sentence in 2A. When the 2C sentence is false, ask students to identify the difference.

• **On- and Higher-level** While you are working with the pre-level students, ask these students to write two false statements and one true statement about their ATM or shopping habits. Have them present the statements to the class. Ask the class to guess which one is true.

3 Read a check

Guided Practice II

15–20 minutes

A 1. Ask: *Can you use an ATM card to pay the rent?* Explain: *Usually we have to write a check or get a money order. Now we're going to read a check.*

2. Direct students to look at the check. Say: *Who is writing this check?* [Kim Ling]

3. Have students work individually to answer the questions. Then go over the answers as a class.

Communicative Practice

10–15 minutes

B 1. Read the question aloud, and give students two minutes to write down their ideas.

2. Call on volunteers and put students' ideas on the board.

 TIP After students have brainstormed six items in 3B, ask them to name whom you write the check to for each item. For example: For clothing items, students might name a department store. For a utility bill, they might name a local utility company. Write company names next to the items. Have students give you a price and write that, too. Draw a blank check on the board. Use the company names and prices on the board to fill it out. Erase your work. Ask volunteers to come up and write the check for one of the other items. Have the class correct their work.

Application

5–10 minutes

BRING IT TO LIFE

With the class, brainstorm a list of places where students can easily observe how people pay. Ask students to tell where they plan to go to complete the assignment.

To compress this lesson: Assign 2D as homework.

To extend this lesson: Give students more practice writing checks.
1. Group students and provide each group with a large piece of paper.
2. Direct them to draw a check on it and fill it out.
3. Have each group hold up its check. Ask the other students to answer the questions in 3A about that group's check.

And/Or have students complete **Workbook 1 page 49** and **Multilevel Activity Book 1 page 82**.

C **Mark the sentences T (true) or F (false).**

_T_ 1. Millions of people use ATM cards every day.

_T_ 2. People get money from ATMs seven days a week.

_F_ 3. Your bank's ATM charges you a fee.

_F_ 4. All ATMs charge fees.

D **Complete the sentences. Use the words in the box.**

free	fees	~~ATM card~~	millions

1. Use your _____ATM card_____ to get money from the bank.

2. Your bank's ATM is _free_____.

3. ATMs at other places often have _fees_____.

4. _Millions_____ of people use ATM cards.

3 Read a check

A **Kim Ling is writing a check. Look at the check. Answer the questions.**

1. Who is writing the check? _Kim Ling_____

2. How much money is she paying? _$ 31.19_____

3. What store is she paying? _Shop and Save_____

B **Think about the question. Talk about the answers with your class.**

What are some things people pay for with checks? Name 6 things.

BRING IT TO LIFE

Go shopping. Watch 5 people pay. Do people pay with cash, checks, or credit cards? Tell your classmates how people pay.

1 Grammar

A Circle *a* or *b*.

1. She has ____ new job at the bank.
   (a.) a   b. any

2. Do you have ____ brothers and sisters?
   a. a   (b.) any

3. We don't have ____ credit cards.
   a. a   (b.) any

4. I have ____ good friends.
   a. a   (b.) some

5. Does he have ____ new shirt?
   (a.) a   b. some

> **Grammar note**
>
> ***a*, *some*, and *any***
>
> **Singular:** *a*
>
>   **A:** Do you have a jacket?
>   **B:** Yes, I have a jacket. *or*
>   No, I don't have a jacket.
>
> **Plural:** *any/some*
>
>   **A:** Do you have any socks?
>   **B:** Yes, I have some socks. *or*
>   No, I don't have any socks.

B Match the questions with the answers.

_c_ 1. Do you want a new jacket?   a. No, she doesn't.

_f_ 2. Is there an ATM near here?   b. Yes, there are.

_d_ 3. Do they need new books?   c. Yes, I do.

_a_ 4. Does she have a new car?   d. No, they don't.

_e_ 5. Does he like to shop?   e. Yes, he does.

_b_ 6. Are there any shirts on sale?   f. No, there isn't.

C Write the answers.

1. What do they want for dinner? (pizza) _They want pizza._
2. How much money does Pedro have? ($100) _He has $100._
3. What color suit does he want? (blue) _He wants a blue suit._
4. What do they need? (a new car) _They need a new car._
5. When do you have lunch? (at 12:30 p.m.) _I / We have lunch at 12:30 p.m._

D Complete the story. Circle the correct words.

Today Emily ((is)/ has) at the mall. She needs ((some)/ any) new shoes. She
(want /(wants)) inexpensive brown shoes. There are some nice brown shoes (in /(on)) sale
for $25. Emily ((has)/ want) $40. She pays the (customer /(salesperson)). Her change
((is)/ are) $15. She (have /(likes)) her new shoes.

Unit 7 Review and expand

Objectives	Grammar	Vocabulary	Correlations
On-, Pre-, and Higher-level: Expand upon and review unit grammar and life skills	*Some/Any*, present-tense questions and answers (*Do you have any socks? Yes, I have some socks.*)	Clothing and shopping words For additional vocabulary practice, see these **Oxford Picture Dictionary** topics: Everyday Clothes, Casual, Work and Formal Clothes, Shoes and Accessories, Money	**CASAS:** 0.1.2, 0.1.3, 1.1.6, 1.3.1, 1.3.3, 1.3.9, 1.8.1, 1.8.2, 4.8.1, 4.8.6, 6.0.1–6.0.4, 6.1.2, 7.2.5–7.2.7, 7.3.1 **LCPs:** 25.01, 25.06, 28.02, 32.01, 32.02, 32.05, 32.13, 33.02 **SCANS:** Creative thinking, Problem solving, Writing **EFF:** Solve problems and make decisions

Warm-up and Review

10–15 minutes (books closed)

1. Review the *Bring It to Life* assignment from Lesson 5.

2. Have students who did the exercise share with the class which stores they went to and how the people they observed paid. Ask other students if they ever go to those stores and what they usually see.

Introduction and Presentation

5–10 minutes

1. Write the *Grammar note* in 1A on the board. Clarify the questions and answers.

2. Write a couple of practice problems on the board to be sure students understand using *any* in questions and negatives. *Do you have _____ dresses? Yes, we have _____ dresses. No, we don't have _____ dresses.* Write *some* and *any* on the board. Then point to each blank, and ask for a show of hands: *Some* or *any*?

3. Write *have, want,* and *need* on the board. Ask individuals: *Do you have a new jacket? Do you need a new jacket? Do you want a new jacket?*

4. State the objective: *Today we're going to ask and answer present-tense questions about shopping using* any, some, have, want, *and* need.

1 Grammar

Guided Practice

40–45 minutes

A Have students work individually to choose the correct answers. Go over the answers as a class.

B Have students work individually to match the questions and answers. Ask volunteers to read the matching questions and answers aloud. Write the number-letter match on the board.

C Have students work individually to answer the questions. Ask volunteers to write the answers on the board.

D Have students work individually to circle the correct word choices. Write the numbers 1–8 on the board, and ask volunteers to write the answers.

Multilevel Strategies

For 1C and 1D, seat same-level students together.

• **Pre-level** For 1C, read each question and help these students form the answer. Give everyone time to copy the answer before moving on to the next question. For 1D, slowly read the paragraph aloud with the correct answers. Tell students to listen and circle the answer.

• **On- and Higher-level** While you are working with pre-level students, ask other students to work together in groups to write another story, like the one in 1D. Give them the first two sentences on the board: *Today Tony is at the clothing store. He needs . . .* Have the groups share their stories with the class.

2 Group work

Communicative Practice

20–35 minutes

A 1. Direct students, in groups of three to four, to focus on the picture on page 77. Ask: *How much are shirts?* [$19.99] *How much are ties?* [$9.99]

2. Set a time limit (five minutes) to complete the exercise. Circulate and answer any questions.

3. Have a reporter from each group read the group's sentences to the class.

Multilevel Strategies

For 2A and 2B, use same-level groups.

• **Pre-level** For 2A, ask these students to write three vocabulary words and one complete sentence. For 2B, allow them to ask and answer the questions without writing.

• **Higher-level** For 2A, ask these students to write two additional sentences about the picture. For 2B, have them ask and answer these questions: *What do you wear to school? What do you wear to work?*

B 1. Have students work in the same groups from 2A to take turns interviewing each other in pairs.

2. Set a time limit (five minutes) to complete the exercise.

C Have a reporter from each group share the group's work.

TIP For more practice with clothing and prices, bring in ads from clothing or department stores. Group students and give each group an ad. Write column heads on the board: *Item, Price, Discount.* Tell them to write the information about several items from the ad. (Use an example to demonstrate that the ad may have prices but not discounts or vice versa.) Ask each group to decide if the prices are good or if it's a good sale. Have a reporter share the group's findings with the class.

PROBLEM SOLVING

15–25 minutes

A 1. Direct students to look at the picture of Joel. Ask: *Where is he?* [at the ATM] *How does he feel?* [confused, worried] Tell students they will read a story about a man with a problem at the ATM. Direct students to read Joel's story silently. Then play the audio, and have them read along silently.

2. Ask: *How much money does Joel want? How much does he get?*

B 1. Read the question and identify the problem. Read the possible solutions.

2. Elicit student ideas for other solutions. Write each one on the board.

3. Discuss whether the statements are appropriate.

4. Ask for a show of hands to see which solution the class likes best.

C Elicit the students' ideas for what Joel can say, and write them on the board. For example, *Excuse me, I'm having a problem with the ATM machine. Can you help me?* Tell students to copy the expressions into their notebooks.

TIP After you write the expressions on the board in 1C, show students how to apply them to other situations. Have students practice using the expressions with their classmates: *Excuse me. I'm having a problem with this exercise. Can you help me?*

Evaluation

30–35 minutes

To test students' understanding of the unit grammar and life skills, have them take the Unit 7 Test in the *Step Forward Test Generator CD-ROM with ExamView® Assessment Suite.*

Learning Log

To help students record and discuss their progress, use the *Learning Log* on page T-178.

To extend this review: Have students complete **Workbook 1 page 50, Multilevel Activity Book 1 pages 83–86,** and the **Unit 7 Grammar Exercises** on the **Multilevel Grammar Exercises CD-ROM 1.**

2 Group work

A Work with 2–3 classmates. Write 5 sentences about the picture on page 77. Talk about the sentences with your class. Answers will vary.

A salesperson is wearing a skirt and blouse. A customer is holding a white shirt. Shirts are on sale. *A man is wearing a suit. A woman is buying a dress.*

B Interview 3 classmates. Write their answers in your notebook.

ASK:

1. Do you have a favorite clothing store?
2. Do you want any new clothes?
3. Do you need any new work or school clothes?
4. Do you pay for clothes with cash, checks, or credit cards?

> *Classmate—Leticia*
> *1. Yes, she does.*
> *2. Yes, she does.*
> *3. No, she doesn't.*
> *4. cash*

C Talk about the answers with your class.

PROBLEM SOLVING

A Listen and read about Joel. What is his problem?
The ATM gave Joe only $20.

Joel is at the bank. He wants $40. He puts his card in the ATM. He takes his card, his money, and his receipt. When he counts the money, he only has $20!

B Work with your classmates. Answer the question. (More than one answer may be possible.)

What can Joel do?
  a. Call the police.
  b. Put the card in the machine again.
  (c.) Ask for help at the bank.
  (d.) Other: __Answers will vary.__

C Work with your classmates. Make a list of things Joel can say.

Eating Well

FOCUS ON
- food
- food shopping
- frequency expressions
- restaurant orders
- healthy eating habits

LESSON 1 Vocabulary

1 Learn food shopping words

A Look at the picture. Where are the people?

B Listen and look at the picture.

C Listen and repeat the words.

1. fruit   2. vegetables   3. basket   4. cart   5. checker   6. bagger

D Look at the picture. Complete the sentences.

1. The man in the white shirt is next to the ___vegetables___, on the right.
2. The ___fruit___ is next to the vegetables, on the left.
3. The ___bagger___ has a yellow tie.
4. One woman has a red ___cart___.
5. One man has a blue ___basket___.
6. The ___checker___ has a green blouse.

Unit 8 Lesson 1

Objectives	Grammar	Vocabulary	Correlations
On-level: Identify food and shopping words **Pre-level:** Recognize food and shopping words **Higher-level:** Talk and write about food and shopping	Simple-present tense (*The bagger has blond hair.*)	Food and shopping For additional vocabulary practice, see these **Oxford Picture Dictionary** topics: Fruit, Back from the Market, A Grocery Store, Vegetables	**CASAS:** 0.1.2, 1.3.8, 7.4.5, 7.4.7 **LCPs:** 28.01, 32.01 **SCANS:** Listening, Participates as member of a team, Seeing things in the mind's eye, Self-management, Speaking **EFF:** Cooperate with others, Listen actively, Observe critically, Speak so others can understand

Warm-up and Review

10–15 minutes (books closed)

Find out which food words students already know. Write *Breakfast, Lunch,* and *Dinner* on the board. Ask students what they like to eat for each meal, and write the words on the board.

Introduction

5 minutes

1. Ask students where they buy their food. Talk about your favorite supermarket.

2. State the objective: *Today we're going to learn words for food shopping.*

1 Learn food shopping words

Presentation

20–25 minutes

A Direct students to look at the pictures. Ask: *How many customers are in the supermarket?*

B 1. Have students listen to the audio. Ask them to point to the correct part of the picture as they listen. Circulate and monitor.

2. Check comprehension by asking *yes/no* questions. Pass out *yes/no* cards to the students (see page T-175), or have them hold up one finger for *yes* and two for *no* in order to get a nonverbal response. Ask: *Is the young man the bagger?* [yes] *Is the basket red?* [no]

C Ask students to listen and repeat the words.

Guided Practice I

15–20 minutes

D 1. Have students complete the sentences using the new vocabulary.

2. Encourage students to take turns reading the completed sentences in pairs.

TIP Draw numbered "aisles" on the board. Put an apple in one, a head of lettuce in another, and other vocabulary items throughout. Have students practice with this conversation: *Where is (the fruit)? It's on (aisle one). Where are (the vegetables)? They're on (aisle two).*

2 Talk about a supermarket

Guided Practice II

35–40 minutes

 A 1. Ask: *Do you like to shop for food?* Introduce the new topic: *Now let's talk about a supermarket.*

2. Group students and assign roles: leader, fact checker, recorder, and reporter. Explain that students work with their groups to match the words and pictures.

3. Check comprehension of the exercise. Ask: *Who looks up the words in the picture dictionary?* [fact checker] *Who writes the numbers in the book?* [recorder] *Who tells the class your answers?* [reporter] *Who helps everyone and manages the group?* [leader]

4. Set a time limit (three minutes), and have students work together to complete the task. While students are working, copy the wordlist on the board.

5. Call "time" and have the reporters from each group take turns calling out the numbers for the wordlist. Record students' answers on the board. If groups disagree, write each group's choice next to the word.

B 1. Ask students to listen and check their answers.

2. Have students correct the wordlist on the board and then write the correct numbers in their books.

3. Tell the groups from 2A to break into pairs to practice the words. Set a time limit (two minutes).

> **TIP** Have students listen again and write the words used to describe the food. [beautiful tomatoes, white bread, favorite soup, sweet onions, healthy grapes, expensive milk, delicious apples]

 C 1. Copy the first line on the board. Do not cross out *lettuce* yet. Say: *Three words are the same. One word is different. Which word is different? Why is* lettuce *different?*

2. Cross out *lettuce* and direct students to complete the exercise independently.

3. Go over the answers as a class, and discuss why the words are alike or different.

Communicative Practice and Application

10–15 minutes

 D 1. Talk with a volunteer about food shopping. Then switch roles.

2. Set a time limit (five minutes). Ask students to practice the conversation with several partners.

Evaluation

10–15 minutes (books closed)

TEST YOURSELF

1. Make a two-column chart on the board with the headings *Food* and *Supermarket*. Have students close their books and give you an example for each column. Then have students copy the chart into their notebooks.

2. Give students five to ten minutes to test themselves by writing the words they recall from the lesson.

3. Call "time" and have students check their spelling in *The Oxford Picture Dictionary* or another dictionary. Circulate and monitor students' progress.

> ### Multilevel Strategies
>
> Target the *Test Yourself* to the level of your students.
>
> • **Pre-level** Have these students work with their books open.
>
> • **Higher-level** Have these students complete the chart and then write two sentences about their shopping habits.

To compress this lesson: Conduct 2A as a whole-class activity. Have students practice 2D with only 1 partner.

To extend this lesson: Have students interview each other: *What's your favorite fruit? What's your favorite vegetable?* Find out what the most popular fruits and vegetables are in the class.

And/Or have students complete **Workbook 1 page 51** and **Multilevel Activity Book 1 page 88**.

2 Talk about a supermarket

A Work with your classmates. Match the words with the picture.

_2_ apples	_9_ chicken	_3_ lettuce	_12_ potatoes
_1_ bananas	_5_ eggs	_4_ milk	_8_ soup
_7_ bread	_11_ grapes	_10_ onions	_6_ tomatoes

B Listen and check your answers. Then practice the words with a partner.

C Cross out (X) the item that does NOT belong in each group.

1. apples   bananas   let̶t̶u̶c̶e̶   grapes
2. checker   e̶g̶g̶s̶   bagger   customer
3. b̶r̶e̶a̶d̶   onions   potatoes   lettuce
4. chicken   bread   soup   c̶a̶r̶t̶

D Work with a partner. Talk about food shopping.

I buy milk, eggs, bread, and fruit every week.

I use a basket. I pay with a credit card.

How about you?

TEST YOURSELF ✔

Close your book. Write 5 food words and 5 supermarket words. Check your spelling in a dictionary.

1 Read about food shopping

A Look at the pictures. Listen.

B Listen again. Read the sentences.

1. The Garcias make a shopping list every Wednesday night.
2. They go to the supermarket every Thursday morning.
3. Mr. Garcia loves oranges. They get oranges every time they shop.
4. Every week, they buy chicken and fish.
5. Once or twice a month, they buy cookies or ice cream.
6. They always look for good prices.

C Check your understanding. Mark the sentences **T** (true) or **F** (false).

  T   1. The Garcias go to the market every Thursday.

  F   2. They make a shopping list every Monday.

  T   3. They buy chicken every week.

  F   4. Mr. Garcia doesn't like oranges.

  F   5. They buy cookies every day.

  T   6. They always look for good prices.

Unit 8 Lesson 2

Objectives	Grammar	Vocabulary	Correlations
On-, Pre-, and Higher-level: Read and write about food shopping	Simple-present tense (*I go to the supermarket every week.*) Frequency expressions (*They go shopping every Saturday.*)	Food and shopping words For additional vocabulary practice, see this **Oxford Picture Dictionary** topic: A Grocery Store, The Farmers' Market	**CASAS:** 0.1.2, 0.2.4, 1.1.6, 1.2.1, 1.2.5, 1.3.8, 6.0.1, 7.4.7, 8.2.1 **LCPs:** 28.01, 32.01, 32.02, 32.13 **SCANS:** Acquires and evaluates information, Interprets and communicates information, Listening, Reading, Responsibility, Self-management, Writing **EFF:** Convey ideas in writing

Warm-up and Review

10–15 minutes (books closed)

Write *yellow, green, red, brown,* and *orange* on the board. Have students line up at the board in two teams. Have team members take turns approaching the board and writing the name of a fruit or vegetable under the correct color. (Some can appear under several colors, like *apple.*) When one team gets "stuck," the game is over.

Introduction

5 minutes

1. Using the fruits and vegetables on the board, find out which ones the students buy every week, every month, every year, and which ones they never buy.

2. State the objective: *Today we're going to read and write about shopping for food.*

1 Read about food shopping

Presentation I

20–25 minutes

A 1. Direct students to look at the pictures. Ask: *Where are they? What are they doing?*

2. Play the audio.

B 1. Play the audio again. Have students read along silently.

2. Check comprehension. Ask: *Do they go shopping every day?* [no] *Does Mr. Garcia love oranges?* [yes]

Multilevel Strategies

Seat same-level students together for 1B and 1C.

• **Pre-level** Reread the sentences in 1B with your pre-level students. Then read each sentence in 1C, and help them locate the answer in 1B.

• **On- and Higher-level** Before you begin working with the pre-level students, write these questions on the board: *What food do you love? What do you buy every week? What do you buy once a month?* Have these students do 1C and then ask and answer the questions on the board with a partner.

Guided Practice I

10 minutes

C Have students work individually to mark the sentences *true* or *false.* Go over the answers as a class.

TIP

After 1C, have students work in groups to make a shopping list for a regular week of shopping. If any group member buys the item every week, it should go on the list. Have groups compare their lists.

2 Write about food shopping

Guided Practice II

20–25 minutes

 1. Pronounce and clarify the *Need help?* sentences. If you did not do the group shopping-list activity from the Tip on page T-90, brainstorm a list of items that the students buy weekly and write them on the board.

2. Copy the sentences in 2A on the board. Read them aloud with your own information.

3. Have students complete the sentences independently. Circulate and assist.

Multilevel Strategies

Adapt 2A to the level of your students.

• **Pre-level** Tell these students to use the words on the board to complete their sentences.

• **Higher-level** Ask these students to complete these sentences as well: *I usually shop at _____. I buy _____ once or twice a month. I never buy _____.*

---

 1. Ask students to read their sentences to a partner.

2. Call on individuals to share what they learned about their partners.

3 Talk about food shopping

Presentation II

20–25 minutes

 Introduce the topic: *Now we're going to look at a supermarket ad.* Write the word *ad* on the board. Direct students to look at the ad. Ask: *Do you look at supermarket ads in the newspaper?* Ask students to identify the items in the ad.

Guided Practice

10–15 minutes

 1. Ask students to put their pencils down and listen for the answer to this question: *What does Mr. Garcia want?* Play the entire audio once.

2. Play the audio in segments. After each food is mentioned, stop the audio and check answers with the students. *Did you check the box in the ad?* If necessary, replay the segment.

3. Check students' listening accuracy: *Are they going to buy peanut butter?* [no] *Are they going to buy tuna fish?* [yes]

Communicative Practice and Application

10 minutes

 1. Direct students to look at the pictures and repeat the names of the food items.

2. Have students read the conversation silently while they listen.

3. Play the audio again, and have students repeat the conversation. Replay if necessary.

4. Model the conversation with a volunteer. Then model it again with other food items.

5. Set a time limit (five minutes). Ask students to practice the conversation with several partners.

6. Ask volunteers to present their conversations to the class.

Evaluation

10–15 minutes (books closed)

TEST YOURSELF

Assign a time limit (three minutes) for students to write their lists independently. Then ask them to read their lists to a partner.

To compress this lesson: Conduct 1C as a whole-class activity. Have students practice the conversation in 3C with only one partner.

To extend this lesson: Group students. Give each group a store flyer, and ask them to choose five items to buy. Ask a reporter from each group to share the group's choices with the class.

And/Or have students complete **Workbook 1 page 52** and **Multilevel Activity Book 1 page 89**.

2 Write about food shopping

A Write about yourself. Complete the sentences. Answers will vary.

I go to the supermarket every _____ .

Every week, I buy _____ , _____ ,

and _____ .

I love _____ .

I always look for _____ .

B Read your story to a partner.

3 Talk about food shopping

A Look at the supermarket ads. Read the items and the prices.

B Listen to the Garcias talk about the supermarket ads. Check (✔) the items they are going to buy.

C Listen. Then practice the conversation with a partner.

A: Let's make vegetable soup.

B: We need some onions. Do we need any potatoes?

A: Yes, we do. Do we need any carrots?

B: No, we have some.

salad   fruit salad   spaghetti

TEST YOURSELF ✔

Close your book. Write a shopping list. Tell a partner what's on your list.

1 Learn frequency expressions

A **Look at Lucy's schedule. Answer the questions below.**

Sunday	Monday	Tuesday	Wednesday	Thursday	Friday	Saturday
	cook dinner at home	have dinner with Alex	cook dinner at home	cook dinner at home	order pizza	have dinner with Alex

1. Does Lucy have dinner with Alex on Tuesdays and Saturdays? __Yes, she does.__
2. When does Lucy order pizza? __On Fridays.__

B **Study the charts.**

FREQUENCY EXPRESSIONS

Frequency expressions	
I cook	every day.
Mary goes shopping	once a week.
We buy cookies	twice a month.
They order pizza	three times a year.

More frequency expressions
every day / week / month / year
once a day / week / month / year
twice a day / week / month / year
three times a day / week / month / year
never (0 times) *We never cook.*

C **Complete the sentences. Use Lucy's schedule in 1A.**

1. Lucy orders pizza __once a week__.
2. Lucy has dinner with Alex __twice a week__.
3. Lucy cooks dinner __three times a week__.
4. Lucy __never__ cooks dinner on Friday.

D **Write sentences with your own information. Read the sentences to a partner.** Answers will vary.

1. (cook dinner) __I cook dinner three times a week.__
2. (eat dinner at home) _____
3. (eat lunch with friends) _____
4. (have breakfast at home) _____

Unit 8 Lesson 3

Objectives	Grammar	Vocabulary	Correlations
On- and Higher-level: Use frequency expressions to talk about eating habits **Pre-level:** Recognize frequency expressions	Frequency expressions (*We buy cookies twice a month.*)	Frequency expressions For additional vocabulary practice, see this **Oxford Picture Dictionary** topic: The Calendar	**CASAS:** 0.2.4, 2.3.2, 7.4.7 **LCPs:** 25.03, 32.01, 32.08, 33.08 **SCANS:** Reading, Self-management, Speaking, Writing **EFF:** Convey ideas in writing, Reflect and evaluate, Speak so others can understand

Warm-up and Review

10–15 minutes (books closed)

Tell students about your eating habits. Write the sentences on the board as you say them. *I eat at a restaurant twice a month. I cook dinner on Monday, Tuesday, and Wednesday. My husband cooks dinner on Thursday, Friday, and Saturday. On Sunday, we eat dinner with my mother.* Ask students about their eating habits. *Do you eat at a restaurant every day? Every week? Once a month?*

Introduction

5–10 minutes

1. Circle the frequency expressions on the board.

2. State the objective: *Today we're going to use these expressions to talk about our eating habits.*

1 Learn frequency expressions

Presentation I

20–25 minutes

A 1. Direct students to look at Lucy's schedule. Read the frequency expressions. Elicit things that the students do once a week, twice a week, three times a week, and never.

2. Give students time to answer the questions. Go over the answers as a class.

B 1. Demonstrate how to read the grammar charts as complete sentences. Read the charts through sentence by sentence. Then read them again, and have students repeat after you.

2. Read the other frequency expressions, and point out that *never* takes a different position in the sentence.

3. Use the schedule in 1A to illustrate points in the grammar charts. Say sentences about Lucy using the frequency expressions. *Lucy orders pizza once a week.*

4. Give students time to silently review the charts.

5. Assess their understanding of the charts. Ask students to say sentences about Lucy using the expressions.

Guided Practice

15–20 minutes

C As a class, complete the sentences. Ask volunteers to write the sentences on the board. Have other students read the sentences aloud.

Multilevel Strategies

For 1C, seat same-level students together.

• **Pre-level** Group these students. Assist them with 1C by eliciting completions for each sentence and having the students write the completions before moving on to the next sentence.

• **On- and Higher-level** Have these students write three to five additional sentences about themselves using frequency expressions. Ask volunteers to share one or two of their sentences with the class.

D 1. Have students work individually to write sentences about themselves.

2. Ask students to read their sentences to a partner.

3. Call on individuals to write their completed sentences on the board.

2 Ask and answer questions with *How often*

Presentation II

20–25 minutes

A Read and have students repeat the questions and answers in the chart. Ask volunteers to say the questions and answers. Assist with the pronunciation of *often*.

Guided Practice

10–15 minutes

B Have students work individually to complete the questions and match them with the answers. Ask volunteers to read the questions and answers aloud.

3 Practice questions about routines

Communicative Practice and Application

20–25 minutes

A 1. Draw the chart on the board, and fill in your own information using frequency expressions.

2. Elicit other possible answers.

3. Give students time (three minutes) to fill in their own information.

B 1. Model the interview with a volunteer. Show where to chart the answers on the board.

2. Check comprehension. Ask: *Do you copy your partner's chart?* [no] *Do you listen to your partner and write?* [yes] *Do you need to write complete sentences?* [no]

3. Set a time limit (three minutes) for students to interview their partners. Circulate and monitor.

Multilevel Strategies

Use mixed-level pairs for 3B.

• **Pre-level** Have these students answer questions first, so they watch their partners charting the answers before they do it themselves.

C Discuss the class's answers. Ask for a show of hands about each question: *How many people eat dinner with friends every day? Twice a week?*

TIP After students complete the chart in 3B, give them more practice with *How often*. Provide pictures of common activities, or use the picture cards on page 94 of *Multilevel Activity Book 1*. Make enough copies so that each student can have one picture. Go over the picture vocabulary. Set a time limit (five minutes). Have students walk around the room asking *How often do you _____?* (filling in the blank using the activity in their picture). Call "time" and have students sit down. As you collect the cards, ask students to make a statement about themselves using the picture card and a frequency expression. *I wash clothes three times a week.*

Evaluation

10–15 minutes

TEST YOURSELF

Ask students to write the sentences independently. Collect and correct their writing.

Multilevel Strategies

Target the *Test Yourself* to the level of your students.

• **Pre-level** Allow these students to write first-person sentences.

• **Higher-level** Have these students write eight sentences about themselves and their partners.

To compress this lesson: Conduct 2B as a whole-class activity.

To extend this lesson: Show students a picture of a famous person. Ask them to write sentences about the person using frequency expressions and their imaginations. *He never washes dishes. He eats in restaurants every day.*

And/Or have students complete **Workbook 1 pages 53–54** and **Multilevel Activity Book 1 page 90**.

2 Ask and answer questions with *How often*

A Study the chart. Ask and answer the questions.

Questions and answers with *How often*	
A: How often do you cook? B: I cook three times a day.	A: How often does he cook? B: He cooks twice a week.
A: How often do you cook? B: We cook every evening.	A: How often does she cook? B: She never cooks.

B Complete the questions. Then match the questions with the answers. Use the schedule from 1A.

_c_ 1. How _often_ does Lucy order pizza?   a. twice a week

_a_ 2. How often do Lucy and Alex _cook_ dinner?   b. never

_h_ 3. How often _does_ Lucy cook on Fridays?   c. once a week

3 Practice questions about routines

A Read the questions. Write your answers in the chart. Answers will vary.

Questions	My answers	My partner's answers
1. How often do you eat dinner with friends?		
2. How often do you order pizza?		
3. How often do you eat dinner at a restaurant?		
4. How often do you cook dinner at home?		

B Interview a partner. Write your partner's answers in the chart.

C Talk about the answers in the chart with your class.

I eat dinner with friends once a week. Mia eats dinner with friends three times a week.

TEST YOURSELF ✔

Write 4 sentences about your partner's answers from 3B.

Martin cooks dinner at home three times a week. He orders pizza once a week.

1 Learn to order food

A Look at the menu. Write the prices.

Pappa's Pizza Place

Menu

Pizza

Small pizza $6.50

Medium pizza $8.50

Large pizza $12.00

Toppings $1.00 each
pepperoni   onions
mushrooms   peppers

Drinks

Soda   Iced Tea

Small $1.50   *Medium* $1.75   *Large* $2.00

1. A large pepperoni pizza is ___$13.00___.
2. A medium mushroom pizza is _$9.50_____.
3. A small pizza with peppers and onions is _$8.50_____.
4. A medium pepperoni and mushroom pizza is _$10.50_____.

B Listen and read.

A: Are you ready to order?

B: Yes, I am—a medium pizza with onions, please.

A: Do you want anything to drink?

B: Yes, I do. I'd like a small iced tea.

A: OK, that's one medium pizza with onions and a small iced tea.

B: That's right.

C Listen again and repeat.

D Work with a partner. Practice the conversation. Use the menu in 1A.

A: Are you ready to order?

B: Yes, I am—a _____ pizza with _____, please.

A: Do you want anything to drink?

B: Yes, I do. I'd like _____.

A: OK, that's one _____ pizza with _____
and _____.

B: That's right.

Unit 8 Lesson 4

Objectives	Grammar	Vocabulary	Correlations
On-, Pre-, and Higher-level: Order food	Simple-present–tense questions and answers (*Are you ready to order? Yes, I am. Do you want salad? Yes, I do.*)	Pizza toppings For additional vocabulary practice, see these **Oxford Picture Dictionary** topics: Fast Food Restaurant, A Coffee Shop Menu, A Menu, Money	**CASAS:** 0.1.2, 0.1.3, 0.1.6, 1.1.6, 1.2.1, 1.2.4, 1.3.8, 2.6.4, 6.0.1–6.0.4, 6.1.1, 7.4.7 **LCPs:** 22.03, 25.01, 28.01, 29.03, 32.01, 32.02, 32.13 **SCANS:** Arithmetic/Mathematics, Self-management, Serves clients/customers, Sociability, Speaking **EFF:** Speak so others can understand

Warm-up and Review

10–15 minutes (books closed)

Draw a pizza on the board (a circle cut into slices). Tell students your pizza is very plain and it needs toppings. Demonstrate a possible pizza topping by drawing a whole mushroom next to the pizza and eliciting the label *mushroom*. Ask volunteers to come up and draw pictures of foods that could be pizza toppings. Have the class guess what each drawing is. When the class gets it right, write the word next to the picture. Encourage students to use their imaginations and be creative with the pizza toppings. When you have some strange toppings on the board, ask *Who wants to eat pizza with _____?* to find out who the adventurous eaters are.

Introduction

5 minutes

1. Say: *People in the U.S. love pizza. Many people order pizza once a week or more.*

2. State the objective: *Today we're going to learn how to order food.*

1 Learn to order food

Presentation

20–30 minutes

A 1. Direct students to look at the menu. Ask: *How much is a medium pizza? What toppings are there?*

2. Give students time to write the prices. Go over the answers as a class.

Guided Practice

20–25 minutes

B Play the audio. Have students read along silently.

C Play the audio again, and have students repeat the conversation. Replay if necessary.

Communicative Practice and Application

15–20 minutes

D 1. Model the conversation with a volunteer using information from the menu in 1A. Then switch roles. Elicit other ways to complete the conversation.

2. Set a time limit (five minutes). Ask students to practice the conversation with several partners.

Multilevel Strategies

For 1D, adapt the oral practice to the level of your students.

• **Pre-level** Have these students read the conversation as written in 1B.

• **Higher-level** Ask these students to use different food and drinks for every conversation.

For more practice ordering food after 1D, pair students and ask each pair to make a simple menu with four food items and four drink choices. Designate each student as Partner A or Partner B. You can pass out A/B cards (on page T-175) to designate roles. After the pairs finish making their menus, tell Partner As to keep the menu. Tell Partner Bs to find new partners and order from their menus. Have them return to their original partners when they finish and switch roles.

1. Direct students to look at the restaurant order forms. Say: *We're going to listen to people ordering pizza.* Tell students to put down their pencils and listen for the answer to this question: *Who orders pizzas with two toppings?* [customer three]

2. Play the audio in segments. After each conversation, check answers with the students: *Did you fill in the order form?* Replay if necessary.

3. While students are listening, draw the order forms on the board. Ask volunteers to complete them.

Multilevel Strategies

After 1E, provide more practice for on- and higher-level students while allowing pre-level students to catch up.

• **Pre-level** Have these students copy the answers from the board if they were unable to finish the exercise.

• **On- and Higher-level** While pre-level students are copying, have these students role-play the customer and counter person, using the order forms in 1E.

2 Practice your pronunciation

Pronunciation Extension

10–15 minutes

A Play the audio. Have students read along silently.

B 1. Tell students to put down their pencils and point to the correct answer as they listen.

2. Replay the audio and have students circle the answers. Go over the answers as a class.

C Have students work individually to match the questions and answers. Ask volunteers to read the questions and answers aloud. Write the number-letter match on the board.

3 Real-life math

Math Extension

10–15 minutes

1. Direct students to look at the menu in 1A and find the price for a large pizza. Ask: *How much are two large pizzas?* [$24.00] *How much are toppings?* [$1.00] *Do both pizzas have a topping?* [yes] *So two large pizzas with toppings are $26.00.* Have students work out the rest of the orders and the total bill prices on their own.

2. Have students share their answers with a partner. Then go over the answers as a class.

Evaluation

10–15 minutes

TEST YOURSELF

1. Model the role-play with a volunteer. Then switch roles.

2. Pair students. Check comprehension by asking: *Who is ordering the pizza?* [Partner A] *Who is listening and repeating?* [Partner B]

3. Set a time limit (five minutes), and have the partners act out the role-play in both roles.

4. Circulate and monitor.

5. Provide feedback.

Multilevel Strategies

Target the *Test Yourself* to the level of your students.

• **Pre-level** Have these students use the skeleton sentences in 1D or read the conversation in 1B.

• **Higher-level** Tell these students they are ordering for a large party.

To compress this lesson: Have students practice the conversation in 1D with only one partner.

To extend this lesson: Provide more practice with ordering.
1. Give students a menu from a fast-food restaurant, or have students use the pictures of fast food in *The Oxford Picture Dictionary*.
2. Teach any new vocabulary.
3. Have students practice ordering and taking orders.
4. Ask volunteers to demonstrate for the class.

And/Or have students complete **Workbook 1 page 55** and **Multilevel Activity Book 1 page 91**.

E Listen and complete the orders.

1

GUEST CHECK

Date	Table	Guests	Server	128354

___2___ large pizzas
with onions

1 _small_ pizza with
pepperoni

___2___ _small_ sodas

Total

Thank you! Please come again.

2

Guest Check

Date	Table	Guests	Server	7742

___1___ medium

pizza with peppers

___2___ large

iced teas

___1___ medium

soda

Total

Thank you! Please come again.

3

GUEST CHECK

Date	Table	Guests	Server	410121

___2___ small

pizzas with __onions__

and __mushrooms__

___1___ small _soda_

___2___ large

iced teas

Total

Thank you! Please come again.

2 Practice your pronunciation

A Listen to the question and answer.

A: Are you ready to order? ↗

B: Yes, I am. ↘

B Listen and circle *question* or *answer*.

1. question ~~(answer)~~
2. ~~(question)~~ answer
3. ~~(question)~~ answer
4. question ~~(answer)~~

C Match the questions with the answers. Then practice with a partner.

__b__ 1. Are you ready to order?   a. I want a small soda.

__c__ 2. Do you want any toppings?   b. Yes, I am.

__a__ 3. Do you want anything to drink?   c. Yes, I do. Mushrooms, please.

3 Real-life math

**Write the prices and the totals for the orders in 1E.
Use the menu in 1A.**
1. 2 large pizzas with onions =$ 26.00;
1 sm. pizza with pepperoni =$ 7.50; 2 sm. sodas = $ 3.00; Total =$ 36.50 **2.** 1 medium pizza
with peppers = $ 9.50; 2 large iced teas = $ 4.00; 1 medium soda = $ 1.75; Total = $ 15.25
3. 2 small pizzas with onions / mushrooms = $ 17.00; 1 small soda = $ 1.50; 2 large iced teas = $ 4.00; Total = $ 22.50

TEST YOURSELF ✔

Work with a partner. Look at the menu on page 94. Partner A: Order a pizza
and a drink. Partner B: Repeat the order. Then change roles.

1 Get ready to read

A **Read the definitions.**

healthy: something that is good for your body

unhealthy: something that is not good for your body

B **Work with your classmates. Complete the chart with healthy food.** Answers will vary.

Healthy food	
apples	

C **Circle the food in the chart that you eat every week.**

2 Read about healthy food

A **Read the article.**

Doctors say, "Eat fruit and vegetables every day!"

Doctors and nutritionists[1] say, "Fruit and vegetables are good for you! Eat a lot of them every day." Some people don't listen. They say, "Fruit is expensive," or, "I don't like vegetables."

Do you think fruit and vegetables are expensive? Look at supermarket ads. Fruit and vegetables are on sale every week.

[1]nutritionist: a person who teaches, talks, and writes about healthy food

Do you eat the same fruit and vegetables every day? Try a new fruit. Eat a different vegetable. Find a new fruit or vegetable you like.

Listen to the doctors and the nutritionists. Don't eat a lot of unhealthy food. Eat fruit and vegetables every day and be healthy!

Source: *www.cdc.gov*

B **Listen and read the article again.**

 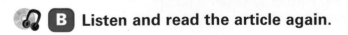 Identify healthy eating habits; interpret nutrition labels

Unit 8 Lesson 5

Objectives	Grammar	Vocabulary	Correlations
On- and Higher-level: Read about and discuss healthy food and food labels **Pre-level:** Read about healthy food and food labels	Imperative (*Eat healthy food.*)	*Healthy, unhealthy, nutritionists* For additional vocabulary practice, see these **Oxford Picture Dictionary** topics: Fruit, Meat and Poultry, Vegetables	**CASAS:** 0.1.2, 1.3.8, 1.6.1, 3.5.1, 3.5.2 **LCPs:** 27.02, 28.01, 32.01–32.06, 32.13 **SCANS:** Acquires and evaluates information, Knowing how to learn, Listening, Reading, Seeing things in the mind's eye, Speaking **EFF:** Read with understanding, Take responsibility for learning

Warm-up and Review

10–15 minutes (books closed)

Write *Every Day, Three Times a Week,* and *Never* on the board. Tell students about your eating habits, and write a food item under each column. Have students tell what they could put in each category and write the food words on the board in the correct column.

Introduction

5 minutes

1. Ask students which of the items on the board are good for your body and which aren't.

2. State the objective: *Today we're going to read about healthy and unhealthy food.* Write *healthy* and *unhealthy* on the board.

1 Get ready to read

Presentation

20–25 minutes

A Direct students to read the definitions of *healthy* and *unhealthy.*

B Copy the chart on the board, and have students help you complete it.

> **TIP** Before reading the article in 2A, find out how much your students know about a healthy diet. Write *Meat, Fruit and Vegetables, Grains, Snacks,* and *Desserts* on the board. Discuss the meanings. Draw a pie chart on the board, giving each item an equal amount of space. Have the students help you adjust the chart to represent a healthier diet.

C Direct students to circle the foods they eat every week. As a class, discuss their answers.

Pre-Reading

Direct students to look at the brochure in 2A. Read the headline aloud. Direct students to look at the picture. Ask: *What foods do you think doctors say to eat every day?*

2 Read about healthy food

Guided Practice I

25–30 minutes

A 1. Ask students to read the article silently.

2. Ask if there are any questions about the reading.

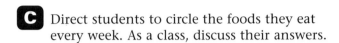

> ### Multilevel Strategies
>
> For 2A–B, seat same-level students together.
>
> • **Pre-level** Group these students, and read the article to them slowly. Give them time to follow along silently. Stop after every section to check comprehension.
>
> • **On- and Higher-level** While you are working with pre-level students, ask these students to write a list of some of the healthy and unhealthy food in their diets. Tell them to be specific—for example, *apples* not *fruit.*

B Play the audio. Have students read along silently.

C 1. Have students work individually to mark the sentences *true* or *false*.

2. Ask additional comprehension questions. *Do doctors say, "Eat fruit and vegetables every day"?* [yes]

> ## Multilevel Strategies
>
> After 2C, replay the audio for 2B to give pre-level students another chance to read.
>
> • **Pre-level** Have these students listen to the audio again and read along silently.
>
> • **On- and Higher-level** Write additional questions on the board for these students to answer. *Are fruit and vegetables always expensive? Is it good to eat the same fruit every day?*

D Have students work individually to complete the sentences with the vocabulary from the box. Go over the answers as a class.

3 Read food labels

Guided Practice II

15–20 minutes

A 1. Say: *Now we're going to look at food labels.*

2. Direct students to look at the pictures. Elicit the names of the soups, and write them on the board for students to copy.

B Have students work individually to complete the sentences. Go over the answers as a class.

> **TIP** Point out that in the food labels in 3A, *water* is the first ingredient because the soup has a lot of water. *Salt* is the last ingredient because it has a little salt.

Communicative Practice

10–15 minutes

C 1. Review the questions.

2. Set a time limit (three minutes). Allow students to think about or write their answers individually.

3. Elicit answers from volunteers, and write their ideas on the board.

> **TIP** To prepare students for the *Bring It to Life* assignment, bring in a real food label and make a transparency of it. Show students the different sections of the label, the nutrition information, and the ingredients. Elicit the words that students recognize and circle them.

Application

5–10 minutes

BRING IT TO LIFE

Discuss what kinds of food with labels students have at home. Have different students sign up to bring different kinds of food.

To compress this lesson: Assign 2D as homework.

To extend this lesson: Have a class discussion about healthy food choices.
1. Show students pictures of different foods, or have them look at pictures of food in *The Oxford Picture Dictionary*.
2. Teach any new vocabulary.
3. As you show each picture, ask for a show of hands to see if it's healthy to eat that food every day, once a week, or once a month.

And/Or have students complete **Workbook 1 page 56** and the **Multilevel Activity Book 1 page 92**.

C Mark the sentences T (true) or F (false).

_T_ 1. Doctors say, "Eat fruit every day."

_F_ 2. Fruit and vegetables are unhealthy.

_F_ 3. Fruit and vegetables are never on sale.

_F_ 4. Nutritionists say, "Fruit is expensive."

D Complete the sentences. Use the words in the box.

| fruit | ~~healthy~~ | sale | nutritionists | vegetables |

1. Eat ___healthy___ food.
2. Doctors and ___nutritionists___ say, "Eat a lot of fruit and vegetables."
3. ___Fruit___ and ___vegetables___ are good for you.
4. Look for fruit and vegetables on ___sale___ every week.

3 Read food labels

A Work with your classmates. Write the names of the soups.

① **Ingredients**
water,
tomatoes,
salt

___tomato soup___

② **Ingredients**
water,
chicken,
onions,
carrots

Salt-free!

___chicken soup___

③ **Ingredients**
water,
onions,
carrots,
mushrooms,
peppers,
tomatoes,
salt

___vegetable soup___

B Look at the food labels. Complete the sentences.

1. The ___chicken___ soup has no salt.
2. The ___vegetable___ soup has a lot of vegetables.
3. The ___tomato___ soup has three ingredients.

C Think about the questions. Talk about the answers with your class.

1. Do you think it's important to read food labels? Why or why not?
2. How often do you read the labels on food you buy?

BRING IT TO LIFE

Bring a food label to class. Talk about the ingredients with your classmates.

1 Grammar

A **Circle the correct words.**

1. I study (**every** / twice) day.
2. She (**always** / once) buys apples.
3. They (**usually** / three times) ride the bus.
4. Pat washes the windows (**twice** / one) a year.
5. They shop (always / **once**) a week.
6. Sharon pays the bills (never / **three times**) a month.

Grammar note

Adverbs of frequency

always ↑ 100%
usually
sometimes ↓
never ↓ 0%

I always eat breakfast.
I usually eat eggs for breakfast.
I sometimes eat breakfast at home.
I never eat pizza for breakfast.

B **Match the sentences with the frequency expressions.**

_e_ 1. Frank watches a movie every Friday.

_c_ 2. Beth cleans the garage in May and October.

_b_ 3. She goes to the bank on the 1st and 15th of the month.

_d_ 4. I feed the cat in the morning, at noon, and at night.

_f_ 5. Gary and Elaine don't drink soda.

_a_ 6. She brushes her teeth in the morning and at night.

a. twice a day
b. twice a month
c. twice a year
d. three times a day
e. once a week
f. never

C **Unscramble the sentences.**

1. never / Lucy / Sunday / eats / on / dinner _Lucy never eats dinner on Sunday._
2. eats / once / Mrs. Mack / a week / ice cream _Mrs. Mack eats ice cream once a week._
3. twice / Ben / does / homework / a week / usually _Ben usually does homework twice a week._
4. Sherman / a week / three / exercises / times _Sherman exercises three times a week._
5. always / Alicia / English / speaks / at home _Alicia always speaks English at home._

D **Write the answers.** Answers will vary.

1. How often do you go shopping? _I go shopping twice a week._
2. How often do you buy ice cream? _____
3. How often do you cook dinner for friends? _____
4. How often do you clean the kitchen? _____

Unit 8 Review and expand

Objectives	Grammar	Vocabulary	Correlations
On-, Pre-, and Higher-level: Expand upon and review unit grammar and life skills	Frequency expressions (*She shops once a week.*)	Frequency expressions For additional vocabulary practice, see this **Oxford Picture Dictionary** topic: The Calendar	**CASAS:** 0.2.4, 1.3.8, 4.8.1, 6.0.1, 7.2.5–7.2.7, 7.3.1 **LCPs:** 28.01, 31.03, 32.01, 32.02, 32.05, 32.13, 33.08 **SCANS:** Creative thinking, Listening, Participates as member of a team, Problem solving, Writing **EFF:** Read with understanding, Solve problems and make decisions

Warm-up and Review

10–15 minutes (books closed)

1. Review the *Bring It to Life* assignment from Lesson 5.

2. While waiting for students to arrive, give students who didn't do the assignment time to create their own label.

3. Have students tell whether they think their label is for a healthy or an unhealthy food.

3. Ask students to tell you words they recognize on the labels.

Introduction and Presentation

5 minutes

1. Using the food items or labels that students brought in, ask: *How often do you eat this food?* Restate the answer in third person. *Su Cheng eats this soup once a week.*

2. Read the *Grammar note* in 1A. Copy the sentences on the board. Draw students' attention to the position of the adverbs. *Other time expressions occur at the end of the sentence, but frequency adverbs usually appear between the subject and the verb.*

3. State the objective: *Today we're going to use frequency expressions to talk about our habits.*

1 Grammar

Guided Practice

40–45 minutes

A Have students work individually to circle the words. Ask volunteers to read the completed sentences to the class.

B Have students work individually to match the sentences and expressions. Call on volunteers to read the matching sentences and expressions. Write the number-letter match on the board.

C Have students work individually to unscramble the sentences. Ask volunteers to write the sentences on the board.

D Have students work individually to answer the questions. Ask volunteers to write their answers on the board.

Multilevel Strategies

For 1B, 1C, and 1D, seat same-level students together.

• **Pre-level** While other students move on to 1C and 1D, go through 1B with these students, reading each sentence and identifying the answers. Skip 1C and help students answer the questions in 1D. After other students have written the answers to 1C on the board, have pre-level students copy the answers into their books.

• **On- and Higher-level** While you are working with pre-level students, ask these students to complete 1C and 1D. Tell them to write three more questions with *How often* and ask a partner the questions.

2 Group work

Communicative Practice

20–35 minutes

1. Direct students, in groups of three to four, to focus on the picture on page 89. Ask: *Is the customer buying healthy food?*

2. Set a time limit (five minutes) to complete the exercise. Circulate and answer any questions.

3. Have a reporter from each group read the group's questions to the class.

> **TIP**
> Review the correct way to ask for spelling: *Please spell your name.* Direct students to ask their partners to spell their names and to listen and write the names rather than copying them.

1. Have students work in the same groups from 2A to take turns interviewing each other in pairs.

2. Set a time limit (five minutes) to complete the exercise.

3. Tell students to make a note of their partners' answers but not to worry about writing complete sentences.

> ## Multilevel Strategies
>
> For 2A and 2B, use same-level groups.
>
> • **Pre-level** For 2A, ask these students to write three vocabulary words and one complete question. For 2B, allow pre-level students to ask and answer the questions without writing.
>
> • **Higher-level** For 2A, ask these students to write two additional sentences about the picture. For 2B, have students ask and answer additional questions. *How often do you eat fruit? How often do you read food labels when you shop?*

 Have a reporter from each group share the group's work.

15–25 minutes

 1. Direct students to look at the picture. Ask: *What are they doing?* [eating dinner] *Why is the mother angry?* [The children don't want to eat.] Tell students they will read a story about a family that has a problem with food. Direct students to read the Ruzika family's story silently. Then play the audio, and have them read along silently.

2. Ask: *Do the girls like vegetables?* [no] *Does Lia cook vegetables?* [yes] *Do the girls eat the vegetables?* [no]

 1. Read the question and identify the problem. Read the possible solutions.

2. Elicit student ideas for other solutions. Write each one on the board.

3. Discuss whether the statements are appropriate.

4. Ask for a show of hands to see which solution the class likes best.

C Elicit the students' ideas for what Lia and Sam can say, and write them on the board.

Evaluation

30–35 minutes

To test students' understanding of the unit grammar and life skills, have them take the Unit 8 Test in the *Step Forward Test Generator CD-ROM with ExamView® Assessment Suite*.

Learning Log

To help students record and discuss their progress, use the *Learning Log* on page T-178.

To extend this review: Have students complete **Workbook 1 page 57, Multilevel Activity Book 1 pages 93–96,** and the **Unit 8 Grammar Exercises** on the **Multilevel Grammar Exercises CD-ROM 1.**

2 Group work

A Work with 2–3 classmates. Look at the picture on page 89.
Write 5 *How often?* questions about the food in the picture.
Talk about the questions with your class. Answers will vary.
How often do you buy bananas? How often do you buy chicken? How often do you buy soup?
How often do you buy bread? How often do you buy oranges?

B Interview 3 classmates. Write their answers in your notebook.

ASK:

1. How often do you eat vegetables
   with your dinner?
2. How often do you order pizza?
3. How often do you cook dinner?

Classmate—Ching Fu
1. every day
2. once or twice
   a month
3. never

C Talk about the answers with your class.

PROBLEM SOLVING

A Listen and read about the Ruzika family. What is
the problem? The girls don't eat vegetables.

Sam and Lia Ruzika have two daughters. Every night at
dinner the children say, "We don't like vegetables." Lia and
Sam think, "Our girls need vegetables." Lia cooks different
vegetables every night. She cooks broccoli, mushrooms,
potatoes, and carrots. The girls never eat them. They say
the same thing, "We don't like vegetables."

B Work with your classmates. Answer the question.
(More than one answer is possible.)

What can Lia and Sam do?
   a. Order pizza with vegetables on it.
   (c.) Tell the girls that vegetables are healthy.
   (b.) Give the girls a lot of fruit.
   (d.) Other: Answers will vary.

C Work with your classmates. Make a list of things Lia and Sam can say.

Your Health

FOCUS ON
- parts of the body/illness and injuries
- medical instructions and advice
- the verb phrase *have to*
- making medical appointments
- preventive care and medicine

LESSON 1   **Vocabulary**

---

1 Learn about parts of the body

A Look at the pictures. Is Mr. Patel healthy? No, he isn't.

🎧 **B** Listen and look at the pictures.

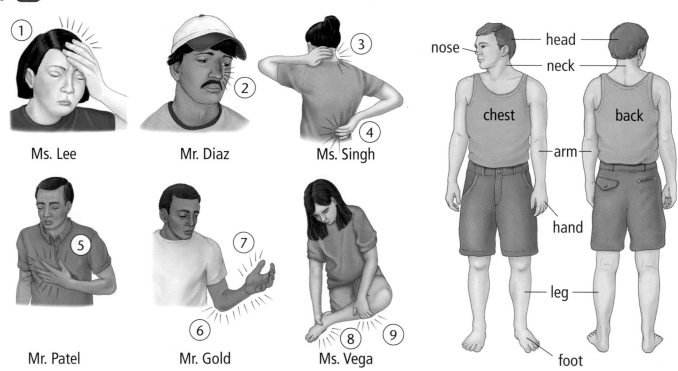

Ms. Lee   Mr. Diaz   Ms. Singh

Mr. Patel   Mr. Gold   Ms. Vega

nose — head — neck   chest   back   arm — hand — leg — foot

🎧 **C** Listen and repeat the words.

1. head	3. neck	5. chest	7. hand	9. leg
2. nose	4. back	6. arm	8. foot*	

*one foot / two feet

D Look at the pictures. Complete the sentences.

1. Ms. Lee's ___head___ hurts.   4. Ms. Singh's ___neck___ and ___back___ hurt.
2. Mr. Diaz's ___nose___ hurts.   5. Mr. Gold's ___arm___ and ___hand___ hurt.
3. Mr. Patel's ___chest___ hurts.   6. Ms. Vega's ___foot___ and ___leg___ hurt.

Unit 9 Lesson 1

Objectives	Grammar	Vocabulary	Correlations
On-level: Identify parts of the body, symptoms, and injuries **Pre-level:** Recognize parts of the body, symptoms, and injuries **Higher-level:** Talk and write about parts of the body, symptoms, and injuries	Simple-present tense (*Her head hurts.*)	Parts of the body, symptoms, and injuries For additional vocabulary practice, see these **Oxford Picture Dictionary** topics: The Body, Symptoms and Injuries	**CASAS:** 0.1.2, 3.1.1, 7.4.5, 7.4.7 **LCPs:** 24.01–24.03, 32.01 **SCANS:** Listening, Participates as member of a team, Seeing things in the mind's eye, Self-management, Speaking **EFF:** Cooperate with others, Listen actively, Speak so others can understand, Reflect and evaluate

Warm-up

10–15 minutes (books closed)

Find out how many body parts your students already know. Point to your head, nose, neck, chest, arm, back, leg, and foot, and see if your students can name them. Repeat, saying each word as you point to the body part and having students repeat. Have students stand and point to the body part as you say it.

Introduction

5 minutes

1. Write *Body* and the words from the warm-up on the board. Say: *These are parts of our body. Sometimes we have a problem with them, and we have to go to the doctor.*

2. State the objective: *Today we're going to learn names of body parts and things to say to the doctor.*

1 Learn about parts of the body

Presentation

20–25 minutes

A Direct students to look at the pictures. Ask: *Is Mr. Patel healthy?* [no]

B 1. Have students listen to the audio. Ask them to point to the correct picture as they listen. Circulate and monitor.

2. Check comprehension by asking *yes/no* questions. Pass out *yes/no* cards to the students (see page T-175), or have them hold up one finger for *yes* and two for *no* in order to get a nonverbal response. Ask: *Does Mr. Patel's leg hurt?* [no] *Does Mrs. Lee's head hurt?* [yes]

C Ask students to listen and repeat the words.

TIP
For more practice with body parts, have students pantomime a pain in the body and practice the following conversation.
A: What's the matter? B: My _____ hurts.
A: Oh, I'm sorry.

Guided Practice I

15–20 minutes

D 1. Have students complete the sentences using the new vocabulary.

2. Encourage students to take turns reading the completed sentences in pairs.

Multilevel Strategies

After completing 1D, seat same-level students together, and provide vocabulary practice targeted to the level of your students.

• **Pre-level** Ask these students to practice together by pointing to the pictures and saying the correct words.

• **On-level** Ask these students to cover the words and test each other on the vocabulary. Have one student point to the pictures while the other student says the correct word.

• **Higher-level** Ask these students to dictate the words to each other.

2 Talk about a doctor's office

Guided Practice II
35–40 minutes

 A 1. Ask: *How often do you go to the doctor?* Introduce the new topic: *Now let's talk about the doctor's office.*

2. Group students and assign roles: leader, fact checker, recorder, and reporter. Explain that students work with their groups to match the words and pictures.

3. Check comprehension of the exercise. Ask: *Who looks up the words in the picture dictionary?* [fact checker] *Who writes the numbers in the book?* [recorder] *Who tells the class your answers?* [reporter] *Who helps everyone and manages the group?* [leader]

4. Set a time limit (three minutes), and have students work together to complete the task. While students are working, copy the wordlist on the board.

5. Call "time" and have the reporters from each group take turns calling out the numbers for the wordlist. Record students' answers on the board. If groups disagree, write each group's choice next to the word.

B 1. Ask students to listen and check their answers.

2. Have students correct the wordlist on the board and then write the correct numbers in their books.

3. Review the pronunciation of *headache, backache, stomachache,* and *earache.*

4. Tell the groups from 2A to break into pairs to practice the words. Set a time limit (two minutes).

C 1. Copy the first line on the board. Do not cross out *stomachache* yet. Say: *Three words are the same. One word is different. Which word is different? Why is* stomachache *different?*

2. Cross out *stomachache* and direct students to complete the exercise independently.

3. Go over the answers as a class, and discuss why the words are alike or different.

Communicative Practice and Application
10–15 minutes

 D 1. Write two skeleton sentences on the board: *His/Her _____ hurts.* and *He/She has a _____.* Write the possible completions under each blank. Say each possibility and have students repeat. *His leg hurts. He has a broken leg. Her ear hurts. She has an earache.*

2. Model the conversation with a volunteer. Then model it again, talking about different patients from the picture in 2A.

3. Set a time limit (five minutes). Ask students to practice the conversation using all of the patients from the picture in 2A.

Multilevel Strategies

For 2D, pair same-level students.

• **Pre-level** While other students practice the conversation in 2D, have pre-level students point to the picture and ask their partners: *What's the matter with the man/woman?* The partners should respond with one of the sentences on the board.

Evaluation
10–15 minutes (books closed)

TEST YOURSELF

1. Make a two-column chart on the board with the headings *Body* and *Illness and Injury*. Have students close their books and give you an example for each column.

2. Have students copy the chart into their notebooks.

3. Give students five to ten minutes to test themselves by writing the words they recall from the lesson.

4. Call "time" and have students check their spelling in *The Oxford Picture Dictionary* or another dictionary. Circulate and monitor students' progress.

To compress this lesson: Conduct 2A as a whole-class activity. Have students practice 2D using only two patients from 2A.

To extend this lesson: Have students pantomime aches and pains and ask each other: *What's the matter?*

And/Or have students complete **Workbook 1 page 58** and **Multilevel Activity Book 1 page 98.**

2 Talk about a doctor's office

A Work with your classmates. Match the words with the picture.

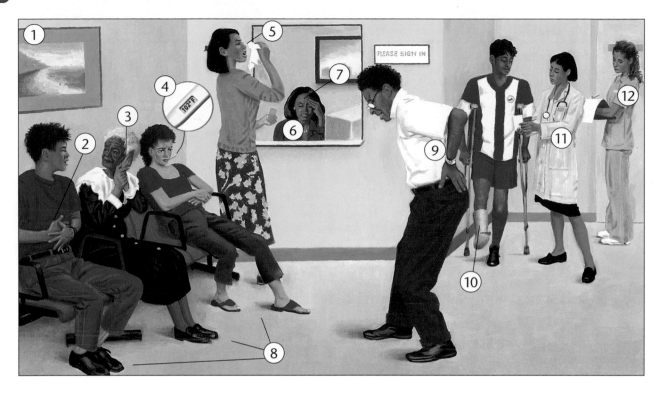

_9_	backache	_11_	doctor	_4_	fever	_8_	patients
_10_	broken leg	_1_	doctor's office	_7_	headache	_6_	receptionist
_5_	cold	_3_	earache	_12_	nurse	_2_	stomachache

B Listen and check your answers. Then practice the words with a partner.

C Cross out (X) the item that does NOT belong in each group.

1. nurse   stomachache   receptionist   doctor
2. patients   earache   stomachache   headache
3. eyes   mouth   cold   nose
4. arms   legs   nose   hands

D Work with a partner. Ask and answer questions. Use the picture in 2A.

A: What's the matter with the man in the white shirt?

B: He has a backache. What's the matter with the receptionist?

A: Her head hurts. She has a headache.

TEST YOURSELF ✔

Close your book. Write 6 body words and 4 illness and injury words. Check your spelling in a dictionary.

1 Read about a doctor's appointment

A Look at the pictures. Listen.

HOWARD CHEN MD

Your blood pressure is normal.

B Listen again. Read the sentences.

1. Miguel is sick today. He's at the doctor's office. He has a sore throat.
2. He gives his insurance card to the receptionist.
3. The nurse takes his temperature and his blood pressure.
4. Miguel opens his mouth. The doctor examines him and writes a prescription.
5. Miguel has to take his prescription medicine twice a day.
6. Miguel has to stay home and rest. He wants to get well.

C Check your understanding. Circle the correct words.

1. Miguel has a sore ((throat) / mouth).
2. Miguel needs his insurance (car / (card)).
3. The nurse takes his ((temperature) / medicine).
4. The doctor examines ((him) / a prescription).
5. Miguel has to take prescription medicine (once / (twice)) a day.
6. Miguel has to stay home and ((rest) / chest).

2 Write about yourself

A Write your story. Complete the sentences. Answers will vary.

Sometimes I have a /an _____, and I go to the
doctor. _____ takes my temperature and blood
pressure. _____ examines me and gives me a
prescription. I _____ to get well.

Need help?

Ways to get well
stay home
rest
take medicine

B Read your story to a partner.

☑ Describe a medical exam; talk about medical advice

Unit 9 Lesson 2

Objectives	Grammar	Vocabulary	Correlations
On-, Pre-, and Higher-level: Read and write about medical exams and doctors' advice	Simple-present tense (*The nurse takes my temperature.*)	Medical-exam words For additional vocabulary practice, see these **Oxford Picture Dictionary** topics: Dental Care, Medical Care, Taking Care of Your Health	**CASAS:** 0.1.2, 3.1.1, 3.2.3, 7.4.7 **LCPs:** 24.01–24.03, 32.01, 32.02, 32.07 **SCANS:** Acquires and evaluates information, Interprets and communicates information, Knowing how to learn, Listening, Participates as member of a team, Self-management, Writing **EFF:** Convey ideas in writing

Warm-up and Review

10–15 minutes (books closed)

Pass out cards or slips of papers with symptoms or injuries on them. Ask students to pantomime the problem on the card. Have the class guess. Encourage students to state the problem in two ways, if possible. *She has a headache. Her head hurts.*

Introduction

5 minutes

1. Referring to your performers, say: *Oh, no! All of my students are sick! You need to make an appointment with the doctor! An appointment is a date and time to see the doctor.* Write *appointment* on the board. Say: *My appointment is on Wednesday at 4:00.*

2. State the objective: *Today we're going to read and write about doctors' appointments.*

1 Read about a doctor's appointment

Presentation I

20–25 minutes

A 1. Direct students to look at the pictures. Ask: *Where is Miguel?*

2. Play the audio.

B 1. Play the audio again. Have students read along silently.

2. Check comprehension. Ask: *Does Miguel have a sore throat?* [yes] *Does the nurse write him a prescription?* [no]

Guided Practice I

10 minutes

C Play the audio. Ask students to listen and circle the correct answers. Go over the answers as a class.

2 Write about yourself

Guided Practice II

20–25 minutes

A 1. Pronounce and clarify the *Need help?* words. Read the final sentence using each of the expressions in the blank.

2. Copy the sentences on the board. Read them aloud with your own information.

3. Have students complete the sentences independently. Circulate and assist. Write the skeleton sentences on the board, or put up a transparency of them, and ask a volunteer to complete them.

Multilevel Strategies

Seat same-level students together for 2A.

• **Pre-level** While other students are completing 2A, reread 1B with the pre-level students. Read each sentence. Ask questions after each sentence.

• **Higher-level** Ask these students to complete two additional sentences.

B Ask students to read their sentences to a partner. Call on individuals to share what they learned about their partners.

3 Talk about ways to get well and to stay healthy

Presentation II

10–15 minutes

 1. Introduce the topic: *Now let's talk about how to get well and how to stay healthy.* Direct students to look at the pictures in 3A. Say: *This is a doctor's advice.* Write *advice* on the board.

2. Read and have students repeat the captions.

Guided Practice

20–25 minutes

 1. Ask students to put their pencils down and listen for the answer to this question: *Who is tired?* [Ms. Mendoza] Play the entire audio once.

2. Play the audio in segments. After each conversation, stop the audio and check answers with the students. *Did you write the letter?* If necessary, replay the segment.

3. Check students' listening accuracy: *Who needs to quit smoking?* [Mr. Wang]

Multilevel Strategies

Replay 3B to challenge on- and higher-level students while allowing pre-level students to catch up.

- **Pre-Level** Have these students listen again for another chance to complete the exercise.

- **On- and Higher-level** Write these questions on the board: *What does Mr. Jones drink? What does Ms. Mendoza do all day? What is Mr. White's problem?* After replaying the audio, have volunteers write the answers on the board.

---

 1. Have students read along silently while they listen.

2. Play the audio again, and have students repeat the conversation. Replay if necessary.

Communicative Practice and Application

10 minutes

 1. Write the conversation skeleton from 3C on the board. Elicit and write possible completions.

2. Model the conversation with a volunteer. Then model it again with different information.

3. Set a time limit (five minutes). Ask students to practice the conversation with several partners.

4. Ask volunteers to present their conversation to the class.

Evaluation

10–15 minutes (books closed)

TEST YOURSELF

1. Write *How do I get well?* on the board. Ask volunteers to give you advice.

2. Assign a time limit (three minutes). Have students listen to their partners and write.

3. Circulate and monitor.

Multilevel Strategies

- **Pre-level** Allow these students to talk without writing.

- **Higher-level** Ask these students to tell their partners four or five ways to get well.

To compress this lesson: Have students practice the conversation in 3D with only one partner.

To extend this lesson: Give students more practice talking about ways to get well and to stay healthy.
1. Provide students with more pictures of symptoms and injuries, or have them look at the pictures in *The Oxford Picture Dictionary*.
2. Have students suggest treatments or remedies for the symptom or injury in the picture.
3. Write their ideas on the board and discuss them.

And/Or have students complete **Workbook 1 page 59** and **Multilevel Activity Book 1 page 99**.

3 Talk about ways to get well and to stay healthy

A Look at the pictures. Read the ways to get well and to stay healthy.

Take medicine.

Rest.

Change your diet.

Exercise.

Drink fluids.

Quit smoking.

B Listen to the conversations. Match the doctor's advice in 3A with the correct patients.

1. Mr. Jones __c__
2. Mrs. Lynn __a__
3. Mr. Martinez __e__
4. Ms. Mendoza __d__
5. Mr. White __b__
6. Mr. Wang __f__

C Listen and repeat.

A: What do you do for a sore throat?
B: I take medicine. What do you do?
A: I drink tea.

D Work with a partner. Practice the conversation. Use your own ideas.

TEST YOURSELF ✔

Close your book. Tell a partner 3 ways to get well. Change roles. Listen and write your partner's ideas.

1 Learn *have to*

A Look at the pictures. Read the sentences. Where does Jeff have to go? To the dentist.

> I have a toothache.

> We have a test tomorrow.

Maria has to leave class early. She has to pick up her son.

Jeff has to leave work early. He has to go to the dentist.

Kim and Rosa have to leave the party early. They have to study.

B Study the chart. Complete the sentences below.

HAVE TO

Statements						
I You	have to	go to the dentist.		We You	have to	go to the dentist.
He She	has to			They		

1. He __has to__ go to the dentist. 2. They __have to__ go to the dentist.

C Look at the pictures. Circle the correct words.

1. Maria ((has) / has to) a son.
2. Jeff ((has to) / have to) go to the dentist.
3. He (has to / (has)) a toothache.
4. Kim and Rosa (has to / (have to)) study.
5. They ((have) / have to) a test tomorrow.
6. They (have / (have to)) leave early.

D Work with a partner. Talk about things you have to do this week.

A: *I have to study. How about you?*

B: *I have to go to the bank.*

Unit 9 Lesson 3

Objectives	Grammar	Vocabulary	Correlations
On- and Higher-level: Use *have to* to talk about obligations **Pre-level:** Recognize *have to*	*Have to* (He has to go to the doctor.)	*Early, toothache* For additional vocabulary practice, see these **Oxford Picture Dictionary** topics: Daily Routines, Symptoms and Injuries	**CASAS:** 3.1.1, 7.1.1–7.1.3, 7.4.7 **LCPs:** 24.02, 32.01, 32.13, 33.02, 33.07 **SCANS:** Seeing things in the mind's eye, Self-management, Speaking, Time, Writing **EFF:** Convey ideas in writing, Observe critically, Plan, Reflect and evaluate, Speak so others can understand

Warm-up and Review

10–15 minutes (books closed)

Write health problems on the board: *stomachache, sore throat, fever, headache, backache, cold*. Write *advice* on the board, and elicit advice for each of the illnesses. Write the advice on the board.

Introduction

5–10 minutes

1. Connect the health problems and advice on the board. *I have a cold. I have to drink fluids.*

2. State the objective: *Today we're going to use* have to *to talk about what we need to do.*

1 Learn *have to*

Presentation I

20–25 minutes

A Direct students to look at the pictures. Ask them to identify where each person is and what time it is in each picture. Read the sentences under the pictures.

B 1. Demonstrate how to read the grammar chart as complete sentences. Read the chart through sentence by sentence. Then read it again, and have students repeat after you.

2. Use the pictures in 1A to illustrate points in the grammar chart. Ask students to underline *has to* and *have to* in each caption in 1A.

3. As a class, complete the sentences under the chart. Ask volunteers to write the sentences on the board. Have other students read the sentences aloud.

4. Give students time to silently review the chart and, if they haven't already, fill in the blanks.

5. Assess students' understanding of the chart. Ask: *What do you have to do tomorrow? What does your (son/daughter/partner/friend) have to do tomorrow?*

Guided Practice

15–20 minutes

C Have students work individually to circle the correct words. Go over the answers as a class.

Communicative Practice

D 1. As a class, brainstorm a list of possibilities for completing the conversation. Write the list on the board.

2. Model the conversation with a volunteer.

3. Set a time limit (five minutes). Ask students to practice with several partners.

4. Ask volunteers to present their conversations to the class.

Multilevel Strategies

Adapt 1D to the level of your students.

• **Pre-level** Have these students practice the conversation using the ideas on the board.

• **Higher-level** Encourage these students to also talk about what their family members or friends have to do. *My daughter has to do her homework. My son has to clean his bedroom.*

---

2 Ask and answer information questions with *have to*

Presentation II

20–25 minutes

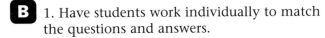 Read and have students repeat the questions and answers in the chart. Underline *have to* in each question and answer. Point out the change from *have to* to *has to* in the third person answer. Say some fill-in-the-blank sentences. Hum or clap to indicate the blank. *I _____ wash the dishes. Leticia _____ make dinner.*

Guided Practice

10–15 minutes

B 1. Have students work individually to match the questions and answers.

2. Ask volunteers to read the matching questions and answers aloud. Write the number-letter match on the board.

3 Practice *have to*

Communicative Practice and Application

20–25 minutes

A 1. Read the question words in the box and the example question and answer.

2. Have students work individually to complete the questions and answers.

3. Write the question completions on the board. Call on several volunteers to share each answer.

B Set a time limit (5 minutes) for students to interview their partners and write the sentences. Circulate and monitor.

> ### Multilevel Strategies
>
> Use mixed-level pairs for 3B.
>
> • **Pre-level** Have these students answer the questions first. Allow them to ask their partners the questions without writing the answers.
>
> • **Higher-level** Ask these students to think of an additional information question with *have to* to ask their partners.

C Discuss the class's answers. Call on volunteers to share what they learned about their partners.

Evaluation

10–15 minutes (books closed)

TEST YOURSELF

Ask students to write the sentences independently. Collect and correct their writing.

> ### Multilevel Strategies
>
> Target the *Test Yourself* to the level of your students.
>
> • **Pre-level** Allow these students to work with their books open. Ask them to write two sentences.
>
> • **Higher-level** Have these students write two additional sentences about what their family members or friends have to do.

To compress this lesson: Conduct 2B as a whole-class activity.

To extend this lesson: Write a list of health problems and health advice on the board, or use the picture cards from page 104 of *Multilevel Activity Book 1*.
1. Group students. If you are using cards, distribute a set to each group. Have students separate the cards into problems and advice.
2. Teach students the expression *I hope you get well soon*. Write this conversation on the board for them to practice using the ideas on the cards or the list on the board:

    A: How are you?
    B: I'm sick. I have a/an _____.
    A: You have to _____.
    B: That's a good idea.
    A: I hope you get well soon.

And/Or have students complete **Workbook 1 pages 60–61** and **Multilevel Activity Book 1 page 100**.

2 Ask and answer information questions with *have to*

A Study the chart. Ask and answer the questions.

Information questions and answers with *have to*	
A: Why do you have to leave early? **B:** I have to pick up my children.	**A:** Why does he have to leave early? **B:** He has to go to the doctor.
A: Why do they have to leave early? **B:** They have to study.	**A:** Why does she have to leave early? **B:** She has to go to the dentist.

B Match the questions with the answers.

_d_ 1. Why do you have to leave early?   a. She has to leave early.

_e_ 2. Why does Jeff have to go to the dentist?   b. He has a sore throat.

_a_ 3. Why does Maria have to talk to the teacher?   c. They have to study.

_c_ 4. Why do the girls have to go to the library?   d. I have to pick up my son.

_b_ 5. Why does Miguel have to see the doctor?   e. He has a toothache.

3 Practice *have to*

A Complete the questions with the words in the box.
Then write your answers.

~~Why~~	What	When	Where

1. __Why__ do you have to come to class every day? __I have to practice English.__
2. __What__ do you have to do after class today? __Answers will vary.__
3. __Where__ do you have to go after class? __Answers will vary.__
4. __When__ do you have to get up tomorrow? __Answers will vary.__

B Ask and answer the questions in 3A with a partner. Then write 4
sentences about your partner's answers.

Teresa has to practice English.

C Talk about the sentences with your class.

Teresa has to practice English. She has to make lunch after class.

TEST YOURSELF ✔

Close your book. Write 5 things you have to do this week. Use complete
sentences.

1 Learn to make an appointment

A Read the appointment card. Answer the questions.

Dear _Vera_____ ,

YOU HAVE AN APPOINTMENT

With: _Dr. Brown___

On: _Monday, May 12th_____

At: ___3:00___ a.m. (p.m)

See you then!

(M)   T   W   TH   F

1. Who has an appointment with Dr. Brown? _____Vera_____
2. What day is the appointment? _Monday_____
3. What's the date of the appointment? _May 12th_____
4. What time is the appointment? _3 p.m._____

B Listen and read.

A: Hello, doctor's office.

B: Hello. This is Carl Lee. I have a terrible cold.
   I have to see the doctor.

A: Let's see. I have an opening on Wednesday at 2:00.
   Is that OK?

B: Yes, it is. Thanks.

A: OK. See you on Wednesday, May 12th at 2:00.

C Listen again and repeat.

D Work with a partner. Practice the conversation. Use your own information.

A: I have a terrible _____. I have to see the doctor.

B: Let's see. I have an opening on _____
   at _____. Is that OK?

A: Yes, it is. Thanks.

B: OK. See you on _____ at _____.

Unit 9 Lesson 4

Objectives	Grammar	Vocabulary	Correlations
On- and Higher-level: Ask and answer questions about doctors' appointments **Pre-level:** Ask questions about doctors' appointments	Simple-present tense (*I have a headache.*)	*Appointment, terrible* For additional vocabulary practice, see this **Oxford Picture Dictionary** topic: Symptoms and Injuries	**CASAS:** 0.1.2, 2.3.2, 3.1.1–3.1.3, 4.8.3, 6.0.1, 7.4.7 **LCPs:** 22.03, 24.02, 24.03, 25.01, 25.03, 32.01, 32.02, 32.13, 33.04, 33.07 **SCANS:** Organizes and maintains information, Responsibility, Serves clients/customers, Sociability, Speaking **EFF:** Speak so others can understand

Warm-up and Review

10–15 minutes (books closed)

Review ordinal numbers. Write the numerals 1–31 on the board. Write a month above the numbers, and say each number as a date using the ordinal. Point to numbers randomly, and call on students to say the ordinals.

Introduction

5 minutes

1. Write on the board: *Doctor's appointment, 5/23, 3 p.m.* Read it aloud and have students repeat. Say: *An appointment is the day and time to see the doctor.*

2. State the objective: *Today we'll learn how to make doctors' appointments.*

1 Learn to make an appointment

Presentation

5–10 minutes

A 1. Direct students to look at the appointment card. Ask: *Who is the doctor?* [Dr. Brown]

2. Give students a minute to answer the questions below the card. Go over the answers as a class.

Guided Practice

20–25 minutes

B Play the audio. Have students read along silently.

C Play the audio again, and have students repeat the conversation. Replay if necessary.

Communicative Practice and Application

15–20 minutes

D 1. Model the conversation with a volunteer. Then model it again with other information.

2. Elicit other ways to complete the conversation.

3. Set a time limit (five minutes). Ask students to practice the conversation with several partners.

Multilevel Strategies

For 1D, adapt the oral practice to the level of your students.

• **Pre-level** Have these students read the conversation as written in 1B.

• **Higher-level** Ask these students to also practice rejecting the receptionist's suggested time. *A: No, it isn't. I have to see the doctor sooner. How about _____?*

1. Direct students to look at the first appointment card. Ask: *Who is the patient?* [Tom]

2. Play the first conversation. Stop and ask for a show of hands of how many students got all of the answers. Replay if necessary before going on to the second conversation. Go over the answers as a class.

2 Learn prepositions *on* and *at*

Grammar Extension

10–20 minutes

1. Read and clarify the *Grammar note*.

2. Have students work individually to complete the sentences.

3. Ask volunteers to read the completed sentences aloud.

1. Read the questions.

2. Have students work individually to write the answers. Ask volunteers to write their answers on the board.

3 Practice your pronunciation

Pronunciation Extension

10–15 minutes

A Play the audio. Have students read along silently.

Replay the audio and have students repeat.

 C 1. Play the audio. Have students circle the words.

2. Replay the audio, so students can check their answers. Go over the answers.

Evaluation

10–15 minutes

TEST YOURSELF

1. Model the role-play with a volunteer. Then switch roles.

2. Pair students. Check comprehension by asking "receptionists" to raise their hands. Ask them for examples of what they can say. Do the same with the "patients."

3. Set a time limit (five minutes), and have the partners act out the role-play in both roles.

4. Circulate and monitor. Encourage pantomime and improvisation.

5. Provide feedback.

> **TIP** Make the *Test Yourself* more intensive. Seat students in two concentric rings facing each other. Tell the inner circle that they are receptionists. Tell the outer circle they are patients. Have the patients "call" the receptionists to make an appointment. Allow time for one call. Then have all students in the outer circle move one seat to the left. Tell them to practice again with the new receptionist. Call "time" when students need to move again. After the circle has gone about halfway around, switch roles. Continue until the circle has gone all the way around.

To compress this lesson: Have students practice the conversation in 1D with only one partner.

To extend this lesson: Practice listening and writing with a memory dictation.
1. Tell students that they should listen without writing as you say three sentences. Say: *I have to leave class early. I have a backache. I'm going to the doctor at 3:00.* Repeat the sentences.
2. Tell students to work with a partner to try to reconstruct your sentences.
3. Ask a volunteer pair to write its reconstruction on the board. Correct it together. Point out to students that these sentences could be a note to a teacher.
And/Or have students complete **Workbook 1 page 62** and **Multilevel Activity Book 1 page 101**.

🎧 **E** Listen and complete the appointment cards.

1

Dear _Tom_,

YOU HAVE AN APPOINTMENT

With: _Dr. Wu_

On: _Tuesday, June 2nd_

At: _4:00_ a.m. (p.m)

M (T) W TH F

2

Dear _Pat_,

YOU HAVE AN APPOINTMENT

With: _Dr. Brown_

On: _Monday, October 23rd_

At: _10:30_ (a.m.) p.m

(M) T W TH F

2 Learn prepositions *on* and *at*

A Complete the sentences with *on* or *at*.

1. I have to leave _____*at*_____ 5:00.

2. Sue has an appointment __*on*__ Tuesday.

3. We want to go to the party __*at*__ 7:00.

4. I have to see the doctor __*on*__ June 17th.

> **Grammar note**
>
> *on* or *at*?
>
> Use *on* for days and dates.
>   on Monday
>   on November 11th
>
> Use *at* for times.
>   at 10:30
>   at noon

B Write your answers. Answers will vary.

1. When do you have to come to class? _____

2. When do you have to go to work? _____

3. When do you have to get up tomorrow? _____

3 Practice your pronunciation

🎧 **A** Listen to the sentences.

1. I **have to** see the doctor.
   I **have a** cold.

2. She **has to** go at 2:30.
   She **has a** new job.

🎧 **B** Listen again and repeat.

🎧 **C** Listen and circle the words you hear.

1. (have to)   have   3. has to   (has)
2. have to   (has to)   4. (have)   has

TEST YOURSELF ✔

Work with a partner. Make an appointment to see a doctor. Partner A:
You're the patient. Partner B: You're the receptionist. Then change roles.

1 Get ready to read

A Look at the picture. Read the definitions.

checkup: a medical examination to check your health when you are not sick

over-the-counter medicine: medicine you don't need a prescription to buy

B Work with your classmates. How often do you do these things?

1. exercise   2. eat healthy food   3. get a checkup

2 Read about good health

A Read the article.

Feeling Fine

It's not always easy to be healthy. Here are some ways to be healthy and feel good.

Exercise

Doctors say it's important to exercise for thirty minutes a day, three days a week.

Eat healthy food

Don't forget to eat fruit and vegetables. They're good for you, and they taste good.

Have regular checkups

See your doctor for a checkup once a year. Always follow your doctor's health instructions.

If you feel sick, you can take over-the-counter medicine. Sometimes over-the-counter medicine helps people feel better. It's important to read and follow the directions exactly.[1] Over-the-counter medicines don't always stop the problem. Then, you have to go to the doctor.

[1]exactly = with no mistakes

B Listen and read the article again.

Unit 9 Lesson 5

Objectives	Grammar	Vocabulary	Correlations
On- and Higher-level: Read about and discuss good health and medicine labels **Pre-level:** Read about good health and medicine labels	Imperative (*Do not take this medicine with milk.*)	*Checkup, over-the-counter medicine, feel, instructions, exactly* For additional vocabulary practice, see this **Oxford Picture Dictionary** topic: Dental Care, Medical Care, Taking Care of Your Health	**CASAS:** 3.3.1, 3.3.3, 3.4.1, 3.5.8, 3.5.9 **LCPs:** 24.02–24.04, 27.02, 32.01–32.06, 32.13 **SCANS:** Acquires and evaluates information, Knowing how to learn, Reading, Seeing things in the mind's eye, Speaking, Writing **EFF:** Read with understanding, Take responsibility for learning

Warm-up and Review

10–15 minutes (books closed)

Put up or draw pictures of various foods, including fruits, vegetables, meats, desserts, snacks, and fast-food items. Have students identify the foods. Then ask volunteers to remove anything from the board they think is not healthy. Discuss the remaining foods: *How often do you eat this?*

Introduction

5 minutes

1. Say: *Eating these foods is not the only way to stay healthy.* Ask: *How else do we stay healthy?* Write some of the students' ideas on the board.

2. State the objective: *Today we're going to read about other ways to stay healthy and look at medicine labels.*

1 Get ready to read

Presentation

15–20 minutes

A Read the words and the definitions. Elicit the names of some over-the-counter medicines that students are familiar with.

B Tell students how often you do each of the three things. Then ask volunteers to share their information. Ask students how often they think it is necessary to do each thing in order to be healthy.

TIP Before students read the article in 2A, have them look through magazines for pictures of healthy and unhealthy behaviors or foods. Discuss the pictures as a class.

Pre-Reading

Direct students to look at the pictures in the magazine article. Use the pictures to have students predict what they will read. Ask them to identify the health recommendation associated with each picture.

2 Read about good health

Guided Practice I

25–30 minutes

A Ask students to read the article silently. Ask if there are any questions about the reading.

Multilevel Strategies

For 2A–B, seat same-level students together.

• **Pre-level** Assist these students by reading each piece of advice separately. Check for comprehension after each section.

• **On- and Higher-level** While you are working with pre-level students, ask these students to evaluate themselves according to the article. Write sentence skeletons on the board for them to fill in with a frequency expression: *I exercise _____. I eat fruits and vegetables _____. I have checkups _____. I _____ follow the directions on medicine labels.*

B Play the audio. Have students read along silently.

C Have students work individually to circle the correct words. Ask volunteers to read the completed sentences aloud.

Multilevel Strategies

Seat same-level students together for 2C and 2D.

• **Pre-level** While other students move on to 2D, allow these students extra time to complete 2C. Have them copy the answers to 2D after they are written on the board.

Higher-level Have these students complete 2C and 2D. Ask them to take turns reading the sentences with a partner before you go over the answers.

D Have students work individually to complete the sentences. Ask volunteers to write the answers on the board.

3 Read directions and warnings on medicine labels

Guided Practice II

15–20 minutes

A 1. Draw students' attention to the medicine labels. Write the word *label* on the board. Say: *Now we're going to look at medicine labels.* Ask: *Which label says, "Do not take with alcohol"? Number 1 or number 2?* [one] *Which medicine says, "Do not take with food"?* [two]

2. Have students work individually to match the sentences with the labels. Go over the answers as a class.

Communicative Practice

10–15 minutes

B Elicit students' ideas about other warnings, and write them on the board. Possibilities include: *Do not drive. Do not operate machinery. Do not take when pregnant. Do not give to children. Do not use with other medicines.*

Application

5–10 minutes

BRING IT TO LIFE

1. Have students brainstorm the names of common over-the-counter medications and choose which ones they are going to look at. Keep the brainstormed list for the introduction to *Unit 9 Review and expand.*

2. Tell students that if they cannot go to a pharmacy, they can complete the assignment using medicine labels in their homes.

To compress this lesson: Assign 2D as homework.

To extend this lesson: Have students turn the ideas from the article in 2A into a plan.
1. Group students and provide each group with a large piece of paper. Ask the group to write a plan for a healthy day. For example: *Wake up at 6:00. Run in the park. Take a shower. Eat fruit for breakfast,* etc.
2. Discuss and correct the papers as a class. As an alternative, have groups describe an unhealthy day, and have the class point out the problem behaviors in it and suggest improvements.

And/Or have students complete **Workbook 1 page 63** and **Multilevel Activity Book 1 page 102**.

C Circle the correct words.

1. It's important to have a checkup every (month /(year)).
2. Eat ((fruit and vegetables)/ over-the-counter medicine) every day.
3. It's important to exercise ((three)/ thirty) days a week.
4. Always (feel /(follow)) the directions with over-the-counter medicine.

D Complete the sentences. Use the words in the box.

checkup   ~~feel~~   exactly   healthy

1. Over-the-counter medicine can help you _____feel_____ better.
2. It's a good idea to go to the doctor for a __checkup_____ every year.
3. Follow all the directions __exactly_____ with over-the-counter medicine.
4. Exercise can help you be __healthy_____ and feel good.

3 Read directions and warnings on medicine labels

A Look at the medicine labels. Match the sentences with the labels.

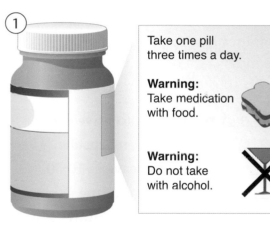

1. Do not take this with milk. __2__   4. Take this medicine twice a day. __2__
2. Take this medicine with food. __1__   5. Do not take this with food. __2__
3. Do not take this with alcohol. __1__   6. Take this medicine three times a day. __1__

B Think about the question. Talk about the answer with your class.

What other warnings are on medicine labels? Name or draw 2 other warnings you know.

BRING IT TO LIFE

Go to a pharmacy. Look at a medicine label. Write the name of the medicine. Write or draw the directions and warnings in your notebook.

1 Grammar

A Circle the correct words.

1. The (**woman** / women) has a cold.
2. This (**child** / children) has to see the dentist.
3. Those (person / **people**) have to ride the bus.
4. His (teeth / **tooth**) hurts.
5. My (foot / **feet**) hurt.
6. The (man / **men**) have to talk to the nurse.

Grammar note

Irregular plural nouns

Singular	Plural
foot	feet
tooth	teeth
man	men
woman	women
child	children
person	people

B Match the questions with the answers.

__e__ 1. What's the matter with Maria?   a. He has to see the doctor.

__d__ 2. When does she have to leave?   b. No, he doesn't.

__a__ 3. Why does Carl have to leave early?   c. We leave early once a week.

__b__ 4. Does he leave early every day?   d. She has to leave at 2:00.

__c__ 5. How often do you leave early?   e. She has a backache.

C Write the questions.

1. _Does Rosa have to leave early?_   Yes, she has to leave early.
2. _What's the matter?_   She has a stomachache.
3. _When does she have to leave?_   She has to leave at 10:30.
4. _Where does she have to go?_   She has to go to the doctor.
5. _Does she always leave early?_   No, she doesn't always leave early.

D Complete the story. Use the words in the box.

~~is~~	have	at	isn't	has	on	receptionist	has to	wants

Today _____is_____ Monday. Mr. Larson _____has_____ an earache.
            1   2

He _has to_ see the doctor. He talks to the _receptionist_.
      3   4

The doctor doesn't _have_ an opening today. There's an
                       5

opening _on_ Tuesday _at_ 10:00.
          6   7

Mr. Larson _isn't_ happy. He _wants_ to see the doctor today.
            8   9

Unit 9 Review and expand

Objectives	Grammar	Vocabulary	Correlations
On-, Pre-, and Higher-level: Expand upon and review unit grammar and life skills	Irregular plurals (*tooth/teeth*) Present-tense questions (*Does he leave early every day?*) *Have to* (*She has to see the doctor.*)	Irregular plurals For additional vocabulary practice, see these **Oxford Picture Dictionary** topics: The Body, Symptoms and Injuries	**CASAS:** 0.1.2, 3.1.1, 4.8.1, 6.0.1, 7.2.5–7.2.7, 7.3.1 **LCPs:** 24.01–24.03, 32.01, 32.02, 32.05, 32.13, 33.04, 33.06, 33.07 **SCANS:** Creative thinking, Participates as member of a team, Problem solving, Speaking **EFF:** Cooperate with others, Solve problems and make decisions

Warm-up and Review

10–15 minutes (books closed)

1. Review the *Bring It to Life* assignment from Lesson 5.

2. Have students who did the exercise share what they saw on the medicine labels.

3. Write common warnings on the board. Ask students who didn't do the assignment to check off warnings they remember seeing before.

Introduction and Presentation

5 minutes

1. Write the list of common over-the-counter medications on the board. For each one, ask: *Why do you take this medicine?*

2. State the objective: *Today we're going to review different ways to talk about illness and health.*

1 Grammar

Guided Practice

40–45 minutes

A 1. Read the irregular plural nouns in the *Grammar note* and have students repeat. Elicit how students know which word is correct. [subject-verb agreement]

2. Have students work individually to circle the correct choice in each sentence.

3. Read the completed sentences aloud, and have students repeat them.

B Have students work individually to match the questions and answers. Ask volunteers to read the matching questions and answers. Write the number-letter match on the board.

C Have students work individually to write the questions. Ask volunteers to write their questions on the board.

D Have students work individually to complete the story. Write the answers on the board. Read the completed paragraph aloud.

Multilevel Strategies

For 1B, 1C, and 1D, seat same-level students together.

• **Pre-level** While other students move on to 1C and 1D, go through 1B with these students, reading each question and having them identify the answers. Skip 1C and help students complete the paragraph in 1D. After other students have written the questions for 1C on the board, have pre-level students copy them into their books.

• **On- and Higher-level** Write *When does _____?, Where does _____?, What time does _____?,* and *Does he _____?* on the board. After these students complete 1C and 1D, ask them to complete the questions with their own ideas and write answers. Have volunteers share their questions and answers with the class.

2 Group work

Communicative Practice

20–35 minutes

 A 1. Direct students, in groups of three to four, to focus on the picture on page 101. Ask: *What's the matter with the receptionist? Why?*

2. Set a time limit (five minutes) to complete the exercise. Circulate and answer any questions.

3. Have a reporter from each group read the group's sentences to the class.

Multilevel Strategies

For 2A and 2B, use same-level groups.

• **Pre-level** For 2A, ask these students to write three vocabulary words and one complete sentence. For 2B, allow them to ask and answer the questions without writing.

• **Higher-level** For 2A, ask these students to write two additional sentences about the picture. For 2B, have them ask and answer these questions: *What do you have to do tomorrow? How often do you have to cook dinner? How often do you have to shop for food?*

B 1. Have students work in the same groups from 2A to take turns interviewing each other in pairs. Set a time limit (five minutes) to complete the exercise.

2. Tell students to make notes of their partners' answers but not to worry about writing complete sentences.

C Have a reporter from each group share the group's work.

> **TIP**
>
> For more practice with *have to* after 2C, do a memory circle. Write on the board: *I have to _____. He/She has to _____.* Have students stand in a circle or in two circles if you have a large class. Have the first student say: *I have to (go to the bank).* The next student says: *She has to go to the bank. I have to (buy bread).* The third student says: *She has to go to the bank. He has to buy bread. I have to (get gas).* Continue until the circle is completed. Put less-verbal students at the beginning of the circle. Go last yourself.

PROBLEM SOLVING

15–25 minutes

 A 1. Direct students to look at the picture of David. Ask: *Where is he? How does he feel?* Tell students they will read a story about a teacher with a problem. Direct students to read David's story silently. Then play the audio, and have them read along silently.

2. Ask: *What is David's job?* [English teacher] *What does he tell his students?* [Come and learn English every day.] *How does he feel today?* [He has a headache and a stomachache.] *Does he want to go home?* [no]

B 1. Read the question and identify the problem. Read the possible solutions.

2. Elicit student ideas for other solutions. Write each one on the board.

3. Discuss whether the statements are appropriate.

4. Ask for a show of hands to see which solution the class likes best.

C Discuss what David can tell his class. Write a skeleton of the conversation on the board. Ask volunteers to present a version of the conversation to the class.

Evaluation

10–15 minutes

To test students' understanding of the unit grammar and life skills, have students take the Unit 9 Test in the *Step Forward Test Generator CD-ROM with ExamView® Assessment Suite.*

Learning Log

To help students record and discuss their progress, use the *Learning Log* on page T-178.

To extend this review: Have students complete **Workbook 1 page 64, Multilevel Activity Book 1 pages 103–106,** and the **Unit 9 Grammar Exercises** on the **Multilevel Grammar Exercises CD-ROM 1.**

2 Group work

A Work with 2–3 classmates. Write 5 sentences about the picture on page 101. Talk about the sentences with your class. Answers will vary.

The girl next to her has a fever. The receptionist has a headache. A man has a broken leg. The nurse is helping him. *A woman is sitting in the chair. She has an earache.*

B Interview 3 classmates. Write their answers in your notebook.

ASK:

1. What do you have to do this afternoon?
2. How often do you have to clean the house?
3. Do you have to work this weekend?

Classmate—Rafik
1. go to the bank
2. once a week
3. yes

C Talk about the answers with your class.

PROBLEM SOLVING

A Listen and read about David. What is his problem?

David is sick today. He has to teach tonight.

David teaches English in the evening. He likes his job and his students very much. Every day he tells his students, "You have to come to school every day. Don't stay home! Come and learn English every day." David has a problem today. He has a terrible headache and a stomachache, too. He doesn't want to go home, but he feels terrible.

B Work with your classmates. Answer the question. (More than one answer is possible.)

What can David do?

a. Call the doctor.
b. Go home now.
c. Stay at school now, but stay home tomorrow.
d. Other: Answers will vary.

C Work with your classmates. What can David tell his students?

UNIT **10**

Getting the Job

FOCUS ON
- jobs and job skills
- looking for a job
- the simple past of *be*
- job interviews
- good employee skills

LESSON **1** Vocabulary

1 Learn names of jobs

A Look at the pictures. Point to the person cleaning a school.

B Listen and look at the pictures.

C Listen and repeat the words.

1. pharmacist
2. homemaker
3. mechanic
4. janitor
5. server
6. childcare worker

D Look at the pictures. Complete the sentences.

1. A _____mechanic_____ works in a garage.
2. A _homemaker_____ works at home.
3. A _childcare worker_____ works in a childcare center.
4. A _janitor_____ works at a school.
5. A _pharmacist_____ works in a pharmacy.
6. A _server_____ works in a restaurant.

Unit 10 Lesson 1

Objectives	Grammar	Vocabulary	Correlations
On-level: Identify job titles and job skills **Pre-level:** Recognize job titles and job skills **Higher-level:** Talk and write about job titles and job skills	Simple-present tense (*He works in a school.*) Present continuous (*He's cooking.*)	Job titles and skills For additional vocabulary practice, see this **Oxford Picture Dictionary** topic: Jobs and Occupations	**CASAS:** 0.1.2, 4.1.6, 4.1.8, 7.4.5, 7.4.7 **LCPs:** 18.02, 19.02, 32.01 **SCANS:** Listening, Participates as member of a team, Seeing things in the mind's eye, Self-management, Speaking **EFF:** Cooperate with others, Listen actively, Observe critically, Speak so others can understand

Warm-up and Review

10–15 minutes (books closed)

Review community places. Have students line up at the board and take turns writing the names of places in the community until they run out of ideas.

Introduction

5 minutes

1. Use the community places on the board to talk about jobs and job skills. *A doctor works at a hospital. She takes care of patients.* Write *skills* on the board, and give more examples.

2. State the objective: *Today we're going to learn job names and job skills.*

1 Learn names of jobs

Presentation

20–25 minutes

A Direct students to look at the pictures and point to the person cleaning a school.

B 1. Have students listen to the audio. Ask them to point to the correct picture as they listen. Circulate and monitor.

2. Check comprehension by asking *yes/no* questions. Pass out *yes/no* cards to the students (see page T-175), or have them hold up one finger for *yes* and two for *no* in order to get a nonverbal response. *Does a server work at a restaurant?* [yes] *Does a janitor work in a pharmacy?* [no]

> **TIP** Replay the audio to challenge your students. Ask more questions. *Why does the pharmacist like his job?* [He helps people.] *Why does the homemaker like her job?* [She loves her family.]

C Ask students to listen and repeat the words.

Guided Practice I

15–20 minutes

D 1. Have students complete the sentences using the new vocabulary.

2. Encourage students to take turns reading the completed sentences in pairs.

> ### Multilevel Strategies
>
> After completing 1D, seat same-level students together, and provide vocabulary practice targeted to the level of your students.
>
> • **Pre-level** Ask these students to practice together by pointing to the pictures and saying the correct words.
>
> • **On-level** Ask these students to cover the words and test each other on the vocabulary by pointing to the pictures.
>
> • **Higher-level** Ask these students to dictate the words to each other.

2 Talk about jobs and skills

Guided Practice II
35–40 minutes

 1. Introduce the new topic: *Now let's talk about more jobs.*

2. Group students and assign roles: leader, fact checker, recorder, and reporter. Explain that students work with their groups to match the words and pictures.

3. Check comprehension of the exercise. Ask: *Who looks up the words in the picture dictionary?* [fact checker] *Who writes the numbers in the book?* [recorder] *Who tells the class your answers?* [reporter] *Who helps everyone and manages the group?* [leader]

4. Set a time limit (three minutes), and have students work together to complete the task. While students are working, copy the wordlist on the board.

5. Call "time" and have the reporters from each group take turns calling out the numbers for the wordlist. Record students' answers on the board. If groups disagree, write each group's choice next to the word.

B 1. Ask students to listen and check their answers.

2. Have students correct the wordlist on the board and then write the correct numbers in their books.

3. Tell the groups from 2A to break into pairs to practice the words. Set a time limit (two minutes).

C 1. Have students work individually to complete the sentences.

2. Ask students to take turns reading the completed sentences in the same pairs from 2B.

TIP

Pantomime one of the occupations from the lesson, and have students guess who you are and what you are doing. Ask volunteers to come up and pantomime other occupations. On the board, write: *Who is he/she? What is he/she doing?* Have the class guess.

Communicative Practice and Application
10–15 minutes

 1. Prepare students for the conversation by eliciting the *–ing* form of each of the verbs in 2C. Point out that a plumber *always fixes* sinks, but *right now* the plumber in the picture *is fixing* the sink. Write the *–ing* form on the board.

2. Model the conversation with a volunteer. Then model it again with other jobs from the picture in 2A.

3. Set a time limit (five minutes). Ask students to practice the conversation with several partners.

Evaluation
10–15 minutes (books closed)

TEST YOURSELF

1. Make a two-column chart on the board with the headings *Jobs* and *Job Skills*. Have students close their books and give you an example for each column.

2. Have students copy the chart into their notebooks.

3. Give students five to ten minutes to test themselves by writing the words they recall from the lesson on the chart.

4. Call "time" and have students check their spelling in *The Oxford Picture Dictionary* or another dictionary. Circulate and monitor students' progress.

Multilevel Strategies

Target the *Test Yourself* to the level of your students.

• **Pre-level** Have these students work with their books open.

• **Higher-level** Have these students complete the chart and then write sentences like the ones in 2D. *He is a plumber. He's fixing the sink.*

To compress this lesson: Conduct 2A as a whole-class activity. Have students practice 2D with only one partner.

To extend this lesson: Teach students how to alphabetize. Write all of the job titles on the board. Show students how to alphabetize using the first letter and then the second. Have students copy the list into their notebooks in alphabetical order.

And/Or have students complete **Workbook 1 page 65** and **Multilevel Activity Book 1 page 108**.

2 Talk about jobs and skills

A Work with your classmates. Match the words with the picture.

GRAND OPENING TODAY!

__4__ bus person	__1__ delivery person	__2__ manager	__6__ plumber
__5__ cook	__8__ gardener	__7__ painter	__3__ server

B Listen and check your answers. Then practice the words with a partner.

C Complete the sentences.

1. A _____plumber_____ fixes sinks.
2. A __bus person__ cleans tables.
3. A __gardener__ works in gardens.
4. A __cook__ cooks food.

5. A __delivery person__ delivers packages.
6. A __manager__ manages a business.
7. A __server__ serves food.
8. A __painter__ paints buildings.

D Work with a partner. Ask and answer questions about jobs. Use the picture in 2A.

A: Who is he?
B: He's a cook.
A: What's he doing?
B: He's cooking.

TEST YOURSELF ✔

Close your book. Write 5 jobs and 5 job skills. Check your spelling in a dictionary.

1 Read about getting a job

A Look at the pictures. Listen.

Here's an application.

See you on Monday.

Great!

B Listen again. Read the sentences.

1. Sergei was a pharmacist in Russia. Now he lives in New York.
2. He's looking for a job.
3. He looks at the help-wanted ads in the newspaper.
4. He sees a sign in a pet store window and applies for the job.
5. He has an interview and gets the job.
6. Sergei is happy. He loves his new job.

C Check your understanding. Mark the sentences T (true) or F (false).

__F__ 1. Sergei lives in Russia now.

__F__ 2. He is a pharmacist in New York.

__T__ 3. He looks in the newspaper for a job.

__F__ 4. He sees a sign on the Internet.

__T__ 5. He gets a job.

__T__ 6. He loves his job.

2 Write about looking for a job

A Write about how to look for a job. Complete the sentences. Answers will vary.

Are you looking for a job?

You can look _____ or look

_____ to find a job.

Then, you _____ and

have an _____. Good luck!

Need help?

You can look...

in the newspaper.
in store windows.
on the Internet.

B Read your sentences to a partner.

☑ Identify ways to find a job; interpret job ads

Unit 10 Lesson 2

Objectives	Grammar	Vocabulary	Correlations
On-, Pre-, and Higher-level: Read and write about looking for a job	Simple-present tense (*The job is part-time.*)	*Sign, applies, wanted, part-time, full-time* For additional vocabulary practice, see this **Oxford Picture Dictionary** topic: Job Search	**CASAS:** 0.1.2, 1.2.5, 2.5.4, 4.1.6, 4.1.8, 6.0.1, 7.4.7 **LCPs:** 19.02, 25.01, 32.01, 32.02, 32.07, 32.13, 33.02 **SCANS:** Acquires and evaluates information, Interprets and communicates information, Knowing how to learn, Reading, Self-management, Writing **EFF:** Convey ideas in writing

Warm-up and Review

10–15 minutes (books closed)

Review job titles and job skills. Say the skill and give students a moment to write the occupation. *1. He cleans buildings. 2. He fixes sinks. 3. She serves food. 4. He fixes cars. 5. She sells medicine.* Put the numbers on the board, and call on individuals to write the job title on the board. Point to each word, and challenge volunteers to remember the skill associated with that job.

Introduction

5 minutes

1. Ask for a show of hands to see how many of your students have a job. Ask how many want a job. Talk about a time when you were looking for a job.

2. State the objective: *Today we're going to read and write about looking for a job.*

1 Read about getting a job

Presentation I

20–25 minutes

A 1. Direct students to look at the pictures. Ask: *What kind of store is this?*

2. Play the audio.

B 1. Play the audio again. Have students read along silently.

2. Check comprehension. Ask: *What was Sergei's job in Russia? Where does he look for work?*

Guided Practice I

10 minutes

C 1. Ask students to put their pencils down and listen to the entire audio once, pointing to the correct answer.

2. Play the audio again, and have students circle the correct answer. Go over the answers as a class.

2 Write about looking for a job

Guided Practice II

20–25 minutes

A 1. Pronounce and clarify the *Need help?* phrases. Write *apply* and *interview* on the board.

2. Copy the sentences on the board. Read them aloud, completing them with the *Need help?* phrases and words on the board.

3. Have students complete the sentences independently. Circulate and assist.

Multilevel Strategies

Seat same-level students together for 2A and 2B.

• **Pre-level** Assist these students with completing 2A. Read it aloud together.

• **Higher-level** Ask these students to write one or two other ways to find a job and share them with the class.

B Ask students to read their sentences to a partner.

3 Read help-wanted ads

Presentation II

20–25 minutes

 A Introduce the topic: *One place to find a job is in the newspaper.* Direct students to look at the help-wanted ads in 3A. Say: *These are help-wanted ads. What are the jobs?*

Guided Practice

10–15 minutes

 B Have students work individually to complete the chart.

> After 3B, provide practice with listening to job information. Post pictures of people with various occupations on the board. Under each picture, write *Where? What job? Hours? Who? Number?* in a column. Give information about the jobs. *Sally's Restaurant needs a part-time cook. Twenty hours a week including Saturdays. Call Barbara, the manager, at (212) 555-4738. That's (212) 555-4738.* Repeat the information and tell students to take notes. Ask volunteers to come up and write short answers to the questions under each picture.

Communicative Practice and Application

10–15 minutes

C 1. Read and have students repeat the questions.

2. Model the questions and answers with a volunteer.

3. Assign a time limit. Have students take turns asking and answering about the jobs with a partner.

4. Ask volunteers to say the questions and answers aloud.

Multilevel Strategies

Seat same-level students together for 3B and 3C.

• **Pre-Level** Give these students extra time to complete 3B and 3C while other students do additional work. Monitor and assist as necessary.

• **On- and Higher-level** While pre-level students are completing 3B and 3C, provide these students with the help-wanted section of a newspaper. Ask them to choose a job title and answer these questions: *How many _____ jobs are there? How many are part-time? How many are full-time?*

Evaluation

10–15 minutes (books closed)

TEST YOURSELF

1. Remind students of the information they'll need to include in their ad: job title, hours, whom to contact, phone number or address.

2. Have them work with a partner to ask and answer the questions in 3C about each other's ads.

> For more practice with the questions in 3C, have students circulate and ask each other about the ads they created for the *Test Yourself.*

To compress this lesson: Conduct 3B as a whole-class activity.

To extend this lesson: Replay the audio from 1C. Ask students to repeat the questions. Ask volunteers to write the questions on the board. Have partners practice the questions and answers.

And/Or have students complete **Workbook 1 page 66** and **Multilevel Activity Book 1 page 109**.

3 Read help-wanted ads

A Look at the help-wanted ads. Read about the jobs.

① **HELP WANTED**

Driver
Evenings, part-time
(18 hours a week)
Call Tom.
555-2298

② **Mechanic Needed**
FT (40 hours a week)
See Bill.
Southside Auto Repair
9245 Clark Avenue

③ **Manager Needed**

Full-time
Apply at Pizza King.
227 Main Street

④ **HELP WANTED**

Cleaning staff
PT (25 hours a week),
late nights
Call Carla for an application.
555-8841

B Look at the help-wanted ads again. Read the sentences.
Check (✔) the correct boxes.

	Job #1	Job #2	Job #3	Job #4
1. This job is part-time (PT).	✔			✔
2. This job is full-time (FT).		✔	✔	
3. This job is on Main Street.			✔	
4. This job is in the evenings.	✔			✔
5. You have to talk to Bill for this job.		✔		
6. You have to talk to Carla for this job.				✔

C Work with a partner. Ask and answer questions
about the help-wanted ads in 3A.

1. What's the job?
2. Is it part-time or full-time?
3. How many hours is the job?
4. Who can I talk to about the job?

TEST YOURSELF ✔

Close your book. Write a help-wanted ad for a job you want. Share your ad
with a partner.

1 Learn the simple past with *be*

A Look at the pictures. Was Rico a student or a gardener in 1992? Rico was a student.

farmer 1980–1991   student 1991–1993   gardener 1994–2002   business owner 2002–present

B Study the charts. Complete the sentences below.

THE SIMPLE PAST WITH *BE*

Statements						
I	was	a gardener.	We		were	gardeners.
You	were		You			
He She	was		They			

1. He __was__ a gardener.   2. They __were__ gardeners.

Negative statements						
I	was not	a gardener.	We		were not	gardeners.
You	were not		You			
He She	was not		They			

Contractions

was not = wasn't
  I wasn't a gardener.
were not = weren't
  They weren't gardeners.

3. He __was not__ a gardener.   4. We __were not__ gardeners.

C Complete the sentences. Use the information in 1A.

1. Rico __was__ a farmer in 1980.

2. Rico and his brothers __were__ gardeners in 1994.

3. They __were not__ gardeners in 1981.

4. Rico __was not__ a student in 2001.

Unit 10 Lesson 3

Objectives	Grammar	Vocabulary	Correlations
On- and Higher-level: Use the simple past of *be* to talk about work experience **Pre-level:** Recognize the simple past of *be*	Simple past of *be* (*He was a farmer.*)	Occupations For additional vocabulary practice, see these **Oxford Picture Dictionary** topics: The Calendar, Jobs and Occupations	**CASAS:** 0.1.2, 4.1.6, 4.1.8, 6.0.1, 7.4.7 **LCPs:** 18.02, 19.02, 22.01, 25.01, 32.01, 32.07, 32.13 **SCANS:** Acquires and evaluates information, Arithmetic/Mathematics, Interprets and communicates information, Seeing things in the mind's eye, Self-management **EFF:** Reflect and evaluate

Warm-up and Review

10–15 minutes (books closed)

Call out letters and ask students to write all the occupations they can think of that begin with that letter. When you finish, ask students to count the number of words on their papers for each letter. Ask the student with the highest number of words for each to write his/her list on the board. After all of the words are on the board, ask the other students if they have any other occupations that begin with that letter not already on the board. Add those jobs to the entire list.

Introduction

5–10 minutes

1. Use the occupations on the board (or add to them if necessary) to talk about yourself. *Now I am a teacher. In 1995 I was a secretary.*

2. State the objective: *Today we're going to talk about our past jobs.*

1 Learn the simple past with *be*

Presentation I

20–25 minutes

A 1. Direct students to look at the pictures. Ask: *Was Rico a gardener in 1992?* [no]

2. Read the captions under the pictures.

B 1. Demonstrate how to read the grammar charts as complete sentences. Read the charts through sentence by sentence. Then read them again, and have students repeat after you.

2. Use the pictures in 1A to illustrate points in the grammar chart. *He was a farmer in 1985. He wasn't a business owner in 1985.*

3. As a class, complete the sentences. Ask volunteers to write the sentences on the board. Have other students read the sentences aloud.

4. Give students time to silently review the charts and, if they haven't already, fill in the blanks.

5. Assess students' understanding of the charts. Ask them to say sentences about Rico and about themselves.

Guided Practice

15–20 minutes

C Have students work individually to complete the sentences. Go over the answers as a class.

Multilevel Strategies

After 1C is corrected, group same-level students together.

• **Pre-level** Have these students copy the sentences from the chart in 1B and quiz each other on the forms. Have one partner say the subject and the other respond with the correct verb form.

• **On- and Higher-level** Ask students to say or write additional sentences with *was/wasn't* and *were/weren't*.

2 Ask and answer *Yes/No* questions

Presentation II

20–25 minutes

1. Read the questions and the corresponding answers in the chart. Have students repeat.

2. Draw students' attention to the reversal of subject and verb in the question and answer. Then give several examples, and have students call out *question* or *answer*. *Was he at school? He was at school.*

3. Write several short answers on the board: *Yes, she was. No, he wasn't. Yes, they were.* Ask questions and have students respond chorally: *Was he a plumber? Was she a teacher? Were they at home?*

Guided Practice

10–15 minutes

Have students work individually to match the questions and answers. Ask volunteers to read the matching questions and answers aloud. Write the number-letter match on the board.

> **TIP** Point out the use of *ago*. Write other phrases on the board that can be used with *ago: two weeks ago, six months ago.*

C Have students work individually to complete the questions and write the answers.

> **TIP** Contrast the present tense with the past tense. Write *Yes, he/she is. No, he/she isn't. Yes, he/she was.* and *No, he/she wasn't.* on the board. Hold up pictures of people in various occupations, and ask *yes/no* questions. *Is she a dentist? Was he a farmer?* Allow students to respond chorally. Then call on individuals to answer the questions.

3 Practice *Yes/No* questions

Communicative Practice and Application

20–25 minutes

A Write the questions on the board. Elicit possible completions and answers. Give students time (three minutes) to write their own questions and answers.

B 1. Model the interview with a volunteer. Switch roles and model with a different volunteer.

2. Check comprehension. Ask: *How many questions do you ask?* [three] *Do you write your partner's short answer?* [no] *Do you write sentences about your partner?* [yes]

3. Set a time limit (two minutes) for students to interview their partners. Circulate and monitor.

4. Discuss the class's answers. Find out what the most commonly held job was. Find out who had an unusual job.

> **Multilevel Strategies**
>
> For 3A and 3B, seat pre-level students together.
>
> • **Pre-level** Assist these students with writing the questions and answers in 3A. Allow them to ask the questions in 3B without writing.
>
> • **On- and Higher-level** After these students have written the third-person sentences about one partner in 3B, encourage them to mingle and ask the questions of several partners.

Evaluation

10–15 minutes (books closed)

TEST YOURSELF

Ask students to write the sentences independently. Collect and correct their writing.

To compress this lesson: Conduct 2B as a whole-class activity.

To extend this lesson: Have students practice short answers with *be* in the present and past.
1. Provide groups of students with pictures of different occupations or use the picture cards on page 114 of *Multilevel Activity Book 1*.
2. Have group members take turns asking questions in the present and past about the pictures. *Is she a homemaker? Yes, she is. Was he a janitor? No, he wasn't.* Model the activity, using correct and incorrect job titles to elicit negative and affirmative answers.

And/Or have students complete **Workbook 1 pages 67–68** and **Multilevel Activity Book 1 page 110.**

2 Ask and answer *Yes/No* questions

A Study the chart. Ask and answer the questions.

Yes/No questions and answers	
A: Were you a doctor ten years ago? **B:** Yes, I was. *or* No, I wasn't.	**A:** Were you at home last night? **B:** Yes, we were. *or* No, we weren't.
A: Was he a student five months ago? **B:** Yes, he was. *or* No, he wasn't.	**A:** Were they at school last week? **B:** Yes, they were. *or* No, they weren't.

B Match the questions with the answers.

__c__ 1. Were they at home yesterday?　　　　a. Yes, he was.

__d__ 2. Was she a student in Brazil?　　　　b. No, I wasn't.

__b__ 3. Were you a student six years ago?　　c. No, they weren't.

__a__ 4. Was he at school last week?　　　　　d. Yes, she was.

C Complete the questions. Then write the answers.

1. __Was_____ Rico a farmer 25 years ago?　__Yes, he was._____
2. __Was_____ Rico a student last year?　__Answers will vary._____
3. __Were_____ you a student in 2004?　__Answers will vary._____
4. __Were_____ you at school yesterday?　__Answers will vary._____

3 Practice *Yes/No* questions

A Complete the questions with a job. Write your answers. Answers will vary.

1. In your home country, were you (a) / an _____gardener_____? _____
2. In your home country, were you a / an _____? _____
3. In your home country, were you a / an _____? _____

B Ask and answer the questions in 3A with a partner. Then write sentences about your partner's answers.

Juan was a gardener in Guatemala.

TEST YOURSELF ✔

Close your book. Write 2 to 4 sentences about your work experience.

I was a homemaker from 1990 to 1998. I was a server from 1998 to 2002.

1 Learn about a job interview

A Read Isabel Monte's job application. Match the questions with the answers.

Applicant name:	Isabel Monte	Position:	Office Assistant
Experience:		Skills:	use a computer, make copies,
Receptionist 2005-present Los Angeles		answer phones, speak English and Spanish	
Office Manager 1995-2005 Guatemala City		Education: English classes,	
Office Assistant 1988-1995 Guatemala City		computer classes, business classes	

___d___ 1. When was Isabel an office manager?   a. Guatemala City

___c___ 2. Does she have office skills?   b. office assistant

___a___ 3. Where was she in 1998?   c. yes

___b___ 4. What job does she want?   d. from 1995 to 2005

B Listen and read.

A: Tell me about yourself, Mr. Tran.

B: I'm from Vietnam. I lived there for thirty years.

A: Do you have work experience?

B: Yes, I do. I was a restaurant manager for two years.
I can cook, serve food, and wash dishes, too.

A: Can you work weekends?

B: Yes, I can.

A: That's great. You're hired!

C Listen again and repeat.

D Work with a partner. Practice the conversation. Use your own information.

A: Tell me about yourself, _____.

B: I'm from _____. I lived there
for _____ years.

A: Do you have work experience?

B: Yes, I do. I was a _____ for _____ years.
I can _____ and _____.

A: That's great. You're hired!

Need help?

A: Do you have work experience?
B: Yes, I do. *or*
No, I don't, but I can learn quickly.

Unit 10 Lesson 4

Objectives	Grammar	Vocabulary	Correlations
On-, Pre-, and Higher-level: Interview for a job and describe abilities	*Can (I can fix sinks.)*	Job skill verbs For additional vocabulary practice, see this **Oxford Picture Dictionary** topic: Job Skills	**CASAS:** 0.1.2, 0.2.1, 4.1.6, 4.1.8, 4.4.7, 4.8.3, 6.0.1 **LCPs:** 18.02, 18.03, 18.06, 19.02, 22.01, 25.01, 32.01–32.03, 32.13, 33.02, 34.01–34.03 **SCANS:** Listening, Seeing things in the mind's eye, Self-management, Sociability, Speaking, Writing **EFF:** Speak so others can understand

Warm-up and Review

10–15 minutes (books closed)

Write *I was* and *I am* on the board. Put an appropriate job for you under each column. *I was a secretary. I am a teacher.* Have volunteers write job titles in each column on the board. Tell them it's OK if they write the same job in both columns.

Introduction

5 minutes

1. Referring to the words from the warm-up, say: *This is our job history. When we go for an interview, we have to talk about our job history.*

2. State the objective: *Today we're going to learn about job interviews.*

1 Learn about a job interview

Presentation

20–30 minutes

A 1. Direct students to look at the application. Ask questions. *What job is Isabel Monte looking for?*

2. Give students a minute to look over the application and match the questions and answers. Go over the answers as a class.

Guided Practice

20–25 minutes

B 1. Direct students to look at the picture. Ask: *Who is the manager?* [the woman] *Who is looking for a job?* [the man]

2. Play the audio. Have students read along silently.

C Play the audio again, and have students repeat the conversation. Replay if necessary.

Communicative Practice and Application

15–20 minutes

D 1. Read the question and answer in the *Need help?* box.

2. Model the conversation with a volunteer. Then model it again with your own information.

3. Elicit other ways to complete the conversation.

4. Set a time limit (five minutes). Ask students to practice the conversation with several partners.

Multilevel Strategies

For 1D, adapt the oral practice to the level of your students.

• **Pre-level** Have these students read the conversation as written in 1B.

• **Higher-level** Ask these students to supply a job history in response to *Do you have work experience?* Put these skeleton sentences on the board: *I was a/an _____ for _____ years. I was a/an _____ for _____ months.*

1. Direct students to read the sentences before they listen.

2. Have students put their pencils down and listen once without writing. Play the audio. Tell them to point to the correct answers.

3. Replay the audio and have students write in the letters that go with each person.

4. Ask follow-up questions. *What was Gladys's job?* [nurse] *Where is she from?* [El Salvador]

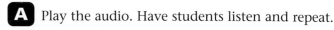 Use pictures of people in different occupations, or the pictures from page 114 of *Multilevel Activity Book 1,* to practice writing job histories. Put up a picture, and as a class, invent a story about the person. Write the story on the board. Group students and provide a picture to each group. Underline or erase key words in the sentences on the board so that students have sentence skeletons to work with. Have the groups write the stories.

2 Learn questions with *can*

Grammar Extension

15–20 minutes

 1. Introduce the new topic: *A plumber can fix sinks. A nurse can help patients. Now let's learn how to use* can.

2. Read and have students repeat the questions and short answers in the chart.

3. As a class, complete the sentences below the chart. Ask volunteers to write the completed questions and answers on the board. Ask other volunteers to read them aloud.

4. Check understanding of the chart by asking questions about the people in 1E. *Can Molly fill prescriptions? No, she can't.*

B 1. Brainstorm a list of possible job skills, and write them on the board.

2. Model the questions and answers with a volunteer using the jobs on the board. Switch roles and model with another volunteer.

3. Assign a time limit (three minutes), and have students practice asking and answering with a partner.

3 Practice your pronunciation

Pronunciation Extension

10–15 minutes

A Play the audio. Have students listen and repeat.

B Play the audio. Have students listen and circle the letter of the correct answer. Go over the answers as a class.

Evaluation

10–15 minutes

TEST YOURSELF

1. Demonstrate the conversation with a volunteer.

2. Pair students. Check comprehension. Ask: *Are you telling about your job history or your job skills?* [job skills] Set a time limit (five minutes), and have the partners talk.

3. Circulate and monitor. Encourage students to switch partners if they finish quickly. Provide feedback.

> ### Multilevel Strategies
>
> Target the *Test Yourself* to the level of your students.
>
> • **Higher-level** Have these students write down their partners' job skills.

To compress this lesson: Have students practice the conversation in 1D with only one partner.

To extend this lesson: Have students talk about the occupations and skills of people they know. Brainstorm a list of people students could talk about, and write them on the board. Give them a sentence skeleton to follow. *My _____ is a/an _____. He/She can _____.* Call on several volunteers to share information about a family member or friend using the sentence skeleton on the board. Assign a time limit (five minutes), and have students practice in pairs.
And/Or have students complete **Workbook 1 page 69** and **Multilevel Activity Book 1 page 111**.

E Listen and match the people with the job skills.

__b__ 1. Gladys   a. He can fix sinks and toilets.

__c__ 2. Ken   b. She can help patients.

__a__ 3. Franco   c. He can fill prescriptions.

__d__ 4. Molly   d. She can cook, clean, pay bills, and take care of children.

2 Learn questions with *can*

A Study the chart. Complete the sentences below.

Questions with *can*		
Can	you he she they	fix cars?

Answers						
Yes,	I he she they	can.		No,	I he she they	can't.

1. A: Can he __fix__ cars?

   B: Yes, he __can__ .

2. A: __Can__ he fix sinks?

   B: No, he __can't__ .

B Work with a partner. Ask and answer questions with *can*.

A: Can you fix cars?

B: Yes, I can.

A: Can you manage a restaurant?

B: No, I can't.

3 Practice your pronunciation

A Listen and repeat.

Can	Can't
I can ride a bicycle.	I can't drive a bus.
Jose can speak English.	He can't speak Chinese.

B Listen for *can* or *can't*. Circle *a* or *b*.

1. a. can   **(b.)** can't   3. **(a.)** can   b. can't   5. a. can   **(b.)** can't

2. **(a.)** can   b. can't   4. a. can   **(b.)** can't   6. **(a.)** can   b. can't

---

TEST YOURSELF ✔

Work with a partner. Tell a partner about 3 job skills you have. Then change roles.

I can fix sinks, I can speak English and Chinese, and I can drive a truck.

1 Get ready to read

A **Read the definitions.**

employee: worker

boss: the person you work for; your supervisor or manager

co-workers: people who work with you; other employees

B **Work with your classmates. Which questions can you ask your boss? Which questions can you ask your co-workers?**

1. Can I leave early today? boss
2. How do I use the photocopier? boss / co-worker
3. Do you like your job here? boss / co-worker
4. Where's the lunchroom? co-worker

2 Read about great employees

A **Read the quiz. Then answer the questions.** Answers will vary.

Are You Good or Are You Great?

Are you a good employee, or a great employee? Check (✔) *yes* or *no* for each sentence. Then count the number of *yes* answers you have. Read what your answers say about you.

1 I always read memos[1] and employee information from my boss.

Yes _____ No _____

2 I ask my co-workers for help or advice.

Yes _____ No _____

3 I come to work on time or a little early every day.

Yes _____ No _____

4 I call my boss on days I can't come to work.

Yes _____ No _____

5 I complete my time card on time.

Yes _____ No _____

What your answers say about you:
5 yes answers: You are an excellent employee!
3–4 yes answers: You are working hard. You're a good employee!
1–2 yes answers: Need help? Ask a co-worker. You can learn something new every day.

[1]memo: a note from a boss to the employee(s)

B **Listen and read the quiz again.**

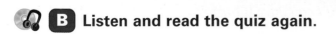

Unit 10 Lesson 5

Objectives	Grammar	Vocabulary	Correlations
On- and Higher-level: Read about and discuss appropriate workplace behavior and time cards **Pre-level:** Read about appropriate workplace behavior and time cards	Simple present-tense questions (*How do I use the photocopier?*)	*Employee, boss, co-workers, memos* For additional vocabulary practice, see these **Oxford Picture Dictionary** topics: The Calendar, An Office, Time	**CASAS:** 2.3.2, 4.1.6, 4.1.7, 4.2.1, 4.4.1, 4.4.2, 4.4.4, 4.6.1, 6.0.1 **LCPs:** 19.01–19.04, 20.02, 25.01, 25.03, 32.01, 32.04–32.06, 32.13 **SCANS:** Arithmetic/Mathematics, Listening, Reading, Speaking, Time **EFF:** Read with understanding, Use math to solve problems and communicate

Warm-up and Review

10–15 minutes (books closed)

1. Draw a blank grid on the board with a number (1–16) in each box. Make sure there is room to write in the boxes. Divide the class into two teams.

2. Play "blackboard concentration" with the following information: 1. bus person; 2. delivery person; 3. fix sinks and toilets; 4. deliver pizzas; 5. plumber; 6. take care of patients; 7. fill prescriptions; 8. manage a business; 9. homemaker; 10. pharmacist; 11. cook, clean, and take care of children; 12. manager; 13. mechanic; 14. fix cars; 15. clean tables; 16. nurse.

3. Ask Team 1 to call out two numbers. Write the corresponding information in the boxes. For example, if the team says one and five, write *bus person* in box 1 and *plumber* in box 5. Ask: *Do they match?*

4. Since they do not match, erase the words. Tell students to put their pencils down and try to remember which words go in which boxes. Call on Team 2 to choose two numbers. Write the words. Ask: *Do they match?* Erase them if they don't match. When a team gets a match, leave the words on the board. Continue until the grid is filled.

Introduction

5 minutes

1. Circle the job skills in the concentration grid. Say: *These are special skills that some employees can do. Today we're going to talk about things every employee can do.*

2. State the objective: *Today we're going to read about good employees and learn how to read a time card.*

1 Get ready to read

Presentation

15–20 minutes

A Read the words and the definitions aloud.

B Read the questions aloud. Ask for a show of hands about each question: *Can you ask your co-workers this question? Your boss?*

Pre-Reading

Direct students to look at the title of the quiz in 2A. Ask for ideas about how students can be great employees. Write their ideas on the board.

2 Read about great employees

Guided Practice I

25–30 minutes

A Ask students to read the quiz silently. Ask if there are any questions about the reading.

Multilevel Strategies

For 2A–B, seat same-level students together.

• **Pre-level** After playing the audio, assist these students by reading the quiz aloud and checking for comprehension as you go.

• **On- and Higher-level** Ask these students to take the quiz and decide if they are "good" or "great" employees.

B Play the audio. Have students read along silently.

1. Have students work individually to circle the correct choice to complete the sentences.

2. Ask volunteers to read the sentences aloud.

3. Ask students for a show of hands to see how many of them are "great" employees. Congratulate them.

 Have the class help you make a "student" version of the quiz on the board. *1. I always read the directions. 2. I ask my classmates for help. 3. I always come to class on time. 4. I tell my teacher when I can't come to class. 5. I complete my homework on time.* Tell students to take the quiz to determine if they are "great" students!

3 Read a time card

Guided Practice II

15–20 minutes

 1. Ask students how many of them have time cards at work. Introduce the topic: *Now we're going to look at a time card.*

2. Direct students to look at the time card. Ask questions. *Who is the employee? Where does he work? What is the rate of pay?*

3. Have students work individually to complete the sentences under the time card.

Multilevel Strategies

Seat same-level students together for 3A.

• **Pre-level** Work with these students to complete the exercise. Read each sentence and help them find the answer on the time card.

• **On- and Higher-level** While you are working with the pre-level students, ask these students to complete the sentences in 3A independently and then check their answers with a partner. Tell them also to discuss the questions in 3B with their partners.

Communicative Practice

10–15 minutes

 Read the questions aloud. Elicit the students' responses.

4 Real-life math

Math Extension

10–15 minutes

1. Read the directions. Have students work individually to answer the questions.

2. Ask a volunteer to write the answers and the math problems on the board.

Application

5–10 minutes

BRING IT TO LIFE

If students don't have magazines at home, ask them to look at magazines at the library, at a newsstand, or in a waiting room. Tell them to mentally choose a picture and remember what it looks like, so they can talk about it in class.

To compress this lesson: Assign 2C as homework.

To extend this lesson: Have students create a list of what it takes to be a great employee.
1. Group students and have each group choose an occupation.
2. Ask students to list what a person in that occupation should do to be "great." For example, for an ESL teacher, they might say: *Speak clearly. Be patient. Come to class on time.*

And/Or have students complete **Workbook 1 page 70** and **Multilevel Activity Book 1 page 112**.

C **Complete the sentences. Circle *a* or *b*.**

1. Ask your co-workers for ____.
   a.) help   b. memos

2. A memo is usually from the ____.
   a. employees   b.) boss

3. Call your ____ on days you can't work.
   a. co-worker   b.) boss

4. Come to work ____.
   a.) on time   b. sometimes

3 Read a time card

A **Look at the time card. Complete the sentences.**

Quick Stop Car Wash   **Employee Time Card**

Name: **White, Joey**   Employee number: **0521**   Rate: **$12.50**   Pay Period: **June 1–June 7**

Day	Time in	Time out	Hours
Monday	8:00 a.m.	2:00 p.m.	6
Wednesday	8:00 a.m.	2:00 p.m.	6
Friday	8:00 a.m.	2:00 p.m.	6
Total hours:			18

1. A pay period at Quick Stop Car Wash is __7__ days.
2. Joey was at work on __Monday__, __Wednesday__ and __Friday__.
3. Joey was at work from __8:00 a.m.__ to __2:00 p.m.__ on Monday.

B **Think about the questions. Talk about the answers with your class.** Answers will vary.

1. Is the rate of pay at Quick Stop Car Wash good?
2. Is Joey's work schedule a good work schedule for you? Why or why not?

4 Real-life math

Look at Joey's time card again. Answer the questions.

Joey works the same schedule every week.

1. How much money does he make every pay period? __$ 225__
2. How much money does he make in a year? __$ 11,700__

⌐ **BRING IT TO LIFE** ⌐

Find magazine pictures of employees and bosses at work. Bring the pictures
to class. Talk about the pictures with your classmates.

1 Grammar

A Complete the sentences with *can* or *can't*.

1. I can speak English,
   and Henry _____can_____, too.
2. My son can cook,
   but my daughter __can't__.
3. I can take care of children,
   and Jackie __can__, too.
4. I can fix sinks, and I __can__ fix bathtubs, too.
5. David __can__ speak English, but he can't speak Spanish.
6. Bill can help patients, but he __can't__ manage a restaurant.

> **Grammar note**
>
> **and/too**
> I can cook. Mary can cook.
> I can cook, **and** Mary can, too.
> **but**
> I can cook. Tom can't cook.
> I can cook, **but** Tom can't.

B Complete the questions and answers. Use *was, wasn't, were,* or *weren't*.

1. __Was__ Mei a doctor in China?   Yes, she __was__.
2. __Were__ they in Hong Kong last month?   No, they __weren't__.
3. __Was__ Mr. Morris at work yesterday?   No, he __wasn't__.
4. __Were__ you at home last Monday?   No, we __weren't__.
5. __Were__ the girls in Texas two weeks ago?   Yes, they __were__.

C Match the questions and answers.

__c__ 1. Where were Tad and Elena yesterday?   a. He was a mechanic.

__e__ 2. Was Elena a plumber in New York?   b. Julio and Elda were their friends.

__a__ 3. What was Tad's job five years ago?   c. They were at school.

__b__ 4. Who were their friends in Chile?   d. They were students in 2005.

__d__ 5. When were they students?   e. No, she wasn't.

D Complete the story. Circle the correct words.

Hector is (for /(from)) Mexico. He ((lived)/ doesn't) there for forty years. He ((was)/ were) a teacher in Mexico. He (was /(can)) teach math and computers. Hector (live /(lives)) in California now. He wants to teach, ((but)/ ago) now he's studying English. He goes to English class (twice /(three)) times a week. His class in on Mondays, Wednesdays, ((and)/ but) Fridays.

Unit 10 Review and expand

Objectives	Grammar	Vocabulary	Correlations
On-, Pre-, and Higher-level: Expand upon and review unit grammar and life skills	*Can (I can speak English.)* Past tense of *be (Was she at work? Yes, she was.)*	Jobs, job skills For additional vocabulary practice, see this **Oxford Picture Dictionary** topic: Job Skills	**CASAS:** 0.1.2, 0.1.3, 2.5.4, 4.8.1, 6.0.1, 7.2.5–7.2.7, 7.3.1 **LCPs:** 18.02, 19.02, 25.01, 32.01, 32.02, 32.05, 32.13, 33.02 **SCANS:** Arithmetic/Mathematics, Creative thinking, Participates as member of a team, Problem solving, Speaking **EFF:** Solve problems and make decisions

Warm-up and Review

10–15 minutes (books closed)

1. Review the *Bring It to Life* assignment from Lesson 5.

2. Have students who did the exercise share their pictures.

3. After students say whether they think the person in each picture is a boss or an employee, ask them to guess the person's job title.

4. Encourage students who did not bring in a picture to do so at a later date.

Introduction and Presentation

5–10 minutes

1. Choose one of the students' pictures that has a clear occupation associated with it. Ask them to guess the person's skills. *Can she drive a truck? Can she fix a sink?*

2. Write the *Grammar note* in 1A on the board. Read the example sentences.

3. Check students' understanding of the note. Write two pairs of sentences on the board. *I can drive a truck. John can't drive a truck. I can play the piano. David can play the piano.* Ask students how to combine them.

4. State the objective: *Today we're going to review how to talk about jobs and job skills.*

1 Grammar

Guided Practice

40–45 minutes

A Have students work individually to complete the sentences. Ask volunteers to read the completed sentences aloud.

B Have students work individually to complete the questions and answers. Ask volunteers to read the completed questions and answers aloud.

C Have students work individually to match the questions and answers. Ask volunteers to read the matching questions and answers aloud. Write the number-letter match on the board.

Multilevel Strategies

For 1C and 1D, seat same-level students together.

• **Pre-level** Work through the exercises with these students one question or sentence at a time.

• **On- and Higher-level** While you are working with pre-level students, ask these students to write additional questions. Provide them with the beginning of the questions. *What was _____? When was _____? Where were _____? When was _____?*

D Have students work individually to circle the correct words. Ask volunteers to write the answers on the board.

2 Group work

Communicative Practice

20–35 minutes

 A 1. Direct students, in groups of three to four, to focus on the picture on page 113. Ask: *What is happening today?*

2. Set a time limit (five minutes) to complete the exercise. Circulate and answer any questions.

3. Have a reporter from each group read the group's sentences to the class.

Multilevel Strategies

For 2A and 2B, use same-level groups.

• **Pre-level** For 2A, ask these students to write three vocabulary words and one complete sentence. For 2B, allow pre-level students to ask and answer the questions without writing.

• **Higher-level** For 2A, ask these students to write two additional sentences about the picture. For 2B, have students ask and answer this question as well: *What job do you want in the future?*

B 1. Have students work in the same groups from 2A to take turns interviewing each other in pairs.

2. Set a time limit (five minutes) to complete the exercise.

3. Tell students to make a note of their partners' answers but not to worry about writing complete sentences.

C Have a reporter from each group share the group's work.

> **TIP**
> Have students write a personal job history. Provide them with this skeleton: *My name is _____. I am from _____. I was a/an _____ from _____ to _____. I can _____. I am looking for a job. I want to be a/an _____.*

15–25 minutes

 A 1. Direct students to look at the picture. Ask: *What is she doing?* Tell students they will read a story about a woman who is looking for work. Direct students to read Mrs. Galvan's story silently. Then play the audio, and have them read along again silently.

2. Ask: *Is Mrs. Galvan new in this city?* [yes] *What was her job in Los Angeles?* [restaurant manager] *What are her skills?* [She can use a computer, cook, and serve food.] *Why is she worried?* [She needs to start work this week.]

B Elicit answers to the question. Ask for a show of hands on which job in the want ads is the best one for Mrs. Galvan.

C 1. Elicit student ideas for other jobs Mrs. Galvan can do. Write each one on the board.

2. Discuss whether the jobs are appropriate.

3. Ask for a show of hands to see which job the class thinks is the best alternative for Mrs. Galvan.

Evaluation

10–15 minutes

To test students' understanding of the unit grammar and life skills, have students take the Unit 10 Test in the *Step Forward Test Generator CD-ROM with ExamView® Assessment Suite.*

Learning Log

To help students record and discuss their progress, use the *Learning Log* on page T-179.

To extend this review: Have students complete **Workbook 1 page 71, Multilevel Activity Book 1 pages 113–116,** and the **Unit 10 Grammar Exercises** on the **Multilevel Grammar Exercises CD-ROM 1.**

2 Group work

A Work with 2–3 classmates. Choose 3 people from the picture on page 113.
Write 2 sentences about each person's work experience. Talk about the
sentences with your class. Answers will vary.

The cook was a restaurant manager in Colombia.   The plumber can fix sinks.
He can cook, serve food, and manage a restaurant.   He can fix bathtubs.

B Interview 3 classmates. Write their answers in your notebook.

ASK:

1. What was your job in your home country?
2. Do you have a job now?
3. Are you looking for a new job?

C Talk about the answers with your class.

> *Classmate—Wen*
> 1. *He was a teacher.*
> 2. *No, he doesn't.*
> 3. *Yes, he is.*

PROBLEM SOLVING

A Listen and read about Mrs. Galvan.
What is her problem? Mrs. Galvan needs a job.

Mrs. Galvan moved to San Diego this week.
She's looking for a job. She can work
weekdays, but she can't work on weekends.
Mrs. Galvan was a restaurant manager in Los
Angeles. She can use a computer, cook, and
serve food. Mrs. Galvan is worried. She needs
to start work this week.

B Work with your classmates. Look at
the job ads and answer the question.
(More than one answer is possible.)

What is the best job for Mrs. Galvan? Answers
will vary.

C Work with your classmates. Make a list
of other jobs Mrs. Galvan can do.

Food Server
PT, M–F 9:00–2:00
$5 per hour

Restaurant Manager
Nights and weekends
$18 per hour

Assistant Manager
FT, M–F 8:30 a.m.–4:30 p.m.
$12 per hour

UNIT **11**

Safety First

FOCUS ON
- traffic signs
- safety at home and at work
- *should* and *shouldn't*
- 911 emergency calls
- traffic safety

LESSON 1 Vocabulary

1 Learn traffic signs

A Look at the pictures. What colors, numbers, and words do you see?

B Listen and look at the pictures.

①

②

③

④

⑤

⑥

C Listen and repeat the words.

1. stop
2. road work
3. school crossing
4. no parking
5. no left turn
6. speed limit

D Look at the pictures. Complete the sentences.

1. The _____no left turn_____ sign with the black arrow means you can't turn left.
2. There's a yellow __school crossing__ sign. Students can walk here.
3. The sign with the number gives the __speed limit__. Drive 35 miles per hour here.
4. There's a red __stop__ sign. You have to stop.
5. There's an orange __road work__ sign. People are working on the street.
6. The __no parking__ sign with the "P" means you can't park here.

Unit 11 Lesson 1

Objectives	Grammar	Vocabulary	Correlations
On-level: Identify traffic signs and work-safety words **Pre-level:** Recognize traffic signs and work-safety words **Higher-level:** Talk and write about traffic signs and work safety	Simple-present tense (*He's careful. He wears a hard hat.*)	Traffic signs and work-safety words For additional vocabulary practice, see these **Oxford Picture Dictionary** topics: Directions and Maps, Traffic Signs, Job Safety	**CASAS:** 0.1.2, 1.9.1, 2.2.2, 2.5.4, 3.4.2, 4.3.2, 4.3.3, 4.6.3, 7.4.5, 7.4.7 **LCPs:** 19.01, 26.04, 27.02, 32.01 **SCANS:** Listening, Participates as member of a team, Responsibility, Seeing things in the mind's eye, Self-management **EFF:** Cooperate with others, Observe critically

Warm-up

10–15 minutes (books closed)

Write the words *safe* and *dangerous* on the board. Circle the words and have the students brainstorm any ideas they associate with them. Create a word map for each idea by clustering the related words. For example, if students say *lion* and *tiger* in reference to *dangerous,* make a circle that says *Dangerous Animals* and connect those words to it.

Introduction

5 minutes

A 1. Pantomime driving and ask students when driving is safe and when it is dangerous. Help them with ideas: *What about driving in the rain? Driving in the snow? Driving without a seat belt?* Write *traffic signs* on the board. Say: *Traffic signs help make driving safe.* Draw a stop sign to illustrate the meaning of traffic signs, and point to any signs you have in your classroom.

2. State the objective: *Today we're going to learn traffic signs and workplace safety words.*

1 Learn traffic signs

Presentation

20–25 minutes

A Direct students to look at the pictures and answer the question.

B 1. Have students listen to the audio. Ask them to point to the correct picture as they listen. Circulate and monitor.

2. Check comprehension by pointing to the signs and asking *yes/no* questions. Pass out *yes/no* cards to the students (see page T-175), or have them hold up one finger for *yes* and two for *no* in order to get a nonverbal response. *Does this mean stop? Does this mean turn left?*

C Ask students to listen and repeat the words.

TIP

Replay the audio and ask students to listen for the "warning" words. [be careful, look out, slow down] Elicit the words and write them on the board.

Guided Practice I

15–20 minutes

D 1. Have students complete the sentences using the new vocabulary.

2. Encourage students to take turns reading the completed sentences in pairs.

Multilevel Strategies

After completing 1D, seat same-level students together, and provide vocabulary practice targeted to the level of your students.

• **Pre-level** Ask these students to practice together by pointing to the pictures and saying the correct words.

• **On-level** Ask these students to cover the words and test each other on the vocabulary. Have one student point to the pictures while the other says the correct word.

• **Higher-level** Ask these students to dictate the words to each other.

2 Talk about work safety

Guided Practice II
35–40 minutes

 1. Direct students to look at the pictures. Ask: *Where are they working?* Introduce the new topic: *Now let's talk about work safety.*

2. Group students and assign roles: leader, fact checker, recorder, and reporter. Explain that students work with their groups to match the words and pictures.

3. Check comprehension of the exercise. Ask: *Who looks up the words in the picture dictionary?* [fact checker] *Who writes the numbers in the book?* [recorder] *Who tells the class your answers?* [reporter] *Who helps everyone and manages the group?* [leader]

4. Set a time limit (three minutes), and have students work together to complete the task. While students are working, copy the wordlist on the board.

5. Call "time" and have the reporters from each group take turns calling out the numbers for the wordlist. Record students' answers on the board. If groups disagree, write each group's choice next to the word.

Multilevel Strategies

For 2A, use mixed-level groups.

- **Pre-level** Assign these students as recorders or create a role of timekeeper (to let the group know when the three minutes are up) giving these students an active to role in the group.

- **On-level** Assign these students as fact checkers and reporters.

- **Higher-level** Assign these students as leaders.

 1. Ask students to listen and check their answers.

2. Have students correct the wordlist on the board and then write the correct numbers in their books.

3. Tell the groups from 2A to break into pairs to practice the words. Set a time limit (two minutes).

 Have students work individually to match the names with the descriptions. Ask volunteers to read each matching name and description aloud. Write the number-letter match on the board.

Communicative Practice and Application
10–15 minutes

D 1. Model the conversation with a volunteer. Then model it again using other characters from 2A.

2. Set a time limit (five minutes). Ask students to practice the conversation with several partners.

Evaluation
10–15 minutes (books closed)

TEST YOURSELF

1. Make a two-column chart on the board with the headings *Traffic Signs* and *Safety Equipment*. Have students close their books and give you an example for each column.

2. Have students copy the chart into their notebooks.

3. Give students five to ten minutes to test themselves by writing the words they recall from the lesson on the chart.

4. Call "time" and have students check their spelling in *The Oxford Picture Dictionary* or another dictionary. Circulate and monitor students' progress.

Multilevel Strategies

Target the *Test Yourself* to the level of your students.

- **Pre-level** Have these students work with their books open.

- **Higher-level** Have these students complete the chart and then write two sentences describing safe or unsafe behavior. *He's careless. He isn't wearing a hard hat.*

To compress this lesson: Conduct 2A as a whole-class activity. Have students practice 2D with only one partner.

To extend this lesson: Show students pictures of other traffic signs, or have them look at pictures of traffic signs in *The Oxford Picture Dictionary*. Discuss the meanings of the signs, and ask if students have seen them near your school.

And/Or have students complete **Workbook 1 page 72** and **Multilevel Activity Book 1 page 118**.

2 Talk about work safety

A Work with your classmates. Match the words with the pictures.

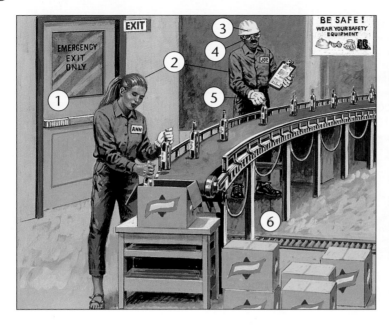

_9_	careful	_2_	factory workers	_6_	safety boots
_11_	careless	_8_	fire extinguisher	_4_	safety glasses
_10_	dangerous/unsafe	_3_	hard hat	_5_	safety gloves
_1_	emergency exit	_7_	safe	_12_	wet floor

B Listen and check your answers. Then practice the words with a partner.

C Look at the factory workers. Match the names with the descriptions.

_b_ 1. Ann   a. He's careless. He doesn't see the wet floor.

_d_ 2. Joe   b. She's careless. She isn't wearing her safety boots.

_a_ 3. Tim   c. She's careful. She wears safety glasses and safety gloves.

_c_ 4. Tanya   d. He's careful. He's wearing safety glasses and safety gloves.

D Work with a partner. Ask and answer questions.
Talk about the factory workers in 2A.

A: Is Tanya careful or careless at work?

B: She's careful. She wears a hard hat. How about Tim?

A: He's careless. He doesn't wear safety boots.

TEST YOURSELF ✔

Close your book. Write 6 words for traffic signs and 4 words for safety equipment. Check your spelling in a dictionary.

1 Read about safe and dangerous behavior

A Look at the pictures. Listen.

Slow down, Frank!

Look out, Frank!

Check the smoke detector, Frank!

SPEED LIMIT 25

Oh, no!

B Listen again. Read the sentences.

1. I always drive fast. I never wear a seat belt. My friends worry, but I don't.
2. I always talk on my cell phone at work.
3. My co-workers say I should be careful, but I don't worry.
4. I never check the smoke detectors at home. My sister worries, but I don't.
5. My sister, my friends, and my co-workers worry too much. They should relax.
6. Oh, no! Here comes a police officer. Maybe I should worry now.

C Check your understanding. Circle the correct words.

1. Frank ((drives) / doesn't drive) fast.
2. His friends ((worry) / don't worry).
3. Frank likes his (sofa / (cell phone)).
4. Frank isn't ((careful) / careless).

2 Write about your behavior

A Write your story. Complete the sentences. Answers will vary.

I _____ drive fast.

I _____ wear a seat belt.

I _____ talk on a cell phone at work or in the car.

I _____ check my smoke detector at home.

Need help?

Adverbs of frequency
always
usually
sometimes
never

B Read your story to a partner.

Unit 11 Lesson 2

Objectives	Grammar	Vocabulary	Correlations
On-, Pre-, and Higher-level: Read and write about safe and dangerous behavior	Adverbs of frequency (*I always drive fast.*)	*Seat belt, smoke detector, safety equipment* For additional vocabulary practice, see this **Oxford Picture Dictionary** topic: Job Safety	**CASAS:** 0.1.2, 0.1.3, 1.4.8, 3.4.2, 4.3.1–4.3.3, 4.6.1, 4.6.3, 6.0.1, 6.4.2, 7.4.7 **LCPs:** 19.01, 25.01, 26.06, 32.01, 32.02, 32.05, 32.13, 33.08 **SCANS:** Listening, Self-management, Speaking, Writing **EFF:** Convey ideas in writing, Use math to solve problems and communicate

Warm-up and Review

10–15 minutes (books closed)

Ask students to identify the safety features in your classroom (*exit sign, fire extinguisher, evacuation map, smoke alarm*). Ask them to name other safety features they find at work or in their homes. Write their ideas on the board.

Introduction

5 minutes

1. Point out that all of the items on the board are *things*, but the most important aspect of safety is *behavior*. Write *behavior* on the board. Say: *Lining up calmly when a fire alarm sounds is an example of safe behavior. Driving the speed limit is an example of safe behavior. Behavior is what you do and how you act.*

2. State the objective: *Today we're going to read and write about safe and dangerous behavior.*

1 Read about safe and dangerous behavior

Presentation I

20–25 minutes

A 1. Direct students to look at the pictures. Ask: *Is Frank careful or careless?*

2. Play the audio.

B 1. Play the audio again. Have students read along silently.

2. Check comprehension. Ask: *Does Frank wear his seat belt?* [no] *Does Frank check his smoke detectors?* [no]

Multilevel Strategies

After the group comprehension check in 1B, challenge on- and higher-level students while working with pre-level students.

• **Pre-level** Reread the sentences in 1B with these students while on- and higher-level students answer additional questions.

• **On- and Higher-level** Write additional questions on the board. After allowing these students to individually answer the questions, have volunteers write the answers on the board.

Guided Practice I

10 minutes

C Have students work individually to circle the correct words to complete the sentences.

2 Write about your behavior

Guided Practice II

20–25 minutes

A 1. Review the frequency adverbs in the *Need help?* box.

2. Copy the sentences on the board. Read them aloud with your own information.

3. Have students complete the sentences independently. Circulate and assist.

B Ask students to read their sentences to a partner. Call on individuals to share what they learned about their partners.

3 Make a safety checklist

Presentation II

20–25 minutes

 1. Introduce the topic: *Now we're going to make a safety checklist.* Direct students to look at the chart and picture in 3A. Ask: *What is her job?*

2. Ask students to put their pencils down and listen for the answer to this question: *How does she say goodbye?* Play the entire audio once.

3. Play the audio in segments. After each piece of advice, stop the audio and check answers with the students: *Did you complete the question?* If necessary, replay the segment.

4. Check students' listening accuracy. Have volunteers read the questions aloud.

5. Direct students to check *Yes, I do.* or *No, I don't.* according to their own behavior.

> ### Multilevel Strategies
>
> Replay 3A to challenge on- and higher-level students while allowing pre-level students to catch up.
>
> **Pre-Level** Have these students listen again for another chance to complete the exercise.
>
> **On- and higher-level** Write these questions on the board: *What should you do at school crossings? What are examples of safety equipment? How often should you check the batteries in your smoke alarm?* After replaying the audio, have volunteers write the answers on the board.

Communicative Practice and Application

10 minutes

 1. Model the conversation with a volunteer. Then model it again with our own information about your safety habits at home, at work, or in the car.

2. Assign a time limit (five minutes). Have students discuss their safety habits with several partners.

4 Real-life math

Math Extension

10–15 minutes

1. Direct students to look at the cartoon. Ask: *Why does he feel bad?*

2. Read the questions aloud. Give students time to write the answers independently.

3. Go over the answers as a class.

> **TIP**
>
> After *Real-life math,* figure out some percentages with the class. Put up sentence strips with safety behavior around the room. *I always wear a seat belt. Sometimes I wear a seat belt. I never wear a seat belt.* Ask students to stand next to the sign that best represents them. Write the total number of students and the number standing at each sign. Estimate or calculate the percentages together. Try again with *I usually drive and talk on the cell phone; I sometimes drive and talk on the cell phone;* and *I never drive and talk on the cell phone.*

Evaluation

10–15 minutes (books closed)

TEST YOURSELF

Give students time to write their ideas. Elicit and write their ideas on the board. Discuss which safety behaviors most people follow and which they need to be more careful about.

To compress this lesson: Have students practice the conversation in 3B with only one partner.

To extend this lesson: Have students make a safety advice poster.
1. Group students and tell them to choose a theme: safety in the home, safety at work, or safety in the car.
2. Ask them to title their posters and write at least three pieces of advice. Have them illustrate their posters with drawings or with pictures from magazines or the Internet.
3. Have groups share their posters with the class.
And/Or have students complete **Workbook 1 page 73** and **Multilevel Activity Book 1 page 119**.

3 Make a safety checklist

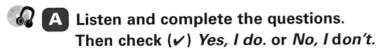

A Listen and complete the questions.
Then check (✔) *Yes, I do.* or *No, I don't.*

Do you...	Yes, I do.	No, I don't.
1. always drive the __speed limit__?	✔	
2. drive fast near __school crossings__?	Answers will vary.	
3. know where the emergency __exits__ are in the building?	Answers will vary.	
4. wear __safety__ equipment at work?	Answers will vary.	
5. have a __smoke__ detector in the kitchen?	Answers will vary.	

Are you safe?

B Work with a partner. Talk about your safety habits at home, at work, and in the car. Use the chart.

A: *Do you wear safety equipment at work?*
B: *Yes, I always wear safety equipment. Do you?*

4 Real-life math

Read about the workers. Answer the questions.

Twenty-five of the one hundred workers at ABC Chemical Factory never wear their safety gloves. That means 25% never wear their gloves and 75% wear them.

Ten of the one hundred workers never wear their safety glasses.

1. What percent of the workers don't wear their safety glasses? __10__ %

2. What percent of the workers wear their safety glasses? __90__ %

Some workers at ABC Chemical Factory

TEST YOURSELF ✔

Close your book. Write 3 things you do to be safe at home, in the car, or at work. Talk about your ideas with the class.

LESSON 3 Grammar

1 Learn *should* and *should not*

A Look at the poster. Read the sentences. How can people be safe at home?

You should:

Know your neighbors.

Lock doors and windows at night.

Tell the manager about problems.

You should NOT:

Open the door to strangers.

Leave the building door open.

Walk alone in the parking lot at night.

B Study the charts. Complete the sentences below.

SHOULD AND SHOULD NOT

Statements					
I You He She	should	lock the door.	We You They	should	lock the door.

1. He ___should___ lock the door.   2. We should ___lock___ the door.

Negative statements						Contractions
I You He She	should not	walk alone.	We You They	should not	walk alone.	should not = shouldn't You shouldn't walk alone.

3. She ___should not___ walk alone.   4. They ___should not walk___ alone.

C Complete the sentences with *should* or *shouldn't*. Use the poster in 1A. Read the sentences to a partner.

1. You ___shouldn't___ leave the front door open.
2. You ___should___ walk in the parking lot with other people.
3. You ___should___ close the building door.
4. You ___shouldn't___ open the door to strangers.

Use *should* and *should not* to describe safety and classroom rules

Unit 11 Lesson 3

Objectives	Grammar	Vocabulary	Correlations
On- and Higher-level: Use *should* and *shouldn't* to talk about safety **Pre-level:** Recognize *should* and *shouldn't*	*Should* and *shouldn't* (*You should lock the door. You shouldn't leave the door open.*)	*Lock, alone* For additional vocabulary practice, see this **Oxford Picture Dictionary** topic: Public Safety	**CASAS:** 0.1.2, 0.1.3, 3.4.2, 4.3.1, 4.3.2, 4.4.3, 4.6.1, 4.6.3, 7.4.7 **LCPs:** 32.01, 33.02, 33.07 **SCANS:** Seeing things in the mind's eye, Self-management, Writing **EFF:** Convey ideas in writing, Observe critically, Reflect and evaluate

Warm-up and Review

10–15 minutes (books closed)

Write *Home, Car,* and *Work* on the board, and elicit safe and dangerous behaviors for each category. Write them on the board neutrally– for example, *drive fast, wear a seat belt, drive and talk on the phone.*

Introduction

5–10 minutes

1. Talk about the behaviors on the board using *you should* and *you shouldn't*. *You shouldn't drive fast. You should wear a seatbelt.*

2. State the objective: *Today we're going to use* should *and* shouldn't *to talk about safety.*

1 Learn *should* and *should not*

Presentation I

20–25 minutes

A 1. Direct students to look at the poster. Ask: *Is this poster in a school?* [no] *Where is it?* [in an apartment building]

2. Have students read the poster silently.

B 1. Demonstrate how to read the grammar charts as complete sentences. Read the charts through sentence by sentence. Then read them again, and have students repeat after you.

2. Use the poster in 1A to illustrate points in the grammar charts. *You should know your neighbors. You shouldn't open the door to strangers.*

3. As a class, complete the sentences. Ask volunteers to write the sentences on the board. Have other students read the sentences aloud.

4. Give students time to silently review the charts and, if they haven't already, fill in the blanks.

5. Assess students' understanding of the charts. Ask students to tell you their ideas from the warm-up using *should* and *shouldn't*.

Guided Practice

15–20 minutes

C Have students complete the sentences individually. Ask them to read the sentences to a partner.

Multilevel Strategies

After 1C is corrected, group same-level students together.

• **Pre-level** Have these students copy the sentences from the grammar charts in 1B. Tell them to read the sentences in the poster aloud to a partner, saying *you should* or *you shouldn't* with every sentence.

• **On- and Higher-level** Ask these students to write four more sentences using *should* and *shouldn't*. Have volunteers write one of their sentences on the board.

2 Ask and answer information questions with *should*

Presentation II

20–25 minutes

A 1. Read and have students repeat the questions and answers in the chart.

2. Copy the questions on the board. Label the subject and verb in each question. Copy the answers and ask students where the subjects and verbs are. Show them how the order reverses for the question.

Guided Practice

10–15 minutes

B Have students work individually to match the questions and answers. Ask volunteers to read the matching questions and answers aloud. Write the number-letter match on the board.

> **Multilevel Strategies**
>
> Group same-level students for 2B.
>
> • **Pre-level** Assist these students with 2B by reading every sentence aloud and giving them time to find the answers before moving on. Have them read the questions and answers together chorally.
>
> • **On- and Higher-level** While you are working with the pre-level students, have these students complete 2B individually. Then have them answer additional questions. *I have the day off tomorrow. Where should I go? My son's birthday is Wednesday. What should I buy?*

3 Use *should* to talk about classroom rules

Communicative Practice and Application

20–25 minutes

A Direct students to look at the poster. Read the title.

> **Multilevel Strategies**
>
> For 3B, use mixed-level pairs.
>
> • **Pre-level** Allow these students to be the "reporters" and read one of the sentences to the class.
>
> • **Higher-level** Ask these students to share any additional ideas that they have.

B 1. Have students work with a partner to complete the poster.

2. Have pairs share their ideas with the class.

TIP After 3B, have students make more "advice" posters addressing their other life roles. Write possible titles on the board. *Be a Great Parent! Be a Great Husband/Wife! Be a Great Soccer Player! Be a Great Cook!* Put the students in groups, and ask the groups to choose one of the topics or create their own. Ask them to write at least four pieces of advice using *should* or *shouldn't*.

Evaluation

10–15 minutes (books closed)

TEST YOURSELF

Ask students to write the sentences independently. Collect and correct their writing.

To compress this lesson: Assign 2B as homework or conduct it as a whole-class activity.

To extend this lesson: Have students practice giving advice.
1. Have students brainstorm a list of problems. Write them on the board. *I'm tired. I have a cold. I have a lot of homework. My daughter is having problems at school. I don't have any money. I want to make friends.*
2. Have students state the problem to a partner and ask: *What should I do?*
3. Call on volunteers to share some good advice that they heard from their partners.

And/Or have students complete **Workbook 1 pages 74–75** and **Multilevel Activity Book 1 page 120**.

2 Ask and answer information questions with *should*

A Study the chart. Ask and answer the questions.

Information questions and answers with *should*	
A: When should she walk with a friend? B: She should walk with a friend at night.	A: What should they do? B: They should lock the door.

B Match the questions with the answers.

_b_ 1. Sara has to walk home at night. What should she do?

_c_ 2. I don't understand. What should I do?

_e_ 3. Bob has a toothache. Where should he go?

_a_ 4. We are students. When should we study?

_d_ 5. Jen has a fever. What should she do?

a. We should study every day.

b. She should walk with a friend.

c. You should ask for help.

d. She should call the doctor.

e. He should go to the dentist.

3 Use *should* to talk about classroom rules

A Work with a partner. Answer the question.
What should students do in class?

B Work with a partner. Complete the poster below with the rules of your class.

Follow Classroom Rules! It's Easy!

Students should . . .	Students shouldn't . . .
1. speak English in class.	4. sleep in class.
2. _____.	5. _____.
3. _____.	6. _____.

TEST YOURSELF ✔

Close your book. Write 3 sentences about your school's safety rules.
Use *should* or *shouldn't*.

1 Learn to call 911

A Look at the pictures. Then answer the questions.

1 There's a traffic accident.

2 There's a robbery.

3 There's a fire.

296
296 GREEN STREET

1. Who needs help?

a man

2. What's the emergency?

a robbery

3. Where's the emergency?

296 Green Street

B Listen and read.

A: 911. Emergency.
B: There's a fire at my neighbor's house.
A: What's the address?
B: It's 412 Oak Street.
A: Is anyone hurt?
B: I don't know.
A: OK. Help is on the way.

Is anyone hurt?

I don't know.

C Listen again and repeat.

D Work with a partner. Practice the conversation. Use emergencies from 1A.

A: 911. Emergency.
B: _____.
A: What's the address?
B: It's _____.
A: Is anyone hurt?
B: _____.
A: OK. _____ is on the way.

> **Need help?**
>
> **Help** is on the way.
> **A police officer** is on the way.
> **An ambulance** is on the way.
>
>

Unit 11 Lesson 4

Objectives	Grammar	Vocabulary	Correlations
On-, Pre-, and Higher-level: Report an emergency and ask for emergency services	*Should/Shouldn't (You shouldn't call 911.)*	*Anyone, ambulance, choking* For additional vocabulary practice, see this **Oxford Picture Dictionary** topic: Medical Emergencies	**CASAS:** 0.1.2, 0.1.3, 1.9.7, 2.1.2, 2.5.1, 3.1.1, 4.3.4, 6.0.1, 7.4.7 **LCPs:** 23.01, 25.01, 27.01, 32.01, 32.02, 32.13 **SCANS:** Acquires and evaluates information, Knowing how to learn, Seeing things in the mind's eye, Self-management, Speaking **EFF:** Speak so others can understand

Warm-up and Review

10–15 minutes (books closed)

Write *Emergency!* on the board, and have students brainstorm a list of emergencies. Write them all—whether you consider them to be emergencies or not.

Introduction

5 minutes

1. Review the emergencies on the board. For each one, ask: *Should you call 911?*

2. State the objective: *Today we're going to learn how to call 911.*

1 Learn to call 911

Presentation

20–30 minutes

A 1. Direct students to look at the pictures. Read the speech bubbles.

2. Give students a minute to answer the questions. Go over the answers as a class.

Guided Practice

20–25 minutes

B Play the audio. Have students read along silently.

C Play the audio again, and have students repeat the conversation. Replay if necessary.

 TIP Teach students to ask for a translator. Write the sentence skeleton on the board: *I need a/an _____ translator.* Elicit the names of the students' languages, and have students practice pronouncing their language names clearly. Direct students to add this sentence to the end of the conversation in 1D.

Communicative Practice and Application

15–20 minutes

D 1. Model the conversation with a volunteer. Then model it again with other information from 1A.

2. Elicit other ways to complete the converation.

3. Set a time limit (five minutes). Ask students to practice the conversation with several partners.

Multilevel Strategies

For 1D, adapt the oral practice to the level of your students.

• **Pre-level** Have these students read the conversation as written in 1B.

• **Higher-level** Ask these students to practice with additional emergencies from the warm-up.

3 1. Direct students to put down their pencils and listen for the answer to this question: *How many of these emergencies are car accidents?* [two] Play the entire audio once.

2. Play the audio in segments. Stop after every conversation, and ask students if they were able to answer all of the questions. Replay that segment if necessary.

3. Ask volunteers to write the answers on the board.

2 Practice your pronunciation

Pronunciation Extension

10–20 minutes

A Play the audio. Ask students to listen and point to *should* and *shouldn't* as they hear them.

B Play the audio. Ask students to circle the letter of the word they hear. Go over the answers as a class.

> ### Multilevel Strategies
>
> Replay the audio in 2B to challenge on- and higher-level students while allowing pre-level students to catch up.
>
> • **Pre-level** Have these students listen again for another chance to complete the exercise.
>
> • **On- and Higher-level** Ask these students to answer these questions for each conversation: *Who is talking? What is the advice?*

C 1. Have students take turns reading the sentences from the chart and giving advice.

2. Ask volunteers to say the sentences and say if they should or shouldn't call 911.

> **TIP**
> Check your students' understanding of 911 by asking them if they should call 911 when there is a very loud party next door, someone stole their bicycle, someone wrote on their fence (graffiti), there is a power outage, there is a loose dog running around the neighborhood, their cat is stuck in a tree. [all <u>no</u>!]

Evaluation

10–15 minutes

TEST YOURSELF

1. Model the role-play with a volunteer. Then switch roles.

2. Pair students. Check comprehension by asking the "911 operators" to raise their hands. Elicit the questions they are going to ask. Do the same with the "callers."

3. Set a time limit (five minutes), and have the partners act out the role-play in both roles.

4. Circulate and monitor. Encourage pantomime and improvisation.

5. Provide feedback.

> ### Multilevel Strategies
>
> Target the *Test Yourself* to the level of your students.
>
> • **Pre-level** Work with these students. Play the 911 operator, and have students take turns calling you.
>
> • **On- and Higher-level** Have these students switch partners and practice again when they finish.

To compress this lesson: Have students practice the conversation in 1D with only one partner.

To extend this lesson: Teach additional medical emergencies.
1. Provide students with pictures, or have them look at the pictures of medical emergencies in *The Oxford Picture Dictionary*. Review the vocabulary.
2. Have students practice a 911 call using the new emergency words.

And/Or have students complete **Workbook 1 page 76** and **Multilevel Activity Book 1 page 121**.

E Listen and write the emergency information.

1. What:	car accident	3. What:	fire
Where:	Pine Ave. and Hope St.	Where:	615 Elm St.
Who needs help:	a man	Who needs help:	a young woman
2. What:	robbery	4. What:	car accident
Where:	3310 Main St.	Where:	1st St.
Who needs help:	the manager	Who needs help:	2 men

2 Practice your pronunciation

A Listen and point to the word you hear.

should   shouldn't

B Listen for *should* or *shouldn't*. Circle *a* or *b*.

1. a. should
   (b.) shouldn't
2. (a.) should
   b. shouldn't

3. (a.) should
   b. shouldn't
4. a. should
   (b.) shouldn't

5. (a.) should
   b. shouldn't
6. a. should
   (b.) shouldn't

C Work with a partner. Read the sentences. Should you call 911? Check (✔) the correct boxes.

A: *I have a headache.*
B: *You shouldn't call 911.*

	Should	Shouldn't
1. I have a headache.		✔
2. My friend has a stomachache.		✔
3. There's a fire in the kitchen.	✔	
4. I need a prescription.		✔
5. There's a bad car accident.	✔	
6. There's a robbery.	✔	

> **TEST YOURSELF** ✔
>
> Work with a partner. Partner A: Report an emergency. Partner B:
> Ask for more information. Tell your partner that help is on the way.
> Then change roles.

1 Get ready to read

A **Read the definitions.**

pull over: to drive the car to the side of the road and stop in a safe place

cause: to make something happen

B **Work with your classmates. Ask and answer the questions.**

1. Why do people have car accidents?
2. Why do people pull over?

pull over

2 Read about safe drivers

A **Read the article.**

Be Safe, Be Smart, Pull Over

Unsafe drivers cause 50% of the car accidents in the U.S. every year. These drivers don't pay attention.[1] Be a safe driver. Pay attention to the road or pull over.

- Sometimes you have to read a map, but you shouldn't read and drive. You should **pull over**.

- Sometimes you're tired, but you can't sleep and drive. **Pull over**!

- Do you have to use your cell phone in the car? Do you have to pay attention to your child? You should **pull over**.

- Don't forget! You have to **pull over** when you have a car accident. It's the law.

---

[1] pay attention – look, listen, and be careful

Source: *New York State DMV*

 B **Listen and read the article again.**

Unit 11 Lesson 5

Objectives	Grammar	Vocabulary	Correlations
On- and Higher-level: Read about and discuss safe drivers and traffic accidents **Pre-level:** Read about safe drivers and traffic accidents	*Should/Shouldn't (You should pay attention when you are driving.)*	*Pull over, cause, pay attention, smart* For additional vocabulary practice, see this **Oxford Picture Dictionary** topic: An Intersection	**CASAS:** 0.1.2, 0.1.3, 1.9.7, 3.4.2, 6.0.1, 6.7.4, 7.4.5 **LCPs:** 25.01, 26.06, 32.01, 32.03, 32.04, 32.06 **SCANS:** Acquires and evaluates information, Listening, Reading, Seeing things in the mind's eye, Speaking **EFF:** Listen actively, Learn through research, Read with understanding

Warm-up and Review

10–15 minutes (books closed)

On the board, write scrambled sentences from previous lessons. *safety should equipment. You wear* [You should wear safety equipment.] *should You smoke check detectors. your* [You should check your smoke detector.] *limit. You the drive speed should* [You should drive the speed limit.] *shouldn't open to You the strangers. door* [You shouldn't open your door to strangers.] *school shouldn't You drive crossings. fast near* [You shouldn't drive fast near school crossings.] Give students a few minutes to unscramble the sentences. Tell them they can look through the unit for the answers.

Introduction

5 minutes

1. Ask students which of the warm-up sentences are safety rules for driving.

2. State the objective: *Today we'll learn more ways to drive safely.*

1 Get ready to read

Presentation

15–20 minutes

A 1. Direct students to look at the picture. Ask: *Is the car stopped?* [yes] *Is someone inside?* [yes] Say: *The driver pulled over.*

2. Read the words and the definitions.

B Read the questions and discuss them as a class. Write the students' ideas on the board.

TIP Discuss the streets near your school. Find out if students know who takes care of traffic-safety improvements and where to make suggestions.

Pre-Reading

Direct students to look at the pictures in the article in 2A. Ask: *What are the people doing?* [looking at a map, sleeping, talking on the phone] *Are they being safe?* [yes]

2 Read about safe drivers

Guided Practice I

25–30 minutes

A 1. Ask students to read the article silently.

2. Ask if there are any questions about the reading.

Multilevel Strategies

For 2A–B, seat same-level students together.

• **Pre-level** Assist these students by reading the article again and stopping after each piece of advice to check comprehension.

• **On- and Higher-level** While you are working with pre-level students, ask these students to list other advice to prevent car accidents. Have the students share their advice with the class. Write their ideas on the board.

B Play the audio. Have students read along silently.

T-132

C Have students work individually to choose the correct words to complete the sentences. Ask volunteers to read the sentences aloud. Write the answers on the board.

D Have students work individually to complete the chart and then read the questions and answers with a partner. Call on individuals to tell you when a driver should pull over. Encourage them to answer without looking at the chart.

Multilevel Strategies

For 2D, seat same-level students together.

Pre-level Assist these students by reading the questions aloud and discussing the answers.

On- and Higher-level Have these students complete 2D and then read the questions and answers with a partner. Write additional questions about driving safety on the board for them to answer. *What should you do when it's raining? When it's snowing? When you see someone with car trouble? If you see an accident? If your tire is flat?* After you go over 2D, elicit and discuss their answers to the additional questions. Write answers to the questions on the board.

3 Learn about traffic accidents

Guided Practice II

15–20 minutes

A 1. Say: Now we're going to look at reasons for traffic accidents.

2. Direct students to look at the pie chart and the key. Read the key.

3. Have students work individually to complete the sentences. Go over the answers as a class.

Communicative Practice

10–15 minutes

B 1. Review the question.

2. Set a time limit (three minutes). Allow students to think about the question and then write their answers individually.

3. Call on individuals to share their ideas.

 Talk about what you should do if you have a traffic accident. *You should pull over. You shouldn't drive away. You should show the other driver your license and insurance information. You should copy the other driver's license and insurance information. If someone is badly hurt, you should call 911. You shouldn't move hurt people,* etc. Write the sentences on the board with a blank for *should* or *shouldn't,* and ask students to supply the correct form.

Application

5–10 minutes

BRING IT TO LIFE

Ask students to write the names of their streets and cross streets. Tell them to pay attention to the traffic on the streets and at the closest intersections.

To compress this lesson: Conduct 2D as a whole-class activity.

To extend this lesson: Bring in copies of the drivers' handbook for your state, or print safety information off your state's Department of Motor Vehicles website. Look at the information together for more ideas about what drivers should and shouldn't do.

And/Or have students complete **Workbook 1 page 77** and **Multilevel Activity Book 1 page 122**.

C Complete the sentences. Use the words in the box.

| read a map | pull over | cell phone | unsafe drivers | ~~pay attention~~ |

1. You should ___pay attention___ when you are driving a car.
2. You shouldn't ___read a map___ when you are driving.
3. You have to ___pull over___ if you have an accident.
4. You should pull over to use a ___cell phone___.
5. ___Unsafe drivers___ cause 50% of traffic accidents.

D Read and check (✔) *yes* or *no*.

Should you pull over...	Yes	No
1. when you are tired?	✔	
2. when you see a stop sign?		✔
3. when you see a road work sign?		✔
4. when you have to read a map?	✔	
5. when you have to use your cell phone?	✔	
6. when you have an accident?	✔	

3 Learn about traffic accidents

A Look at the pie chart. Complete the sentences.

1. ___3___ % of car accidents happen because drivers drink ___alcohol___.

2. ___50___ % of car accidents happen because drivers aren't paying ___attention___.

3. ___11___ % of car accidents happen because of ___bad___ weather.

4. ___4___ % of car accidents happen because of car ___problems___.

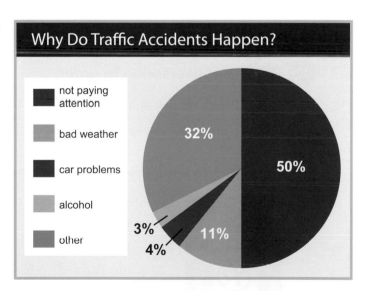

Why Do Traffic Accidents Happen?

- not paying attention
- bad weather
- car problems
- alcohol
- other

32%   50%   3%   4%   11%

B Think about the question. Talk about the answer with your class.

What other things can cause accidents?

┌─ **BRING IT TO LIFE** ─

Watch the traffic in your neighborhood. Are the drivers paying attention?
Tell your classmates about the drivers in your neighborhood.

1 Grammar

A Write the answers to the questions.

1. There's a school crossing sign. Should I slow down?
   <u>Yes, you should.</u>

2. Teo is driving to work. Should he wear his seat belt?
   <u>Yes, he should.</u>

3. The floor is wet. Should Min and Janet walk on it?
   <u>No, they shouldn't.</u>

4. I'm driving home, but I'm very tired. Should I pull over?
   <u>Yes, you should.</u>

> **Grammar note**
>
> *Yes/No questions* with *should*
>
> **A:** Should I call 911?
> **B:** Yes, you should. *or* No, you shouldn't.
>
> **A:** Should he wear gloves?
> **B:** Yes, he should. *or* No, he shouldn't.

B Match the questions with the answers.

<u>c</u> 1. What's the emergency?   a. A man and a woman.

<u>e</u> 2. What should I do?   b. 122 Pine Street.

<u>a</u> 3. Who needs help?   c. There's a car accident.

<u>b</u> 4. Where's the emergency?   d. No, they shouldn't.

<u>d</u> 5. Should people drink and drive?   e. You should call 911.

C Put the conversation in order.

<u>4</u> It's 2386 3rd Avenue.   <u>1</u> 911. Emergency.   <u>3</u> What's the address?

<u>5</u> Help is on the way.   <u>2</u> There's a fire.

D Look at the signs. Read the sentences. Write your advice. Answers will vary.

1. Luis isn't paying attention.
   <u>He should watch for children.</u>

2. Anne is looking for a place to park.
   _____

3. Ted is driving fifty-five miles per hour.
   _____

4. Molly is driving and talking to her friend.
   _____

Unit 11 Review and expand

Objectives	Grammar	Vocabulary	Correlations
On-, Pre-, and Higher-level: Expand upon and review unit grammar and life skills	*Should/Shouldn't (Should I call 911? Yes, you should.)*	Emergencies, driving words For additional vocabulary practice, see these **Oxford Picture Dictionary** topics: Medical Emergencies, Directions and Maps, Traffic Signs	**CASAS:** 0.1.2, 0.1.3, 1.4.8, 1.9.1, 1.9.7, 2.2.2, 2.4.1, 2.5.1, 3.4.2, 4.8.1, 6.0.1, 7.2.5–7.2.7, 7.3.1 **LCPs:** 19.01, 23.01, 26.04, 26.06, 27.01, 27.02, 32.01, 32.02, 32.05, 32.07, 33.02, 33.07 **SCANS:** Creative thinking, Problem solving **EFF:** Solve problems and make decisions

Warm-up and Review

10–15 minutes (books closed)

1. Review the *Bring It to Life* assignment from Lesson 5.

2. Have students who did the exercise discuss the drivers in their neighborhoods. Have other students discuss what they have noticed about their neighborhoods.

3. Determine if anybody has a serious traffic problem in his/her neighborhood that should be reported to the city.

Introduction and Presentation

5 minutes

1. Read the questions and answers in the *Grammar note* in 1A. Check student comprehension by eliciting a choral response. Then use the students' information about their neighborhoods to write sentences and questions with *should*. *Maria's neighbor shouldn't drive so fast. Bing's neighbors should stop at the corner. Where should the city put in a stop sign?*

2. State the objective: *Today we're going to review using* should *to give safety advice.*

1 Grammar

Guided Practice

40–45 minutes

A Have students work individually to answer the questions. Ask volunteers to write the answers on the board.

B Have students work individually to match the questions and the answers. Ask volunteers to read the matching questions and answers aloud. Write the number-letter match on the board.

Multilevel Strategies

For 1B and 1C, seat same-level students together.

• **Pre-level** Read each 1B question aloud, and give these students time to find the answer before reading the next one. Have them write in the answers to 1C when the class corrects.

• **On- and Higher-level** While you are working with the pre-level students on 1B, have these students complete 1B and 1C. Ask those who finish early to read the 1C conversation with a partner.

C Have students work individually to put the conversation in order. Ask a volunteer to read the sentences aloud in order.

D Have students work individually to write the advice. Ask volunteers to put their sentences on the board.

Multilevel Strategies

For 1D, seat same-level students together.

• **Pre-level** Read each situation aloud, and have these students give you suggestions. Write the sentence with *should* for them to copy into their books.

• **On- and Higher-level** While you are working with pre-level students, ask these students to write one sentence with *should* and one with *shouldn't* for each situation.

2 Group work

Communicative Practice

20–35 minutes

 A 1. Direct students, in groups of three to four, to focus on the pictures on page 125. Ask questions about the picture. *Which picture shows a safe workplace? Which picture shows a dangerous workplace?*

2. Set a time limit (five minutes) to complete the exercise. Circulate and answer any questions.

3. Have a reporter from each group read the group's sentences to the class.

> ### Multilevel Strategies
>
> For 2A and 2B, use same-level groups.
>
> • **Pre-level** For 2A, ask these students to write three vocabulary words and one complete sentence. For 2B, allow them to ask and answer the questions without writing.
>
> • **Higher-level** For 2A, ask these students to write two additional sentences about the pictures. For 2B, have them ask and answer additional questions: *How often do you talk on the phone and drive? How often do you drive faster than the speed limit?*

B 1. Review the placement of frequency adverbs *always, usually, sometimes,* and *never.*

2. Have students work in the same groups from 2A and take turns interviewing each other in pairs.

3. Set a time limit (five minutes) to complete the exercise.

4. Tell students to make a note of their partners' answers but not to worry about writing complete sentences.

C Have a reporter from each group share the group's work.

TIP For more practice with *should*, have students write different kinds of advice. Post enough pieces of butcher paper around the room so that groups of four can stand at each poster. Write a problem on each poster. Keep the activity lighthearted by making some of the problems silly. Have each group write one piece of advice on the poster. Call "time" after one minute. Have groups move to the next poster. Tell them their advice must be different from the previous group. Repeat until every poster has three or four pieces of advice on it.

PROBLEM SOLVING

15–25 minutes

A Direct students to look at the picture. Ask: *What happened?* Tell students they will read a story about a car accident. Ask students to read Mr. Brown's story silently. Then play the audio, and have them read along silently. Ask: *Where is Mr. Brown? How does he feel?*

B 1. Identify the problem. Read the question. Read the possible solutions. Elicit student ideas for other solutions. Write each one on the board.

2. Discuss whether the statements are appropriate. Ask for a show of hands to see which solution the class likes best.

C 1. As you elicit student ideas, write the note on the board. Ask students to copy the note into their notebooks.

Evaluation

10–15 minutes

To test students' understanding of the unit grammar and life skills, have them take the Unit 11 Test in the *Step Forward Test Generator CD-ROM with ExamView® Assessment Suite.*

Learning Log

To help students record and discuss their progress, use the *Learning Log* on page T-179.

To extend this review: Have students complete **Workbook 1 page 78, Multilevel Activity Book 1 pages 123–126,** and the **Unit 11 Grammar Exercises** on the **Multilevel Grammar Exercises CD-ROM 1**.

2 Group work

A Work with 2–3 classmates. Look at the pictures on page 125.
Write 5 sentences with *should* or *shouldn't*.
Talk about the sentences with your class. Answers will vary.

Ann should wear safety glasses. Tim shouldn't listen to music at work.
Ann should wear safety boots. Tim should be careful. Tim should wear a hard hat.

B Interview 3 classmates. Write their answers in your notebook.

ASK:
1. How often do you wear your seat belt?
2. Do you check your smoke detector batteries every 6 months?
3. How often do you wear safety glasses or gloves?

> Classmate—Lina
> 1. She always wears her seat belt.
> 2. Yes, she does.
> 3. She sometimes wears safety glasses.

C Talk about the answers with your class.

PROBLEM SOLVING

A Listen and read about Mr. Brown. What is his problem?
Mr. Brown has a car accident. The driver of the other car is not there.

Mr. Brown is in the parking lot at the supermarket. He's very tired. He's parking his car and he doesn't see the car next to him! He has a small accident. He looks around the parking lot, but the driver of the other car is not there.

B Work with your classmates. Answer the question.
(More than one answer is possible.)

What should Mr. Brown do?
- (a.) Call the police.
- b. Call 911.
- (c.) Talk to the market manager.
- (d.) Other: Answers will vary.

C Work with your classmates. Write a note that Mr. Brown can put on the car for the driver.

UNIT 12
Free Time

FOCUS ON
- weather and seasons
- leisure activities
- the future with *be going to*
- making future plans
- holidays

LESSON 1 Vocabulary

1 Learn weather words and holidays

A **Look at the pictures. When are the holidays?** 1. January 2. February 3. May 4. June 5. July
6. November

B **Listen and look at the pictures.**

C **Listen and repeat the words.**

1. snowing   2. raining   3. cloudy   4. sunny   5. hot   6. cold

D **Look at the pictures. Complete the sentences.**

1. It's ____hot____ this Independence Day.
2. It's ___cold___ this Thanksgiving.
3. It's ___sunny___ this Father's Day.
4. It's ___snowing___ this New Year's Day.
5. It's ___cloudy___ this Mother's Day.
6. It's ___raining___ this Presidents' Day.

Unit 12 Lesson 1

Objectives	Grammar	Vocabulary	Correlations
On-level: Identify weather, holiday, and leisure activity words **Pre-level:** Recognize weather, holiday, and leisure activity words **Higher-level:** Talk and write about weather, holidays, and leisure activities	Simple-present tense (*It's cold this winter.*)	Weather, holidays, and leisure activities For additional vocabulary practice, see these **Oxford Picture Dictionary** topics: Weather, Holidays, Places to Go	**CASAS:** 0.1.2, 0.2.4, 2.3.3, 7.4.5, 7.4.7 **LCPs:** 29.04, 30.01, 32.01, 32.02, 32.13 **SCANS:** Listening, Participates as member of a team, Seeing things in the mind's eye, Self-management, Speaking **EFF:** Cooperate with others, Reflect and evaluate, Speak so others can understand

Warm-up and Review

10–15 minutes (books closed)

Write *Winter, Spring, Summer,* and *Fall* on separate sheets of butcher or poster paper. Have students brainstorm words they associate with each season, including months, holidays, weather, clothing, and activities. List them on the paper. Save these posters for the extension activity at the end of the lesson.

Introduction

5 minutes

1. Read the words on the posters.

2. State the objective: *Today we're going to learn more words for weather, holidays, and things to do.*

1 Learn weather words and holidays

Presentation

20–25 minutes

A Direct students to look at the pictures. Discuss the holidays and ask when they are.

B 1. Have students listen to the audio. Ask them to point to the correct picture as they listen. Circulate and monitor.

2. Check comprehension by asking *yes/no* questions. Pass out *yes/no* cards to the students (see page T-175), or have them hold up one finger for *yes* and two for *no* in order to get a nonverbal response. Ask: *Is it cold on Thanksgiving Day?* [yes] *Is it raining on Father's Day?* [no]

Multilevel Strategies

After the group comprehension check in 1B, call on individuals and tailor your questions to the level of your students.

• **Pre-level** Ask *or* questions. *Is it snowing on New Year's Day or on Presidents' Day?* [New Year's Day]

• **On-level** Ask information questions. *Which day is hot?* [Independence Day]

• **Higher-level** Ask these students to use the vocabulary. *How's the weather on New Year's Day?*

C Ask students to listen and repeat the words.

TIP Find out if and when students celebrate Independence Day, New Year's Day, Mother's Day, and Father's Day in their countries of origin.

Guided Practice I

15–20 minutes

D 1. Have students complete the sentences using the new vocabulary.

2. Encourage students to take turns reading the completed sentences in pairs.

2 Talk about leisure activities

Guided Practice II

35–40 minutes

 1. Ask: *What is your favorite season? Winter, spring, summer, or fall?* Introduce the new topic: *Now let's talk about things to do in different seasons.*

2. Group students and assign roles: leader, fact checker, recorder, and reporter. Explain that students work with their groups to match the words and pictures.

3. Check comprehension of the exercise. Ask: *Who looks up the words in the picture dictionary?* [fact checker] *Who writes the numbers in the book?* [recorder] *Who tells the class your answers?* [reporter] *Who helps everyone and manages the group?* [leader]

4. Set a time limit (three minutes), and have students work together to complete the task. While students are working, copy the wordlist on the board.

5. Call "time" and have the reporters from each group take turns calling out the numbers for the wordlist. Record students' answers on the board. If groups disagree, write each group's choice next to the word.

> ### Multilevel Strategies
>
> For 2A, use mixed-level groups.
> - **Pre-level** Assign these students as recorders or create a role of timekeeper (to let the group know when the three minutes are up) giving these students an active role in the group.
> - **On-level** Assign these students as fact checkers and reporters.
> - **Higher-level** Assign these students as leaders.

B 1. Ask students to listen and check their answers.

2. Have students correct the wordlist on the board and then write the correct numbers in their books.

3. Tell the groups from 2A to break into pairs to practice the words. Set a time limit (two minutes).

C 1. Have students circle the correct words to complete the sentences.

2. Ask students to take turns reading the completed sentences in the same pairs from 2B.

Communicative Practice and Application

10–15 minutes

 1. Model the interview with a volunteer. Then switch roles and model it again.

2. Set a time limit (five minutes). Ask students to interview several partners.

Evaluation

10–15 minutes (books closed)

TEST YOURSELF

1. Make a two-column chart on the board with the headings *Hot Weather* and *Cold Weather*. Have students close their books. Ask a volunteer to give you an example of his/her favorite activity for each type of weather.

2. Have students copy the chart into their notebooks. Give students five to ten minutes to test themselves by writing the words they recall from the lesson on the chart.

3. Call "time" and have students check their spelling in *The Oxford Picture Dictionary* or another dictionary. Circulate and monitor students' progress.

> ### Multilevel Strategies
>
> Target the *Test Yourself* to the level of your students.
> - **Pre-level** Have these students work with their books open.
> - **Higher-level** Have these students complete the chart and then write three complete sentences using this skeleton: *I like to _____ in the _____.*

To compress this lesson: Conduct 2A as a whole-class activity. Have students practice 2D with only one partner.

To extend this lesson: Have students add any words they learned during the unit to the posters from the warm-up. Ask them to look through magazines and cut out seasonal pictures to decorate the posters.

And/Or have students complete **Workbook 1 page 79** and the **Multilevel Activity Book 1 page 128**.

2 Talk about leisure activities

A Work with your classmates. Match the words with the pictures.

_7_	go out to eat	_8_	go to the movies	_4_	play soccer
_6_	go swimming	_3_	have a picnic	_1_	stay home
_5_	go to the beach	_2_	make a snowman		

B Listen and check your answers. Then practice the words with a partner.

C Look at the pictures. Circle the correct words.

1. In the winter, it's ((cold)/ hot). They like to (play soccer /(stay home)).
2. The flowers are beautiful in the (fall /(spring)). They like to have (movies /(picnics)).
3. The weather is ((hot)/ cold) in the summer. They like to ((go)/ stay) to the beach.
4. In the fall, they like to go ((out to eat)/ to the beach). Other people like to go (swimming /(to the movies)).

D Work with a partner. Ask and answer the questions.

1. What is your favorite time of the year?
2. What do you like to do at that time of the year?

TEST YOURSELF ✔

Close your book. Write your 5 favorite activities for hot and cold weather.
Check your spelling in a dictionary.

1 Read about a trip to a baseball game

A Look at the pictures. Listen.

RIVERSIDE BASEBALL STADIUM

B Listen again. Read the sentences.

1. I can't wait for the weekend. I don't have to work or go to school on Saturdays or Sundays.
2. On Saturdays, I have fun with my son.
3. This Saturday, we're going to see a baseball game.
4. We're going to watch the game and eat hot dogs.
5. My son wants to catch a ball at the game.

C Check your understanding. Circle *a* or *b*.

1. He _____ on Saturday.
   a. works
   b. doesn't work

2. They're going to see a baseball game _____.
   a. on Saturday
   b. on Sunday

3. He's going to see the game with his _____.
   a. boss
   b. son

4. His son wants to catch a _____ at the game.
   a. ball
   b. hot dog

Unit 12 Lesson 2

Objectives	Grammar	Vocabulary	Correlations
On-, Pre-, and Higher-level: Read and write about plans and bus schedules	*Be going to* future (*I'm going to see a baseball game.*)	*Can't wait, catch* For additional vocabulary practice, see this **Oxford Picture Dictionary** topic: Team Sports	**CASAS:** 0.1.2, 0.1.3, 0.2.4, 2.2.2–2.2.4, 2.6.1, 6.0.1, 7.4.7 **LCPs:** 22.03, 25.01, 32.01, 32.02, 32.13 **SCANS:** Listening, Reading, Seeing things in the mind's eye, Self-management, Speaking, Time, Writing **EFF:** Convey ideas in writing, Listen actively, Observe critically

Warm-up and Review

10–15 minutes (books closed)

Write *Sports* and *Free-time Activities* on the board. Have volunteers come to the board and write words in each category. When students run out of ideas, go over the lists. Correct spelling, clarify meaning, and discuss whether each word is in the right column.

Introduction

5 minutes

1. Using the activities on the board, say: *How often do you _____? When we're going to do one of these activities, we are very happy and excited. We say: I can't wait to go!*

2. State the objective: *We're going to read about a father who can't wait for Saturday. We're going to write about things we can't wait to do.*

1 Read about a trip to a baseball game

Presentation I

20–25 minutes

A 1. Direct students to look at the pictures. Ask: *Where does he work? What's he going to do on his day off?*

2. Play the audio.

B 1. Play the audio again. Have students read along silently.

2. Check comprehension. Ask: *When are his days off?* [Saturday and Sunday] *What are they going to do at the baseball game?* [watch the game and eat hot dogs]

Multilevel Strategies

After 1B, seat same-level students together.

• **Pre-level** Reread the sentences in 1B with your pre-level students while on- and higher-level students go on to 1C. Have them copy the answers to 1C from the board.

• **On- and Higher-level** Have these students work individually to complete 1C. Ask students who finish early to ask a partner: *What do you like to do on the weekend?*

Guided Practice I

10 minutes

C Have students circle the correct letter to complete the sentences. Have volunteers write the answers on the board.

When students learn the expression *can't wait for*, they may be inclined to follow it with a verb instead of a noun. (*I can't wait for go to the movies* instead of *I can't wait for Saturday.*) Show students how to use *can't wait to + verb* or *can't wait for + noun*.

2 Write about your plans

TIP In preparation for their 2A writing exercise, have students brainstorm a list of things they like to do, and write them on the board under the columns *Verb* and *Noun*. Have students practice saying *I can't wait* with the expressions on the board.

Guided Practice II

20–25 minutes

A 1. Copy the sentences on the board. Read them aloud with your own information.

2. Have students complete the sentences independently. Circulate and assist.

⋮ 1. Ask students to read their sentences to a partner.

2. Call on individuals to share what they learned about their partners.

3 Use a bus schedule to plan a trip

Presentation II

20–25 minutes

1. Introduce the topic: *Now we're going to look at a bus schedule.* Direct students to look at the schedule in 3A. Ask: *Is this the Wednesday schedule or the Saturday schedule?* [Saturday]

2. Ask students to put their pencils down and listen for the answer to this question: *What time is the baseball game?* [5:00] Play the entire audio once.

3. Play the audio in segments. After each conversation, stop the audio and check answers with the students: *Did you write the time?* If necessary, repeat that segment of the audio before moving on.

4. Check students' listening accuracy: *When does Bus 2 get to Front Street School?* [12:15]

Multilevel Strategies

Replay 3A to challenge on- and higher-level students while allowing pre-level students to catch up.

• **Pre-Level** Have these students listen again for another chance to complete the exercise.

• **On- and Higher-level** Write this question on the board: *Where do numbers 3, 4, and 5 go?* After replaying the audio, have volunteers write the answers on the board.

Guided Practice

10–15 minutes

B Have students work individually to match the questions with the answers. Go over the answers as a class.

Communicative Practice and Application

10 minutes

C 1. Model the conversation with a volunteer. Then model it again with other information from the schedule in 3A.

2. Set a time limit (five minutes). Ask students to practice the conversation with several partners.

3. Ask volunteers to present their conversations to the class.

Evaluation

10–15 minutes (books closed)

TEST YOURSELF

Have students work independently to write their sentences. Collect and correct their writing.

To compress this lesson: Assign 1C as homework. Have students practice the conversation in 3C with only one partner.

To extend this lesson: Make a transparency of a local bus schedule and go over it with the class.

And/Or have students complete **Workbook 1 page 80** and **Multilevel Activity Book 1 page 129**.

2 Write about your plans

A Write your story. Complete the sentences. Answers will vary.

I can't wait for _____.

I don't _____ on _____.

On _____, I'm going to _____.

B Read your story to a partner.

3 Use a bus schedule to plan a trip

A Listen to the conversation. Complete the schedule below.

Metro Bus West Line–Weekend Schedule

	Grant Street	Front St. School	Town Mall	Riverside Baseball Stadium	City Park
Bus #1	8:00	8:15	8:30	8:45	9:00
Bus #2	12:00	12:15	12:30	12:45	1:00
Bus #3	4:00	4:15	4:30	4:45	5:00

B Match the questions with the answers.

Pedro and his son have to get on the bus at Grant Street. The baseball game is at 1:00.

_b_ 1. What bus do they have to take?   a. 12:45

_c_ 2. How many stops are between Grant Street and the stadium?   b. Bus #2

_d_ 3. What time do they have to take the bus?   c. two

_a_ 4. What time will they stop at the stadium?   d. 12:00

C Work with a partner. Practice the conversation. Use the bus schedule in 3A.

You are on Grant Street.

A: Excuse me, I have to be at the mall at 5:00.
   Can I take the bus from here?

B: Yes. Take the number 3 bus at 4:00.

A: Thank you.

TEST YOURSELF ✔

Close your book. Write 3 sentences about places you are going to go this weekend.

I'm going to go to the mall this weekend.

1 Learn the future with *be going to*

A Look at the pictures. What season is it? Answers will vary.

It's going to be sunny on Friday.   It's going to be cloudy on Saturday.   It's going to rain on Sunday.

B Study the charts. Complete the sentences below.

THE FUTURE WITH *BE GOING TO*

Statements							
I	am	going to	have a picnic.	We	are	going to	have a picnic.
You	are			You			
He She	is			They			
It	is	going to	be sunny.				

1. She is __is going to__ have a picnic.   2. They __are__ going __to__ have a picnic.

Negative statements							
I	am	not going to	have a picnic.	We	are	not going to	have a picnic.
You	are			You			
He She	is			They			
It	is	not going to	be sunny.				

3. I am __not__ going to have a picnic.   4. We are not __going to__ have a picnic.

C Look at the pictures in 1A. Match the parts of the sentences.

__b__ 1. They are going to   a. rain on Saturday.

__d__ 2. It is going to   b. have a picnic on Friday.

__c__ 3. They are not going to   c. stay home on Saturday.

__a__ 4. It is not going to   d. rain on Sunday.

Unit 12 Lesson 3

Objectives	Grammar	Vocabulary	Correlations
On- and Higher-level: Use the future with *be going to* to talk about leisure activities **Pre-level:** Recognize the future with *be going to*	Future with *be going to* (*We're going to have a picnic.*)	Leisure activities For additional vocabulary practice, see this **Oxford Picture Dictionary** topic: The Park and Playground	**CASAS:** 0.1.2, 0.2.4, 2.3.3, 7.4.7 **LCPs:** 30.01, 32.01, 33.02, 33.06, 33.09 **SCANS:** Listening, Seeing things in the mind's eye, Self-management, Speaking **EFF:** Listen actively, Observe critically, Plan, Reflect and evaluate, Speak so others can understand

Warm-up and Review

10–15 minutes (books closed)

Ask students about their plans for the weekend, the summer, the holidays, or an upcoming vacation. Write the phrases on the board. *Visit my sister, have a party, go dancing.*

Introduction

5–10 minutes

1. Say sentences about your class using the information from the warm-up and *be going to.*

2. State the objective: *Today we're going to use be going to to talk about our plans.*

1 Learn the future with *be going to*

Presentation I

20–25 minutes

A 1. Direct students to look at the pictures and answer the question: *What season is it?*

2. Read the captions under the pictures.

B 1. Demonstrate how to read the grammar charts as complete sentences. Read the charts through sentence by sentence. Then read them again, and have students repeat after you.

2. Use the pictures in 1A to illustrate points in the grammar chart. *It's going to rain on Sunday.*

3. As a class, complete the sentences under the charts. Ask volunteers to write the sentences on the board. Have other students read the sentences aloud.

4. Give students time to silently review the charts and, if they haven't already, fill in the blanks.

5. Assess students' understanding of the charts. Ask students to tell you their plans for the weekend using the phrases from the warm-up and *be going to.*

Guided Practice

15–20 minutes

C Have students work individually to complete the sentences. Go over the answers as a class.

Multilevel Strategies

After 1C is corrected, group same-level students together.

• **Pre-level** Have these students read the sentences in 1C to each other.

• **On- and Higher-level** Ask these students to say or write sentences using *be going to* and the phrases from the warm-up.

2 Ask and answer questions with *be going to*

Presentation II

20–25 minutes

 1. Read and have students repeat the questions and answers in the chart.

2. Copy the questions and answers on the board. Underline *are going to do* in the first question. Say: *This verb has four parts.* Elicit all four parts of the verb (*be going to* + main verb) for the rest of the questions and answers.

3. Ask a student: *What are you going to do tonight?* Then ask another student to answer the third-person question: *What is (first student) going to do tonight?* Do this with several volunteers, asking them to respond with complete sentences. Then have a volunteer ask you the question.

Guided Practice

10–15 minutes

B Have students work individually to write the questions. Ask volunteers to put their questions on the board.

> ### Multilevel Strategies
>
> • **Pre-level** While other students are completing 2B, ask these students to write three sentences with: *This weekend, I'm going to _____.* Once the 2B questions are on the board, have the pre-level students copy them.
>
> • **On- and Higher-level** Have these students complete 2B and write the questions on the board. Correct the questions. While pre-level students are copying from the board, have these students ask and answer the questions with a partner.

3 Practice questions with *be going to*

Communicative Practice and Application

20–25 minutes

 Have students work individually to complete the questions and write the answers. Write the questions on the board. Elicit different answers.

> ### Multilevel Strategies
>
> For 3B, use mixed-level pairs.
>
> • **Pre-level** Have pre-level students answer the questions.
>
> • **On- and Higher-level** Encourage these students to ask the questions from memory when they are ready.

B 1. Model the interview with a volunteer. Then switch roles and model it again.

2. Set a time limit (three minutes) for students to interview their partners. Circulate and monitor.

Evaluation

10–15 minutes (books closed)

TEST YOURSELF

Ask students to write the sentences independently. Collect and correct their writing.

To compress this lesson: Assign 2B as homework or conduct it as a whole-class activity.

To extend this lesson: Practice different forms of *be going to*.
1. Put students in groups and tell them to discuss their weekend plans.
2. Direct them to write one third-person sentence for each group member and one plural sentence for all of the group members with *We are all. Jun is going to go shopping. Katia is going to go to a party. We are all going to watch TV.*
3. Ask a reporter from each group to read the sentences to the class.
And/Or have students complete **Workbook 1 pages 81–82** and **Multilevel Activity Book 1 page 130**.

2 Ask and answer questions with *be going to*

A Study the chart. Ask and answer the questions.

Information questions with *be going to*	
A: What are you going to do tonight? **B:** I'm going to study.	**A:** What are we going to do next week? **B:** We're going to (go to) Mexico.
A: What is he going to do tomorrow? **B:** He's going to see a movie.	**A:** What are they going to do next year? **B:** They're going to buy a house.

B Write the questions.

1. <u>What is she going to do tonight?</u>   She's going to watch TV tonight.
2. <u>What are you going to do on Saturday?</u>   I'm going to have a picnic on Saturday.
3. <u>What are you / we going to do this weekend?</u>   We're going to have fun this weekend.
4. <u>What are they going to do tomorrow?</u>   They're going to study tomorrow.
5. <u>What is he going to do tonight?</u>   He's going to feed the dog tonight.

3 Practice questions with *be going to*

A Complete the questions. Use the words in the box. Then write your answers.

What	Who	When	~~Where~~

1. <u>Where</u> are you going to go after class?
   <u>I'm going to go home.</u>

2. <u>What</u> are you going to do tomorrow?
   Answers will vary.

3. <u>When</u> are you going to see a movie?
   Answers will vary.

4. <u>Who</u> are you going to talk to after class?
   Answers will vary.

B Ask and answer the questions in 3A with a partner. Then write sentences about your partner's answers.

Juan is going to go to work.

TEST YOURSELF ✔

Close your book. Write 2 sentences about your future plans and 2 sentences about your partner's future plans.

I'm going to study tomorrow. Juan is going to go to work.

1 Plan to see a movie

A Read the movie ads. Say the titles and the times of the movies.

B Listen and read.

A: What are we going to do tonight?

B: Let's see a movie. *The Action Man* is playing at 6:00.

A: OK. How much are tickets?

B: The 6:00 show is only $6.00.

A: $6.00? That's a bargain. Let's go!

C Listen again and repeat.

D Work with a partner. Practice the conversation. Use the movie ads in 1A.

A: What are we _____ do tonight?

B: _____ see a movie? _____ is playing at _____.

A: Sure. How much are _____?

B: _____.

A: _____? Let's go!

E Listen to the conversation. Answer the questions.

1. What movie are they going to see? _____Rain in My Eyes_____

2. What time are they going to meet? _At 9:00._

3. What time is the movie? _At 9:30._

4. Can they take the bus? _Yes, they can._

Unit 12 Lesson 4

Objectives	Grammar	Vocabulary	Correlations
On- and Higher-level: Ask and answer questions about movies **Pre-level:** Ask questions about movies	Future with *be going to* (*What are we going to do today?*)	*Bargain, bargain matinee, running time* For additional vocabulary practice, see this **Oxford Picture Dictionary** topic: Places to Go	**CASAS:** 0.1.2, 0.1.6, 0.2.4, 2.6.1–2.6.3, 6.0.1, 7.4.7 **LCPs:** 25.01, 32.01, 32.02, 32.13 **SCANS:** Acquires and evaluates information, Arithmetic/Mathematics, Knowing how to learn, Reading, Speaking **EFF:** Speak so others can understand, Use math to solve problems and communicate

Warm-up and Review

10–15 minutes (books closed)

Write *Event, Place, Time,* and *Price* on a large piece of butcher paper as column heads. Ask a volunteer what he/she is going to do this weekend, and write the answer under *Event*. Ask where and when the event is going to occur and how much it's going to cost. Write all of the information in the chart. (Write *free* for activities like going to the park or going to a family party.) Continue asking until you have four or five events listed in the chart. Save the paper for an extension activity at the end of the lesson.

Introduction

5 minutes

1. Restate the information in the chart. *Su is going to watch her son's soccer game in the park. It's going to start at 10:00, and it's going to be free!*

2. State the objective: *Today we're going to ask and answer questions about going to the movies and other weekend plans.*

1 Plan to see a movie

Presentation

20–30 minutes

A 1. Direct students to look at the movie ads. Ask questions. *Which movie do you like? Which movie is good for children?*

2. Give students a minute to read the movie titles and times. Ask students to identify the meaning of the asterisk next to 5:30, 6:00 and 4:00. [bargain matinee]

Guided Practice

20–25 minutes

B Play the audio. Have students read along silently.

C Play the audio again, and have students repeat the conversation. Replay if necessary.

Communicative Practice and Application

15–20 minutes

D 1. Model the conversation with a volunteer. Then model it again with other information from 1A.

2. Elicit other ways to complete the conversation.

3. Set a time limit (five minutes). Ask students to practice the conversation with several partners.

Multilevel Strategies

For 1D, adapt the oral practice to the level of your students.

- **Pre-level** Have these students read the conversation as written in 1B.
- **Higher-level** Write the names of some current movies on the board, and ask these students to practice additional conversations using the real movies.

E 1. Read the questions aloud.

2. Play the audio. Tell students to answer as many questions as they can. Replay the audio, so students can write the answers they missed. Go over the answers as a class.

2 Practice your pronunciation

Pronunciation Extension

10–15 minutes

A Play the audio. Have students read along silently.

B Play the audio. Tell students to circle *formal* or *relaxed*. Replay the audio and stop after each sentence to check the students' answers.

> **TIP** Bring copies of recent newspaper movie sections to the class. Group students and provide each group with a page of the paper. Ask them to find a movie, the name of a theater where it is playing, and the show times. Have a reporter from each group share his/her findings with the class.

C Have students work with a partner to read the questions and answers in 2A.

3 Real-life math

Math Extension

10–15 minutes

1. Direct students to read question 1. Have them look at the ads on page 142 and find *Rain in My Eyes*. Ask: *How long is the movie?* [120 minutes] *How many hours is that?* [two] *Can Emily take the 11:15 bus home?* [no]

2. Direct students to read question 2 and find the answer to the question. Ask a volunteer to share the answer with the class.

> **TIP** Tell parents that if they are concerned about the movies their children are seeing, they can find much more detailed rating systems on the Internet. Typing *movie ratings for parents* into an Internet search engine will point them to various sites.

Evaluation

10–15 minutes

TEST YOURSELF

1. Model the role-play with a volunteer. Then switch roles.

2. Pair students. Elicit questions that partners may want to ask. *What time is the movie? How much are the tickets?*

3. Set a time limit (five minutes), and have the partners act out the role-play in both roles.

4. Circulate and monitor. Encourage improvisation.

5. Provide feedback.

> **Multilevel Strategies**
> Target the Test Yourself to the level of your students.
> • **Pre-level** Allow these students to use the conversation in 1B.
> • **Higher-level** Have these students say the conversation using real movie information from the newspaper or Internet.

To compress this lesson: Have students practice the conversation in 1D with only one partner.

To extend this lesson: Have student discuss other weekend plans.
1. Adapt the questions from this lesson to the activities discussed during the warm-up.
   What are you going to do?
   What time are you going to get there?
   How are you going to get there?
   How much is it going to cost?
2. Have students ask and answer the questions in pairs, using the events from the warm-up or their own information.
And/Or have students complete **Workbook 1 page 83** and the **Multilevel Activity Book 1 page 131**.

2 Practice your pronunciation

 A **Listen to the sentences. What is different in the "relaxed" pronunciation?**

	Formal	Relaxed
1. going to	A: What are we **going to** do today? B: We're **going to** go to the park.	A: What are we **going to** do today? B: We're **going to** go to the park.
2. want to	A: Do you **want to** go to a movie? B: Yes. I **want to** go to a movie.	A: Do you **want to** go to a movie? B: Yes. I **want to** go to a movie.

B **Listen and circle** *formal* **or** *relaxed*.

1. (formal)   relaxed
2. formal   (relaxed)
3. (formal)   relaxed
4. formal   (relaxed)
5. formal   (relaxed)

C **Work with a partner. Read the questions and answers in 2A.**

3 Real-life math

Work with your classmates. Use the running times in the movie ads in 1A to answer the questions.

1. Emily is going to see *Rain in My Eyes* at 9:30.

   Can she take the 11:15 bus home?

   <u>No, she can't.</u> .

2. Asha is going to take her children to see *My Friend, Green George* at 6:00.

   They live ten minutes from the movie theater. Can they be home at 7:30?

   <u>Yes, they can.</u> .

TEST YOURSELF ✔

Work with a partner. Use the movie ads in 1A to make plans this weekend.
Partner A: Name a movie you want to see. Partner B: Ask about the times
and ticket prices. Then change roles.

1 Get ready to read

A **Read the definitions.**

occasion: a holiday, birthday, or other special day
greeting cards: cards for holidays, birthdays, and other special occasions

B **Work with your classmates. Can you name the month for each holiday?**

① Be My Valentine

February

② HAPPY HOLIDAYS

December

③ Happy Mother's Day

May

④ HAPPY FATHER'S DAY

June

2 Read about greeting cards

A **Read the article.**

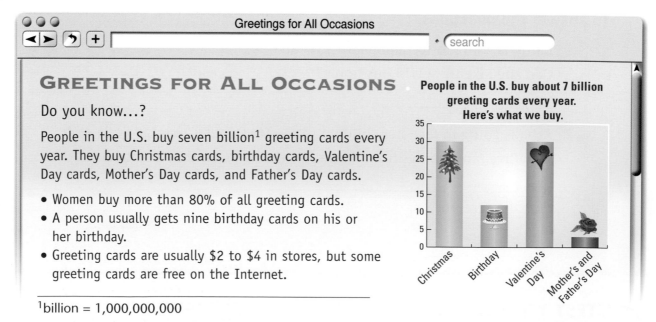

Greetings for All Occasions

search

GREETINGS FOR ALL OCCASIONS

Do you know...?

People in the U.S. buy seven billion[1] greeting cards every year. They buy Christmas cards, birthday cards, Valentine's Day cards, Mother's Day cards, and Father's Day cards.

- Women buy more than 80% of all greeting cards.
- A person usually gets nine birthday cards on his or her birthday.
- Greeting cards are usually $2 to $4 in stores, but some greeting cards are free on the Internet.

[1]billion = 1,000,000,000

People in the U.S. buy about 7 billion greeting cards every year. Here's what we buy.

Christmas Birthday Valentine's Day Mother's and Father's Day

Source: *www.greetingcard.org*

B **Listen and read the article again.**

Unit 12 Lesson 5

Objectives	Grammar	Vocabulary	Correlations
On- and Higher-level: Read about and discuss greeting cards and using the phone book **Pre-level:** Read about greeting cards and using the phone book	Simple-present tense (*People buy greeting cards for birthdays.*)	*Occasion, greeting card, balloon* For additional vocabulary practice, see this **Oxford Picture Dictionary** topic: Holidays	**CASAS:** 0.1.2, 1.1.3, 2.3.2, 2.5.3, 2.7.1, 6.0.1 **LCPs:** 25.01, 29.04, 32.01–32.06 **SCANS:** Acquires and evaluates information, Knowing how to learn, Listening, Reading, Seeing things in the mind's eye, Speaking **EFF:** Read with understanding, Take responsibility for learning

Warm-up and Review

10–15 minutes (books closed)

Elicit the names of the months, and write them on the board. Ask students which holidays occur in which months. Have volunteers come up and write a holiday under its month. Continue until students run out of ideas.

Introduction

5 minutes

1. Show students greeting cards from different holidays. Say: *On some holidays and at other special times, Americans like to send greeting cards.* See if students know which of the holidays on the board have a greeting-card tradition.

2. State the objective: *Today we're going to read about greeting cards and look for a card store in the phone book.*

1 Get ready to read

Presentation

15–20 minutes

A Direct students to look at the picture of the birthday card. Ask: *What kind of card is this?* Read the words and the definitions aloud.

B Have students look at the pictures. Elicit the month of each holiday. Add any new holidays to the list on the board.

TIP Display some greeting cards. Ask students to guess which occasions they go with. Teach students that cards that say *sympathy* are for a person who has lost someone.

Pre-Reading

Direct students to look at the chart in the article in 2A. Ask: *How many cards do people buy?* [seven billion] Draw students' attention to the footnote. *How many zeros in a billion?* [nine]

2 Read about greeting cards

Guided Practice I

25–30 minutes

A 1. Ask students to read the article silently.

2. Ask if there are any questions about the reading.

B Play the audio. Have students read along silently.

Multilevel Strategies

For 2A–B, seat same-level students together.

• **Pre-level** Assist these students by reading the article again and checking for comprehension after each section. *Do Americans buy seven billion or 17 billion greeting cards every year? Do men or women buy more greeting cards? Are some greeting cards free at the store or on the Internet?*

• **On- and Higher-level** While you are working with pre-level students, ask these students to interview their partners: *Do you ever give greeting cards? For what occasions? Where do you buy them?* Compare their results with the bar graph. *Do students give the same number of Christmas cards as birthday cards?*

C Have students work individually to complete the sentences. Go over the answers as a class.

> Teach students some simple phrases to use in greeting cards. *I hope you have a (wonderful/great/beautiful) day. Have a wonderful holiday season. Best wishes on your birthday. Thank you for everything.*
>
> In some languages, the expression for *I love you* can be used to signify respect or admiration. Teach students that in English, *I love you* is used only with close friends, family members, and romantic partners.

D 1. Have students work individually to answer the questions. Ask volunteers to write the answers on the board.

2. Ask additional comprehension questions. *What are the two most popular greeting-card occasions?* [Christmas and Valentine's Day]

3 Learn to use a phone book

Guided Practice II

15–20 minutes

A 1. Show students a phone book. Say: *Now we're going to look at phone-book listings.*

2. Have students work individually to look at the phone-book page and answer the questions.

Multilevel Strategies

Seat same-level students together for 3A.

- **Pre-level** Go through the questions with these students, and help them find the answers on the phone-book page.
- **On- and Higher-level** Give these students a copy of a real page from the party-supplies section of your local phone book. Ask them to find the name, location, and hours of a party store.

Communicative Practice

10–15 minutes

B 1. Review the questions.

2. Set a time limit (three minutes). Allow students to think about the questions and then write their answers individually.

3. Elicit and discuss student responses.

Application

5–10 minutes

BRING IT TO LIFE

Direct students to look in their phone books for a store near their home.

To compress this lesson: Conduct 2D and 3A as whole-class activities.

To extend this lesson: Have students make a greeting card. There are several ways to do this:
  a) If you have access to the Internet in class, use an online greeting-card maker. Show students how to choose an occasion, personalize the greeting card, and print it out.
  b) If you don't have access to the Internet in class, use an online greeting-card maker to print out covers for birthday cards. Give one cover to every student and help students write personalized messages inside.
  c) Give each student a sheet of card stock, and have them create their own cards.

Choose the best way for your class. Regardless of which method you use, have students create a rough draft of their cards. Collect the rough drafts, and go over any common mistakes. Allow students to keep the final drafts of their cards, so they can use them.

And/Or have students complete **Workbook 1 page 84** and **Multilevel Activity Book 1 page 132**.

C Complete the sentences. Use the words in the box.

holidays	birthday	~~greeting cards~~	Internet

1. Americans buy seven billion ___greeting cards___ every year.
2. People buy greeting cards for birthdays and __holidays__.
3. Some greeting cards are free on the __Internet__.
4. A person usually gets nine greeting cards on his or her __birthday__.

D Read the sentences. Write the answers.

1. Name three occasions when people buy greeting cards. __Answers will vary.__
2. Name two places you can buy or get greeting cards. __Answers will vary.__

3 Learn to use a phone book

A Look at the phone book. Answer the questions.

▶ **Holiday/Party Supply Stores**

BALLOONS AND THINGS ············· 555-2759
(see our display ad this page)

Hall's Card Shop ······················· 555-0225

Nancy's Cards and Gifts ············ 555-7730

Paul's Flowers ··························· 555-3151

SPECIAL MOMENTS GIFTS ········· 555-1351
(see our display ad this page)

HAPPY BIRTHDAY
BALLOONS AND THINGS
All your party decorations here!
Open 9:00 a.m.–8:00 p.m.
7 days

Special Moments Gifts
Birthdays!
Anniversaries! Valentines Day!
Something for everyone.
Open 9–9. Closed on Sundays
10% OFF THE PRICE WITH THIS AD

1. What's the phone number for Hall's Card Shop? __The phone number is 555-0225.__
2. Where can you shop for flowers? __At Paul's Flowers.__
3. What time does Balloons and Things open every day? __At 9:00 a.m.__
4. Where can you get 10% off the price of gifts? __At Special Moments Gifts.__
5. What store is closed on Sunday? __Special Moments Gifts.__

B Think about the questions. Talk about the answers with your class.

1. What information can you find in the phone book?
2. What are some other ways to find information about places in your city?

BRING IT TO LIFE

Look in the phone book. Is there a holiday or greeting card store near your home? Bring the address to class.

1 Grammar

A Circle *a* or *b*.

1. Was it cloudy yesterday?
   a. Yes, it was.
   b. No, it isn't.
2. Is it raining today?
   a. Yes, it was.
   b. No, it isn't.
3. Is it going to snow tomorrow?
   a. Yes, it was.
   b. No, it isn't.
4. Was it hot yesterday?
   a. Yes, it was.
   b. No, it isn't.

> **Grammar note**
>
> **Questions with *be***
>
> **Present**
> A: Is it sunny today?
> B: Yes, it is. *or*
> No, it isn't.
>
> **Past**
> A: Was it sunny yesterday?
> B: Yes, it was. *or*
> No, it wasn't.
>
> **Future**
> A: Is it going to be sunny tomorrow?
> B: Yes, it is. *or*
> No, it isn't.

B Match the questions with the answers.

___d___ 1. Is it going to be sunny tomorrow?   a. He's going to work.

___b___ 2. Is Joe going to study this evening?   b. Yes, he is.

___a___ 3. What's he going to do tomorrow?   c. No, I'm not.

___c___ 4. Are you going to cook next weekend?   d. Yes, it is.

C Unscramble the sentences.

1. next / be / going to / It's / cloudy / week   It's going to be cloudy next week   .
2. this / going to / He's / at home / be / evening   He's going to be at home this evening   .
3. They're / going to / test / next / have / a / Friday   They're going to have a test next Friday   .
4. tomorrow / are / What / going to / do / you   What are you going to do tomorrow   ?

D Complete the story. Use the words in the box.

going   it's   clean   be   ~~is~~   sleep   Sunday   to

Max ___is___ listening to the weather report for the weekend. It's going to
___be___ sunny on Saturday. Max is ___going___ to have a picnic. It's going ___to___
rain on Sunday morning. Max is going to stay in bed and ___sleep___. ___It's___ going
to be cloudy on ___Sunday___ afternoon. Max is going to ___clean___ the house.

Unit 12 Review and expand

Objectives	Grammar	Vocabulary	Correlations
On-, Pre-, and Higher-level: Expand upon and review unit grammar and life skills	Past, present, and future of *be* (*It was warm. It's hot. It's going to be cloudy.*)	Weather For additional vocabulary practice, see this **Oxford Picture Dictionary** topic: Weather	**CASAS:** 0.1.2, 0.1.3, 2.3.3, 2.6.3, 4.8.1, 7.2.5–7.2.7, 7.3.1 **LCPs:** 30.01, 32.01, 32.02, 32.05, 32.13, 33.02 **SCANS:** Arithmetic/Mathematics, Creative thinking, Listening, Participates as member of a team, Problem solving, Speaking **EFF:** Solve problems and make decisions

Warm-up and Review

10–15 minutes (books closed)

1. Review the *Bring It to Life* assignment from Lesson 5.

2. Have students who did the exercise tell where the nearest party store is to their home. Provide phone-book pages for students who were unable to complete the assignment.

3. As students talk about the stores, write the stores' names and locations on the board.

Introduction and Presentation

5 minutes

1. Ask about the weather: *How's the weather today?* Write the response on the board. *It's warm.* Ask about the last time the weather was different. *How was the weather (yesterday/last week/in March)?* Write the response. *It was cool in March.* Ask about a time in the future when the weather is likely to be different. *How's the weather going to be in November?* Write the answer. *It's going to be cold in November.*

2. Underline the verb in each of the sentences. Say: *This is the verb* be *in the past, present, and future.*

3. State the objective. *Today we're going to review the past, present, and future of the verb* be *and talk about the weather.*

1 Grammar

Guided Practice

40–45 minutes

A 1. Read the questions and answers in the *Grammar note*. Check understanding of the note by asking questions about the real weather. *Is it cloudy today?*

2. Have students work individually to circle the correct answers. Go over the answers as a class.

B Have students work individually to match the questions and answers. Ask volunteers to read the matching questions and answers aloud. Write the number-letter match on the board.

C Have students work individually to unscramble the sentences. Have volunteers write the sentences on the board.

D Have students work individually to complete the paragraph. Ask volunteers to write the answers on the board. Do a choral reading of the paragraph.

Multilevel Strategies

For 1C and 1D, seat same-level students together.

• **Pre-level** Dictate the 1C sentences to these students word by word, so they can write them in order. Have them copy the answers to 1D from the board and then join in the choral reading of the paragraph.

• **On- and Higher-level** While you are working with pre-level students, ask these students to complete 1C and 1D. Then challenge them to create their own scrambled sentences and give them to partners to solve.

2 Group work

Communicative Practice

20–35 minutes

A 1. Direct students, in groups of three to four, to focus on the picture on page 137. Ask: *Which season is it now?* Ask students if they are going to do any of the depicted activities next weekend.

2. Set a time limit (five minutes) to complete the exercise. Circulate and answer any questions.

3. Have a reporter from each group read the group's sentences to the class.

Multilevel Strategies

For 2A and 2B, use same-level groups.

• **Pre-level** For 2A, ask these students to write three vocabulary words and one complete sentence. For 2B, allow them to ask and answer the questions without writing.

• **Higher-level** For 2A, ask these students to write two additional sentences about the picture. For 2B, have them ask and answer additional questions. *What are you going to do after class? What are you going to do next summer/winter? When are we going to have a test?*

B 1. Have students work in the same groups from 2A and take turns interviewing each other in pairs.

2. Set a time limit (five minutes) to complete the exercise.

3. Tell students to make notes of their partners' answers but not to worry about writing complete sentences.

C Have a reporter from each group share the group's work.

TIP If you have access to the Internet in class, teach your students how to look up the weather. Or bring in the weather page from the newspaper and show students the information they can find on that page. Talk about the times local TV stations provide weather reports.

PROBLEM SOLVING

15–25 minutes

A 1. Direct students to look at the picture. Ask: *Where is she? How does she feel?* Tell students they will read a story about bad weather. Direct students to read Linda's story silently. Then play the audio, and have them read along silently.

2. Ask: *Where is Linda going for Thanksgiving?* [her brother's house] *How many hours does she have to drive?* [two hours] *What does the radio say?* [It's going to snow all night tonight and all day tomorrow.] *Why is Linda worried?*

B 1. Identify the problem. Read the question. Read the possible solutions.

2. Elicit student ideas for other solutions. Write each one on the board.

3. Discuss whether the statements are appropriate.

4. Ask for a show of hands to see which solution the class likes best.

C Discuss what Linda should tell her brother. Give students time to write their sentences. Ask volunteers to present their sentences to the class.

Evaluation

10–15 minutes

To test students' understanding of the unit grammar and life skills, have them take the Unit 12 Test in the *Step Forward Test Generator CD-ROM with ExamView® Assessment Suite.*

Learning Log

To help students record and discuss their progress, use the *Learning Log* on page T-179.

To extend this review: Have students complete **Workbook 1 page 85, Multilevel Activity Book 1 pages 133–136,** and the **Unit 12 Grammar Exercises** on the **Multilevel Grammar Exercises CD-ROM 1.**

2 Group work

A Work with 2–3 classmates. Write 5 questions and answers about the pictures on page 137. Use *be going to.*
Talk about the sentences with your class. Answers will vary.

What are they going to do this summer?   What are they going to do this spring?
They're going to go to the beach.   They're going to have a picnic.

B Interview 3 classmates. Write their answers in your notebook.

ASK:

1. Are you going to see your friends this weekend?
2. Are you going to go to a party this weekend?
3. What are you going to do on Sunday?

> *Classmate #1 —Ben*
> *1. Yes, he is.*
> *2. No, he isn't.*
> *3. He's going to go to the library.*

C Talk about the answers with the class.

PROBLEM SOLVING

A Listen and read about Linda. What is her problem?
Linda wants to drive to her brother's house on Thanksgiving. Its going to snow.
Linda lives in Chicago. Every year she drives two hours to her brother's house on Thanksgiving Day. Tomorrow is Thanksgiving. Linda is cooking and listening to the radio. The radio says that it's going to snow all night tonight and all day tomorrow. Linda doesn't like to drive in bad weather.

Snow...

B Work with your classmates. Answer the question.
(More than one answer is possible.)

What should Linda do?
  a. Drive to her brother's house now.
  b. Stay home and watch TV.
  c. Take the bus to her brother's house.
  d. Other: Answers will vary.

C Work with your classmates. What should Linda tell her brother? Write 3 sentences.

THE FIRST STEP: Names and Numbers

Pg. 2 Exercise 1C

M = Man, W = Woman
1. W: Maria. M-A-R-I-A.
2. M: Lee. L-E-E.
3. W: Tom. T-O-M.
4. M: Rebecca. R-E-B-E-C-C-A.
5. W: Kumar. K-U-M-A-R.
6. M: David. D-A-V-I-D.

Pg. 3 Exercise 3C

M = Man, W = Woman
1. W: Twenty
2. M: Forty
3. W: Ninety
4. M: One hundred

UNIT 1   In the Classroom

Pg. 4 Lesson 1—Exercise 1B

M = Man, W = Woman
1. W: Listen to the letter "A."
2. M: Point to the letter "B."
3. W: Say the letter "C."
4. M: Repeat the letter "D."
5. W: Open the notebook.
6. M: Close the book.
7. W: Sit down, please.
8. M: Stand up, please.

Pg. 5 Lesson 1—Exercise 2B

M = Man, W = Woman, N = Narrator
1. W: What is it?
   M: It's a board. This is a white board. There are numbers on the white board today.
   N: board
2. M: Who is he?
   W: He's a teacher, Mr. Terrel. He's a good teacher.
   N: teacher
3. M: What is it?
   W: It's a clock. The clock is on the wall. It is 10:00.
   N: clock
4. W: Who are they?
   M: They're students. There are two students.
   N: students
5. M: What is it?
   W: It's a dictionary. The dictionary is open.
   N: dictionary
6. W: What are they?
   M: They're notebooks. There are three red notebooks.
   N: notebooks
7. M: What are they?
   W: They're pens. There are five blue pens.
   N: pens
8. W: What is it?
   M: It's a desk. There are many things on the desk.
   N: desk
9. W: What are they?
   M: They're books. There are four books.
   N: books
10. M: What are they?
    W: They are chairs. The chairs are black. They're two black chairs.
    N: chairs

Pg. 6 Lesson 2—Exercise 1A

S = Woman school clerk, J = Jim Santos
S: Tell me your first name.
J: Jim.
S: Please spell your last name.
J: S-A-N-T-O-S.
S: Complete the form. Please print your address.
J: OK.
S: Write your telephone number with the area code. Then write your email address. Sign your name on line five. Please give me the form. Welcome to school.

Pg. 7 Lesson 2—Exercise 3A

W = Woman, M = Man
1. W: Circle the last name.
2. M: Circle the telephone number.
3. W: Circle the area code.
4. M: Circle the email address.
5. W: Circle the first name.
6. M: Circle the signature.

Pg. 7 Lesson 2—Exercise 3B

W = Woman, M = Man
1. W: Print your first name.
2. M: Write your telephone number.
3. W: Print your last name.
4. M: Write your address.
5. W: Sign your name.
6. M: Write your area code.

Pg. 11 Lesson 4—Exercise 2B

W = Woman, M = Man
1. W: What is your name?
2. M: I'm John.
3. M: Who's your teacher?
4. W: My teacher is Carol Brown.
5. M: What's your name?

UNIT 2   My Classmates

Pg. 16 Lesson 1—Exercise 1B

W = Woman, M = Man
1. W: What time is it?
   M: It's eight o'clock in the morning. Jun is at home.
2. M: What time is it?
   W: It's nine fifteen a.m. Jun's at work.
3. W: What time is it?
   M: It's noon. Time for lunch.

4. M: What time is it?
   W: It's eight thirty p.m. He's at school.
5. W: What time is it?
   M: It's nine forty-five. Jun's at home.
6. M: What time is it?
   W: It's midnight. Jun's at home.

Pg. 17 Lesson 1—Exercise 2B

W = Woman, M = Man, N = Narrator
1. W: The month is March.
   N: month
2. W: What is the first day of the work week?
   M: Monday is the first day.
   N: day
3. W: The date for my first English class is March 8th, 2007.
   M: 3/8/07 is the date.
   N: date
4. M: One week is seven days. The week is from Sunday to Saturday.
   N: week
5. M: What day was yesterday?
   W: Yesterday was Monday, March 5th.
   N: yesterday
6. M: What day is today?
   W: Today is March 6th. It's a beautiful day today.
   N: today
7. W: Tomorrow is March 7th.
   M: I'll see you tomorrow.
   N: tomorrow
8. M: How many months are in a year?
   W: There are twelve months in a year.
   N: year

Pg. 19 Lesson 2—Exercise 3A

W1 = Woman 1, W2 = Woman 2, M1 = Man 1,
M2 = Man 2
1. W1: What's your name?
   M1: My name is James. That's J-A-M-E-S.
   W1: Where are you from?
   M1: I'm from China.
2. M1: What's your name?
   W1: My name is Lan. That's L-A-N.
   M1: Where are you from?
   W1: I'm from Vietnam.
3. M2: What's your name?
   W2: My name is Linda. That's L-I-N-D-A.
   M2: Where are you from?
   W2: I'm from Mexico.
4. W2: What's your name?
   M2: My name is Pedro. That's P-E-D-R-O.
   W2: Where are you from?
   M2: I'm from the Philippines.

Pg. 19 Lesson 2—Exercise 3B

W = Woman, M = Man
1. W: What's your name?
2. M: Where are you from?
3. W: What's your date of birth?
4. M: What's your favorite color?

Pg. 23 Lesson 4—Exercise 1E

M = Man, W = Woman, W2 = Woman 2, A = Announcer
1. M: What's your name?
   W: Pat Tyson. Mrs. Pat Tyson.
   M: Nice to meet you, Mrs. Tyson.
2. M: Good evening. I'm Pat Song. Welcome to class.
   W: Good evening, Mr. Song.
3. M: I have an appointment with Ms. Terry Miller.
   W: Yes. Ms. Miller can see you now.
4. W: Excuse me. My registration form says my teacher is Mrs. Terry Farmer.
   W2: I'm Mrs. Farmer. Welcome to class.
5. W: Hello. I'm Jean Silver.
   W2: Hello, Ms. Silver. Nice to meet you.
6. A: Attention! Paging Mr. Gold. Paging Mr. Gene Gold. Please come to the office. You have a phone call.

Pg. 23 Lesson 4—Exercise 2B

M = Man, W = Woman
W: OK, Mr. Milovich. I need to complete this form with you. Let's see, the date today is October 26th, 2007. Let me write that down...ten, twenty-six, oh-seven. What is your first name?
M: My first name is Sasha. That's S-A-S-H-A. Sasha.
W: OK. Are you married or single?
M: I'm single.
W: OK. Single. Let's see. What's your date of birth?
M: My date of birth is June 10th, 1971.
W: That's 6/10/71. Alright. Where are you from, Mr. Milovich?
M: I'm from Russia.
W: What's your address?
M: It's 1769 Rose Avenue, Chicago, Illinois, 60601.
W: What's your phone number?
M: My phone number is area code three one two, five five five, one six six nine.
W: Did you say three one two, five five five, one six six nine?
M: Yes, that's right.

UNIT 3   Family and Friends

Pg. 28 Lesson 1—Exercise 1B

M = Man, W = Woman, W2 = Woman 2, A = Announcer
A: The Martinez family.
1. W: This picture is from June 22nd, 1997. Carlos and Anita are married. It's their wedding day.
   M: Carlos is a new husband today. He is very happy to be a husband.
2. W2: Anita is his new wife. She is happy to be a wife.
   W: This picture is from November 15th, 1999. That's Carlos and Eric.
3. M: Carlos is a father today. He's a little nervous about being a father.
4. W2: Eric is his new son. Eric's a beautiful boy.
   W: This picture is from April 20th, 2003.
5. W2: Anita is a wonderful mother.
6. W: Her new daughter is Robin. She's a beautiful girl.
   W2: This is a photograph of the Martinez family on June 30th, 2006.

7. M: Carlos and Anita are busy parents. Soon they'll be very busy parents.
8. W: Eric and Robin are the only two children in this picture. Soon there will be three children.

Pg. 29 Lesson 1—Exercise 2B

E = Eric (age 10), N = Narrator
    E: Hi. I'm Eric and this is my family. They are all great people.
1. E: These are my grandparents. They are the best grandparents in the world.
    N: grandparents
2. E: This is my grandmother. Her name is Helen, but I call her Grandma. She's a really great grandmother.
    N: grandmother
3. E: My grandfather is Ramiro. We play together a lot. My grandfather is really funny.
    N: grandfather
4. E: My parents are Carlos and Anita, but they are Mom and Dad to me. I love my parents very much.
    N: parents
5. E: Hector is my uncle. Uncle Hector and my dad are brothers.
    N: uncle
6. E: That's my aunt. Her name is Sue. Aunt Sue makes the best chocolate cake.
    N: aunt
7. E: This is Robin. She is my sister. She's a good little sister—most of the time.
    N: sister
8. E: This is my new brother. He's one year old. My brother's name is Jimmy.
    N: brother
9. E: I have a cousin. Her name is Sandra. I visit my cousin every Sunday.
    N: cousin

Pg. 31 Lesson 2—Exercise 3A

M = Man, W = Woman
1. M: Simon is Paulina's husband. He is the man with gray hair and brown eyes.
2. W: Karina is Paulina's daughter. She is the girl with brown hair and blue eyes.
3. M: Sam is Paulina's son. He is the boy with blond hair and brown eyes.

Pg. 34 Lesson 4—Exercise 1A

W = Woman
W: Today is March 1st. March is my favorite month. There are a lot of special days in March. Look at my calendar. March 2nd is my friend Ashley's birthday. The first day of spring is March 20th. My friend Julie's birthday is on March 23rd.

Pg. 35 Lesson 4—Exercise 2A

M = Man, W = Woman
1. Digital answering machine voice: October 5th, 3:00 p.m.
    M: Hi. It's me, Tim. Please call me at 555-9241. I'll be here all afternoon. Again, that's 5-5-5, 9-2-4-1.

2. Digital answering machine voice: February 21st, 9:45 a.m.
    W: Hello, Martha. It's Jackie calling. It's about 9:45 on February 21st. I just wanted to say, "Happy Birthday." Hope you are having a great day. Call me if you can. 555-7737. That's 5-5-5, 7-7-3-7.
3. Digital answering machine voice: May 18th, 7:30 p.m.
    M: This is Jim calling. My number is 5-5-5, 1-0-8-9. It's about 7:30 in the evening, Friday, May 18th. Are you there? Hello? Hello? Hello? OK. See you Monday.

Pg. 35 Lesson 4—Exercise 3B

M = Man, W = Woman
1. F: Teresa's birthday is January third.
2. M: My birthday is July twenty-sixth.
3. F: Armando's birthday is October seventh.
4. M: My mother's birthday is April fourteenth.
5. F: My birthday is September first.
6. M: My daughter's birthday is August twenty-third.

UNIT 4 At Home

Pg. 40 Lesson 1—Exercise 1B

M = Man, M2 = Man 2, W = Woman, W2 = Woman 2
1. W: Is the bathroom pink?
    W2: Yes, it is. The bathroom is a very pretty pink.
2. M: Is the bedroom brown?
    M2: No, it isn't. The bedroom is blue.
3. W: What color is the garage?
    M: The garage is gray.
4. M: What color is the living room?
    M2: The living room is green.
5. W: What color is the dining area?
    W2: The dining area is yellow.
6. M: Is the kitchen green or white?
    W: The kitchen is white.

Pg. 41 Lesson 1—Exercise 2B

L = Lisa, K = Ken, N = Narrator
L: Hi, I'm Lisa. I live in an apartment on the second floor. I really like my apartment.
1. L: Here's the bedroom. This is my dresser. It's new.
    N: dresser
2. L: Look at my bookcase. I have many books in the bookcase.
    N: bookcase
3. L: Here's my bed. The bed is new, too.
    N: bed
4. L: Here's the bathroom. Look at the sink. The bathroom sink is new.
    N: sink
5. L: The bathtub is great. It's a big, old bathtub.
    N: bathtub
    K: Hello. My name is Ken. My apartment is on the first floor.
6. K: There's my living room. My sofa looks good there. It's a comfortable sofa.
    N: sofa

7. K: Do you see that chair? It's my favorite chair for reading.
    N: chair
8. K: The living room rug is old. Maybe I'll get a new rug soon.
    N: rug
9. K: My TV is perfect there. I like to watch TV.
    N: TV
10. K: I spend a lot of time in the kitchen. That's my kitchen table. I eat and do homework at that table.
    N: table
11. K: I like the stove. It's a gas stove.
    N: stove
12. K: The refrigerator is nice, too. It's a big refrigerator.
    N: refrigerator

Pg. 43 Lesson 2—Exercise 3A

T = Tina, S = Sally
T: Sally, how about this TV? It's perfect for our house.
S: No, this TV is so small. Look at that TV! It's big. It's beautiful. It's perfect for our apartment.
T: Ummm…are you sure?
S: Tina, look at these chairs. They look comfortable and brown is a great color.
T: No, these chairs are terrible! Look at those chairs. They're beautiful. Green is my favorite color. They're perfect for our place.
S: Uhhhhh…are you sure?

Pg. 46 Lesson 4—Exercise 1B

M1 = Man 1, M2 = Man 2, M3 = Man 3, M4 = Man 4,
W1 = Woman 1, W2 = Woman 2, W3 = Woman 3,
W4 = Woman 4
1. M1: Please pay the gas bill today. It's seventeen dollars.
    W1: Seventeen dollars? That's not bad.
2. W2: What's the date?
    M2: It's September 29th.
    W2: Oh! Don't forget to pay the phone bill. It's twenty-six dollars.
    M2: Yes, dear. Twenty-six dollars. I'm paying it right now.
3. M3: When is the electric bill due?
    W3: It's due on October 1st. Please pay it. It's eighty-two dollars.
    M3: Eighty-two dollars? That's a lot of money.
4. M4: Is today the 14th?
    W4: Yes, it is. We need to pay the water bill. It's fourteen dollars and fifty cents and it's due tomorrow.
    M4: Fourteen fifty? OK, I can pay it tomorrow morning.

UNIT 5   In the Neighborhood

Pg. 52 Lesson 1—Exercise 1B

M1 = Man 1, M2 = Man 2, W1 = Woman 1,
W2 = Woman 2
1. W1: Excuse me, where's the school?
    M1: The high school is on 2nd Street.
2. M1: Is there a supermarket on 2nd Street?
    W1: Yes, there's a supermarket on 2nd Street.
3. M1: Excuse me, where's the hospital? I think I'm lost.
    M2: The hospital is on Elm Street between 2nd and 3rd.
4. W1: Is there a bank nearby?
    W2: Yes. The bank is on Oak Street on the corner of 1st and Oak.
5. M1: Can you tell me where the fire station is?
    W1: No problem. The fire station is on 1st Street.
6. M1: Can I help you?
    W1: Yes, please. Where is the police station?
    M1: The police station is on Pine Street.

Pg. 53 Lesson 1—Exercise 2B

M = Man, N = Narrator
    M: Hello. My name is Mark. I live in Riverside. This is my neighborhood.
1. M: I go to the supermarket every Monday. Fast Mart is a good supermarket.
    N: supermarket
2. M: The pharmacy is on the corner. When I need medicine, I go to the pharmacy.
    N: pharmacy
3. M: I go to the movies every Friday. Tonight I'm going to see *Hometown Friends* at the movie theater.
    N: movie theater
4. M: The car on the street is blue. That's my friend Sam driving the car.
    N: car
5. M: There's a stop sign on the corner. Don't forget to stop at the stop sign!
    N: stop sign
6. M: Here comes the school bus. The children are riding the bus to school.
    N: bus
7. M: A girl is waiting at the bus stop. She goes to the bus stop every morning at 7:45.
    N: bus stop
8. M: Bob's Restaurant is my favorite restaurant in town!
    N: restaurant
9. M: The gas station is near the park. I work at that gas station.
    N: gas station
10. M: The parking lot is over there. There is one parking lot on this street.
    N: parking lot
11. M: Town Savings is my bank. It's a good bank.
    N: bank
12. M: There's a boy riding a bicycle. Do you like to ride a bicycle?
    N: bicycle

Pg. 55 Lesson 2—Exercise 3A

M1 = Man 1, M2 = Man 2, M3 = Man 3, M4 = Man 4,
M5 = Man 5, W1= Woman 1, W2 = Woman 2,
W3 = Woman 3, W4 = Woman 4, W5 = Woman 5
1. W1: Excuse me, where's the parking lot?
    M1: It's behind the pharmacy.

2. M2: (Sneezing) Excuse me. Where is the clinic?
   W2: The clinic is between the parking lot and the apartment building.
3. W3: Where's the supermarket?
   M3: It's in front of the apartment building.
4. M4: Excuse me. Is there a hospital on Lee Street?
   W4: Yes, it's across from the pharmacy.
5. W5: Is there a fire station on this street?
   M5: Yes. The fire station is next to the post office.

Pg. 58 Lesson 4—Exercise 1B

W = Woman
W: 1. Let me give you directions to the clinic from here. Go straight on Grand Avenue.
   2. Turn right on 12th Street.
   3. Go two blocks on Maple Street.
   4. Turn left on 14th Street.
   5. It's across from the park.
   6. It's next to the pharmacy.

UNIT 6   Daily Routines

Pg. 64 Lesson 1—Exercise 1B

M = Man, W = Woman
M: Good morning! My name's Brian.
W: And I'm Jen.
M: This is our daily routine.
1. M: In the morning, we get up at 7 a.m.
   W: Yes. We get up at 7:00.
2. W: We get dressed at 7:15.
   M: Uh-huh. 7:15 is when we get dressed.
3. M: At 7:30 we eat breakfast.
   W: That's right. Before we go to work, we eat breakfast.
4. W: In the evening, we come home at 5:30.
   M: It's nice to come home together.
5. W: We make dinner at 6:00.
   M: Yes, we make dinner together.
6. W: We usually go to bed at 11:00 p.m. Right, honey?
   M: Yes, that's right. We go to bed at 11:00.
   M and W: That's it. That's our daily routine!

Pg. 65 Lesson 1—Exercise 2B

W = Woman, N = Narrator
1. W: On school days, Deka and her friend walk to school together. They practice English while they walk.
   N: walk to school
2. W: After class, Deka and her friends have lunch. They usually have lunch in the cafeteria.
   N: have lunch
3. W: Deka has to ride the bus for 15 minutes. She likes to ride the bus to her job.
   N: ride the bus
4. W: Deka works at a supermarket. She has to work there Monday through Friday.
   N: work
5. W: In the evening, Deka has to do housework. She likes to do housework.
   N: do housework

6. W: When the house is clean, she takes a shower. She likes to take a hot shower and relax.
   N: take a shower
7. W: Deka drinks coffee to stay awake. She likes to drink coffee.
   N: drink coffee
8. W: Deka thinks that doing homework is very important. At the end of the day, Deka has time to do homework.
   N: do homework
9. W: Deka is tired after a long day. At midnight, it's time for her to go to bed.
   N: go to bed

Pg. 67 Lesson 2—Exercise 3A

MB = Mel Brown
Mel: I'm Mel. I work at Joe's Market and I like my job a lot. Joe's is a small market in my neighborhood. I work on Monday, Wednesday, and Friday from 10:00 in the morning to 3:00 in the afternoon. In the morning, I mop the floor and wash the windows. In the afternoon, I help the manager and answer the phone. The hours are good and the people are nice. It's a great job for me.

Pg. 71 Lesson 4—Exercise 1E

M = Man, W = Woman, W1 = Woman 1, W2 = Woman 2
1. M: Excuse me. The copy machine is out of paper. Can you help me?
   W: Sure. You need to fill the machine. Put the paper here.
   M: Oh, that's easy. Thanks for your help.
2. W: I think the printer is broken. It doesn't print.
   M: No, it's OK. Just turn on the printer. Push this button.
   W: Oops! My mistake. I'll turn it on.
3. M: Excuse me. The stapler is empty. Do you have another one?
   W: No, let's fill the stapler. Put the staples here.
   M: OK. Thanks.
4. W1: Excuse me, Mrs. Blake. Can you help me? How do you turn off the computer?
   W2: Push this button.
   W1: Oh! OK, thank you.

UNIT 7   Shop and Spend

Pg. 76 Lesson 1, Exercise 1B

M1 = Man 1, M2 = Man 2, W1 = Woman 1,
W2 = Woman 2, B1 = Boy 1, B2 = Boy 2
1. W1: Can I have a penny? I need to buy a one-cent stamp.
   M1: Sure. Here's a penny.
2. B1: Can I have a nickel? I want some gum.
   W2: Yes, honey. Here's a nickel.
3. B1: Candy is 10 cents. I need a dime.
   B2: Here's a dime.
4. W1: I need to buy a pencil. It costs a quarter.
   W2: A pencil is a quarter? I'll buy one, too.
5. M1: How much is coffee? I only have a one-dollar bill.
   W1: That's OK. Coffee is one dollar.

6. M2: I have a five-dollar bill. Is that enough for the book?
  W2: Yes, the book is five dollars.
7. W1: The gas bill is forty-five dollars this month. Please write a check.
  M1: I have the check right here.
8. M1: We need a money order for the rent.
  W2: I have a money order for $300 right here.

Pg. 77 Lesson 1—Exercise 2B

W = Woman, N = Narrator
1. W: There are many customers in the store. One customer is waiting in line.
  N: customer
2. W: The cashier takes money and gives change. It's important to give correct change.
  N: change
3. W: The lady in line is buying a dress. It's a blue dress.
  N: dress
4. W: She is also buying some shoes. The shoes are on the counter.
  N: shoes
5. W: There are some socks next to the shoes. The socks are on sale.
  N: socks
6. W: That man with the bag is wearing a suit. It's a brown suit.
  N: suit
7. W: Men's shirts are on sale. For only $19.99, you can buy this shirt.
  N: shirt
8. W: Ties are on sale, too. Do you need a tie?
  N: tie
9. W: The salesperson is wearing a blouse. Her blouse is yellow.
  N: blouse
10. W: The salesperson is also wearing a skirt. She usually wears a skirt to work.
  N: skirt
11. W: The salesperson is helping a young man in a T-shirt. He's wearing a red T-shirt.
  N: T-shirt
12. W: The young man is also wearing gray pants. He might buy some new pants today.
  N: pants

Pg. 79 Lesson 2—Exercise 3A

J = John
J: My name is John. These are the clothes I like to wear. At home, I usually wear a T-shirt and jeans. I also wear my favorite sneakers. At work, I wear a hat, a uniform, and a belt. On special occasions, I like to look good. I wear my favorite suit, tie, and shoes. How about you? What clothes do you like to wear?

Pg. 83 Lesson 4—Exercise 1E

M = Man Customer, S = Salesperson, W = Woman Customer
1. M: Excuse me. Is this jacket a large? I need a large.
  S: Yes, it is. It's eighty dollars.
  M: Did you say eighteen or eighty?
  S: It's eighty dollars.
  M: OK, thanks. I'll think about it.
2. S: Can I help you with something?
  W: Yes. This blouse and this skirt are beautiful. What size are they?
  S: They're both small.
  W: Are they on sale?
  S: Yes, they are. The blouse is seventeen dollars and the skirt is only sixteen dollars.
  W: Great! I'll take them both in small.
3. M: Excuse me. I need a medium jacket and a medium T-shirt.
  S: These are medium.
  M: How much are they?
  S: The jacket is nineteen ninety-nine and the T-shirts are on sale for five dollars each.

Pg. 83 Lesson 4—Exercise 2C

M = Man, W = Woman
1. M: How much are the shoes?
  W: They're fifty dollars.
2. W: How much is the shirt?
  M: It's sixteen dollars.
3. W: That's one dress and one sweater. Your total is forty twenty-eight.
4. M: OK. Here you go. Your change is twelve sixty.
5. W: That tie is on sale. It's ten eighteen.
6. M: Thank you very much. Your change is six dollars and ninety cents.

UNIT 8   Eating Well

Pg. 88 Lesson 1—Exercise 1B

M1 = Man 1, M2 = Man 2, W1 = Woman 1, W2 = Woman 2
1. W1: I need to buy fruit.
  M1: Fruit? We have a special on bananas.
2. M1: What vegetables are fresh today?
  W1: Vegetables? We have fresh lettuce and carrots.
3. M1: The man in the white shirt is carrying a basket.
  W1: The basket is blue.
4. M1: The red shopping cart is outside.
  W1: A woman is pushing the cart.
5. M1: What is the checker doing?
  M2: The checker is ringing up the food.
6. W1: The young man is the bagger.
  W2: The bagger is putting the food in bags.

Pg. 89 Lesson 1—Exercise 2B

W = Woman, N = Narrator
1. W: I go to the supermarket every week. This week, I'm buying bananas. Everyone in my family eats bananas.
  N: bananas

2. W: These apples look delicious. I always put apples in the kids' lunches.
    N: apples
3. W: Lettuce is on sale this week. I can make a salad with lettuce for dinner.
    N: lettuce
4. W: Milk is expensive this week, but my kids drink milk every day.
    N: milk
5. W: I'm buying a dozen eggs. There's a sale on eggs this week.
    N: eggs
6. W: Look at these beautiful red tomatoes. My husband loves tomatoes.
    N: tomatoes
7. W: I buy bread every week. My kids like white bread.
    N: bread
8. W: This is my favorite soup. I like to have soup for lunch.
    N: soup
9. W: I'm making chicken for dinner tonight. My whole family likes chicken.
    N: chicken
10. W: These are nice sweet onions. My son loves onions.
    N: onions
11. W: I buy grapes when they are on sale. Grapes are a healthy snack.
    N: grapes
12. W: I'm also buying potatoes. Tomorrow, we'll have potatoes with dinner.
    N: potatoes

Pg. 91 Lesson 2—Exercise 3B

M = Mr. Garcia, MS = Mrs. Garcia
  MS: OK, let's see what's on sale this week. Ground beef is $1.89 a pound. That's great. We need ground beef. Peanut butter is $3.99. No, that's too expensive. We need tuna fish and carrots. We don't need beans and we don't need spaghetti this week. Oh, that's my favorite cheese! It's $2.10 a pound. It's on sale this week. I can have a little cheese. Ramon? Do you need anything special from the supermarket?
  M: Well, don't forget my oranges.
  MS: OK, oranges.

Pg. 95 Lesson 4—Exercise 1E

P1 = Pizza Store Employee 1, P2 = Pizza Store Employee 2,
P3 = Pizza Store Employee 3, C1 = Woman Customer 1,
C2 = Man Customer, C3 = Woman Customer 2
1. P1: Are you ready to order?
    C1: Yes, I am. I'd like two large pizzas with onions and one small pizza with pepperoni.
    P1: Anything to drink?
    C1: Yes, please. I'd like two small sodas.
    P1: That's two large pizzas with onions, one small pizza with pepperoni, and two small sodas.
    C1: Yes, that's right.

2. P2: Are you ready to order?
    C2: Yes, I'm ready. I'd like one medium pizza with peppers.
    P2: That's one medium pizza with peppers. Anything to drink?
    C2: Yes. Two large iced teas and one medium soda.
    P2: One medium pizza with peppers, two large iced teas, and one medium soda coming up.
3. P3: Are you ready to order?
    C3: Yes, I'm ready. I'd like two small pizzas with onions and mushrooms.
    P3: OK, anything to drink?
    C3: Yes, please. I'd like one small soda and two large iced teas.
    P3: That's two small pizzas with onions and mushrooms, one small soda, and two large iced teas.
    C3: That's right. Thank you.

Pg. 95 Lesson 4—Exercise 2B

M = Man, W = Woman
1. M: I'd like a large pizza.
2. W: Do you want anything to drink?
3. M: Are you ready to order?
4. W: I never eat lunch at home.

UNIT 9   Your Health

Pg. 100 Lesson 1—Exercise 1B

R = Receptionist, W1 = Woman 1, W2 = Woman 2,
W3 = Woman 3, M1 = Man 1, M2 = Man 2, M3 = Man 3
1. R: Doctor's office. How can I help you today?
    W1: This is Ming Lee calling. My head hurts.
2. R: Doctor's office. How can I help you today?
    M1: Hello. This is Miguel Diaz. I hurt my nose.
    R: I'm sorry to hear that.
    M1: Yes. I got hit in the nose with a baseball. It really hurts!
3. R: Hello, Ms. Singh. I understand that you need to see the doctor.
    W2: Yes. My neck hurts.
4. R: Is there anything else?
    W2: Yes. My back hurts, too.
5. R: Doctor's office. Can I help you?
    M2: This is Raji Patel. My chest hurts.
    R: Mr. Patel, do you need an ambulance?
    M2: No, it's not that bad. I just want to see the doctor.
6. R: Doctor's office? Can I help you?
    M3: Yes. This is Niles Gold. I have to see the doctor about my arm. My arm hurts.
7. R: Does anything else hurt?
    M3: Yes, my hand hurts, too.
8. R: So, Ms. Vega, do you need to see the doctor this week?
    W3: Yes I do. My foot hurts.
9. R: OK, Ms. Vega. The doctor can see you tomorrow at 11 a.m. Is there anything else?
    W3: Yes, my leg hurts, too.

Pg. 101 Lesson 1—Exercise 2B

M = Man, N = Narrator, N1 = Nurse

1. M: Hi. My name is Michael. I'm at the doctor's office. It's very busy at the doctor's office today.
   N: doctor's office
2. M: I'm sick. I have a stomachache. It's no fun having a stomachache.
   N: stomachache
3. M: The lady next to me has an earache. She says she gets bad earaches twice a month.
   N: earache
4. M: I think the girl over there has a fever. Her face is hot and red. It's probably a fever.
   N: fever
5. M: The woman at the receptionist's window has a cold. I hope I don't get her cold!
   N: cold
6. M: The receptionist is talking to the woman with a cold. The receptionist is working hard today.
   N: receptionist
7. M: In fact, I think she has a headache. She has her hand on her head. Yes, I'm sure she has a headache.
   N: headache
8. M: The lady next to me, the girl over there, and I are all patients today. There are other patients here, too.
   N: patients
9. M: The man in the center of the room has a backache. It's terrible to have a backache.
   N: backache
10. M: Wow! That soccer player has a broken leg. I know from experience. It's no fun to have a broken leg.
    N: broken leg
11. M: The doctor is giving the man a prescription for some medicine. That's Doctor Kim. She's a great doctor.
    N: doctor
12. M: There's the nurse. She has a chart. I think she's looking for me.
    N1: Michael? Michael Chen?
    M: Excuse me, the nurse is calling me.
    N: nurse

Pg. 103 Lesson 2—Exercise 3B

D = Doctor, M1 = Man 1, M2 = Man 2, M3 = Man 3, M4 = Man 4, W1 = Woman 1, W2 = Woman 2

1. D: What's the matter today Mr. Jones?
   M1: Well, Dr. Moss, I don't feel well. I have a stomachache.
   D: When did it start?
   M1: Yesterday.
   D: Tell me about your diet, Mr. Jones.
   M1: I don't eat lunch. I drink a lot of soda and coffee.
   D: Mr. Jones, you have to change your diet.
2. D: How are you today, Mrs. Lynn?
   W1: Not so good. I have a terrible headache.
   D: Take this medicine.
   W1: Thanks, Doctor.

3. D: What seems to be the problem, Mr. Martinez?
   M2: Oh, Doctor Moss, I have a bad cold.
   D: Say "Ahhhh."
   M2: "Ahhhhhhhhhhhhhhhhhhhhhh."
   D: Yes, you have a cold. Drink a lot of fluids. Try hot tea or juice.
   M2: OK, Dr. Moss. Achoo!
   D: Bless you.
4. W2: I don't feel well. I sit at my desk and I'm tired all day, Dr. Moss.
   D: Ms. Mendoza, you have to exercise three or four times a week.
5. M3: I have a terrible backache today, Dr. Moss.
   D: You have to stay home and rest for forty-eight hours, Mr. White.
6. D: I'm worried about your blood pressure, Mr. Wang. You have to quit smoking.
   M4: Yes, Dr. Moss. I know.

Pg. 107 Lesson 4—Exercise 1E

MR = Man Receptionist, WR = Woman Receptionist, M1 = Man 1, M2 = Man 2

1. MR: Good morning. Dr. Wu's Dental Clinic.
   M1: This is Tom Garcia. I have to make an appointment with the dentist.
   MR: OK. The first opening I have is on Tuesday, June 2nd at 4:00 in the afternoon. Is that OK?
   M1: 4:00 on Tuesday? Yes, that's fine.
   MR: OK, Tom. We'll see you at 4:00 on Tuesday, June 2nd.
2. WR: Dr. Brown's office. Can I help you?
   M2: Yes, this is Pat McGee. I have to see Dr. Brown for an eye examination.
   WR: OK, Pat. I have an appointment available on October 23rd at 10:30 a.m. Is that OK?
   M2: October 23rd? Yes, that's a Monday. That's fine.
   WR: OK, then. Thanks, Pat. See you on Monday, October 23rd at 10:30.

Pg. 107 Lesson 4—Exercise 3C

M = Man, W = Woman
1. W: What does he have to do today?
2. M: She has to work at 9:00.
3. W: Who has a new car?
4. M: We have two children.

UNIT 10 Getting the Job

Pg. 112 Lesson 1—Exercise 1B

M1 = Man 1, M2 = Man 2, M3 = Man 3, W1 = Woman 1, W2 = Woman 2, W3 = Woman 3

1. M1: I work at the pharmacy. I fill prescriptions. I like my job because I help people feel better. I'm a pharmacist.
2. W1: I work in my home. I take care of my family and our home. It's a lot of work, but I love my family. I'm a homemaker.
3. M2: I work in a garage. I fix a lot of cars. My friends love my job because I fix their cars, too. I'm a mechanic.

4. M3: I work at a school. I keep the school buildings clean. I'm a janitor.
5. W2: I work at Fran's Fancy Restaurant. I am a server. I am the best server in the restaurant.
6. W3: I work at a day care center. I take care of children all day. I love my job. I'm a childcare worker.

Pg. 113 Lesson 1—Exercise 2B

M1 = Man 1, N = Narrator, M2 = Man 2, M3 = Man 3, M4 = Man 4, M5 = Man 5, M6 = Man 6, W1 = Woman 1, W2 = Woman 2
1. M1: Hi. I'm Lars. I'm delivering food to the restaurant. I'm a delivery person.
   N: delivery person
2. W1: I'm Young Hee. Today is a very big day for me. I manage the restaurant. I'm the manager.
   N: manager
3. W2: I'm Nancy. Today is my first day. I serve food to the customers. I'm a server.
   N: server
4. M2: Hi. I'm Henry. I clean the tables and help Nancy. I'm the bus person.
   N: bus person
5. M3: Hello. I'm Tomas. I can't talk now. I'm busy. I have to cook the food. I'm the cook.
   N: cook
6. M4: I'm Pat. I'm fixing the sink now. I'm the plumber.
   N: plumber
7. M5: I'm Oliver. I'm painting the building for the big grand opening. I'm the painter.
   N: painter
8. M6: I'm Nate. I plant flowers. These are going to be beautiful. I'm a gardener.
   N: gardener

Pg. 119 Lesson 4—Exercise 1E

M1 = Man 1, M2 = Man 2, W1 = Woman 1, W2 = Woman 2, W3 = Woman 3
1. W1: My name is Gladys. I lived in El Salvador for twenty years. I was a full-time nurse. I can help patients.
2. M1: My name is Ken. I lived in Japan and studied English. I was a pharmacist. I can fill prescriptions.
3. M2: My name is Franco. I was a plumber in Mexico for many years. I can fix sinks and toilets.
4. W3: My name is Molly. I studied business and stayed home with my children for five years. I can cook, clean, pay bills, and take care of children.

Pg. 119 Lesson 4—Exercise 3B

M = Man, W = Woman
1. W: I can't fix the sink.
2. M: I can plant flowers.
3. W: I can take care of children.
4. M: I can't fill prescriptions.
5. W: I can't speak Spanish.
6. M: I can cook Mexican food.

UNIT 11 Safety First

Pg. 124 Lesson 1—Exercise 1B

M = Man, W = Woman
1. M: Be careful. There's a stop sign. You have to stop and look for other cars at a stop sign.
2. W: Be careful. That's a road work sign. You have to watch for people working on the street when you see a road work sign.
3. W: Look out! There's a school crossing sign. You have to slow down and look for children at a school crossing sign.
4. M: Don't park there. There's a "no parking" sign. You can't park next to a "no parking" sign. You have to park somewhere else.
5. W: The sign says "no left turn." You can't turn left. You can only turn right.
6. M: Slow down! The speed limit sign says "35." You have to pay attention to the speed limit sign.

Pg. 125 Lesson 1—Exercise 2B

W = Woman, N = Narrator
1. W: There's an emergency exit on the left. The emergency exit is always open during the workday.
   N: emergency exit
2. W: Ann and Joe are factory workers. These factory workers come to work at 7:30 a.m.
   N: factory workers
3. W: Joe is wearing his hard hat. He knows that a hard hat will keep his head safe.
   N: hard hat
4. W: Joe is also wearing safety glasses. He always wears his safety glasses at work.
   N: safety glasses
5. W: Joe is also wearing his safety gloves. Sometimes he works with chemicals. He always wears safety gloves then.
   N: safety gloves
6. W: Joe is wearing his safety boots, too. He wears his safety boots every day.
   N: safety boots
7. W: This warehouse is a safe workplace. A safe workplace is important for everybody.
   N: safe
8. W: There's a fire extinguisher on the wall. All the workers learn to use the fire extinguisher.
   N: fire extinguisher
9. W: Tanya is very careful at work. She pays attention and wears her safety equipment. She's a careful worker.
   N: careful
10. W: This warehouse is dangerous, or unsafe. It's important to pay attention to dangerous situations and things.
    N: dangerous, unsafe
11. W: Tim is careless at work. He never pays attention and he doesn't wear safety equipment. He's a careless worker.
    N: careless

12. W: Look out, Tim! The floor is wet! Tim doesn't see the wet floor.
    N: wet floor

Page 127 Lesson 2—Exercise 3A

NA = News Anchor
  NA: Good evening. This is Leticia Gomez at Channel 13 News with tonight's special edition: Are you safe on the road, at work, and at home? Take the following quiz to find out.
1. Do you always drive the speed limit?
2. Do you drive fast near school crossings?
3. Do you know where the emergency exits are in the building?
4. Do you wear safety equipment at work?
5. Do you have a smoke detector in the kitchen? Remember to be safe. This is Leticia Gomez reporting. Good night.

Pg. 131 Lesson 4—Exercise 1E

M1 = Man 1, M2 = Man 2, M3 = Man 3, W1 = Woman 1, W2 = Woman 2, W3 = Woman 3
1. M1: 911. What's the emergency?
   W1: A car accident on my street.
   M1: Where is the accident?
   W1: On the corner of Pine Avenue and Hope Street.
   M1: Is anyone hurt?
   W1: Yes, a man.
   M1: OK. Help is on the way.
2. W2: 911. What's the emergency?
   M2: There's a robbery.
   W2: What's the address?
   M2: 3310 Main Street.
   W2: Is anyone hurt?
   M2: Yes, the manager.
   W2: OK, sir. A police officer is on the way.
3. W2: 911. What's your emergency?
   W3: There's a fire in the house across the street.
   W2: What's the address?
   W3: It's 615 Elm Street.
   W2: Is anyone hurt?
   W3: Yes, a young woman.
   W2: OK, I'll send an ambulance.
4. W2: 911. What's your emergency?
   M3: There's been a bad car accident.
   W2: Where's the accident?
   M3: It's on 1st Street.
   W2: Is anyone hurt?
   M3: Yes. Two men are hurt.

Pg. 131 Lesson 4—Exercise 2A

M = Mother, B = Boy, D = Daughter, F = Father
M: You should eat your vegetables.
B: Why? Why should I eat vegetables?
M: You should eat vegetables because they're good for you.
M: You shouldn't smoke.
D: I know I shouldn't. I shouldn't smoke because it's bad for me. Don't worry, Mom. I know.
M: You should wash the car.
F: I know I should. The car is dirty. I should wash it today.
M: You're right. You should wash it and I should help you.

Pg. 131 Lesson 4—Exercise 2B

M = Man, W = Woman
1. W: You shouldn't park there.
2. M: For a healthy diet, you should eat these.
3. W: At work, you should do this.
4. M: When you have a cold, you shouldn't do this.
5. M: When you are driving, you should do this.
6. W: At home, you shouldn't do this.

UNIT 12 Free Time

Pg. 136 Lesson 1—Exercise 1B

WM = Weatherman
1. WM: Hello and Happy New Year! It's snowing this New Year's. It's going to keep snowing all day.
2. WM: Yes, it's raining this Presidents' Day, so don't forget your umbrella. It's raining hard.
3. WM: It's a little cloudy this Mother's Day. It's cloudy, but there's no rain. Go ahead and take Mom to the park for some fun.
4. WM: Hello, and Happy Father's Day. It's a beautiful sunny day today, so go out and enjoy the sunny weather with Dad.
5. WM: It's hot this Independence Day. It's hot at the park. It's hot at the beach. Wherever you go, drink lots of water and have a great 4th of July.
6. WM: Happy Thanksgiving, everyone. Brrrr! It sure is cold out. I'm going to get out of the cold and have some turkey with my family. Enjoy your holiday, everybody.

Pg. 137 Lesson 1—Exercise 2B

W = Woman, N = Narrator
1. W: In the winter, the weather is very cold in our city. We like to stay home. On snowy days, we stay home and relax together.
   N: stay home
2. W: When we have enough snow, the kids make a snowman. My son is outside making a snowman now.
   N: make a snowman
3. W: In the spring, the weather is usually nice. We like to go to the park and have a picnic. My daughter and I are getting ready to have a picnic now.
   N: have a picnic
4. W: My husband and my son love to play soccer. They are playing soccer now.
   N: play soccer
5. W: It's hot in our city in the summer. We like to go to the beach. In the summer, we go to the beach every weekend.
   N: go to the beach
6. W: There's a boy swimming in the ocean. On a hot summer day, it's great to go swimming.
   N: go swimming
7. W: The weather changes a lot in the fall here. Sometimes it's sunny. Sometimes it's cloudy and windy. When it's nice, we like to go out to eat. We go out to eat once or twice a month.
   N: go out to eat

8. W: We also like to go to the movies in the fall. Look. Some people across the street are going to go to the movies.
   N: go to the movies

Pg. 139 Lesson 2—Exercise 3A

M = Man, W = Woman
1. W: I'm taking the number one bus. What's the first stop?
   M: The number one bus stops at Grant Street at 8:00 a.m.
2. M: What time does the number two bus stop at the school?
   W: It stops at Front Street School at 12:15.
3. W: I work at the mall. I have to be there at 9:00.
   M: You can take the number one bus. It stops at the mall at 8:30.
4. W: I'm taking my children to the baseball game. It starts at 5:00. What time does the number three bus stop at the baseball stadium?
   M: The number three bus stops at the Riverside Baseball Stadium at 4:45.
   W: Great!
5. W: Let's go to the park today for lunch. What time does the number two bus stop there?
   M: The number two stops at the park at 1:00. That's a good time for lunch!

Pg. 142 Lesson 4—Exercise 1E

N = Norma, G = Gloria
G: Hi, Norma.
N: Hi, Gloria. What are you doing?
G: I'm going to see a movie. Do you want to go with me?
N: Sure. What are you going to see?
G: I want to see *Rain in My Eyes*. It's a love story. It's playing at 9:30.
N: *Rain in My Eyes*? That sounds good. Let's go then.
G: OK. If we go at 9:30, and it's over by 11:30 we can take the last bus.
N: That's great! I'll meet you at the bus stop at 9:00.
G: OK. Bye.

Pg. 143 Lesson 4—Exercise 2B

M = Man, W = Woman
1. M: I'm going to go to the market.
2. W: I wanna eat dinner at 6:00.
3. M: I want to study at the library tomorrow.
4. W: I'm gonna call my mother this evening.
5. M: Do you wanna go to the beach with us tomorrow?

THE SIMPLE PRESENT WITH *BE*

Statements		
I	am	
You	are	a student.
He She	is	
It	is	a book.
We You They	are	students.

Negative statements		
I	am not	
You	are not	a student.
He She	is not	
It	is not	a book.
We You They	are not	students.

Contractions	
I am = I'm	I am not = I'm not
you are = you're	you are not = you're not / you aren't
he is = he's	he is not = he's not / he isn't
she is = she's	she is not = she's not / she isn't
it is = it's	it is not = it's not / it isn't
we are = we're	we are not = we're not / we aren't
they are = they're	they are not = they're not / they aren't

Yes/No questions		
Am	I	
Are	you	
Is	he she it	happy?
Are	we you they	

Answers							
Yes,	I	am.	No,	I	am not.		
	you	are.		you	aren't.		
	he she it	is.		he she it	isn't.		
	we you they	are.		we you they	aren't.		

Information questions		
Where	am	I?
How	are	you?
Who	is	he? she?
When	is	it?
Where What	are	we? you? they?

THE PRESENT CONTINUOUS

Statements		
I	am	
You	are	
He She It	is	sleeping.
We You They	are	

Negative statements		
I	am not	
You	aren't	
He She It	isn't	sleeping.
We You They	aren't	

Yes/No questions		
Am	I	
Are	you	
Is	he she it	eating?
Are	we you they	

Answers						
Yes,	I	am.	No,	I	am not.	
	you	are.		you	aren't.	
	he she it	is.		he she it	isn't.	
	we you they	are.		we you they	aren't.	

Information questions			
Where	am	I	going?
When	are	you	
Who Why	is	he she	calling?
How	is	it	working?
What	are	we you they	doing?

THE SIMPLE PRESENT

Statements

I You	work.
He She It	works.
We You They	work.

Negative statements

I You	don't	
He She It	doesn't	work.
We You They	don't	

Contractions

do not = don't
does not = doesn't

Yes/No questions

Do	I you	
Does	he she it	work?
Do	we you they	

Answers

Yes,	I you	do.	No,	I you	don't.
	he she it	does.		he she it	doesn't.
	we you they	do.		we you they	don't.

Information questions

What	do	I you	study?
Who	does	he she	see?
How	does	it	work?
Where When Why	do	we you they	work?

THE SIMPLE PAST WITH *BE*

Statements

I	was	
You	were	
He She It	was	here.
We You They	were	

Negative statements

I	wasn't	
You	weren't	
He She It	wasn't	here.
We You They	weren't	

Contractions

was not = wasn't
were not = weren't

Yes/No questions

Was	I	
Were	you	
Was	he she it	late?
Were	we you they	

Answers

Yes,	I	was.	No,	I	wasn't.
	you	were.		you	weren't.
	he she it	was.		he she it	wasn't.
	we you they	were.		we you they	weren't.

Information questions

Where	was	I	yesterday?
Why	were	you	in Texas?
Who	was	he? she?	
What	was	it?	
When	were	we	here?
How	were	you they	yesterday?

THE FUTURE WITH *BE GOING TO*

Statements

I	am		
You	are	going to	have a party tomorrow.
He She	is		
It	is	going to	rain in two days.
We You They	are	going to	visit friends next week.

Negative statements

I	am not		
You	aren't	going to	have a party tomorrow.
He She	isn't		
It	isn't	going to	rain in two days.
We You They	aren't	going to	visit friends next week.

Yes/No questions

Am	I		
Are	you	going to	work?
Is	he she		
Is	it	going to	snow?
Are	we you they	going to	go?

Answers

	I	am.		I	am not.
	you	are.		you	aren't.
Yes,	he she it	is.	No,	he she it	isn't.
	we you they	are.		we you they	aren't.

Information questions

Who	am	I	going to	see?
	are	you		
When What	is	he she it	going to	eat?
How Why What	are	we you they	going to	study?

CAN AND *SHOULD*

Statements

I You He She It We You They	can should	work.

Negative statements

I You He She It We You They	can't shouldn't	work.

Contractions

cannot = can't
should not = shouldn't

Yes/No questions

Can Should	I you he she it we you they	work?

Answers

	I you he she it we you they	can. should.		I you he she it we you they	can't. shouldn't.
Yes,			No,		

Information questions

Who What	can should	I you	see?
When Why How	can should	he she it	help?
Where	can should	we you they	travel?

THERE IS/THERE ARE

Statements

There	is	a pencil.
	are	pencils.

Negative statements

There	isn't	a pencil.
	aren't	pencils.

Yes/No questions

Is	there	a pencil.
Are		pens?

Answers

Yes,	there	is.		No,	there	isn't.
		are.				aren't.

Questions with How many

How many	pens	are	there?

Answers

There	is	one pen.
	are	two pens.

THIS, THAT, THESE, AND THOSE

Singular statements / Notes

Singular statements		Notes
This That	sofa is new.	Use *this* and *these* when the people or things are near.
This That	is new.	

Plural statements / Notes

Plural statements		Notes
These Those	sofas are new.	Use *that* and *those* when the people or things are far.
These Those	are new.	

Yes/No questions

Is that sofa new?

Answers

Yes, it is.

Yes/No questions

Are these sofas new?

Answers

Yes, they are.

A, AN, ANY, AND SOME

Singular questions

Do you have	a tomato? an onion?

Answers

Yes, I have an onion.
No, I don't have an onion.

Plural questions

Do you have	any	tomatoes? onions?

Answers

Yes, I have some tomatoes.
No, I don't have any tomatoes.

NOUNS

To make plural nouns	Examples	
For most nouns, add -s.	chair—chairs	office—offices
If nouns end in -s, -z, -sh, -ch, -x, add -es.	bus—buses	lunch—lunches
If nouns end in consonant + -y, change -y to -ies.	family—families	factory—factories
If nouns end in vowel + -y, keep -y.	boy—boys	day—days
For most nouns that end in -o, add -s.	photo—photos	radio—radios
For some nouns that end in -o, add -es.	tomato—tomatoes	potato—potatoes
For most nouns that end in -f or -fe, change -f or -fe to v. Add -es.	wife—wives	half—halves
Some plural nouns do not end in -s, -es, or -ies. They are irregular plurals.	child—children	person—people

PRONOUNS AND POSSESSIVE ADJECTIVES

Subject pronouns	Object pronouns	Possessive adjectives
I	me	my
you	you	your
he	him	his
she	her	her
it	it	its
we	us	our
you	you	your
they	them	their

POSSESSIVES

Singular nouns		Notes
Tom's The manager's The factory's The woman's The person's	office is big.	Use -'s after a name, person, or thing for the possessive. Tom's the factory's

Plural regular nouns		Notes
The managers' The factories'	offices are big.	For plural nouns, change -s to -s'. the managers'

Plural irregular nouns		Notes
The women's The people's	office is big.	For irregular plurals, add -'s. women's

Information questions			
What color is	my your Tom's Sara's the cat's our your their	hair?	

Answers	
My Your His Her Its Our Your Their	hair is black.

PREPOSITIONS

Times and dates		Notes
The party is	on Tuesday. on June 16th.	Use *on* for days and dates.
The party is	at 9:30. at 9 o'clock.	Use *at* for times.

Locations		
The bank is	next to behind in front of across from	the library.
The bank is	between	the library and the store.

FREQUENCY AND TIME EXPRESSIONS

Frequency expressions			
I You	exercise		
He She It	exercises	every once a twice a three times a	day. week. month. year.
We You They	exercise		

Adverbs of frequency		
I You		exercise.
He She It	always usually sometimes	exercises.
We You They	never	exercise.

Questions and answers with *How often*	
A: How often do they exercise? B: They exercise every month.	A: How often does she exercise? B: She always exercises.
A: How often does he exercise? B: He exercises once a day.	A: How often do you exercise? B: I never exercise.

STATEMENTS WITH *AND, BUT, OR*

Notes	Examples
To combine sentences, use *and*. Change the first period to a comma.	I need a quarter. Amy wants a dime. I need a quarter, and Amy wants a dime.
For sentences with different ideas, use *but*. Change the first period to a comma.	I have a nickel. I don't have a quarter. I have nickel, but I don't have a quarter.
To combine two options, use *or*. Change the first period to a comma.	I want 10¢. I need a dime. I need ten pennies. I want 10¢. I need a dime, or I need ten pennies.

VOCABULARY LIST

ACADEMIC SKILLS

Grammar

Graphs, Charts, Maps

Listening

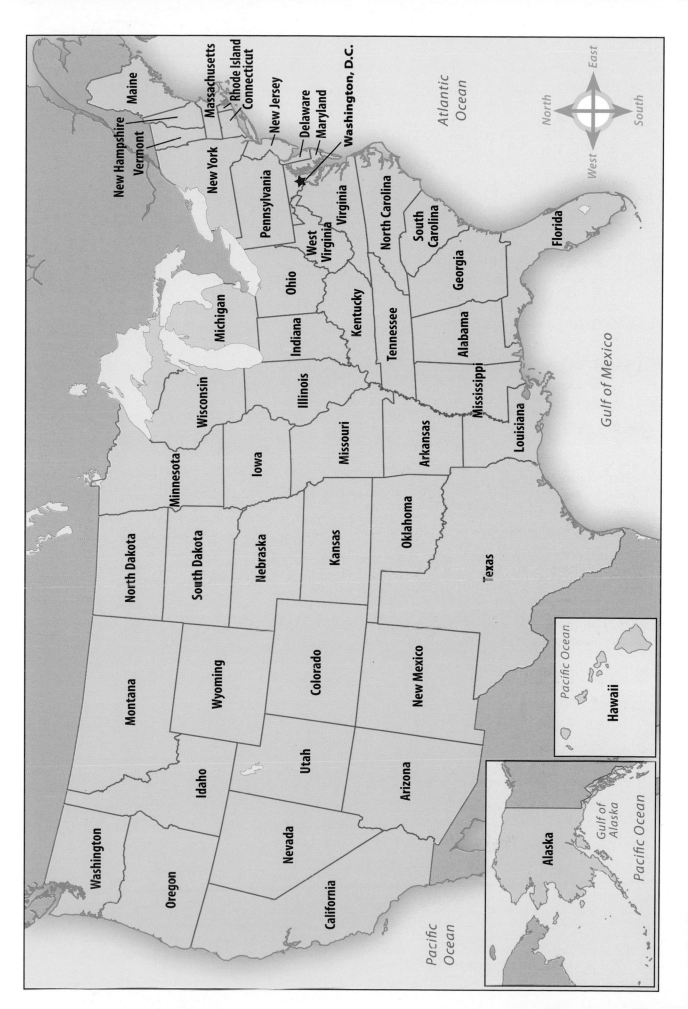

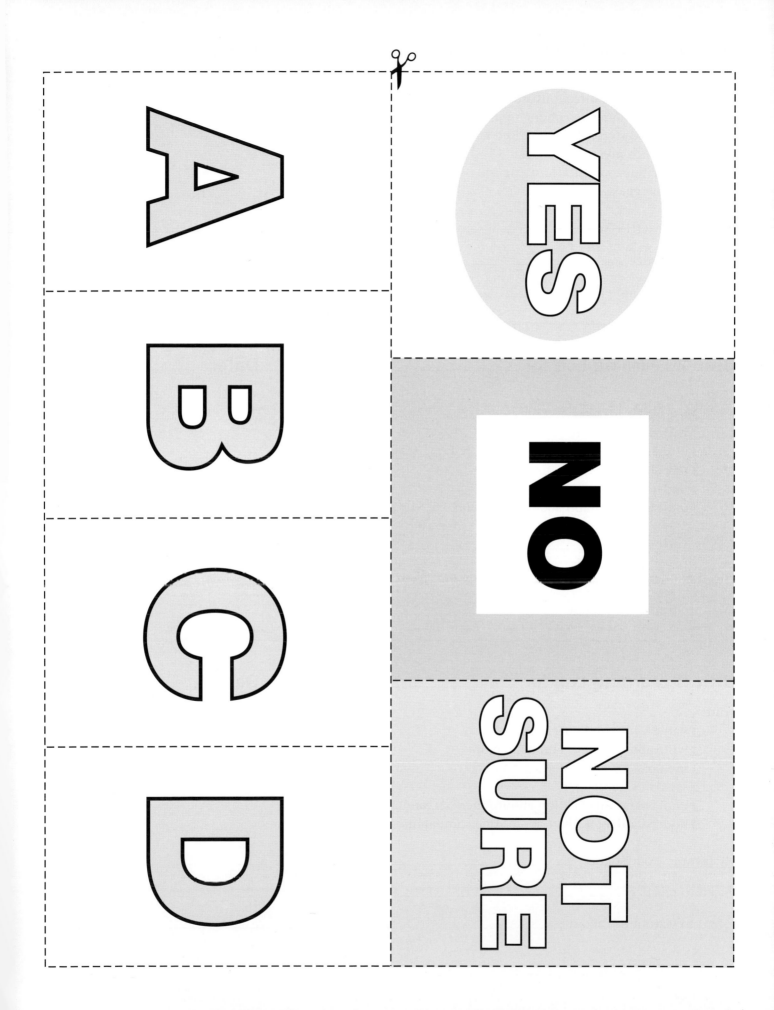

Unit 1 Learning Log for _____ Date: _____
(name)

I can

- ❏ use classroom directions and name things in the classroom.
- ❏ write my name, telephone number and signature.
- ❏ use the verb *be*. (*I am a student. She is a teacher.*)
- ❏ introduce myself to people.
- ❏ understand ways to learn English.
- ❏ say my goals.

My favorite exercise was _____.

I need to practice _____.

I want to learn more about _____.

Unit 2 Learning Log for _____ Date: _____
(name)

I can

- ❏ use words for time and the calendar.
- ❏ write about myself.
- ❏ use *yes/no* questions and answers. (*Is Trang happy? Yes, she is.*)
- ❏ talk about marital status.
- ❏ understand a population map.
- ❏ understand a graph about population.

My favorite exercise was _____.

I need to practice _____.

I want to learn more about _____.

Unit 3 Learning Log for _____ Date: _____
(name)

I can

- ❏ name family members.
- ❏ write about my eye and hair color.
- ❏ use possessives. (*Her eyes are brown.*)
- ❏ say dates.
- ❏ understand information about American families.
- ❏ understand a pie chart about American families.

My favorite exercise was _____.

I need to practice _____.

I want to learn more about _____.

Unit 4 Learning Log for _____ Date: _____
(name)

I can
- ❏ name places in the house and furniture.
- ❏ write about a day at my home.
- ❏ use the present continuous. (*I'm eating She's eating.*)
- ❏ talk about a utility bill.
- ❏ understand how to save money.
- ❏ address an envelope.

My favorite exercise was _____.

I need to practice _____.

I want to learn more about _____.

Unit 5 Learning Log for _____ Date: _____
(name)

I can
- ❏ name places and things in the neighborhood.
- ❏ write about my neighborhood.
- ❏ use *There is* and *There are*. (*There is a supermarket on 4th St. There aren't any schools.*)
- ❏ ask for and give directions.
- ❏ prepare for emergencies.
- ❏ read an emergency exit map.

My favorite exercise was _____.

I need to practice _____.

I want to learn more about _____.

Unit 6 Learning Log for _____ Date: _____
(name)

I can
- ❏ use words for everyday activities.
- ❏ write about my school schedule.
- ❏ use the simple present. (*I exercise. She exercises.*)
- ❏ ask for help with office machines.
- ❏ understand daily routines.
- ❏ understand a graph.

My favorite exercise was _____.

I need to practice _____.

I want to learn more about _____.

Unit 7 Learning Log for _____ Date: _____
(name)

I can

❏ use words for money and clothes.
❏ write about shopping.
❏ use simple present *yes/no* questions. (*Does he need a jacket?*)
❏ ask questions in the clothing store.
❏ use an ATM.
❏ write a check.

My favorite exercise was _____.

I need to practice _____.

I want to learn more about _____.

Unit 8 Learning Log for _____ Date: _____
(name)

I can

❏ use words for food shopping.
❏ write about shopping.
❏ learn frequency expressions. (*I cook every day.*)
❏ order food.
❏ understand information about healthy eating.
❏ understand a food label.

My favorite exercise was _____.

I need to practice _____.

I want to learn more about _____.

Unit 9 Learning Log for _____ Date: _____
(name)

I can

❏ name parts of the body, illnesses, and injuries.
❏ write about going to the doctor.
❏ use *have to*. (*She has to leave class early.*)
❏ make an appointment with the doctor.
❏ understand information about health.
❏ read medicine labels.

My favorite exercise was _____.

I need to practice _____.

I want to learn more about _____.

Unit 10 Learning Log for _____ Date: _____
(name)

I can
- ❏ name jobs and talk about job skills.
- ❏ write about looking for a job.
- ❏ use the simple past with *be*. (*He was a farmer. They were gardeners.*)
- ❏ answer job interview questions.
- ❏ take a quiz about good employees.
- ❏ understand a time card.

My favorite exercise was _____.

I need to practice _____.

I want to learn more about _____.

Unit 11 Learning Log for _____ Date: _____
(name)

I can
- ❏ understand traffic signs and talk about work safety.
- ❏ write about driving safety.
- ❏ use *should* and *should not*. (*You should lock the door. You shouldn't leave the door open.*)
- ❏ call 911.
- ❏ follow driving safety advice.
- ❏ understand a pie chart about car accidents.

My favorite exercise was _____.

I need to practice _____.

I want to learn more about _____.

Unit 12 Learning Log for _____ Date: _____
(name)

I can
- ❏ describe the weather and talk about holidays.
- ❏ write about my plans.
- ❏ use the future with *be going to*. (*I'm going to have a picnic. It's going to be sunny.*)
- ❏ ask and answer questions about a movie schedule.
- ❏ understand information about greeting cards.
- ❏ use a phone book.

My favorite exercise was _____.

I need to practice _____.

I want to learn more about _____.

MULTILEVEL CLASSROOM TROUBLESHOOTING TIPS

Instructional Challenge	Try this	Read this
Activities seem to run too long and students go off task.	1. Set time limits for most activities. An inexpensive digital timer will keep track of the time and allow you to focus on monitoring your learners' progress. You can always give a time extension, if needed. 2. Assign timekeepers in each group and have them be accountable for managing the time limits.	Donna Moss, "Teaching for Communicative Competence: Interaction in the ESOL Classroom," *Focus on Basics*, http://www.ncsall.net/index.php?id=739 (2006)
There are so many different needs in my classroom, I just don't have time to teach to them all.	1. Use a corners activity to help learners identify shared goals, resulting in more realistic expectations for the group. (See the *Step Forward Professional Development Program* for more information on corners activities.) 2. Encourage learners to identify what they have to do to meet their learning goals. Having learners complete open-ended statements such as *Good students* _____ creates a forum for a class discussion of the learners' responsibilities in the learning process.	Lenore Balliro, "Ideas for a Multilevel Class," *Focus on Basics*, http://www.ncsall.net/index.php?id=443 (2006)
I'm worried that assigning pre-level learners tasks that are different from the higher-level learners stigmatizes them.	Provide three levels of the same task and have your learners identify which one they want to tackle. Most pre-level learners appreciate being given tasks that match their ability in the same way that higher-level learners appreciate being given tasks that match their abilities.	Betsy Parish, *Teaching Adult ESL: A Practical Introduction* (New York: McGraw Hill, 2004), 195.
Students in groups finish tasks at different times and often start speaking in their first language.	1. Supply a follow-up task for every exercise. Often a writing task makes a good follow-up. (See the Multilevel Strategies throughout this book.) 2. Create a set of self-access materials that students can work on while they wait for other groups to complete the main task—for example, magazine pictures with writing prompts, level-appropriate readings with comprehension questions, grammar worksheets from the *Step Forward Multilevel Grammar Exercises CD-ROM 2, Step Forward Workbook 2*, etc.	Jill Bell, *Teaching Multilevel Classes in ESL*, (San Diego, Dominie Press, 1991), 134–146.
I like the high energy of group interaction, but it's hard to get the groups' attention once they've been engaged in group work.	1. Establish a quiet signal such as a bell, harmonica, train whistle, or music to bring the groups back into "whole-class" mode. 2. Give group leaders the job of getting the group quiet once the group timekeeper calls time.	Peter Papas, "Managing Small Group Learning," *Designs for Learning*, http://www.edteck.com/blocks/2_pages/small.htm (2006).